CW00393588

Four Centuries of Modern Iraq

Note on Production

This book has been photographed from the original first edition. The quality of the type as reproduced on the pages therefore reflects the printing technology available at that time. A slight distortion of the type has also occurred during the photographic process, but this should not impair the reading of the text. We feel that the benefits of capturing the original style of the book and its period outweigh the disadvantages of any minor distortions to the type.

THE FOLIOS ARCHIVE LIBRARY

FOUR CENTURIES of MODERN IRAQ

STEPHEN HEMSLEY LONGRIGG

FIRST PUBLISHED IN 1925
BY OXFORD UNIVERSITY PRESS

Garnet
PUBLISHING

FOUR CENTURIES OF MODERN IRAQ

Published by
Garnet Publishing Limited
8 Southern Court
South Street
Reading
RG1 4QS
UK

This edition copyright © Garnet Publishing, 2002

All rights reserved.
No part of this book may be reproduced in any form or by any electronic or mechanical means, including information storage and retrieval systems, without permission in writing from the publisher, except by a reviewer who may quote brief passages in a review.

New edition 2002
First published in 1925 by Oxford University Press

ISBN 1 85964 169 5

British Library Cataloguing-in-Publication Data
A catalogue record for this book is available from the British Library.

Printed in Lebanon

PREFACE

The territory whose history during the four latest centuries forms the subject of this book is that—with differences in detail only—of the Turkish provinces of Mosul, Baghdad, and Baṣrah in their final form. The propriety with which the name 'Iraq can be thus applied may, indeed, be disputed; during most of the period itself it was not in general use with this significance, and it has been used at times to denote a quite different territory; but no more convenient name suggests itself, and none more readily intelligible to a public now well accustomed to it as the name of the present kingdom of 'Iraq.

Had there existed a reasonably adequate history of the country in modern times—from the early sixteenth to the close of the twentieth century—the present writer would not have entered the field. As it is, nothing of the kind has been published in English, and in other European languages, but a single unsatisfying monograph; while the published—and, as far as has been ascertained, the manuscript—writings of western Asia contain no work whose mere translation would fill the gap. The ancient and medieval records of the 'Iraq have long since received and still receive from archaeologists and historians the care due to a very cradle of man's civilization, to a centre of the earliest great Empires, to lands trodden by great captains of Greece and Rome, to the scene, for many generations, of the glories of 'Abbasid Islam; but this ancient fame has singularly failed to attract a glance of curious sympathy at the subsequent vicissitudes and sufferings of the same country. The long age of poverty, confusion and neglect that followed the Mongol inroad has repelled the historians alike of Hammurabi and of Cyrus, of Seleucus and Khasrau and Harun. Darkness of varying depth falls over 'Iraq history from the hour when the light of the Khalifate was extinguished until the present century. From the conquest by Hulaku, indeed, to the birth of Ṣafawi Persia much that is relevant may be found recorded among the obscure histories of Mongol, Tartar, and Turkoman; into these the present historian has not entered. He has confined himself to the latest and least studied period.

But his excuse for pages so many and so often tedious lies not only and not principally in the long-faded splendours of antiquity. He deals with lands great in extent, important by their position, once marvellously and still potentially wealthy: with constant natural and social conditions which, whether unique or not, are well worthy of study as a background of history: with a country whose most recent past has involved the lives and fortunes of thousands of our countrymen, and whose future is to-day a problem exciting the keenest—too often the most ignorant—controversy. On this last ground the writer ventures to hope that the appearance of these pages may be opportune—that they may, by their contribution of the actual relevant facts of history, be welcome to such as value these as a basis for their opinions.

In themselves, meanwhile, the records of 'Iraq since the days of Sulaiman the Magnificent contain striking figures too long debarred from a place in history, incidents barren neither in dramatic nor in historic interest, and materials to illumine a neglected subject, the Asiatic provinces of the Sultan's empire in zenith and decline. The historian of Arabia must turn here for an aspect of the nomad tribes, the fierce Revivalists, of his deserts and oases : the historian of Persia for the scene of an age-long religious and imperial bitterness between Heresy and Tradition, where renowned champions of both empires gained and regained Hamadan, the Kurdish valleys, and Baghdad : the historian of the Kurds (yet to appear) for the dealings of his southern valley-states with their suzerains and with each other : the student of British enterprise for the first humble establishments of her trade with Baṣrah, and its slow increase to diplomatic and economic dominance.

The writer who thus ambitiously hopes to interest historian, statesman and orientalist has faced his task under conditions of much preoccupation, of exacting climate, of remoteness from libraries. He cannot hope to conceal the shortcomings of an *editio princeps.* He has felt, however, that his rare fortune of access to the oriental sources, his advantage of help from local scholars, his long residence in 'Iraq (necessarily bringing knowledge of conditions, topography, and languages) obliged him to attempt a work attractive (and indeed possible) to few. He would welcome its early supersession by a work from abler hands, to which his own researches will lie ready.

The generous help of many 'Iraqi friends—in provision of manuscript materials, loan of rare Turkish works, and secretarial services—cannot here be fully acknowledged.

It would, however, be improper to omit the names of Ḥamdi Beg Baban (member of the famous family so often mentioned in the narrative), of Ya'qub Effendi Sarkis, of Maḥmud Beg ul Shawi, of Ḥasan Beg of Ḥillah, of Daud Beg ul Ḥaidari, and of Shaikh Aḥmad ul Basha'yan. Valuable notes on the later history of particular localities have been contributed by Ḥaji 'Adhar of Baṣrah, Ḥaji Shukri Beg of Ḥillah, Ḥamid Khan of Najf, 'Abdu'l Majid Beg Ya'qubizadah of Kirkuk, and by numerous others in lesser degree. The secretarial help of Zahad Effendi, 'Abdu'l Jabbar Effendi, and Yusif Malik has greatly lightened the task of compilation.

BAGHDAD,
February 1925.

CONTENTS

NOTE ON TRANSLITERATION

No attempt has been made to subject Turkish and Kurdish words (which in the original language allow a wide latitude in spelling) to any but phonetic rules of transliteration. Each word is treated on its merits in respect of sound and familiarity of form. Similarly with European and other foreign words strict Arabic transliteration has not been pressed, even though they appear in Arabic guise and context.

Arabic names and words are generally transliterated on the accepted system: but lapses from uniformity (sometimes probably indefensible) will be discovered, and in particular the following points contain partial exceptions.

(*a*) In the Arabic of ‘Iraq, ث has the value of th (in "thing"), and is rendered accordingly. The three letters ذ ض and ظ have usually almost identical value as dh (as English th in "this"), and are rendered respectively by dh, ḍh, and d̲h̲; although Turkish, borrowing Arabic words containing these letters, gives them quite different values (as z or d). ص is transliterated as ṣ, ح as ḥ, خ as kh, ط as ṭ, ع as ‘, غ as gh, ق as q, hamzah as ’.

(*b*) Initial and usually final Hamza is not transliterated.

(*c*) In some common words, the popular has been preferred to the correct form, to avoid embarrassing non-Arabist readers: e. g. Mosul for Mauṣil, Sultan for Sulṭan.

(*d*) For a similar reason in certain compound names a looser form has been allowed—Kut ul Amarah for Kutu'l Amarah, Suq ul Shuyukh for Suqu'l Shuyukh, Ḥamid ul Ḥasan and Harun ul Rashid for Ḥamidu'l Ḥasan and Harunu'l Rashid. Other compounds, where it seemed unobjectionable, have been correctly rendered—e. g. ‘Abdu'l Qadir, Fakhru'l Din.

I

'IRAQ AND THE TURKISH CONQUEST

§ 1. *The country in 1500.*

Few lands of ancient renown have faded before the eyes of the later world to more obscurity than that spread over the Tigris and Euphrates valleys in the early sixteenth century. Successive inundations from the further East, with the rise and fall of a score of dynasties, had swept the old glories of the land into legend. The new things of the Renaissance, the new world of Columbus, the policies of brilliant monarchs in Europe wielding new powers of concentrated nations, left to the 'Iraq but a feeble claim on the interest of the West. Few thought of Babylon, Nineveh, and Baghdad as sites in a living land; fewer had heard of the rare exchanges of diplomacy between the viceroys of 'Iraq and the courts of Europe. The tales of travellers were scanty and unreal. Only the seafaring states of southern Europe cared for countries east of the Levant as the source, or routes to the source, of the silks and spices exchanged in Syria and Egypt. For them already the voyages of Diaz and da Gama had quickened interest in the Indies. The fleets of Portugal had sailed Indian seas before the fifteenth century was out, and settled in the Gulf the great fortress-mart of Hormuz in 1507. Merchants of Venice and Genoa used, little but persistently, the land-bridge joining Mediterranean to Persian waters, had slept in khans of " Badget " or " Babylon ", seen Najf, and halted at Zubair.

Thus meagre was the place of 'Iraq in the world before the growing fame of the Persian " Sophy ", the eastern conquests of the Sultan, and the expansion in trade and venture of the western Powers (cause and effect of a wide increase in knowledge) served to bring it again—still humbly enough—into general observation.

Meanwhile, it had in itself little enough to tempt the avarice of neighbours. The country—whatever its past, whatever treasures might yet await science and enlightened rule—lay now long ruined by callous oppression, wild, desolate, and disordered from the rock-fortress of Mardin to the Shaṭṭ ul 'Arab. The traveller passing along routes fixed by age-long usage, faced the exacting but not pestilent climate and bore the particular hardships of each region. From southern to central 'Iraq he journeyed by the Euphrates to Ḥillah, or by Euphrates and Gharraf[1] and Tigris to Ctesiphon. He passed the splendid highway of the Shaṭṭ ul 'Arab, traversed swamps of sedge and bulrushes, was dragged by his "trackers" along willow or date-lined streams ever dividing and reforming, saw rare patches of sown maize and barley, herds of buffaloes, reed-matting villages of the marshmen, and black-tented camps of the shepherd tribes forced by drought from steppe to river-side. Above Baṣrah lay the great tower of Dair, above Qurnah to the Gharraf mouth Nahr 'Antar, Manṣuriyyah, Kut ul Mu'ammir—the most populous or permanent of a thousand such clusters of tribal homes. On the Gharraf none of the modern townships had yet appeared save Ḥai by the ancient Wasiṭ. On the Tigris, 'Amarah, Kut, Bughailah, 'Aziziyyah, Ṣirah were all unborn. The middle Euphrates swept by 'Arjah, Samawah, Lamlum, past Ḥiskah (now Diwaniyyah) and past a score of well-settled villages in their date-gardens, to Ḥillah. To the west, over ground floodable in spring, lay Rumaḥiyyah, Kufah, and the Holy Places. The Pallacopas or Hindiyyah channel of the Euphrates was dry and forgotten. Kifl (like 'Uzair on the Tigris) was a Jewish shrine, Ṭuwairij was yet unbuilt, Musayyib busy with pilgrim traffic to Karbala. From there in three, from Ḥillah in four stages lay the road by land to Baghdad.

Such were the scenes and such the townships of lower 'Iraq. Similar as it was to the same tract to-day, it yet differed more than the northern regions. River courses were not identical, the marshes commenced higher upstream and covered wider areas,

[1] From Sassanian times to 1500 the bulk of Tigris water took the Gharraf course, a lesser volume past the modern 'Amarah to Qurnah. By 1575 it was equally divided, and by 1650 the eastern route was preferred. The Gharraf branch is now commonly called the Ḥai.

spring floods were wholly uncontrolled. There was less of cultivation, more of nomad stock-breeding. Willow and poplar, rare to-day, then lined the banks. The visible traces of old greatness were less deeply buried.

Above Fallujah, above Samarra, across the Jabal Ḥamrin, the level of the country rose and its character altered. No trace remained of swamp and willow, of marshman and buffalo, of capricious rivers without banks. Silt gave place to gravel and rock, flatness to undulation, signs of mineral wealth appeared. For the few cultivators, waterwheels and the more copious rain replaced flood-channels and the karid, mud-huts the tent or reed-hut. Greater flocks of sheep or camels led their masters over wider and less scanty pastures.

The route to Syria crossed the Euphrates at Fallujah and followed it north-westward by the stages familiar to every age. Except Ramadi, the townships of the upper river were identically those of to-day in name, scale, and conditions, as the pure desert air and dry rising downs are the same.

The Tigris above Baghdad was little seen by travellers. From the shrines of Kadhim and Abu Ḥanifah to Ḥamman Ali, the spa of Mosul, no towns were passed save Sumaikah on the Dujail channel, Samarra, and Takrit. The much-trodden route to Mosul—to-day unchanged in alinement and halting-places—lay through the Khaliṣ country and across the Jabal Ḥamrin. On the northern outskirts of Baghdad two roads diverged at a fine angle. The eastern passed a Khan—later the Orta Khan of the Turks—and reached the Diyalah ferry at Buhriz, then skirted the dense gardens of the Ba'qubah group and the fortress of Shahroban, and passed across the low hills to Khaniqin and into Kurdistan. This was the old and famous Khurasan Road of the 'Abbasids. East of Ba'qubah lay a village on the Ruz canal, the half-way post to Mandalchin, where Arab at last gave way to Lur, and the drought of the flat-lands to rapid hill-streams. The Mosul road ran past Mu'adhdham and the Khaliṣ villages to cross the canal at Dali 'Abbas.[1] Leaving the nomads of the Ghurfah on the left, it mounted the Jabal by a stiff climb, and debouched on the undulating plain of

[1] The present place-names are Turkish; but every age inevitably left a bridge and caravansarai at the same spot.

Qara Tepe. Zangabad was the next halt, whence, passing the older site of Kifri, the way ran by Ṭuz Khormatu and Tauq to Kirkuk. North from there the road crossed a low range past a cluster of rude oil-wells, and across a plain to the Lesser Zab at Altun Kupri. To the Greater Zab past Qush Tepe and the ancient fortress of Arbil, the road passed through the same pleasant sloping wheat-lands. The stream was crossed by two ferries and Mosul reached after another stage. Christian villages and an ancient monastery lay on the road. Mosul was the natural gate to northern 'Iraq. It was approached from the north and west by two main routes. One reached the hill-top city of Mardin by Urfah from Aleppo, and ran by Qara Dere to Nisibin, thence across steppe to the Tigris below Jazirah ibn 'Umr. The other ran from the great city and fortress of Diyarbakr to Jazirah ibn 'Umr and thence to Mosul by Zakho and Al Qush.

By such paths would a traveller journey from Anatolia and Syria to the shores of the Gulf. The country he would traverse was that most characteristically 'Iraqi—the upper and the lower zone of the long plain of the Two Rivers. The present survey would pass at once to the conditions of town and tribe which he would witness, were it not bound to deal first with the lands flanking the 'Iraq on every side. 'Iraq's immediate neighbours, profoundly as they may differ from it in aspect and society, are historically inseparable. Through some lay the routes essential to its traffic. Some passed through phases of vassaldom or subjection or enmity to its rulers, some were permanently part of the Baghdad province. All were in constant intercourse with its people, and all affected by the same external pressures as itself.

The great desert west of Euphrates—geographically and culturally distinct from 'Iraq, though no barrier divides them—served the triple purpose of keeping Syrian influences remote, of providing a storehouse of Arab tribes wherefrom to fill whatever pastures of 'Iraq should tempt invasion, and of keeping the western frontier from age to age frightened and insecure. At the names of the countless tribe-sections who grazed and raided over it, it would be folly to guess: of their politics and history it is needless to speak, for they were those of nomadism and Arabia in every age. Of the remoter tribes of the Najd oases, of Al Ḥasa and the Gulf shores, it will be time to speak when later years brought contact. In the Gulf itself we have glanced already at the successful entry of the Portuguese into waters sailed otherwise only by the pirates and pearl-fishers of Baḥrain, the coasting traders of 'Uman and the tiny ports of Arabia and Fars. More will be said of their long tyranny of these seas.

In the flat marsh-lands of 'Arabistan, tribe after obscure tribe of Arab rice-growers and buffalo-breeders took toll from the river-traffic, and grazed unhindered over a frontier later to trouble the great Powers of the world. Ruler of these was the Wali of Ḥuwaizah, representative of an old Arab line[1] whose origins vanish in legend. His power was felt as far west as Qurnah and the Shaṭṭ. The emergence of his state had followed, perhaps, the fall of the fourteenth-century Atabegs of Khuzistan. His power was increased by skilful play between Portuguese and Persian and the Arabs of Baṣrah, and safeguarded by the poverty and difficulty of his country.

East and west of the Wali's territory lay the tribes and valley principalities into which the old kingdom of the Atabegs had disintegrated. Khuzistan and Bakhtiyari together formed the old Lur i Buzurg, Greater Luristan. It was split now into small, proud, and isolated tribe-states whose relations to neighbour and to suzerain has scarcely changed from that day to this. The usual tendencies had worked towards the decomposition of larger into smaller groups, coagulating momentarily under the attractive force of a personality or a common danger. Lesser Luristan, lying along the well-marked 'Iraq frontier both sides of the Zagros, was still under the old Atabeg line as vassal of the King of Kings. Their rule extended a few miles into the plain west of their foothills, covering the villages of Jaṣṣan and Badrah, where Lurish population still predominates.

North of Pusht i Kuh, south of Sirwan (Diyalah) river, and astride the Baghdad-Karmanshah route, was the ancient Kurdish tribe-group of the Kalhur. Represented by a small remnant to-day, they had occupied their present area from great antiquity. North and north-west of the Kalhur, the country fell into three zones—the "hot country" between the Qara Dagh range and the road from Zangabad to the Zab, the Shahrizor valleys, and the

[1] Probably connected with the Rabi'ah, through their section the Buwaish.

territories of Ardalan. The former two were bounded on the north by the Lesser Zab, and divided from Ardalan (now Persian Kurdistan) by the Aoroman Mountain and the modern international boundary. This whole tract of Kurdistan was ruled in the twelfth century by the ancient family of the "bani Ardalan". Conflicting legends surround the name. The family sprang, probably, from a noble house of Diyarbakr, whence one of them migrated to the Guran section of the Kalhur. Rapidly extending his influence, he had gained suzerainty over the tribes of Shahrizor and the valleys east of Aoroman. Jenghis Khan confirmed his rule. His son Kalul took tribute from Arbil itself. The state remained peaceful and united under two more princes of the same line. Early in the fourteenth century, the rise of the Jala'irs in 'Iraq corresponded with the rule of a weak prince in Ardalan, who was forced to relinquish the northern and western parts of his empire. The Jala'irs failed in all attempts to gain more, thanks to courage and wisdom in the succeeding Ardalan ruler, Ḥasan; and late in the fifteenth century, in the firm government of Ma'mun, the northern area was regained. The Greater Zab again became the northern limit and Ruwanduz was garrisoned. None of 'Iraq's neighbours, as our period finds them, could compare for royal state and culture with Ardalan.

The Shahrizor held as yet few of its later tribes and families. Zanganah, Hamawand, and Jaf were still in Persia. The religious founders of the Shaikhan, Ṭalabani, and Jabbari had yet assumed no tribal character. Farman-holders from Turkey who were to settle in the Zuhab and Daudiyyah lands were still many generations distant. The valleys east of Kirkuk were in the possession of a mixed Kurdish peasantry united here and there in groups long since dissolved and forgotten, in villages to whose faint names no site can be assigned. The ruins of hill-forts and occasional place-names recall to-day the vivid, fiercely individual, not uncivilized life of medieval Kurdistan, so little remembered yet scarcely changed to-day. Darnah and Panjvin on the passes of the later frontier, Keui, Ḥarir, and Ruwanduz between the Zabs, 'Aqrah on the Greater Zab, were among the fortress-states.

Above the Greater Zab, 'Amadiyyah had already a long history. Its dependencies were 'Aqrah, Dair and Dohuk, and sometimes Zakho. From the twelfth to the fourteenth centuries it had formed part of the Ardalan dominions. This suzerainty was followed by that of the Jala'irs, until they too passed away. Uncertain as is the early record of the place, later survivals and tradition point to an aristocracy of great sanctity—the Baḥdinan family—ruling there from the later fourteenth century over the peasant Hakari Kurds. From that age to our present period the city had passed from son to son, resisted the aggression of White Sheep armies, but failed to escape the suzerainty of Ardalan.

North of the Ardalan dominions (in Persia), and east of Ruwanduz athwart the modern frontier, lay the tribe-group of the Mukri. Boasting a great antiquity, they never unified their constituent tribes nor produced a strong ruling house. An early Kurdish kingdom—perhaps in Seljuk times—was connected with the name of Mukri; but in our period they had none but a shadowy bond, and could not but fall under the influence of Ardalan. As late as 1750 there are mentions of a Beg of the Mukri; but though no doubt such title was confined to a single family, nothing is on record of the reality and chronology of their sway. The head-quarters of the group was at Sauj Bulaq.[1]

As famous as the Mukri were their rivals in purity and age, the Hakari. These ebbed and flowed over an area stretching north to Bitlis, east nearly to the Urmiyyah lowlands, and south (east of Tigris) to a distance ever varying in effective sway. Their earlier history is that of a distinctive branch of the Kurdish race, with a Seljuk ruling family. The medieval Prince of Bitlis was the strongest of Kurdish potentates. Representatives of the family in successive ages founded dependent dynasties at Jazirah ibn 'Umr and Julamark: but these by the end of the fifteenth century no longer owned the sway of the Hakari prince. Each had its separate dynasty, claimed separate treatment from successive conquerors, and spread the influence of its Beg as widely as might be over the tribes and villages surrounding.

[1] The great tribe of the Pishdar and the family of Soran were of the Mukri.

§ 2. *Races and society.*

The plains of 'Iraq were thus encircled by territories very different from itself in land surface and populace. A glance embracing the pure Arab nomads of the Syrian Desert, the mixed coastmen of the Gulf, and Lur and Kur on the east and north, emphasizes by apparent contrast the single language and more uniform terrain of 'Iraq proper. Arabic, indeed, was spoken from Mosul to the Karun. The traditions of the country were by now generally Arab traditions. Islam was almost universal. There was much of the unity of common scenes, and none but a single culture. The rivers linked north to south. Yet in blood, in religion, in the unit of society, this seeming uniformity contained varieties full of significance.

In race the 'Iraq was never an Arab country. From Sumerian to Mongol, wave after wave of conquest had added new elements to its blood, which in the dawn of history was neither Arab nor Semitic. Its Arab nationality was partly of recent date, preserving the memory of but one of many conquerors; but partly represented the element which, since the break-down of Khalifate greatness, had more and more submerged the rest. We find, therefore, no purity in type: and when we find rallying to a claim of common origin, such claim has no foundation in history. A few tribes still unsettled, a few families in the towns, alone could boast of such purity of race as Islamic marriage-custom had left them. Otherwise, the 'Iraqi of that century, as of this, was the heir of a score of peoples.

More than this, there were communities up and down the country in which not even this general prevalence of the Arab strain held good. Persians were domiciled in the Holy Cities, Indians and negroes at Baṣrah. The "Sabaeans"—quiet silversmiths in river-side villages—were scattered over southern 'Iraq. Kurdish and Turkish families were long settled in Mosul and Baghdad, where Jews in thousands also plied the trades of their race. Christians were of many sects and origins. In Mosul they formed a great part of the townspeople, and their populous villages covered the low hills to the north. Throughout Kurdistan small Christian societies rallied round a monastery and maintained a priesthood. Jabal Sinjar and hill-tracts north-east of Mosul held the fierce Yazidis, their hand against all men and every government. Turkoman remnants of earlier immigration lingered at Tel 'Afar and in a long string of villages along the Mosul highway from Dali 'Abbas to the Greater Zab, with their greatest concentration at Kirkuk. Kurds, in tribe and city-state, looked down from their hills on the down-country of all northern 'Iraq. The Lurs of Pusht i Kuh spread over the outermost villages of the eastern frontier. On the west, the pure bedouin scorned as a different and degenerate race the tribes whom watered lands had tempted to settle and mix with cultivators.

With the conflict in religion—the perpetual discord of the Sunni and Shia' sects of Islam—this record is concerned only as it affected history, and this aspect—vital to 'Iraq politics both foreign and internal—is considered elsewhere as an abiding difficulty of its rulers. A cleavage as deep, as productive of problems of government, was that of town and tribe. In favourable areas—the upper-middle Euphrates, the Khaliṣ country, the lower Diyalah, villages of the Kurdish border, the groves of Baṣrah—there were societies which partook of both types, cultivating folk of tribal origin still unforgotten, but of settled habit and interest. Otherwise, the line between town and tribe was clear. They agreed in little. The tribesman robbed the caravan of the merchant, the live stock of the peasant. Of no town-produce had he need, save the grain and dates which he bartered yearly for young camels. The townsman despised and feared the nomad as a destructive savage. Yet such relations did not preclude occasional intercession by a townsman for a tribal friend, or the invitation of tribal forces to aid in revolt or faction behind city-walls.

The riverain half-permanent settlements of lower 'Iraq were tribal in all essentials and dominated by this or that shaikhly governor, self-appointed. For the rest, the 'Iraq towns had various but simple origins. Remarkable uniformity of interspace shows the birth of many as caravan-stages. Some grew at the river-crossings on main routes. Some had gathered round the fort at a tribal outpost, and marked the leadership or generosity of a forgotten chief. Of others, a shrine was the centre and pilgrim-traffic the support. Need of a market for wool and garden produce, grain and leather, had elsewhere called for shops and granaries, a mosque and bath and coffee-house. Of the greater towns rather more may be said. The Baṣrah of the time was enclosed, with garden and waste land, in mud walls ill repaired. Its suburb on the Shaṭṭ ul 'Arab had but a few houses. Itself was a decayed but not idle port of some ten thousand houses, many of these mere reed huts whose owners were but lightly tied to city-life. A few pretentious buildings faced the creek, two miles inland. Some years later an Englishman[1] (almost the first to visit it) saw it as " a towne of great trade of spices and drugges which come from Ormus. Also there is a great store of wheat, rice, and dates growing thereabout, where-with they serve Babylon and all the country, Ormus, and all the parts of India ".

Ḥillah had its present character, a large tribal market and centre of exchange, and an important (because a rich) governor-ship. The Baghdad of the day was " a towne not very great but very populous, and of great traffike of strangers, for that is the way to Persia, Turkie, and Arabia : and from thence doe goe Caravans for these and other places ". A bridge of boats " tyed to a great chaine of yron, which is made fast on either side of the river ", connected the eastern and western parts of the town. The former was walled and bastioned in some fashion, the Kirkh suburb completely open. The most pretentious buildings were the palace and barracks of the governor, the public baths and mosques, and the roofed bazaars. The rest was of shabby, huddled, one-storied houses, with windowless walls on the narrow winding alleys. Dates and rice came up from lower 'Iraq, wool from the grazing tribes, wood from Kurdistan, grain from Mosul. Indian goods were brought from Baṣrah, Levantine from Aleppo by 'Anah, Persian from Karmanshah by Khaniqin. Learning was not entirely dead, security fair within the walls, government venal and capricious, craft and industry at their lowest level, the phrases of religion, as ever, on every lip.

Kirkuk was admired by travellers as "a glorious fine city "[2] where the corrupt Turkish and the Kurdish of the Shahrizor were the current speech. The Q̰al'ah was strong in defence and dominated the lime-built alleys at its base. The quarters east of the wide stream-bed were yet unbuilt. Arbil—strikingly similar to Kirkuk in natural structure and in race—was as

[1] Ralph Fitch. [2] Rauwolff.

remote from its Arab and closer akin to its Kurdish neighbours. A Christian monastery lay near. Mosul, natural capital of the Jazirah and base for the cities of central Kurdistan, had the advantage of abundant building materials, lime, stone, and timber. Pretentious walls were belied by shabby disrepair within. The khans and baths were ill found, mosques few. The important commerce in Kurdish produce—gall-nuts, raisins, gum —was mainly in the hands of settled merchants of that race. Trade was brisk, agriculture in constant danger of drought and locusts. The quarrels of Christian sects outdid in bitterness the chronic factions of the Mosul families.

To reconstruct urban conditions of the time in greater detail is neither needful nor possible. In the interests, the minds, the topography, the very language of these sixteenth-century cities there was little to surprise a twentieth-century visitor. In the tribes, still less is altered of essential elements. The same conditions produced the same local variations in subsistence and in degree of settlement. To one community the camel, to one the sheep, to one the buffalo was the means and business of life. The structure of tribal society, its ideals and shames, its law and sanctioned lawlessness, its intolerance of other codes, had long been and were to be the greatest difficulty of successive rulers. If that difficulty has lessened in the last four centuries by increasing settlement of the nomad, it has increased by their equipment with fire-arms and by the easier targets—railway, telegraph, and wheel-road—now offered to their malice.

To name even the greatest of the tribe-groups ranging 'Iraq in 1500 would be (were it possible) but a slight aid to the historian. The particular feuds and alliances, raids and revolts of this or that, the personalities of shaikhs, their allegiance or defiance to the city-ruler, are for ever forgotten. One by one the names of modern tribes will creep into the record. Some—Qash'am, Rabi'ah, Muwali—were even then in their present dirah. Of some of the greatest, a later page—dealing with an age two centuries on—will speak of the first appearance. We can now but ignore the tangled varieties of name and station, and emphasize the general uniformity of the tribes by which the settled areas of 'Iraq were surrounded, isolated, and far outnumbered.

§ 3. *The recent past.*

Such was the land whose fortunes this history is to trace from the early sixteenth to the late nineteenth century. The contrast of its desolation to the populous wealth of 'Abbasid times tempts a backward glance at the course of recent history which had thus maimed and despoiled it: and the ease of its subsequent fall to Persian and Turkish conquerors will be better explained if their predecessors are passed rapidly in review.

The dawn of the thirteenth century had found Baghdad still the incomparable sacred city of the Khalifs, 'Iraq still that paradise of grain and gardens known to Sargon, Seleucus, Al Rashid. For three centuries before that, indeed, the Commander of the Faithful had been the puppet of his guards and governors; the wide empire of Harun had shrunk to a single province: yet the Khalif, chastised or tolerated by overlords, intriguing with remote Mongol princes against Muslim neighbours, still feebly held the countless watercourses, the teeming settlements, the luxurious art and learning and industry of his famous land of the Rivers. North and west to the decadent Caesars on the Bosphorus, east to the now gathering hordes of Turkistan, lay the Amirates of a host of dynasties thrown up as the great flood of Seljuk conquest had broken and subsided. Meanwhile, still brilliant, wealthy, and revered—but factious, corrupt, and lacking every essential of power—the Abode of Peace enjoyed the Indian summer of its greatness. This passed for ever when in 1258 Hulaku, grandson of Jenghis Khan, extinguished for ever the Khalifate of Baghdad, looted its uncounted riches, slew or scattered its poets, traders, scholars, and divines, reduced it in a day from the peerless seat of Islamic dominion to a shabby outpost of the Il Khan empire. The three centuries separating his annihilating visit from the conquest by Sulaiman the Magnificent falls into four periods. For eighty years Baghdad was a government of the Mongol emperors of Iran. For seventy more it was the southern capital of a state carved by a vassal from the weakened body of that empire. It fell in 1410 to a half-tribal dynasty of Turkomans, to be reft from them by compatriot rivals; and in 1508 it was absorbed in the growing kingdom of Ṣafawi Persia.

The Il Khan empire, confined as was its throne for a century to a single family, was none the less ill knit and ill controlled. It was based neither on consent nor wealth, but on a superior virility which must itself give way to a greater. The Mongols had a tradition of conquest, none of empire. In administration neither apt nor well intentioned, they bore in their greatest power the stamp of impermanence. These weaknesses were reflected typically in their province of 'Iraq. In the governments of Baṣrah, Baghdad, and Jazirah—for these now formed no single unit—the appointment of royal princes showed that the post was not without honour; the elevation of intriguing favourites showed the corrupt basis of such rule; the rare works of charity—a canal, a mosque—showed that no mere savages were there enthroned. Ghazan Khan, in particular, was a genuine benefactor of Baghdad. His reforms in law and government, his Shia' pieties, his frequent presence in 'Iraq might well raise hopes of a revival. But this could scarcely be. The Il Khan writ ran precariously outside the towns. Routes could not be secure, and few would sow where another might reap. Most ruinous of Hulaku's acts had been the studied destruction of dykes and headworks whose ancient and perfected system had been the sole source of wealth. Disordered times, and the very fewness of the spiritless survivors, forbade repair; and the silting and scouring of the rivers once let loose, soon made the restoration of control the remote, perhaps hopeless, problem to-day still unsolved. Tribe after tribe of nomads from the steppes of Najd and the Jazirah crossed the Euphrates to the pastures of 'Iraq. Grazing-grounds were allotted by the unending processes of tribal war and policy. From the Lurish hills to the Sinjar, 'Iraq became a country of few and small towns, while round and between lay tracts grazed and dominated by the tribes alone.

The death of Ghazan in 1314 fatally weakened the family of Hulaku. The dynasty, even while pilgrims and traders followed the Mongol court to Baghdad and brought some humble prosperity with them, was far gone in disruption. The childless death of its last effective monarch Abu Sa'id in 1336 was followed by civil war. Each of the great provinces of Iran produced candidates for the throne, puppets for ambitious courtiers and vassals. Many months of fighting cleared the issue to two competitors. The viceroy of Baghdad now sent troops to help this Amir or that, now sheltered fugitives from a victor. Its own fate was in the balance. Finally, on a partition of the empire, it fell to the share of Ḥasan Jala'ir, a Mongol (but now Muslim) Amir of the highest rank, and became in 1339 the winter capital of the Jala'ir state.

This in its great days was no mean empire. Its ruler held the provinces of Jazirah, Adharbaijan, 'Iraq, and Jibal. Tabriz was his summer capital. The early rulers of the line were martial and ambitious, but religious and not inhumane. They restored to the 'Iraq, if little prosperity, some self-respect. The government of Ḥasan the Great and his son Uwayyis gave for more than a generation peace from aggression and some patronage to the arts. Ḥusain, third of the line, was of feebler stuff, and faced the greater difficulties of an empire already dangerous with ambitious rivals. He succumbed to mutiny in his own Court, and the usurpation of his brother, 'Ali. The latter could not hold Baghdad against Sulṭan Aḥmad, the remaining brother, who in 1383 again united it with Tabriz in a single state, and gave it ten years of peace under his viceroys.

But worse catastrophes than any since Hulaku were in store. Already Qara Yusif, ruler of the Turkoman kingdom of the Black Sheep based on Van, had made good his promotion from the role of Jala'ir vassal to that of powerful ally; and Timur the Lame, last and greatest of the Mongols, was passing from conquest to conquest at the head of vast armies from the east. In 1393 he appeared at the gates of Baghdad. The Jala'ir bowed to the storm, re-arose as it passed, and expelled the Mongol governor. In 1401 it broke in fury. Sulṭan Aḥmad with Qara Yusif fled to the court of Yilderim Bayazid, fourth of the Ottoman Sultans; Baghdad fell easily to the arms of Timur. Thousands were massacred, mosques, schools, and dwellings demolished. If the scenes and losses were less dreadful than those of the ruin of the Khalifate, it was that Baghdad in 1401 had not the same pride to be humbled, the same materials for atrocity.

The death of Timur in 1405 allowed—by a fortune rare even in Eastern vicissitude—the return of the Jala'ir and Turkoman princes to their thrones. 'Iraq was reorganized, Baghdad refortified with walls which, tested by a score of sieges, still stood to be peacefully dismantled in the nineteenth century. But the possession of Tabriz, needful to both Black Sheep and Jala'ir, was one of several pretexts leading first to jealousy, then to war between them. Defeated in a great battle, Sulṭan Aḥmad lost life and empire together. The name of Jala'ir was heard no more. The son of Qara Yusif entered Baghdad, and in the rough manner of the time sold or bestowed its governorships, received the homage or bore the turbulence of the tribes.

The new masters of 'Iraq differed in culture little from the Jala'irs. They conferred upon the distracted province one generation of what passed for peace. Shah Muḥammad reigned for twenty-three years. His end was stormy, in flight and murder; but his successor held the viceroyalty for ten more years, until 1444. In the later of these years, war between the heirs of Qara Yusif and the Emperor of Iran (who claimed the suzerainty) had confirmed the Black Sheep as Timurid vassals; but the death of Shah Rukh in 1447 allowed Jihan Shah to extend the Black Sheep empire from Tabriz to the Shaṭṭ ul 'Arab, to throw off the least allegiance to the Timurids, to add Fars and Karman to his kingdom. From an obscure tribe, the Black Sheep had become a wide and rich but unstable empire. Baghdad held its own as capital of 'Iraq 'Arabi, one of a dozen provinces.

This golden age of Jihan Shah was short lived. In frontier wars with the Timurid, he lost ground and prestige. Vassals and generals ceased not to raise rebellion in province after province. Pir Budaq, his son, rewarded for loyalty with the rule of 'Iraq, followed their example after a few years. He proclaimed his independence. A year's siege restored the city to Jihan in 1465. But his tottering empire was already doomed to an end similar to that inflicted on the Jala'irs by Qara Yusif. Bitter enmity had sprung up between the Black Sheep dynasty and a growing rival, similar in origin as in race, the White Sheep state of Diyarbakr. Uzun Ḥasan, grandson of their founder (a Turkish officer of Timur), had inherited ambition and hatred which neither Jihan nor his Timurid overlord could restrain. The crash came in 1467. Jihan was defeated and murdered, Abu Sa'id the Timurid worsted in council and field alike. The rule of the White Sheep spread over 'Iraq and Persia. Baghdad, still held by a Black Sheep governor, for a moment resisted. The commander sent by Uzun Ḥasan was beaten off. Ḥasan arrived in person to find shut gates. Battle and siege forced them open. Alwand was killed. Ḥasan installed governors of 'Iraq 'Arabi, of Jazirah, of Jibal. The dynasty of the Black Sheep had vanished for ever.

The change made little difference to 'Iraq, and the struggles of ambition rent the provinces of the White Sheep as of the Black. The forces and governor of 'Iraq were ever involved in the rivalries of sons of Uzun Ḥasan for the throne. Prince followed prince, intrigue and violence rent the loose and mutinous empire. The arms and diplomacy of Stambul, of Diyarbakr, of Iṣfahan were involved on this side or that, but none could secure peace or control. And when in 1499 a precarious agreement was reached between the warring cousins, it was to be torn up not (for once) by their own hands, but by the new monarch of a Persia revived and reinspired.

§ 4. *The Persian occupation and the Turkish threat.*

The rapid rise of the Ṣafawi[1] power could not fail to threaten and displace the distracted empire of the Turkomans. In 1499 Shah Isma'il led troops to Shirwan and annexed that region. This brought him into direct contact with Alwand, ruler of the northern provinces of the White Sheep. The Turkoman was completely defeated in the critical battle of Nakhchawan. The conqueror ascended at Tabriz the throne which his family were to hold for two centuries and a half; the vanquished fled to Arzinjan, to Baghdad, to Diyarbakr. Death removed him from the Shah's path. Within a year all western Persia to the Gulf was the Ṣafawi's, his officers in every town. Within

[1] The ancestor of the Ṣafawis, Shaikh Ṣafi, a pious Shi'i of Ardabil, traced his descent from the seventh Imam. His son was signally favoured by Timur the Lame. Successive sons—'Ali, Ibrahim, Junaid—increased the reputation of the family for religion and patriotism. The last named, driven from home by Shah Jihan, took refuge at Diyarbakr with Uzun Ḥasan, whose daughter (given to Haidu his son) became mother of the future Shah Isma'il. The family now passed through the stormy times common to the period and place. Finally Isma'il, young but already learned, returned to rally the following of his family in Gilan (1497). Baku and Shamakhah fell to him. From man of religion he had become leader of a loyal and hopeful army. Now came his White Sheep campaigns.

The "Arch of Ctesiphon" in 1747

two more his power had spread far into Asia Minor. Murad, the terrified White Sheep emperor still holding 'Iraq, turned where he could for help. In 1507 he and his allies were defeated; he fled to the court of the Turkish Sultan, and 'Iraq fell to the little more than nominal sway of his kinsman Sulṭan Ya'qub. Barik was governor of Baghdad. The Shah, turning with deadly rapidity from conquest to conquest, dispatched Lala Ḥusain to capture the city. It was easily done. Late in 1508 Baghdad was occupied and another page turned.

That 'Iraq was long since habituated to disorder, to poverty, to change and bloodshed, to alien rulers, needs not to be said. For eight generations each year had seen the country sink further back into tribalism, insecurity, dependence. Each month had brought news of dynastic rise and fall, to herald a fresh governor to Baghdad. Each day saw a new outrage of robbers on the roads, or the seizure of some river-side city by a tribesman usurper. To Lala Ḥusain was accorded a welcome stale by repetition.

Better than the mullas and merchants of that day we can see that the moment was a great one. None of the previous conquerors since Hulaku had had the stuff of permanence. All were distracted by feuds, some were scarce-settled tribesmen. The Ṣafawi empire, infant and still growing, was the visible product of a tremendous national and religious revival. It marked the birth of modern Persia. It was founded upon ardent Shia'ism, highly civilized and refined; it was to outlast nine generations of men. Had not chance brought into a single age the eastern expansion of the Ottoman and the rise of this powerful Persia, no doubt 'Iraq would have been Persian soil from that day to our own.

The accession of the new province to his Shia' throne brought the Shah hot-foot on pilgrimage. In Baghdad he levelled to the dust the tombs of Sunni worthies, and put to death some of the chief apologists of that sect; news of a Sunni massacre ran through Turkey. With the non-Muslims he dealt yet more strictly. He visited the Holy Cities of the Euphrates, and repaired and named after himself the "Nahr ul Shah". At the tomb of Musa ul Kaḏhim he began a stately building: then, leaving Ibrahim Khan to the government of 'Iraq, he returned to other conquests. Adding Mosul to his empire, he had become by 1510 unquestioned master of all Persia and 'Iraq.

In the years between the Shah's visit and his death in 1524, central and lower 'Iraq passed half a generation of peace. The powerful influences of the Holy Cities favoured the new rule. Persian merchants flocked to Baghdad. The religious prestige of the Ṣafawi attracted even the lawless riverain tribes. In Baṣrah an Arab governor paid annual tribute to the Shah; a Khan was deputed to govern Mosul; and in Kurdistan Persia could claim the nominal allegiance of all the castled hill-states, until a rival and greater claimant knocked at the door.

In the Ottoman dominions, the deposition of Bayazid II ended a generation of comparative calm. He was succeeded in 1512 by his son Salim, a man remarkably gifted with the opposite attributes of culture and ferocity, brilliant prowess and the callousness of an idiot. Peace had given time to survey the world, to lament the heresies that disgraced Islam, to hear from frontier Pashas of the new greatness of Shia' Persia. The massacre of Sunnis in Baghdad had created a deep impression. Although the identification of Sultan and Khalif was yet a few years distant, and Turkey therefore less explicitly the guardian of orthodoxy, there was yet abundant material for religious antagonism between Stambul and Tabriz: and championship of the Sunni cause was Salim's first pretext for war. In any case a clash was inevitable. The Ṣafawi advance westward could not be ignored. The buffer state of the Aq Qoiyunlu was no more. Kurdish states, Turkish tribes of Anti-Taurus, and Christian communities of Armenia were claimed as realms of the Shah. Stambul imperialists declared that Persia had, by the annexation of 'Iraq and Kurdistan and Armenia, violated the boundaries of the Ottoman, besides recently sheltering the fugitive brothers of Salim himself. The young Sultan had ambitions coterminous with his knowledge of the world. He marked his first months of power by a careful massacre of his Shia' subjects wherever found. The usual prelude of bombastic letters was then exchanged with the Court of Persia. Nothing could come of these; but the responsibility for war-making was made to rest upon the Turk. After careful preparation Salim embarked upon his campaign.

The terrific battle of Chaldiran near Urmiyyah gave victory to Salim, and drove the Shah wounded from the field. Turkish forces entered Tabriz, though disease and indiscipline forbade them to hold it. The campaign profoundly affected the policy of the Kurds. Bitlis, Ardalan, 'Amadiyyah, Jazirah ibn 'Umr, and their smaller dependencies hastened to make terms with a potential overlord. Though Turkish acquisition of central Kurdistan and northern 'Iraq—the nominal fruits of Salim's great raid—involved no more than the distribution of robes and farmans, the reception of homage and presents, Persian rule there had meant no more. Turkish governors were installed in Diyarbakr, Mardin, and Mosul, a strong garrison placed in the Van area. For the rest, definite devolution, organized units, permanent loyalties, all the phenomena of occupation and government, were lacking. The mixed tribes of the northern Jazirah heard of new-comers at Mosul and Raqqah ; Mosul lost a Khan and gained a Pasha ; the Kurdish principalities could now balance Persian culture against Sunni religion, and play at flattery and evasion with two great Powers instead of one. In vain Tahmasp Shah bestowed the title of "Khalif of Khalifs" on his governor of Baghdad. In vain viceroys came and went. More and more letters left Baghdad for the Bosphorus, while the Khan of the moment barely upheld his authority in central 'Iraq.

The last episode of the Persian occupation, and the best recorded, is the usurpation of Dhu 'l Faqar. Neither his antecedents, nor the mode of his assumption of government in Baghdad, are clear. He belonged perhaps to a frontier Lurish family, and had gained the following of the powerful Kalhur group. The Khan of Baghdad[1] had marched to the foot-hills on his way to rejoin the Shah. By night in the first pass Dhu 'l Faqar attacked and slew him. Pressing on to Baghdad, he entered and besieged the Citadel. It fell to his vigorous and not unwelcome arms. He assumed sovereign powers. By a sudden stroke Baghdad had been lost to Persia. Dhu 'l Faqar became unquestioned master of central 'Iraq ; but the

[1] The version of Gulshan is here followed, but it is full of difficulties. The Turkish authorities (Ferdi and Pashawi), followed by von Hammer (vol. v, Bk. XXVIII, p. 204), make Dhu 'l Faqar an ordinary viceroy appointed by Tahmasp.

times were not for small rulers in places so exposed; and he wisely ordered public worship and coinage to proclaim the suzerainty of the Sultan. Messages reached Stambul begging acceptance and protection of the new vassal.

Tahmasp, still but sixteen though he had reigned six years, heard with bitter annoyance the defection of 'Iraq. In 1530 he marched by Karmanshah to Baghdad. Several assaults availed him nothing. Dhu 'l Faqar was as stubborn in defence as bold to seize. Treachery succeeded where the Ṣafawi arms had failed. The Shah, seducing by promises the two brothers of the usurper, secured his assassination. He died fighting desperately in his own house; his short reign, and the suzerainty of Stambul, were over. The traitor brothers were loaded with favours; the government of Baghdad was given to Muḥammad Khan of the Anatolian province of Tekke. The Shah appointed loyal officers to the governorships of Kirkuk, Ḥillah, Mandali, Jaza'ir, and Rumaḥiyyah, and himself returned to Qasvin.

But the end was at hand. The Sultan had not forgotten the petitions of the famous city which had begged his protection. The Lawgiver, the Lord of his Age, the Magnificent, was already on the march.

§ 5. *Sultan Sulaiman.*[1]

In the winter of 1525 the Persian Court had heard with alarm of giant warlike preparations at Stambul. The Sultan, in tardy letters of congratulation to the boy-Shah Tahmasp, had used phrases of menace. The Ṣafawi's advisers had addressed the King of Hungary and the Emperor to make common cause. Sulaiman replied by execution of the Persian prisoners then detained at Gallipoli. A great campaign against Persia appeared imminent. But the arms of Turkey were diverted instead to Hungary; and 'Iraq, as we have seen, remained Persian (save for the episode of Dhu 'l Faqar) for nine years more.

[1] Authorities: the "Journal" of Sultan Sulaiman is the most important for his own operations. The rest of the campaigns of 1533 and 1534 are collected by von Hammer (vol. v, Bk. XXVIII, pp. 202 ff.), from Jalalzadah, Pashawi, and Ferdi. Knolles (pp. 649–53 of 1603 ed.) is interesting. Internal affairs at Baghdad are from Gulshan, the only source, as noted by Huart (p. 38, foot-note). The Persian sources used by Malcolm and Sykes are jejune. The events are briefly noticed in the lesser 'Iraqi sources.

But with Turkish power at its apex of aggressive pride, the feud of Shia' and Sunni deep and bitter, and the eastern expansion of Salim yet incomplete, a Persian war could be postponed but not avoided. For immediate pretext there were frontier incidents. The Khan of Bitlis had left Turkish for Persian service; while Ulamah Beg, a waverer between the two empires, had now kissed hands at Stambul. He was made Beglerbegi of Ḥasankif. The governors of neighbouring Turkish provinces, ordered to install him, failed to force entrance against the army of Sharif of Bitlis. To this indignity to Ottoman arms was added the appeal of Sunni Baghdad for rescue. Fatwahs justifying war and urging unsparing massacre of Shia' heretics were easily obtained.

In the early autumn of 1533, the Grand Wazir Ibrahim Pasha left for Bitlis. He found his work done. Sharif Beg was dead. The son of Ulamah was appointed governor. The Wazir returned to Aleppo, whence he broke camp in April 1534. Crossing the Euphrates at Birijik, he reached Diyarbakr on May 14. Here a halt of six weeks was made. Van and many more Kurdish fortresses of the frontier sent in their keys. Early in July Ibrahim Pasha left Diyarbakr. The Sultan marched from Scutari on the same day. The Wazir entered Tabriz without further trouble and without bloodshed. Expeditions in the hill-country of Adharbaijan confirmed the conquest. Late in September the Sultan joined forces with his Minister. Generous largesse and a general reception of Khans and Begs flocking to do homage marked the short stay at Tabriz.

Baghdad was the next objective. The march began under conditions of early autumn. The Sultan passed by Miyanah to Zanjan, and on to Sulaimaniyyah. News here reached him that the expected Persian forces had fallen back, and several of their vassals were eager to change sides. No enemy therefore lay between the Turkish army and Hamadan; but the cold and rains of November, and the little-trodden passes of the last hundred miles of mountain, made the passage of the army difficult and costly. Swollen streams swept away part of the artillery. Hundreds of animals were abandoned. Tempers were short, high officers were disgraced. Gun-carriages were burnt and the cannon buried to avoid enriching the enemy. With immense relief the Sultan at last saw the Lurish hills break and fall lower and the plains of 'Iraq lie before him.

In Baghdad all was division. Ulamah Beg, left by the Sultan in the north, had already sent letters of seduction to Muḥammad Khan, the "Tekkeli" governor installed by Shah Tahmasp. They appealed to his Turkish race, to a new and truer loyalty, to the terror of the Sultan's arms. The Khan replied in insulting terms, and prepared for defence. In this resolution he was strengthened by a message from Tahmasp, but weakened by the Shah's retreat and the Sultan's nearer approach. He decided upon flight, but flight to Persia. Feigning receipt of a summons from the Shah, he convoked his officers and told his plan. The Tekke tribesmen, his natural followers, refused and mutinied. The Khan still hoped to regain Persia with a body-guard of another tribe: and in fact at this moment arrived a courtier of the Shah with similar orders. Rumour was strong that royal reinforcements were at hand, the Shah already at Khaniqin. The Tekke contingent were again assembled, again refused to leave the city. Muḥammad Khan sent out the criers: let those stay behind who fancied a hopeless siege, while lovers of their Sovereign would follow him. Seven hundred families rallied to him. The bulk of the citizens, it may be, cared little what Khans or Sultans came or went: but the men of Tekke, a last time urged to leave, threw off the dying authority of their Khan, formed their ranks, and seized as base and fortress the old college of Mustanṣiriyyah.

The Khan played his last card. He summoned their leaders, declared his changed intentions: he had decided to welcome the Turk. All were agreed and eager. The chief captains left the city with the keys to present to Sulaiman: their rank and file stayed leaderless behind. The ruse of Muḥammad Khan had perfectly succeeded. Without trouble he collected his whole household and belongings, crossed to the right bank, and gained Persian soil by a long circuit to the south.

News of his flight from a defenceless city reached the Sultan some stages from Baghdad. The Grand Wazir was sent ahead. Entering unopposed, he closed the gates to prevent looting and sent back to welcome his Sovereign. The exhausted army camped north of the town. Sulaiman Qanuni in pomp and ease entered Baghdad. At long last a Khalif had come back to the Abode of Peace.

The need to rest his forces till spring, no less than to organize the new provinces, led him to stay for some months in 'Iraq. The official and perpetual allegiance of the country to his throne was announced. All notables and tribal leaders offered their homage. Generous rewards and promotions were bestowed on officers of the victorious army. The notables of Baghdad surveyed for some months at closest quarters the full pomp of the Sultan's court. His Head-quarters was in camp outside the city, and the ritual was rather of camp than palace. The uneasy Baghdadis, and frequent curious visitors from all parts of 'Iraq and its hill-fringes, could appraise the wealth of the new masters and their military machine invincible from Danube to Shaṭṭ ul 'Arab. In the callous execution in Baghdad of a personal enemy of the Grand Wazir, they could see the caprice, the avarice, from which even Sulaiman was not exempt.

The learned of Baghdad, doubtless, spared their guests no detail of a truly glorious past. Ruins less deeply buried then than now, huge mounds and canal banks, giant masonry thrown down, the shattered pottery of mighty cities—these must impress Sultan and sutler that they stood in the ruins of a great civilization. Many a flattering tongue foretold that the Sultan would revive and surpass the former glories. The appeal to religion was yet more poignant. It was now thirty years since Salim I had taken the trinkets of the Khalifate from Cairo to Stambul. The re-creation, in very fact, of the city and land of his spiritual forebears might well have roused a thrill in the Sultan's heart.

To the religious appeal he responded suitably. In his age the flame of Islam burned very bright. His predecessor, the Ṣafawi, had had high claims to spiritual sovereignty: he must not have less. With real reverence he made pilgrimage to the tomb of 'Abdu 'l Qadir ul Gailani and to the twin Shia' shrines of Musa ul Kadhim and Muḥammad Taqi. He ordered completion of the great mosque begun by Shah Isma'il and entailed generous estates to Sunni and Shia' incumbents alike. No duty of religion more exercised him than to discover and restore the tomb of Abu Ḥanifah, founder of one of the four Sunni sects.

The Shi'i occupiers had thrown down the shrine, desecrated the very remains; but the ancient custodian of the place was guided miraculously to discover the holy body, perfectly preserved. Divine protection had saved it from infidel Shi'i hands. The Sultan raised upon the spot a stately dome that became for centuries a great Sunni pilgrimage.

His next care was to visit the Holy Places of the middle Euphrates, and there to outdo the Ṣafawi pilgrim of the last régime. He found the sacred city of Karbala distraught between flood and drought. The swollen Euphrates in spring inundated the depressions all round the town, and did not spare the shrines themselves; while at low river, tens of thousands of pilgrims depended upon scanty and brackish wells. The "Rauf ul Sulaimaniyyah"—a dyke still standing and effective—was raised to protect the town from flood. The Ḥusainiyyah canal was deepened and widened to bring constant water and to convert dusty wastes round it into gardens and corn-lands. It flowed over land which all had pronounced higher than the parent river. All hailed a miracle, and praise and wonder were divided between the martyred Ḥusain and the Turkish Sovereign. After visiting the shrine of 'Ali at Najf, Sulaiman returned to Baghdad.

His stay was nearly over. The Arab tribesman[1] who had hitherto ruled Baṣrah with shadowy allegiance to the Shah, had hastened now to send his son Rashid (راشد) with the keys and obsequious messages to the Sultan. Baṣrah was thus easily incorporated in the Ottoman dominions, and received the titular status of an ayalat. Rashid himself was appointed governor. His injunctions were to look for his orders to the Pasha of Baghdad, to hold to the Shara' law as his rule of government, to honour the name of his new Sovereign in the coinage and public prayers. Similar envoys brought the submission of the Jaza'ir and Gharraf regions, of the Lurish hills, of the Ḥuwaizah marshes, even of distant Qaṭif and Baḥrain.[2] Garrisons were

[1] The sequence and dates of accession of these Baṣrah rulers are inconsistently given in the Calendar, Basha'yan, and Gulshan. A compromise is adopted in the text.

[2] Knolles adds (p. 653, ed. cit.) that ambassadors "came unto him as far as Ormus, a city in the mouth of Euphrates, where it falleth into the Persian Gulfe" (*sic*).

sent to the provincial towns, now known as the Head-quarters of a Sanjaq Begi. This rank and smaller estates, each with its feudal liability of service, were bestowed on soldiers distinguished in the last campaign.[1] Orders were given for the charting of the new province, and for a fair assessment of its tax-farms.

The troops formed for the long return march and struck camp. The former governor of Diyarbakr, Sulaiman Pasha, was appointed the first Ottoman Viceroy of Baghdad. With him were left a thousand Musketeers and as many Fusiliers.[2] By the road of the Khaliṣ and Saqaltutan, Sultan Sulaiman left Baghdad. No incidents are preserved of the long journey to Maraghah and Tabriz. Mosul was off the line of march; but this did not prevent the granting of fiefs[3] in that ayalat and the bestowal of its government upon a tried vassal, Sayyid Aḥmad of Jazirah ibn 'Umr.

[1] That the fief system, now introduced by Sultan Sulaiman into such parts of 'Iraq as he could control (von Hammer, v, p. 220), never took root as in other provinces, we shall see elsewhere. According to the Qanunnamah of Sulaiman, the seven Baghdad Sanjaqs of Ḥillah, Zangabad, Jawazir, Rumaḥiyyah, Janqulah, Qara Dagh, and one other, were thus distributed in fiefs, and the remaining eleven Sanjaqs of the Ayalat undivided.

[2] The actual strength of the garrison, which must have included Janissaries, regular Sipahis, and artillery, cannot be gathered from this short reference in Ferdi.

[3] According to Auliya, sixty-six zi'amats and a thousand and four timars. Mosul, on his classification, had only three Sanjaqs.

II

THE SIXTEENTH CENTURY

§ 1. *Hopes and fears for 'Iraq as a Turkish province.*

There was reason for fair hopes that the new rule in the Arab world which, 'Iraq with the rest, had fallen with little effort to the great period of Ottoman expansion, would prove a blessing. These countries had for centuries lacked the advantages of Imperial rule. Local governments where strong were oppressive. The Sultan might well be greeted as deliverer. Yet another great empire had arisen in western Asia, and only by inclusion in it could the weak and factious hope for firm and paternal government. A better organization, reformed laws, new rights, had been published by the enlightenment of the great monarch who patronized the sovereigns of Europe. Taxation was light and reasonably equitable. Little fanaticism was directed against non-Muslim races. Forces for the preservation of order were found in the renowned Janissaries, still the most formidable military body in the world. In the many families of Turkish blood scattered through the new provinces were elements of assured loyalty; while the assumption by Salim the Grim of the most sacred character in Islam had given certainty that the whole Sunni world, as long as their religion held them, could not look elsewhere than to Stambul.

So might have reasoned a spokesman of the Arab provinces newly conquered. But there were factors as potent on the other side, reasons as good why hopes of contented inclusion in the Ottoman Empire were to be disappointed. It is needless to insist—for few in that age and place would see force in such criticism—that the very conception of Turkish dominion condemned the governed to selfish and partial rule. The Empire existed and must ever be widened for the greater glory of the Sultan, the spread of the true religion, the replenishing of the treasury, the settlement of fiefs and recruitment of vassal-forces. Not to the Lawgiver himself—far less to ambitious viceroys—occurred the paradox that rule was for the ruled, that Ministers should be ministers indeed.

And in the Empire of the middle sixteenth century the high summer of greatest extent and glory showed the first signs of autumn. The abuses which ruined later Turkey were even now discernible. Capricious promotion of a eunuch or a favourite might bring to Cairo or Baghdad a governor grotesquely unsuitable. The vast opportunities for self-enrichment offered by the distant Pashaliqs soon made them a marketable asset. The tax-farm, which was the government of the province, fell to the highest bidder. The costly presents necessary to retain a lucrative office must themselves be provided by the provincial victims, who thus not only suffered but paid for ill government. In the eastern and southern provinces, by their very remoteness, the excesses of governors were less visible from Stambul, and appeal more difficult. Loyalty could not grow fast among a people who saw the outer fringes of their Sovereign's power, and felt the ungentle touch of his furthest officers. These in their turn must regard banishment to 'Iraq or Palestine as a hated duty or a rich opportunity. Racially there was nothing in common between the inhabitants and their new governors. Intercourse was to reveal the profoundest differences in genius. Arabs, with their long past of desert life, their impatience and inconstancy, remain the most difficult of subject races. The Turkish character—unimaginative and inelastic—could least of all appreciate their vagaries. The very appearance, manner, and language of the Turkish Aghas was strange and foreign to Arab eyes and ears.

To 'Iraq, in full measure, these fears and doubts applied. And they were emphasized by the inner conditions of the province. Northern 'Iraq and Kurdistan were Sunni, Baghdad divided; but the central and southern regions were strongly Shia' and scorned the pretentions of the new Khalif. From the Holy Cities radiated influence strong in its appeal, hostile to the Sultan and by reaction friendly to the Shah; and for the struggles of those rivals 'Iraq—as three centuries were to prove—was a natural stage. There was small hope of religious concord or peaceful frontiers. In the province itself there was as little. The new rulers were faced with a torrid unfamiliar climate, the difficulties of waterless steppe and trackless marsh, long and unguarded communications. The towns, asking little and easily bullied, were yet fickle and disloyal: the tribes were a problem in government then unsolved, and unsolved to-day. Covering the whole face of the country, powerful in their numbers, infinitely mobile and intangible in their retreats, and by nature and tradition impatient of restraint, patriarchal in government and followers of a desert code incompatible with any rule, the tribesmen of 'Iraq were never to acquiesce in the sway of Pashas, never to surrender the lawless freedom in which they held nine-tenths of the country now proclaimed subject to the house of 'Uthman.

§ 2. *Internal 'Iraq, 1534 to 1620.*[1]

There is reason why the earliest generations of Turkish rule in 'Iraq should be the most significant. The Empire was at its apex. It had, in the provinces, no past to live down but great reputation to justify. In 'Iraq lay a new field to test its prowess in government. Unhappily, the materials do not exist from which an adequate picture of its success or failure can be drawn. The few known facts, which will be shortly told, may render disservice to history if they distort proportions and lay stress on unessentials. Our best but perilous guides are the constant conditions of 'Iraq, and deductions from contemporary Turkey. The naïve records of the travellers little assist the historian, and few traditions survived the subsequent loss and recapture of Baghdad.

The general position of the 'Iraq territories was that of a distant but regular portion of the Sultan's dominions. The terminology and official forms of Turkish government held the field, never to be displaced. Crime was kept down by Turkish constables, and corrected by a Qadhi from Stambul. In favour of the complete surrender of 'Iraq to Turkish rule were the new bureaucracy, the garrisons, the feudal tenants, and a part of the divines. Against it were the tribes, the Shia' and Persian influences, local

[1] Authorities are scanty. For Baṣrah troubles and a few other facts, Gulshan and Basha'yan. For Cicala, von Hammer, Bk. VII, pp. 219–20. The principal travellers are Rauwolff, Sidi 'Ali, Fitch and his companions, Balbi, Teixeira. For Mosul, see p. 36, foot-note.

ambitions favouring non-government, and the peculiarities of the country itself.

The dominant feature of the century was the almost ceaseless hostilities[1] of the Empire against Persia—a condition which affected the public and garrisons of 'Iraq to a degree difficult to estimate. If influenced, certainly, the flow of pilgrims to the shrines, and the exchanges of commerce with Iṣfahan and Tabriz. It called for the occasional rally of Janissary and feudal tenant to contribute to Imperial armies in the north. Grain and transport-animals were requisitioned. The panic of a threat to the city-walls, the secession of fickle Kurdish princes, the royal reception of a Persian ambassador *en route* for the Bosphorus, were among the incidents familiar to 'Iraq in these years. If, in contrast to the great Persian wars of the eighteenth century, those of the sixteenth did not call the Pashas or timariots of 'Iraq to a leading part, yet a few vivid episodes stirred more than a languid interest in the Baghdadis. In 1586 five thousand Turkomans, refugees from the heroic Ḥamza Mirza, flocked into the city. Not long afterwards a furious battle was fought close to it between Farhad Pasha, the Turkish Commander-in-Chief, and a strong Persian force under high commanders. It is remembered for the facetious messages that passed between the generals, and for the rich spoil of boys and slave-girls with which victory enabled the Pasha to delight his Sovereign. In 1604 a sudden raid of the Persian captain Allah Werdi Khan captured three hundred prisoners outside the very walls of Baghdad and spread panic within them. A partial blockade of the town was established in the year following.[2] In 1616 Mandali was sacked by Persian forces,[3] but was promptly and

[1] These conditions are fully recorded in general Turkish and Persian history, to which they belong. Their main stages were marked by the Peace of 1555 which endured for twenty years: by an Armistice in 1578, quickly broken: by another Peace in 1590, lasting till 1603. Fresh hostilities then ensued till 1618. Ambitions, jealousies and pretexts were ever present on both sides. Until the end of the century the Ottoman was the aggressor, thereafter the ascendancy and the offensive passed to the Ṣafawis. The succession of feeble rulers in Turkey, and the reign of 'Abbas the Great in Persia, did much to turn the tide of success.

[2] Malcolm, followed by Sykes, makes the whole of 'Iraq fall to Persia in 1605 after the defeat of Cicala in the Urmiyyah battle. This is certainly incorrect.

[3] Della Valle (Letter I of 1617).

vigorously recovered by the Pasha of Baghdad. Of the effect of these conditions on the Kurdish states more will be said on a later page. Other characteristics of the period sprang partly from the Persian menace, partly were endemic in 'Iraq. Its status as a frontier province brought it the benefit of large garrisons to impress town and tribe, and taught it ever to look to the fountain-head of its protection; while the Sultan in turn saw Baghdad dear for its great name and its very precariousness. Within, the nomad and half-settled tribes' impatience of any government at all was a feature of this and every succeeding age. In these earliest days, particularly, tribal scorn of their rulers was habitual, while in settled areas there were cases enough of government within government, of Imperial rule here completely inoperative, and here shared with local potentates. While Mosul and Baghdad, indeed, ran their course as fairly normal seats of an ayalat, the detached provinces of Baṣrah and Shahrizor were barely kept from complete secession.

Sulaiman Pasha, first Wali of Baghdad, gave way to we know not whom. The governor in 1546 was Ayas Pasha. To him fell for the first time a task which till far into the seventeenth century was to weary Pashas of Baghdad—the reduction of Baṣrah and its turbulent tribes. In southern 'Iraq the government conferred by Sultan Sulaiman on Rashid ul Mughamis endured for a decade. Giving and receiving nothing, he kept on passable terms with his northern colleague, the ever-changing Pasha of Baghdad. But friction gradually appeared. Familiarity with the Sultan's rule bred contempt. Fugitives from central 'Iraq found welcome and refuge at the port. The Pasha demanded them in vain. The distant Sultan ordered an expedition; Baṣrah must be annexed in earnest. In 1546 Ayas left Baghdad at the head of an imposing force. Large columns marched down the Tigris,[1] while three hundred sailing-craft conveyed the stores. The Baṣrah ruler advanced north to the Jaza'ir region[2] and was completely defeated. Ayas entered Baṣrah, announced the abolition of taxes levied by the Arab

[1] So Basha'yan. Gulshan makes the march by the Euphrates, and mentions a visit to Najf.

[2] Gulshan suggests that Rashid stayed in Baṣrah to flee tamely when all was lost, while the resistance to Ayas was that of the Qash'am Shaikh, who was defeated and slain.

governor, and substituted the strict dues of religious sanction. His wise benevolence was lauded, and blessings invoked on the Khalif. Ayas remained in Baṣrah as its ruler.[1]

But the work was yet imperfect. In 1549 the tribesmen of the Baṣrah marshes cut all routes to the town. The Pasha of Baṣrah, since he took no part in the subsequent campaign, perhaps could not maintain his own position. The Sultan's orders to punish the insurgents were addressed to 'Ali Pasha Tamarrud, captain of the Janissaries in Baghdad (or possibly its governor). His place in Baghdad was taken by the Mirmiran of Siwas, Muḥammad Pasha Baltachi, who brought a small personal force to his new command. 'Ali Pasha completed his preparations, marched and halted on the Gharraf. Here he was joined by 'Ali Beg, Sanjaq Begi of the district. The united army descended to the main Euphrates. Madinah, head-quarters of the rebel leader 'Ulayyan, was besieged. It fell after an assault which, spread over three days, broke the spirit of the tribesmen; 'Ulayyan fled among his scattered followers. These did not abandon such resistance as raids and brigandage could produce. 'Ali Pasha erected strong redoubts to control the water-ways. Pacification, nominal and temporary, was at last complete. He retired to Baghdad.

When in the spring of 1554 the famous admiral-author "Sidi 'Ali" visited Baṣrah, he found normal government in the city. The navy was in ill repair. Fifteen unsound galleys were handed to him. Relations with Hormuz were friendly enough to let him try, without success, to re-equip them from there. With five ships he co-operated with the Baṣrah governor, Muṣṭafa Pasha,[2] against riverain enemies in 'Arabistan.[3] Janissaries from Egypt were among the Baṣrah garrison. The instability of these caused the expedition to fail, with the loss of a hundred lives.

The Baṣrah Pasha lived, in the clearer intervals, in a pomp

[1] Baṣrah Calendar, p. 62, gives "Wazir Ayas Pasha" as Wali in A. H. 539. This account blends Gulshan and Basha'yan.

[2] Not in the list of Walis in the Baṣrah Calendar. But the list is evidently incomplete, names being merely taken from the few incidents of the Basha'yan history.

[3] "Sidi 'Ali" says the "island of Ḥuwaizah". Possibly an island held by that power, unless Jazirah is used in its other sense. But if so, how could ships co-operate?

based on the sure and copious revenues of his Customs House. His rule, however, scarcely extended beyond the town-ditch; many river-side forts were needed to protect shipping from the Ḥuwaizah robbers; and the marshmen of the lower Tigris and Euphrates showed little signs of coming permanently to terms: "... some the Turks cannot subdue, for that they hold certain Ilandes in the river Euphrates which the Turk cannot win of them. They be theeves all and have no settled dwelling".[1] The governor of Baṣrah was faced, more than his colleagues elsewhere, with something of nationalist feeling in the habitual resistance to government. Merchants objected to no government that could give security; but the town-rabble, with perhaps some religious elements, objected to the Turks as foreigners. Compromises and concessions were attempted, as well as active punishment; but, as will be told, local influences in the end extinguished Turkish government altogether, after a short and flickering life.

Meanwhile in the Shahrizor province secession and recovery were running a different course. The towns—Kirkuk, Arbil, Altun Kupri—were firmly held. The Sultan's rule, indeed, was perhaps more welcome here than in any district in 'Iraq. Only in the northern and eastern areas of the province was opposition found and government nominal and precarious. Of this, as it concerns the neighbouring state of Ardalan, more will be said in the survey of 'Iraq's neighbours.

A few bare facts remain to record of the Baghdad rulers of these years. A later page will speak of the dismissal of 'Ali Pasha Tamarrud, his replacement by Baltachi Muḥammad, and the mission of the Pasha of Aleppo to Kurdish frontier duty. The successor of Darwish 'Ali, who had restored order in Baṣrah in 1567, was perhaps Murad Pasha, an early appointment of Salim II.[2] It is commemorated by the stately minaret of the Muradiyyah, bearing an inscription of A.H. 978. The Pasha of 1575 was seen (but is not named) by Rauwolff, from whom he tried to extract presents. Two or three years later the post was held by a man famous in his time, Alwandzadah 'Ali Pasha.

[1] Ralph Fitch (in Horton Ryley, p. 53).

[2] To the same reign should be ascribed a shadowy incident, gathered by Rauwolff from half-understood diwan-talk, of a raid on Baghdad and the capture and ransom of "the Shah's son". This may refer to some foot-hill trouble with Kurd or Lur.

His pious works embraced the holy places of both sects. He rebuilt the great dome of Ḥusain at Karbala, and the hospice of ʻAbdu ʼl Qadir ul Gailani in Baghdad. Poets of his time applauded a wise and reforming government. Historians found a theme in his expeditions against turbulent neighbours of the province. One of these was directed at the neighbouring Ḥuwaizah state.[1]

The campaign of the great Farhad Pasha near Baghdad about 1589 has been mentioned. He was never governor of Baghdad; but that office was held, almost or quite contemporarily, by yet a greater figure of the age—Jighalzadah,[2] known in Europe as Cicala. His romantic career cannot be recorded here; but the high commands he had already held in the Empire show the importance attached to the Baghdad province. His tenure was marked by important reforms. He called the attention of Stambul to the perils of the Ḥaj pilgrims in traversing, unorganized, the deserts of Arabia. He proposed to organize armed and protected parties to set forth from Baghdad and Damascus, under the governors of these cities. The Shiaʻ shrines of the Euphrates had become almost abandoned by pilgrims through the excessive shortage of water; for the pious canal-works of his predecessors had silted and dried up. Cicala strove to revive the flow both of water and of pilgrims. His schemes were not adopted; but they showed a benign and vigorous mind. His campaigns in southern Persia formed part of the struggle closed only by the peace of 1590. A fraternal conflict in Dizful city-state enabled him to intervene decisively. Dizful and neighbouring fortresses fell into his hands, and Persian vassal-forces were defeated. For a time his power spread far into the Bakhtiyari country.

At the beginning of the last decade of the century Sinan Pasha[3] Jighalzadah held the Pashaliq and enriched it with

[1] A work in Turkish, the "Hunrnamah" of Niyazi (believed to exist but not found by the author) deals with such an expedition in A. H. 992 (A. D. 1584). An abridged form exists under the title "Dhafarnamah".

[2] For his Baghdad governorship cf. von Hammer, VII, pp. 219 f. and 409, VIII, p. 38.

[3] Not to be identified with the "Conqueror of Yaman". But Gulshan (1) does not mention the Pashaliq of Cicala himself, (2) does not know that the great Sinan was Pasha of Mosul in 1594 (see p. 37 sub). Although in the text "Sinan Pasha, son of Jighal" has been taken at its face value, yet this juxtaposition of great names is suspicious.

a caravansarai and other buildings long known by his name. The connexion of the great Cicala with Baghdad was thus prolonged, and was yet again to be renewed. By buildings, likewise, was commemorated the reign of another Pasha of this decade, Ḥasan. In the last year of the century one Dali Ḥusain was governor of Baghdad. He is mentioned only in passing as the brother of the famous outlaw 'Abdu 'l Ḥalim Qarayazichi, whose revolt in Asia Minor terrorized the Ottoman Empire. How far the part played by Dali Ḥusain implicated 'Iraq troops or interests is doubtful. The public of the 'Iraq provinces, probably, were but distant spectators of the dangerous brother rebels.

The new century opened without incident. The governor of the time, Wazir Ḥasan Pasha,[1] protected the Kirkh suburb with a deep and wide ditch and earth-rampart, and adorned it with several buildings. Subsequent Pashas cannot be identified with confidence. The post was conferred on an outgoing Qa'im-maqam of Stambul, Qasim Pasha, at the beginning of 1604. He did not proceed beyond Yenishahr, but there joined the forces of rebellion. At Baghdad he never appeared.[2] Instead came Muṣṭafa Pasha Ṣariqchi. His stay was short. In the autumn of 1604 the state procession of fifteen Qapuchis brought the farman and robe, the sword and golden chain of appointment to a Circassian eunuch, Yusif Pasha. In his time occurred an important rising in Karbala, where the Turkish garrison were slain and despoiled by the townspeople.[3]

The best-recorded incident of the time belongs, in the general history of Turkey, to a range of widespread internal disturbances against which Murad Pasha, Grand Wazir, directed his armies after the Peace of Silvatorek. In 1607 one Muḥammad bin Aḥmad ul Ṭawil, a Janissary captain of the Baghdad garrison, assumed the chief power in the city under circumstances now obscure.[4] Naṣuh Pasha, sometime Grand Wazir and now

[1] Teixeira (ed. cit.), p. 61. He is there called " Acem Baxa ".
[2] Gulshan says that he remained at Brusa, and was there put to death.
[3] Teixeira (ed. cit.), p. 53.
[4] Briefly told in Ghayatu 'l Muram, the Baghdad Calendar, and Basha'yan. More fully in von Hammer (VIII, p. 113), and fullest in Gulshan. The latter two accounts contain discrepancies, but not in essentials. There are references in Della Valle.

governor of Diyarbakr, was detailed to suppress him. He marched southward in 1608 with 40,000 men. In the battle following, Naṣuh was defeated by the treachery of his own troops. Wali Pasha, accompanying him, was slain. An ignominious truce was followed by formal recognition of Muḥammad as Pasha of Baghdad. Although he fell after a few days of power to the dagger of an enemy, his ascendancy had been such as to pass now to his younger brother, Muṣṭafa. But such inheritance could not be tolerated. Maḥmud, son of the great Cicala, was at the time in winter quarters at Urfah. His family connexions in 'Iraq, the devotion of Abu Rishah,[1] of the noble Kurdish family of Soran, of the Qash'am and other 'Iraq tribes, led to his appointment as governor of Baghdad. He was bidden to restore it to the Empire it had flouted. From Mosul he launched a bloodless campaign of missives. Captains and lieutenants of the Baghdad Janissaries received his secret letters bidding them have done with a perverse and hopeless allegiance. These did their work. Muṣṭafa was besieged in the Citadel. Dispatches brought Maḥmud in hottest haste to Baghdad. He reached the walls in the midsummer of 1609. The defenders,[2] superior in guns, offered firm resistance and showed an unexpected loyalty to their leader. After some weeks of costly deadlock a compromise was reached. Muṣṭafa agreed to hand over the government to the son of Cicala, and himself received the rich Sanjaq of Ḥillah. Peace and obedience were restored. Maḥmud Jighalzadah was twice to be ruler of Baghdad, and is remembered in the village-name of Maḥmudiyyah which he founded a stage south of Baghdad. His present term of office was short. In 1610 Baghdad was awarded to 'Ali Pasha Qadhizadah, and subsequently to others whose bare name and title are recorded—Dilawir, Muṣṭafa, and Ḥafidh Ahmad. Of this last much more will be told.

The Mosul[3] records open only at the second millennium of the Hijrah. From the terms in which a European in Mosul mentions

[1] p. 39 sub.

[2] Gulshan, in putting these at more than 20,000 horse and foot, must greatly exaggerate, as the Citadel could not hold the half of that number.

[3] Authority: the Mosul Calendar, which has a list of Walis and "historical information". The author of the latter, Ḥasan Taufiq, notes that, according to Minhalu 'l Auliya, the Pashas before A.H. 1000 are not preserved.

the Pasha of "Carahemit" (Qara 'Amid, Diyarbakr), it would seem that his influence at Mosul as a powerful neighbour exceeded that of Baghdad. If so, the orientation of the Mosul ayalat differed in the sixteenth century from that of the eighteenth, looking upstream instead of down for a colleague who was almost an overlord. We hear of severe earthquakes in Adharbaijan in 1572, felt as far south as Mosul. A solar eclipse, in the same year, filled the sky with stars at midday. The great drought in central 'Iraq from 1574 to 1576—thirty rainless months—stimulated the river-borne export of Mosul wheats to Baghdad. The first recorded Pasha is Amir Ḥusain, the second Piyalah Pasha. Nothing is preserved save the exact period of their tenures. In 1593 Sinan Pasha held the government of Mosul[1] for ten months. He was followed by officials of whom no particulars are preserved. Their terms were of a few months each. Only Ḥusain Pasha, appointed in 1594, reigned for almost three years. In 1600 the province was given to "Ḥasan Pasha, ruler of 'Amadiyyah". The Baḥdinan family had, indeed, been highly favoured by Sultan Sulaiman, and their internal quarrels composed by Farhad Pasha. As Mosul had been given to the prince of Jazirah in 1535,[2] so it may well have been given in 1600 to the Beg of 'Amadiyyah. He held office for nearly four years. Nothing is known of his successors save their names. It was not unusual for the same official to return a second or third time to the same Pashaliq; and there are traces of transfers between the various provinces or sub-provinces of 'Iraq. In 1617 Muḥammad Pasha, who had held the Mutasallimate of Baṣrah, was appointed to Mosul. Three years later the post was awarded, possibly for the first time, to a local candidate. The famous 'Umari family were brought there during this period, that their sanctity might still the alarming earthquakes which had shaken the town. Bakr Pasha was not, however, an 'Umari. He was appointed in 1620, stayed a year, and was transferred to other Pashaliqs. He returned five years later, when the Persians were

[1] The Mosul Calendar gives such particulars as make certain, at first sight, his identification with the great Sinan. There is nothing repugnant to this in Sinan's career, though Turkish historians are silent upon his Mosul governorship; and the Calendar, after making it clear that this was the "Conqueror of Yaman", puts a foot-note denying it. The identification should on the whole be accepted.

[2] p. 26 *supra*.

already in Baghdad. The appointment in 1623 of one Aḥmad Pasha, brother of an officer of the ruler of Baghdad, further suggests that Stambul was forced to give preference to notables of the province itself.

§ 3. *The fringes.*

Such are the scanty surviving facts of this first period of Turkish rule in ‘Iraq proper. It is convenient to survey separately its outlying dependencies and nearest neighbours.

On the desert side, west and south-west of Euphrates, the tribes and oases of Najd were still, pending the great Revival of the eighteenth century, too divided and too uninspired to trouble the ‘Iraq outposts. An occasional exchange of raids on the spring pastures was the only contact. The Bani Khalid of Al Ḥasa (never an ‘Iraq tribe) lorded it in their own country,[1] just touching, at some seasons, the furthest tents of the Euphrates tribes. The desert powers that more concern us are two nomad confederations through whose territories travellers from the Gulf to Aleppo passed for several stages of their route. Mir Naṣir, or Naṣir bin Muhanna, was in 1604 the "king" of the more southerly, which stretched from Najf to Fallujah. Najf, always fanatical and now impoverished since death cut off the bounties of Shah Tahmasp, admitted the power of this desert ruler. Karbala, not less intolerant but larger and more prosperous, was the centre of his dirah. Travellers from Baghdad to Fallujah were met but a few miles from the capital by his agents and paid his tolls. Naṣir, one of the line of some shaikhly house momentarily dominant—Muwali or ‘Anizah—professed allegiance to the Sultan. An occasional present, it may be, reminded the Pasha of this humble servant. But his autocracy of the wilds, his tolls and customs-bars for travellers, his intimidation of pilgrims, told another tale. Small Turkish garrisons were usually stationed in the Holy Cities; but they held their ground on sufferance of the

[1] It is clear from the Institutes of Sultan Sulaiman that Stambul claimed the allegiance of Al Ḥasa (as it did of Abyssinia). Auliya effendi remarks that there were no fiefs there and that, whereas the governors were formerly installed as Beglerbegis, they now ruled without authority, but sent presents to the governor of Baghdad. If shaikhs of Qaṭif and Baḥrain sent messages of welcome to Sulaiman in 1534, this was far from a true submission. Briefly, a baseless and unreal claim to Al Ḥasa was maintained, in the Turkish manner, unsupported by history or present power.

Shaikh, and in 1604 (as has been told) that of Karbala met an ignominious end.[1]

North and west of Naṣir's territory, with perhaps a wild no-man's-land between, was the more famous power of Abu Rishah.[2] The name was hereditary to the paramount chief of the tribe-group. 'Anah was his base. His dirah stretched from Hit to Birijik and the fringes of the Syrian tribes. Ṭayyibah and Maskanah were his. To the Pashas of Diyarbakr, Baghdad, and Aleppo, Abu Rishah was a formidable name. His dynasty existed before Ottoman arms appeared in Syria or 'Iraq. The Turk—strange to desert politics—found an enemy inaccessible, contemptuous, rarely subservient. By 1574 this "King of Arabia" had had many a brush with the Sultan's officers. He had installed his son in a river-side castle at "Galantza", only to be captured and beheaded in Stambul. This neither broke his power nor modified his habits of toll and raid. The Venetian consul at Aleppo sent him presents. Travellers knew him as a King. The Turks admitted his Amirate of 'Anah, and brought him into their bureaucracy as Sanjaq Begi of his own area.[3] The customs collected at his posts were nominally shared by him with the Turkish Treasury; the power to molest and to protect the traveller was his alone. By an agreement made shortly before 1575, he was to be paid 6,000 ducats a year by the Sultan, and his hereditary rule admitted. In the opening years of the new century the reigning Amir was Aḥmad (or Ḥamid), whose rebellious nephews were increasing the normal insecurity by raids in defiance of his power.

Camel-caravans made the journey from Baghdad to Aleppo in fifty days, from Baṣrah and Zubair in seventy. The general conditions of desert travel were those of every age. Such as readily fell in with the realities of bedouin life (whereof courtesy is a part) and could yield equably item after item of their baggage, would reach Baghdad with little danger. Every lord of twenty camels was both authorized guide and wandering

[1] Teixeira (ed. Sinclair and Ferguson), p. 53.

[2] Mentioned by nearly all the travellers. See Teixeira (op. cit., p. 84, foot-note) for summary of the references to him. Rauwolff (not there mentioned) is important also.

[3] Compare their treatment, centuries later, of similar powers in Arabia—the Sanjaq conferred upon the nineteenth-century rulers of Najd and Kuwait, and the rank of Qa'immaqam bestowed upon ibn Hadhdhal.

customs-barrier. To pay the fees of the one and freely declare your goods to the other, while avoiding both when possible, were the easy but expensive rules of the road. By occasional expeditions, by subsidy and favour, and by the digging of desert wells, the Turks did something to open the route. But the task for four centuries was too much for them, and meanwhile the outpost Turkish authorities were as rapacious as the Arab. Christian traders, in particular, of whom some number traded from Syria eastward to Persia, Hormuz, or even India, were subject to "many unjust taxes . . . to their great loss and damage"; and might easily be arrested as spies.

Earlier pages[1] mentioned the Portuguese invasion of the Gulf waters in the late fifteenth century, and the foundation of Hormuz by de Albuquerque in 1507. Besides this fortress (which, forced to leave, he easily regained in 1515), he left a string of trading-posts on the Gulf shores. From the native coasters the Doms had nothing to fear. Only rare and feeble opposition told of deep resentment at their intrusion and brutality. But a serious rival was at hand. By 1520 Salim the Grim had conquered Egypt and the Yaman, and the Turks were finding their sea-legs. By 1529 a Turkish fleet had entered the Gulf. They touched at Baṣrah, and in no friendly guise; for the ruler of that port agreed with the Portuguese to keep them at bay in exchange for help against his own tribal enemies. A Portuguese captain visited Baṣrah and penetrated some way up the Rivers. The Arab governor refused (as usual) to fulfil his bargain, whereat the Portuguese burnt some reed-villages and withdrew. In 1538 a large Turkish fleet from Egypt raided the Indian coast. In 1550 Qaṭif, expelling its ruler, appealed to the Turks at Baṣrah to protect them from the Portuguese. Murad Beg occupied Qaṭif, but was dislodged by the Portuguese and pursued into the Shaṭṭ ul 'Arab. The Turks replied by raids on Masqaṭ and Qishim and threats to Hormuz. The leader of this sally, Pir Beg, was beheaded in Stambul. His successor, Murad Beg, could accomplish nothing. A later commander, 'Ali Chalabi, was defeated in battle in 1553. But threats to the Portuguese depots continued. In 1559 a Turkish fleet conveying Janissaries landed at Baḥrain, at that time subject to the titular Shaikh of

[1] pp. 1 and 5 *supra*.

Hormuz. The local ruler was helped by a Persian force, and reinforced by the Portuguese from Hormuz. The Turks surrendered on humiliating terms. In 1581 Masqaṭ was seized, but not held, by the Turkish captain 'Ali Beg. So profitless were the Gulf waters to the rulers of Baṣrah, whose Qaptan Pasha played, it seems, no part in fighting the intruder.

'Iraq's remaining neighbour of Arab race was the powerful Wali of Ḥuwaizah. His embassy of submission to Sultan Sulaiman had been but the precautionary politeness of a moment. Throughout the century his relations with his Persian suzerain varied from servility to defiance, from tribute paid to blackmail demanded. His amphibious followers on the Shaṭṭ ul 'Arab were undeterred by Qaptan Pasha or by Portuguese from theft and piracy. Voyagers on the Shaṭṭ were impressed by the precautions against this audacity: "we cast anchor", says one,[1] "against a fort that the Turks held . . . they have many others such to protect their land and their vessels therein against Arab forays." The Wali of the time, Mubarak bin Muṭlab, was no less nervous of his Turkish neighbours. His riverain lands were left uncultivated, his claim to the rule of Baṣrah itself maintained with Arab persistence but little hope. He had, however, some part yet to play in its affairs.[2]

The sixteenth and early seventeenth centuries saw developments in the relations of the 'Iraq Pashas with the Kurdish and Lurish fringes of their command. In Jazirah ibn 'Umr, the great days of the ruling house did not outlast the life of Sayyid Aḥmad upon whom Mosul itself had been bestowed. His son ruled in peace, but in the reign of Mir Ibrahim, his successor, family quarrels led as usual to the scurrying of rivals to the rival Powers. One fled for support to Farhad Pasha at Van, the other invoked Tahmasp Shah. The Shah interfered, and captured and slew the Mir; but the rule of Jazirah and its vassal Korkil seems still to have been determined by Turkish farmans, and its position on a main marching-route kept it in fairly close Ottoman control. There was little interference, however, with the local dynasty as long as it kept its limits. Subjection to Bitlis was long forgotten.

The 'Amadiyyah state was equally torn by faction. Hasan,

[1] Teixeira (ed. cit.), p. 27.

[2] See pp. 121–2 sub.

its Baḥdinan prince in 1500, had early submitted to the rising Ṣafawi, and gained high favour. Such dependence on Ardalan as still remained was by this manœuvre thrown off; and Baḥdinan ambition was again well served by the *volte-face* of instant adhesion to Sultan Salim on his appearance. To Sulaiman the Magnificent the next prince, Ḥusain, was able to render special service, and the little state had for a time the status of an ayalat. But the death of Ḥusain plunged it into civil war. Of his two sons, Quhad and Bairam, the second fled for help to the Shah. Meanwhile the Mazuri tribesmen expelled Quhad and installed his cousin Sulaiman. The Hakari prince of the day, Zainab Beg, now took a part; he interceded with the Shah to release Bairam. Quhad fled to Stambul, secured the favour of the Grand Wazir, and obtained a farman for the government of 'Amadiyyah. Bairam Beg was meanwhile installed at Zakho, and Sulaiman at 'Amadiyyah. Quhad, farman in hand, reached Dohuk and busied himself with the removal of enemies; but Sulaiman with a Mazuri force was able to capture him and scatter his followers. Bairam hastened from Zakho to Dohuk, and escorted Sulaiman to the palace of 'Amadiyyah where he assumed his government. The sons of Quhad, however,—Sayyidi Khan and another—fled to Stambul. Murad III took up their case. 'Amadiyyah was given to Sayyidi Khan, and Farhad Pasha authorized to call upon the Pashas of Baghdad and Kirkuk, and the vassal princes of Kurdistan, for help in installing him. By setting rival against rival, by intrigue and the demand for bribes, by a mock trial before a Shara' judge, Farhad Pasha succeeded in handing 'Amadiyyah to Sayyidi Khan in 1585. He ruled it for many years.

These circumstances, of small interest and uncertain perspective, are taken from the chronicles of the time to illustrate thus early the main feature of Kurdish history—the endless self-seeking quarrels of brothers for their petty thrones, and their ready appeals to tribesman, Turk, and Persian. Were materials to hand, and did space allow, the same story with only names and places changed could doubtless be told of Zakho, Dohuk, and 'Aqrah, of Raniyyah, Ḥarir, and the rest. In every valley, in every hill-side village, the same disunity was lit by the same fires of selfish ambition, and fed by the same fuel of intrigue and violence. The Turkish part was that of the occasional bestower of farmans, receiver of nominal homage and contributions of military force. Even these could be withheld by the stronger Begs if a correct tone were maintained. This was not government; yet modern experience finds it difficult to quarrel with so light a hold on a region inaccessible, alien, and (to the Sultan) profitless. The general Turkish policy to the Kurdish states was one of commitments avoided, of the fruits of Empire expected without the labours. It was that which any government, so placed, must have adopted. It would have succeeded better if more firmness and goodwill had been behind it, if Kurdish pride and fickleness had been studied, and if a rival Empire had not been striving constantly to regain the place of suzerain.

The clash of Turkish and Persian land-hunger is most marked (among what concerns these pages) in the valleys of Shahrizor. Here the resistance to Turkish claims lay not in the independence of native princes, but in the counter-claims of the royal house of Ardalan. Their influence in Shahrizor was doubly formidable. Before Turk and Ṣafawi had appeared, they had claimed empire over it; and since the rise of Isma'il Shah—with a brief apostasy to Salim the Grim—the Ardalan prince had been a loyal vassal of Tabriz. He claimed south-eastern Kurdistan, then, both for himself and for his overlord. Unchecked, he had spread his power south and west over the (later) frontier, and dominated the Shahrizor country. The Lesser Zab, the Aoroman, Shahribazar, the Qara Dagh, even the "warm country", owned the vague sway of Ma'mun. This was little agreeable to Ottoman claims, to the location of a Janissary garrison at Kirkuk, and to the need to control the eastward routes. Local collision with Ardalan officers and influence was inevitable. To Sultan Sulaiman, the Wali of Ardalan appeared too strong and rich a neighbour, and a displeasing contrast to the docile states of 'Amadiyyah and Bitlis. In 1538 he sent a force under Ḥusain Pasha against Ma'mun. With the Pasha were associated many Kurdish Begs, including the Baḥdinan; the thorough conquest of Shahrizor, if not of Merivan and Sannah, was the objective. Ma'mun [1] offered a noble resistance. In the end he retired to

[1] Gulshan i Khulafa differs from the Sharafnamah in (1) making Ma'mun Beg a mere hostage taken (? in 1535) by Sultan Sulaiman from his father to

the ancient fortress of Qal'ah i Dhulm. A siege followed; Ma'mun, seeing all lost, fled to Stambul but only to be kept in captivity. The Turks devastated and withdrew. Surkhab, uncle of the fugitive Ma'mun, renewed his allegiance to the Shah. Others of the family fled to Turkey. Ma'mun was released, awarded the rich fief of Ḥillah, and dispatched to accompany the Sultan's troops for his reinstation.

'Ali Pasha, governor of Baghdad, had meanwhile sent his dispatch to the capital. The reply surprised him. It contained his dismissal and the elevation of Muḥammad Baltachi, mentioned before as deputy-governor of Baghdad in 1549. The Shahrizor campaign was, however, entrusted not to him but to 'Uthman Pasha of Aleppo, who was dispatched in command of regular infantry and the feudal contingents of several ayalats. Baltachi Muḥammad, now installed in his Baghdad Sarai, sent a large contingent, well equipped with artillery, to join the Aleppo general. Loyal Kurdish vassals supplied forces to help the Pasha in his encirclement of Surkhab's fortress. His guns failed to effect a breach. For complete blockade he had too small a force. He died of weariness and unsuccess. His troops melted away.[1] Our two authorities here completely diverge. The Turkish chronicler wipes out the failure of 'Uthman by a successful campaign closely following, and makes Shahrizor a Turkish province for the whole second half of the century. In his account Muḥammad Baltachi was commissioned to restore the Shahrizor. He marched, leaving as Qa'immaqam in Baghdad Suhail Beg, governor of the Rumaḥiyyah Sanjaq. The first campaign launched by Baltachi was one of diplomacy. Terms were concluded, the fortress gates thrown open, and Surkhab

secure the loyalty of Shahrizor. Ma'mun, after a Turkish official career, settled in Ḥillah; (2) in confining his narrative to the years 1552–4, and dealing with the "sieges" of Shahrizor solely from the Baghdad point of view. Ardalan is never mentioned; (3) in saying that after 1554 Shahrizor was "rejoined" to the Ottoman Empire. The account in the text is generally that of the Sharafnamah, but embodies Gulshan where they are not actually discrepant.

[1] This is Gulshan's account of 'Uthman Pasha's campaign. The Sharafnamah agrees in the identity of the Turkish commander, and in the unsuccessful outcome. It adds, however, that the fortress besieged was "Dhulm", that the siege was preceded by a pitched battle and lasted for two years. Dhulm was then relieved by forces sent by Tahmasp under one Ḥusain Beg. Muḥammad Beg, the fugitive Ardalan prince, died at the same time as 'Uthman Pasha.

left the town in safety. Shahrizor was restored to the Empire of the Khalifs. A sufficient guard was posted with Wali Beg as governor. The ayalat, thus regularized in 1554 for the first time, was confirmed as Turkish territory by the treaty of 1590.

The Ardalan account has nothing of this. Surkhab, relieved by his suzerain, retained Ardalan and Shahrizor for a long reign and with high favour at the Ṣafawi court.[1] The subordination of Shahrizor to Turkey, in this version, was the voluntary act of a later Ardalan ruler, Timur. He had seen the feebleness of the rulers of Persia. He transferred his allegiance to Stambul, and obtained farman and bounty from Murad III. His whole kingdom thereafter admitted the overlordship of the Khalif, while the valleys of Ḥarir, Bazyan, and Shahrizor were directly administered from Kirkuk. Thus by the eighth decade of the century (if not by an earlier date) Shahrizor took its place as a Turkish province, and the Ardalan as a high-standing vassal realm of the Sultan. An area for many miles round Kirkuk had from the first been administered by the Sanjaq Begi of that place.[2]

By 1600 the wind had changed again. The successor of Timur attempted independence, but succumbed instead to the seductions of Shah 'Abbas. Khan Aḥmad Khan in 1605 ascended the royal government of Sannah as one of the vassal-kings of Persia. He was used at once by his suzerain as a means of offensive on Kurdish tribes that leaned to Turkey. The first act of Khan Aḥmad was to raid and punish the Mukri group and the Bilbas. In subsequent years he took possession of Ruwanduz and 'Amadiyyah, putting his own lieutenants into these places and into Keui and Ḥarir; but the interruption of local dynasties was short-lived. The first twenty years of Khan Aḥmad Khan were a period of great Ardalan glory and prosperity. He enjoyed the continual favour of Shah 'Abbas, and recovered for a time almost the whole of the ancient Ardalan dominions. He was, it is certain, the alarm and envy of the Pashas of Mosul and Baghdad. Turkish and 'Iraqi historians deny by their silence his successful invasion of Ottoman soil, and means indeed are lacking to dis-

[1] He sent his son Bahram as governor of Ruwanduz, where he founded a dynasty which endured for three centuries.

[2] It was perhaps not an ayalat till late in the reign of Sulaiman Qanuni. The fiefs allotted in it by him may belong to various dates.

tinguish between raid and acquisition. Khan Aḥmad did not, perhaps, rob the Sultan of any soil directly administered from Kirkuk. He tampered with the vassaldom of half-independent waverers, and exchanged farmans for presents with princes whose loyalty was anyhow valueless. Many, no doubt, held the letters-patent of Shah and Sultan together.

In Luristan the last years of the sixteenth century saw a revolution—the fall of the Atabegs. Those of Fars and of Luristan i Buzurg had long since given way to local Khans. In 1585 the last Atabeg of Lesser Luristan was still ruling. This was Shah Werdi Khan, attacked by Timur Khan of Ardalan in that year. But the line did not survive the strong rule of Shah 'Abbas and his special wish for devoted subjects on his western border. The Atabeg was deposed in the last years of the century, and replaced by one Ḥusain Khan, a man of great personality and the most prominent of the Lurish chiefs. His achievements both in war and in peaceful development earned him the title of Buzurg, the Great.

§ 4. *The Government.*

References have been made to the peculiar difficulties of 'Iraq as a field for government—its tribes, its religions, its frontier position—and the question asked with what hopes and doubts its new masters could be viewed. Now that the little known has been told of the first three generations of Turkish government, an answer must be attempted to the question: what sort of rule were the Turks, in fact, producing?

Although many of the town-amenities of to-day—conservancy, schools, town-planning, hospitals—were lacking, town life was secure and not uncomfortable. The greatest cities in history have lacked sanitation not less completely. Dark and narrow streets were a half-intended protection from summer glare. The settled people of 'Iraq have at all times felt pride in their township, with a love of simple and decorous social intercourse. "Baladiyyahs" on the later pattern did not yet exist; but there was in every settlement an informal council of leading citizens. Medicine was represented by the Sayyid whose sole drug was the Qur'an, by the barber ready with razor and lancet, by an occasional Persian mendicant with herbs. Education was found at the feet of the Mullas in the Mosque-schools which Sultan Sulaiman had founded or suffered to remain. The work of police fell to the Janissary garrison aided by private watchmen appointed by the merchants. The Qadhi, sole civil and criminal judge, looked to no code but the Shara' law. Corruption could not but be general; but, as we hear from travellers[1] of police officers efficient and benign, so doubtless there were rare judges wise and honest. In such matters, the tone of the public service closely followed the character of the Pasha of the day.

Rule in the towns, then, if unprogressive was tolerably conservative. Religious oppression was less than anywhere in Turkey. If there was bullying and extortion, it was not confined to Baghdad, to Turkey, or to that age. Jew and Christian paid a moderate poll-tax to the tax-farmer; Muslims their customs, their octrois, date and sheep-tax, their bazaar-dues on weighing and vending. The Pasha was no economist: the incidence of taxation obeyed no rule but that of maximum and immediate yield.

Of government in the tribes there is little evidence. The recorded turbulence of the Baṣrah tribes suggests conditions like those of later centuries, or more restless as the attempted control was stranger. Travellers from Syria paid more tolls to tribal potentates than to Government, and learnt the futility of appeal. Here and there the favour of Pasha or Agha—a robe, a tax-farm, help in a tribal war—would be sought by the Shaikh of an inlying dirah: compliments and promises cost nothing even to one remote in steppe or marsh: but for regular obedience, loyal subjection, it would be foolish to look.

The military garrisons of this century varied with the course of relations with Persia. The signature of Peace, in 1555 and in 1590, would be followed by the paying off of temporary levies, by the return of Janissary and Sipahi companies to Stambul, by the dismissal of feudal troops; and in peaceful years no Pasha would waste his treasury on the repairing of bastions. At all times, however, armed forces were the mainspring of government. To assert a minimum of authority, and for frequent tribal suppressions, garrisons were necessary in every town: and settlements

[1] Teixeira (ed. cit.), p. 67. He writes of 1604.

of all sizes required strong mud walls with loopholed towers. The governors of the four capital cities had each a troop of armed personal attendants, as well as a regiment or more of guards locally raised and armed with matchlocks. These were paid and permanent, but provincial and not imperial,[1] troops. They were increased at need by bodies of the timariots. For a campaign, temporary levies of urban Arabs and foot-hill Kurds would be raised, while the fief-holders, rallying to their Sanjaq, must serve by the obligations of their estate.[2] The backbone of the whole was the regular army of the Sultan, under his own and not the Pasha's officers. Imperial gunners manned the greater fortresses, imperial infantry—the Janissaries—were in every Sanjaq. To the 'Iraqi their drill and arms made them formidable, while their quarrelsome oppression made them hated. Their function in the province was to enforce government. They were the town-police, the official messengers, the tax-collectors where force or fear were required, and a ubiquitous regular army. Nice specialization of function was not attempted; the day, however, had not yet come when a Janissary might live anyhow and anywhere, while still remaining enrolled. Baghdad, perhaps, had now one or two thousand, the other ayalat centres half those numbers. They were increased, at times replaced, by the less honourable corps of the sagbans or siemans. The imperial troops, like the local, were paid from the Pasha's treasury, but at imperial rates.

As the government of the Empire was an autocratic monarchy with religious sanction, so the government of each province was absolute. In the remoter provinces especially there existed little to prevent the Pashas governing, as a traveller says, " at their

[1] The general basis of Turkish military forces is the distinction of imperial and local troops. The former, the " Qapu Quli ", were in every particular a centralized body merely loaned or temporarily posted to the provinces: they included the corps of Janissaries and subordinate corps (sagbans, bustanchis, &c.) later incorporated with them, the regular (not the feudal) sipahis, the topchis, jebechis, and saqqas. The local troops included the personal guards, the occasional levies, and the tribal contingents of a Pasha; in practice also the feudal forces of the province, though the obligations of these were really imperial.

[2] But the feudal rally, the basis of the Turkish provincial system, was never a leading phenomenon in 'Iraq. It was found little in Baghdad, not at all in Başrah. Only in Mosul and Shahrizor it approached the normal of other provinces. See p. 26 *supra*.

own will and pleasure". In the absence of a true and benign principle of government, of any wish to govern a subject race to its profit, the restraints against oppressive self-enrichment were slight. For the hard treatment of foreigners a religious sanction could be employed; and to the ruthless squeezing of the public at large a Pasha was forced by the expensive outlay necessary to his own office. But entirely without restraints he was not. He was a Muslim. In the annually-appointed Qaḏhi was a constant witness of his methods, and one soon to return to the capital. The Daftardars, similarly, were appointed from Stambul and thither rendered their accounts, though in practice they could not but support the Pasha who held their lives in his hand. Appeal by the subjects themselves to their Sovereign was not unknown. The Diwan must be consulted at times and could not be entirely flouted. References are made[1] to a permanent official at Baghdad and at Aleppo deputed by the Sovereign himself to watch the merchants' interests, while those of Baṣrah[2] could sometimes obtain redress through the Portuguese agent there. Finally, the half-independent status of the Janissaries set a limit to the caprices of the Pasha, whom they had no reason to court. Stronger than all these checks was the ultimate limit of popular endurance; and this was the less remote in a country of wild undisciplined tribes. No Pasha could have withstood a general revolt.

His appointment was in theory annual. But in practice the highest officers sometimes could not be displaced, some were too loyal and valuable, some had bought a longer term. This last was the dominant consideration. The appointment of Beglerbegi to a great government—Cairo, Baghdad, Tabriz—was honourable and highly profitable. Too frequently the Sultan could not resist the candidate who paid a round sum of revenue in advance. The transition is easy from this to a mere bribe, and its effect on the resultant government in the ayalat was the same. The first care of the incoming Pasha, for more than three centuries, was to divide up the lands of his province into the usual number of farmable units, from a single canal to a huge tribal territory, and lease them to the highest reasonable bidder. The farmers

[1] e. g. Teixeira (ed. cit.), p. 64.
[2] Rauwolff.

were indistinguishable from governors—at times were specifically both. This Sanjaq Begi, that Agha or ḍhabiṭ, would bring his hundred Janissaries to Ḥillah, sublet its lands and taxes, employ his force in stimulating payment or hire them out to the rapacious collectors.

Provincial administration, in fact, was in a transitional state, between its origin as a fief-group and its later place as a devolved government. The relations of the governor to his Sovereign in the rallying of forces beneath the Banner were those of the old Beglerbegi; and he in turn called upon his Sanjaqs, and they upon the Za'ims and timariots, upon the aghas of the smaller towns, and the tamer shaikhs. But the Pasha of the day was more than the mere chief of feudal levies. He was collector of the Sultan's revenues, custodian of shrines and their Auqaf, lord of a palace and a staff of ministers, president of a council, responsible for all the few functions of civil and military government. Meanwhile, from the moment of his gorgeous entry to his no less impressive supersession, he lived the life of an independent prince.[1]

[1] Cf., in particular, Rauwolff's account of the court of Aleppo. The remarks of Dr. Ponqueville (in Thornton, i, p. 160) are typical for all periods.

III

THE ṢU BASHI AND SULTAN MURAD

§ 1. *Bakr the Ṣu Bashi.*

If, eighty-seven years after the conquest of Sulaiman the Magnificent, 'Iraq was now to fall partly to peaceful secession from within, partly to treachery ending in a second Persian occupation, the reason is not to be sought only in the province itself. Its remoteness and peculiar problems largely explain it; but the conditions were provided no less by the weakness of the Empire. The signature of peace with Persia in 1619 was followed by no peace in Turkey. The Sultan, Murad IV, was still a child. His feeble predecessors had allowed disorder to gather strength on every hand.

> "The rebel Abaza was lord and tyrant over Asia Minor. The tribes of the Lebanon were in open insurrection. The governors of Egypt and other provinces were wavering in their allegiance. The Barbaresque regencies assumed the station of independent powers. . . . The fleets of the Cossack marauders . . . even appeared in the Bosphorus, and plundered the immediate vicinity of the Capital. In Constantinople itself there was an empty Treasury, a dismantled arsenal, debased coinage, exhausted magazines, a starving population, and a licentious soldiery." [1]

In Baghdad, remotest corner of an Empire so distraught, the usurpation of Bakr the Ṣu Bashi was to hand 'Iraq for half a generation to the Shah.[2] For that alone, the well-remembered

[1] Creasy, p. 246.
[2] The episode of the Ṣu Bashi is the most famous in modern 'Iraq history. Its fullest record is in Gulshan and in the historiographers followed by von Hammer (Bk. IX, pp. 5 ff.). These two sources are independent, and differ considerably in detail; cf. R. P. Phillipe, *Voyage d'Orient*, pp. 87–8. On the Persian side, cf. Ta'rikh i 'Alam Arai i 'Abbasi, of Iskandar Beg Turkoman.

episode is important; and in the history of humanity the story deserves a place as a *locus classicus* of treachery.

Bakr was a Janissary of Baghdad. Promotion brought him the rank of Ṣu Bashi,[1] Lieutenant of Police. He became captain of his company, and rose to a paramount position in the garrison. Wealth and alliances, with ruthless ambition, more and more magnified his power. Twelve hundred 'Azabs[2] followed his personal command. By 1619 his influence exceeded that of the weak ruler, Yusif Pasha. He was uncrowned King of Baghdad, inspiring devotion and hatred and exposed to the intrigues of envy. In 1621 his affairs took him with a force of 'Azabs and Janissaries to the lower Euphrates. Baghdad officialdom with shaking head watched him depart, and had leisure to reflect on his ambitions and severities and their own station beneath him. Leader of the malcontents was his ancient enemy, Muḥammad Qanbar. In his hatred of the upstart, Qanbar could count on strong support. The moment was opportune. He summoned to secret conclave the officers and nobles of the city. All agreed on the dethronement of the Ṣu Bashi. News of the plot was carried to 'Umr his Kahya, and to Muḥammad his son.[3] 'Umr could not profess the loyalty he still felt. He undertook so to lay the case before the Pasha that Bakr must fall. These professions did not deceive the conspirators. They felt that 'Umr, right-hand man of the Ṣu Bashi, should be the first to go. Qanbar himself waited upon Yusif Pasha. To him he described the factions in Baghdad: 'Umr with his large following must be reckoned of Bakr's party; and the ambitions of Bakr could not stop short of the Pashaliq. Yusif was persuaded, but foolishly sought to win over 'Umr by the bestowal of honours. Priceless time was lost. The Ṣu Bashi's party, led by 'Umr and Muḥammad, rallied their supporters, shut gates, blockaded streets, and

[1] The title, whatever its origin as water-warden or as irrigation official, by this time connoted police duties; cf. Père Anastase, p. 197 (foot-note); Teixeira (ed. cit.), p. 103; Huart, p. 48 (foot-note).

[2] Originally a special corps in charge of the magazines; here evidently light mercenary troops.

[3] The part played by the son Muḥammad is doubtful. Accounts followed by von Hammer make him privy to the plot and subsequently a leader in the attack on Yusif Pasha in his Citadel. Gulshan gives him as loyal to his father. The latter is here accepted. Von Hammer's version has perhaps been influenced by his later treachery.

seized strategic buildings. The loyal troops of the Pashaliq, massed in the Maidan and Citadel, suffered heavily from their fire. A sortie of the Pasha's men led to a fierce street battle in which victory rested with the rebels. The siege of the Citadel was closely pressed.

Qanbar fell back upon another plan. By swift and secret messenger he dispatched a letter to his son, who had accompanied Bakr on campaign. It bade him make away with the upstart tyrant. The letter fell instead into the hands of the Ṣu Bashi, whose tribal expedition had now ended in victory. Horrified, he marched on Baghdad. The Tigris was crossed under heavy fire from the Citadel, where the hopes of the besieged grew fainter and vanished entirely when a stray shot slew Yusif Pasha.

Under promise of personal safety, Qanbar surrendered to his ancient enemy. The inrushing troops of Bakr spared nothing. Of the garrison, a few escaped to the streets and the desert, many fell into captivity. To Qanbar and his two sons Bakr showed the extremes of hatred and cruel revenge. They were placed in chains in a boat loaded with sulphur and bitumen and burned to a terrible death. The Ṣu Bashi feasted his eyes and ears till the last charred ashes sank in the Tigris. The common prisoners met as dreadful a fate. The names of Hulaku and Timur were on men's lips. The victims included the venerable Mufti of Baghdad. Backed by the treasures of the Sarai, the Ṣu Bashi emerged unquestioned master of Baghdad.

This could not be the end; Stambul had heard nothing of these events. Bakr meanwhile produced a forged farman, and proclaimed his appointment to the Pashaliq. Simultaneously he wrote to Ḥafidh Aḥmad Pasha, Beglerbegi of Diyarbakr, and to the Sovereign himself. He had, his letters declared, rescued Baghdad from faction and violence, and ridded the Empire of Yusif Pasha, a traitor: the government of Baghdad was the recompense he asked. While his messengers still toiled on the road, heavy blows fell upon the city. Fear drove many cultivators to the desert. The rains failed. Famine set in. From Najd trooped up starving thousands, intensifying the deadly hunger in central 'Iraq. Looting of provision-stores was followed by the eating of every abomination. Cannibalism was not unknown. After weeks of misery the crisis passed. Flocks from Persia and laden rafts from Mosul fed Baghdad until the next season.

Meanwhile the envoys of the Ṣu Bashi reached the Sultan's Diwan. The Grand Wazir, Mir Ḥusain, was not deceived. He bestowed Baghdad upon Sulaiman Pasha; dispatched one 'Ali Agha as Mutasallim, to hold Baghdad until the new Wali should arrive; and sent orders to Ḥafidh Aḥmad at Diyarbakr to support Sulaiman Pasha with his armies. 'Ali Agha reached Baghdad, where the Ṣu Bashi was scarcely restrained from putting him to death.

Sulaiman Pasha presently arrived at Diyarbakr, where Ḥafidh Aḥmad rallied the Pashas of Mosul, Shahrizor, Mar'ash, and Siwas. His own forces were twenty thousand. Contingents from the Kurdish Begs joined him. In a last council of war at Diyarbakr, his captains urged the dangers of the campaign. Ḥafidh Aḥmad rejected such warnings, and gave word to march. A halt was made at Mosul. The Kurdish forces were here reviewed. Contingents of 'Amadiyyah and Siwas arrived, those of Urfah and Mar'ash were long awaited. The army at Mosul began to suffer from disease. News, however, reached Ḥafidh Aḥmad of whispers in Stambul that fear or the rebel's gold were keeping him from Baghdad. He could delay no more. He moved to Kirkuk, and thence sent an army ahead—Sulaiman and Bustan[1] Pashas, with chiefs of the noble house of Soran. With a halt at Buhriz, these reached the walls of Baghdad and camped north of the town by A'dhamiyyah.[2]

The Ṣu Bashi first kept behind his walls, then, by a sudden sortie, wrought havoc on the besiegers and drove them to a more distant camp. A fierce battle on the following day ended in a rebel victory. These withdrew to their walls, the Sultan's forces re-formed and camped by the Diyalah. A few days later they were joined by Ḥafidh Aḥmad and a large body of vassals, who included all the hereditary rulers of the Kurdish states. The Sardar at once pressed the assault. A ruse brought

[1] Wali of Mosul in 1619 (Mosul Calendar).

[2] In the ensuing operations, the account of von Hammer (based on Na'imah and Pashawi) is to be preferred to Gulshan, in which there are chronological and topographical difficulties.

the city garrison into the open, but after a day and a night of close contact it fled within its gates, leaving four thousand dead and wounded upon the field. The Kurdish leaders urged their Pasha to press home the attack, for mourning and lamentation filled the town; but the good advice was rejected, and he retired to his camp. In the wanton slaughter of prisoners and beheading of the dead was shown his bitterness against the city he had once ruled. Mutiny among his own irregulars increased his disgust, and was barely allayed by his bounty.

Negotiations had already passed between the leaders on either side. Bakr would accept no terms but the Pashaliq. This was unthinkable. Food was now scarce in Baghdad, the garrison weakened. He turned to his supreme act of betrayal. Messengers left Baghdad for Persia, bearing the keys of the city to Shah 'Abbas. They were received with the liveliest pleasure. Urgent orders were sent to the vassals of Luristan, Ardalan, and the Afshar to rally to the governor of Hamadan, Ṣafi Quli Khan. An army speedily formed and reached the frontier. No effort was to be spared to profit by this heaven-sent chance of regaining 'Iraq and its holy shrines.

While the first Persian force under Karchghai Khan was still short of Shahroban, and Persian envoys had been welcomed in Baghdad, the Ṣu Bashi addressed the besieging general. A Persian army was reported from the frontier: would Ḥafidh Aḥmad Pasha join in defending Baghdad against the enemy of their country? Ambassadors came and went. Ḥafidh could not admit the usurper as Beglerbegi of Baghdad: Bakr would accept no less. The Persian menace was confirmed, the besieging troops were war-weary and footsore. An envoy of Karchghai reached the camp. "Baghdad was Persian; would the Pasha consent to retire from the vicinity, to keep the peace between the two nations?" "This is no Persian soil," replied the Sardar; "our task is to punish a rebel." The Persian with threatening words returned to his master.

But, as the Shah's armies loomed up from the east, some solution must be found. A council was held and decision reached to grant the Pashaliq to Bakr. Then—true Turkish diplomat—Ḥafidh Aḥmad prepared farmans in a different sense, naming Bakr governor of Raqqah. The bearer of these documents to the Ṣu Bashi was received with fury. He barely escaped to report their angry rejection. The Sardar still would not yield the final point, had not such tidings reached him as left no choice. A spy or deserter brought news that Bakr was minting coins in the Persian name. His treason stood apparent, but the case was not less desperate for that: at any cost the Shah's armies must be repelled. An infamous traitor was vested with the great Pashaliq of Baghdad.

2. *The second Persian occupation.*

The embassy of Ṣafi Quli was still in Baghdad. Suspicious of the enemy without, they pressed for the final reply of the Ṣu Bashi. The farman at last secure in his hands, he dictated a message of exaggerated and sarcastic servility. It reached Ṣafi Quli, to be read with angry surprise. The Khan sent it to the Shah, who summoned forces from every province to meet him on the frontier. Meanwhile the Ṣu Bashi with morbid cruelty was hanging Persians head-downwards from the walls of Baghdad. Ḥafidh Aḥmad had left for Mosul.

Karchghai Khan now appeared before the walls. He demanded submission. Bakr suavely offered him his expenses of the campaign, and nothing more: Baghdad would never be surrendered. The hot season of 1623 was well begun when the Shah reached Baghdad. He found that, in a first brush, the garrison troops had been sharply defeated. The desperate messages of the Ṣu Bashi to Diyarbakr and to Stambul brought no response. In the city famine assumed horrible forms. The flesh of dogs, of children, of corpses, was consumed. The blockade was vigorously pressed, the air rent constantly with the crash of exploding mines.

The third month of the siege began. Deserters left the city night by night for the Persian camp, among them relations of the Ṣu Bashi. By their means his son Muḥammad, entrusted with the defence of the citadel, opened secret negotiations with the Shah. He was promised the province of Baghdad as the reward of the abject treachery he contemplated. On the night of November 28, 1623, he opened the gates. Thousands of Persian troops entered the town. At dawn every housetop and minaret rang with the blast of Persian trumpets. The Shah was proclaimed, amnesty promised, terror allayed, the bazaars opened.

If a terrible death were ever deserved, it had been deserved by the Ṣu Bashi. Captured and dragged before the Shah, he found his son seated in state beside the monarch, and listened to his reproaches. In the manner of his death no cunning and lingering cruelty was spared, while Muḥammad watched and assisted.

The amnesty promised to the city had been but a ruse. All arms were demanded, all troops and thousands of the Sunni inhabitants seized. To the wealthy torture was applied. Hundreds or thousands paid with their lives for their faith and late resistance. Thousands of women and children were sold as slaves, and vanished for ever into Persia. A handful of earnest Sunnis escaped from the town and sought refuge in Turkey.[1] The religious resentment of the Shah grew as it gratified itself. From his savage intention to spare no single Sunni he was turned by the entreaties of the guardian of the shrine of Karbala. The Sayyid gained without difficulty the lives of the Baghdad Shi'is, and, submitting the roll of these, included the names of many Sunnis. To the buildings of the city the recent struggle had brought general dilapidation. Schools became stables. Houses stood ruined. The great mosques of Abu Ḥanifah and 'Abdu 'l Qadir ul Gailani were largely destroyed.

Gradually peace descended, government was established, life stirred in the markets and alleys of Baghdad. The Shah, after pilgrimage to the Holy Cities, returned to Persia. Ṣafi Quli[2] was left as governor of Baghdad. Persian merchants flocked in from Hamadan and Tabriz. Their advantage as Shi'is, Persian nationals, and experts in Persian produce soon procured them the bulk of the commerce. In architecture and the few industries, Persian influences regained a sway they had never entirely lost; while the Holy Cities committed themselves more deeply than ever to the Shah. The towns accepted Persian garrisons; the desert tribes fawned on and raided the new-comers as the old. Muṭlaq, the Abu Rishah of the moment, professed feelings still

[1] It is on the accounts of these that Na'imah bases his history. Among them was the poet Nadhmi, father of Martaḍha, the author of Gulshan i Khulafa (Huart, Introduction, pp. 1 and 58).

[2] So Gulshan; Na'imah says Ṣari Khan.

loyal to the Turks. Such devotion was of potential value should they return, and meanwhile gave excuse for flouting their successors. Naṣir ul Muhanna hailed the Persians as deliverers. Two years later, however, he was attempting, with the forced levy of a strong passing caravan, to drive them out of Karbala. Samawah, Ḥiskah, Ḥillah, and the Holy Places had garrisons. That of 'Anah was quickly expelled by Abu Rishah. In taxation the Khans were unlikely to be less extortionate than the Pashas.[1] Their garrisons were less disciplined and as foreign. In the half-generation of their occupation many grants of land and privilege were made, for Sultan Murad to cancel.

Karchghai and Qasim Khan were early sent to account for the northern ayalats of Mosul and Shahrizor. Bustan Pasha at Kirkuk saw no hopes of a successful resistance, and retired to Mosul and beyond. At Mosul a brief defence was offered. The city then received Qasim Khan as its governor. He moved against Diyarbakr but could take it neither by assault nor by intrigue. Here the tide turned. Aḥmad the Little, a gallant Albanian, was dispatched by Ḥafidh Aḥmad against Mosul. The Khan retired precipitately before his advance. Mosul was again the Sultan's. Sulaiman, nephew of the Albanian, was made Governor.[2] Kirkuk remained a few months longer under a rule especially hateful to its Turkish and Kurdish population.

§ 3. *Ḥafidh Aḥmad.*[3]

The Persian occupation of Baghdad brought them neither wealth nor honour. No works of development or improvement marked the period. Insecurity in central 'Iraq and the desert kept its normal level. Less and less, as Turkish armies held Kirkuk and Mosul and spent years under the walls of Baghdad,

[1] Cf. Phillipe (op. cit.), p. 33. This French Carmelite seems the only European who has left an account of 'Iraq in these years.

[2] Mosul Calendar dates this appointment 1625, probably a year too late.

[3] Authorities: von Hammer (Bk. XI), following Na'imah and three special histories of the Baghdad campaign—two by 'Abdu 'l 'Aziz Qarachelebizadah, and one by Nuri. Gulshan is full and valuable. Basha'yan is derived from Gulshan, cf. Thévenot, *Voyage fait au Levant* (1645), pp. 569–76; Tavernier (ed. cit.), pp. 84–5; Boullaye-le-Gouz, pp. 323–5; Phillipe (op. cit.), pp. 38, 88, and 528–9, and many minor references in both European and oriental writers.

could Ṣafi Quli Khan control more than the capital itself and freedom of pilgrimage to the Holy Cities.

From the moment of its loss, the recapture of Baghdad was a pressing ambition of the Ottoman Court. It was entrusted in 1625 to Ḥafidh Aḥmad, who had become Grand Wazir in the previous year. After a campaign stained with unwisdom, mutiny, and failure, he abandoned the task. In the autumn of 1630 Khasrau Pasha met no better success. Only in 1638, when the terrible Padishah marched in person on 'Iraq with the cream of the Imperial forces, did Baghdad fall to his attack.

Ḥafidh Aḥmad Pasha had never relinquished the Pashaliq of Diyarbakr, and the insignia of the Grand Wazarat reached him in his own province. In May 1625 his camp was outside Diyarbakr. The intention to march upon Baghdad was recognized; and a first blow was at once struck by the mission of Charkis Ḥasan against the Persians at Kirkuk. A small force of Circassians routed the ten thousand Persians; Kirkuk was reoccupied. The valleys of Shahrizor were cleared of the forces if not the influence of the Shah. Bustan Pasha again assumed the government of the province.

The main army of the Wazir spent the summer in camp, whither information came of a great pilgrimage of the Baghdad garrison to Najf, by which the city lacked, for the moment, the bulk of its defenders. On this news Alyas Pasha, Beglerbegi of Anatolia, was dispatched with a light force to cut the Baghdad-Karbala road and prevent their return. The attempt failed, but doubtless it further weakened Persian hold on the Euphrates and expelled for a time the garrisons. Meanwhile a council of war was held in the camp at Diyarbakr. The optimism of the Wazir was but partly contagious. "The keys of Baghdad", he cried, "are in my hand." More careful soldiers hesitated over the season, the lightness of the Turkish guns, and the strength of the Baghdad garrison. The march began. At Kirkuk it was learnt that strong reinforcements had succeeded in entering Baghdad under Persian captains, Ṣari Khan and Mir Fattaḥ. A messenger from the Persian general himself bade the Wazir, in terms of sarcasm, to delay his invasion for the few days necessary to bring the Shah in person to the war. This was decisive. The Pasha of Mosul was sent back to amass stores and dispatch them downstream by kallak. Bustan was left at Kirkuk. Ill found in artillery and stores, ill served in leadership and intelligence, the main army followed the familiar road by Zangabad and Buhriz to the walls of Baghdad.

While a column under Murad Pasha ravaged the country towards the Euphrates, Ḥafidh Aḥmad took up his siege positions. In twelve days the trenches, emplacements, and redoubts were complete. The trenches were manned by the contingents of Karman, Rumelia, Anatolia, Siwas, and Mar'ash. The Pasha of Aleppo rested his flank on the river, while Khasrau Pasha pressed nearer to the east gate of the defenders. For two months the siege was pressed. Fifty mines were exploded beneath the walls. The picked troops of the Persian garrison never left the bastions. By night a thousand torches banished the darkness, while wakeful sentries chanted monotonously at their posts. The attackers were allowed no profit from their scanty artillery, nor from the date-logs cast down to cross the moat. The waste land within the eastern wall was patrolled incessantly by Persian cavalry. On the seventy-second day a desperate assault was launched, heroic courage displayed, heavy losses suffered in vain. Next day came news of a relieving army from the Shah, its strength variously estimated at six to eighty thousand men. At Shahroban they had cut off three thousand of a Turkish foraging-party. Council of war was held again. The case for retirement was plainly put. The Janissaries would have none of it, and the decision was to renew the siege.

Monotony increased as hope and spirit grew less. Ṭayyar Muḥammad Pasha tried vainly to dislodge Zainal Khan (the general of the relieving army) from his camp on the Diyalah, where a bridge of boats had been constructed. Murad Pasha was no more successful. Discipline grew lax. Chalabi 'Ali, son of the Qasim Khan who had surrendered Mosul to Kuchuk Aḥmad, was allowed to force his way past the Turkish lines into Baghdad. Another symptom of demoralization was the episode of 'Umr Pasha, Quartermaster to the army, when the camp rang with rumours that he had sold stores to the enemy. Morale was not improved by the noisy demonstrations of the defenders' joy as the approach of the Shah was reported. A moment's relief was given when a convoy of Persian money and munitions stumbled by error into the Ottoman camp.

Six months had passed when a morning of early summer in 1626[1] found Ḥafidh Aḥmad and his staff practising the jarid, as their custom was. Dust was seen on the horizon. A few minutes later a messenger of the Shah rode up with a missive to the Pasha. He read it, mounted and lance in hand. The game went on. Later the messenger was sent about his business with a verbal message, " Come for your reply when the battle 's over ". The force was arrayed and disposed for battle, but little came of the first contact of the armies save casualties sustained and prisoners taken. Simultaneously raft-loads of ordnance arrived downstream. The Persians, cutting all the left-bank approaches from their camp on the Diyalah, threatened to make the Pasha's camp immobile by constant harrying of watering and grazing-parties. 'Umr Pasha, sent upstream to collect fresh transport animals, was cut off; a rich convoy fell to the Persians, who captured also the Fallujah bridge-head.

Messages meanwhile passed between the royal and viceregal commanders. In one the Shah declared that he was demanding the formal secession of Baghdad from the Sultan, to form a province for the royal Prince of Persia. In another he reproached the Turk for lack of ardour in battle and diplomacy alike: would he make neither war nor peace? The Pasha picked up his pen: " Pursuing the dove, the hawk recks nothing of daw and raven: the jackal's baying does not disturb the lion." A second battle was fought near the walls of the city, with no more result than the shedding of blood. An attempt to set fire to the wooden gates of Baghdad did not succeed.

The Turkish position was now desperate. Within the city, indeed, every palm-frond had been stripped of its leaves, and many convoys of provisions, attempting to slip through to the besieged by land or river, had been interrupted. But these trophies could not suffice for the Pasha's army. They were surrounded on every side by the Shah's forces, a powerful outer ring more numerous,

[1] In assigning this incident and the third battle after the Shah's arrival to January 16, 1627 and May 27, 1627 respectively, von Hammer (Bk. IX, pp. 72-4) certainly errs, conflicting with Gulshan and the Persian authorities, as well as with his own narrative.

more inspirited, and better provided than themselves. Disease of body and spirit alike gained ground among them. A third main battle was fought late in May 1626. The Persians attacked the camp simultaneously in three places. The engagement was the fiercest of the whole campaign. On either side the highest commanders charged impetuously at the head of their men. The Persians were inspired by the banner and presence of their king, the Turks by the personal prominence of their Pashas and the long tradition of their corps. Murad, Alyas, and Khasrau again and again rallied their contingents. Ḥafidh Aḥmad showed a valour inferior to none. The camp was saved. A "sacred band" of fifteen hundred Persians, after incredible exploits, was cut down to the last man. Both sides retired, leaving dead heaped upon the field.

A fortnight later the Shah again suggested negotiation. Ḥafidh Aḥmad sent his Chamberlain and other officers to the Persian camp. They returned with the Shah's Ambassador. The Persian renewed his claims to Baghdad. At a later meeting he renounced Baghdad to the Turks, if Najf might be his. Every stone of Najf, replied the Wazir, was worth a thousand lives: Baghdad was but its guard-house. No argument or compromise could bring a settlement nearer. But the endurance of the Turk had reached breaking point. Mutiny broke out. The tent of the Grand Wazir was torn down. Before the eyes of the Persian Ambassador the Pasha himself was made prisoner in the shrine of Abu Ḥanifah. After hours of disorder a semblance of discipline was restored. A fresh tent was erected and the Wazir brought back to it. "Your meaning?" he asked: "where are my heroes who would capture Baghdad or die?" His voice was drowned in cries for retreat. The desperate Janissaries would listen neither to orders nor argument. The siege was abandoned.

The Turkish force was able, by the carelessness of the enemy, to accomplish the first day's march unmolested. At the second halt a Persian squadron rode up to demand the person of their Ambassador, whom the Wazir had retained. He was surrendered. In the third night Persian forces attacked the rear and were barely driven off. The retreat was by the Tigris line, a route little used; stores were nowhere to be bought or seized.

A few raft-loads captured on the river kept the force alive. Food, in the moving camp, changed hands at enormous prices. Transport animals were killed and eaten. The winding river could not always be followed; thirst was added to fatigue and famine. Mob-rule prevailed. Only when the Lesser Zab was crossed were some supplies of grain to be had. Mosul, and comparative plenty, were reached at last. Its government was given to Qara Bakr,[1] the garrison to Charkis Ḥasan.

§ 4. *A respite and a second failure.*

Ḥafidh Aḥmad moved into winter quarters at Aleppo. His dispatch to Stambul was accepted by his Sovereign, and a robe of honour rewarded him for his loyalty; but such was the venom against him among his rivals that it needed all the power of the Sultanah, and all the old intimacy of Wazir and Sultan, to give so favourable a reception. He was deposed from the Wazarat, but consoled by the bestowal of the Sultan's own sister upon him.

His successor, Khalil Pasha, was too much occupied by internal troubles to move against Baghdad. Early in 1628 a Persian Ambassador reached Stambul formally to demand Baghdad as the government of the Persian heir, and to ask for a treaty of peace. There was no result. In 1628 Khalil's place as Grand Wazir fell to Khasrau Pasha, a truculent Bosnian whose implacable energy had raised him from the ranks. A year elapsed before an army moved from its camp at Scutari for the East.

Baghdad and central 'Iraq enjoyed two years of peace. The retreating rabble of Ḥafidh Aḥmad had left stores to be plundered at leisure. Two crops were sown and harvested. Ṣafi Quli continued his long rule of Baghdad. The garrisons of the Euphrates towns were restored. Tribesmen held Hit and upwards. From Fallujah to 'Arjah the Khan's writ ran fitfully; on the Tigris below Diyalah there was little control. Baṣrah had for years past been an independent state,[2] little concerned with the fate of empires north of the marshes. Southern Kurdistan

[1] "Accuru de Bussra au secours de l'armée" says von Hammer (Bk. IX, 80), following Na'imah. This does not accord with what we know of Baṣrah affairs at the time. See ch. V sub.

[2] Chapter V deals with this.

was a no-man's-land of Turkish and Ardalan influences and intrigues, of Begs who courted both and served neither. Mosul had its garrison of Turkish regulars. The Pasha of Kirkuk had given place to a Persian Khan, under pressure of the Persian armies in the south and the bold ruler of Ardalan eastward.

These were months of uneasy waiting for the next storm. News of the death of Shah 'Abbas, early in 1629, depressed the Khan of Baghdad and delighted the camp at Scutari. His grandson and successor, Shah Ṣafi, went far to ruin his line and country by a blood-thirst heedless of merit, age, or services. Shah 'Abbas had reigned for forty-two years, and died at the age of seventy. Had he held his throne for ten more years a true struggle of Titans would have settled the fate of Baghdad History was spared the spectacle of conflict between the greatest of Persian monarchs and the cruel brilliance of Murad IV.

Khasrau Pasha commenced his march in May 1629. The route, by Aqshahr and Konia to Aleppo, was marked by the severities of the general. Crossing the Euphrates at Birijik, he ordered the construction of great rafts[1] to convey supplies to Fallujah. A halt was made at Diyarbakr, where his troops were reinforced by the first contingents of the Kurdish Begs. At Mosul the army was rejoined by its artillery, which thousands of oxen had drawn by another route.

The season[2] was of exceptional severity. Rain and floods had made central 'Iraq impassable to all transport. The snow lay feet deep round Diyarbakr, at Mosul no greybeard could recall so heavy a fall. An advance on Baghdad was unthinkable. Meanwhile, arrangements were made for supplies, and kallaks prepared for transport. An army moved east and south across the Great Zab. A general council of war was held near Arbil, of which the Persian governor, with his colleague of Kirkuk, had fled to Baghdad. It was attended by all leaders of the Turkish regulars, timariots, and mercenaries, by a score of Kurdish Begs, by Arab shaikhs from the Tigris. A campaign to the south was prohibited alike by the sodden country and by the pressure of hostile Ardalan in the rear. The first campaign, it was decided,

[1] The flat-bottomed "shakhturs" of all ages. They still ply downstream from Birijik to Musayyib.

[2] Midwinter 1629–30

should be against Persian vassals in and beyond the Shahrizor country.[1]

Khan Aḥmad Khan of Ardalan was still a loyal servant of the Shah.[2] He had distinguished himself in the 'Iraq campaigns of 'Abbas the Great. Among his relations, however, were many who favoured the Empire of the Sunnis. These lost no time in approaching the Grand Wazir with presents. As the army moved eastward from Kirkuk many begs of the Ardalan kingdom, and twenty more Khans of Kurdistan, approached to kiss the hand of the Wazir. Passing from the low to higher passes, the Turkish force halted at Gulanbar, where a solemn council was held: should the old frontier-fortress built by Sulaiman Qanuni, and demolished by Shah 'Abbas, be restored? Sentiment demanded its repair. Seven weeks' toil completed the task. The work was useless and ill timed. Isolated hill-fortresses in this wild country could not keep the Sultan's frontiers.

This much time wasted, the Wazir sent his advanced troops against the Ardalan country. The first objective was the strong castle of Mihriban. It fell and was garrisoned; but, while the main body under the Wazir still tarried in the Shahrizor, Zainal Khan, the Persian Commander-in-Chief, and Khan Aḥmad of Ardalan moved rapidly up from Hamadan. Their army was 40,000 strong. Ignoring wise advice to make straight for the Shahrizor (thus cutting off the Turks from their base), they offered battle near Mihriban. The struggle was long and savage. Reinforcements sent up by Khrasau arrived at the critical moment. Zainal Khan retired in rout; his losses reached many thousands. Summary death, the price of failure, awaited him in the Shah's camp. Rustam Khan took his command. The Shah moved towards Iṣfahan.

Khasrau Pasha, after completing his fortress, appeased a mutiny, held a grand Durbar of victory at Mihriban, and moved

[1] The authorities for this campaign are Na'imah and Ḥaji Khalifah. Not only the route and topography but the Kurdish politics are unsatisfactory—and this although Ḥaji Khalifah was himself with the army.

[2] According to the Turkish historians, he (1) was expected by Khasrau to be an enemy, (2) made submission, with his Sunni brother, at the Turkish crossing of the Lesser Zab, (3) fled from his palace at Ḥasanabad at the Turkish approach. These inconsistencies cannot wholly be resolved. It is certain that, at a later stage, Khan Aḥmad broke with Shah Ṣafi, who put out his son's eyes.

deeper into Ardalan. The castle of Khan Aḥmad at Ḥasanabad was completely sacked. Persian stragglers and deserters were rounded up, not one to escape the severity of the Ottoman general. Through rich and populous country their march brought them in June 1630 to Hamadan. The pitiless destruction of this great city does not belong to 'Iraq history. After six days of blood and fire, the army moved by the Qasvin road to Darguzin. It was destroyed. Ten waterless marches lay between this place and Qasvin, the intended quarry. But, at a council held here, other views prevailed. Baghdad, first and last, was the objective: Qasvin and Ardabil, attractive to loot and desecrate, lay far from the road enjoined by the Padishah.[1] The summer was far advanced. 'Iraq would now be tolerable. The army turned westward.

No incident, save a successful skirmish with the Lurish Khans, marked the long march to the frontiers of 'Iraq. Once in the flat lands of the middle Diyalah, the Wazir found reinforcements awaiting him from Mosul with the welcome support of artillery. A month was spent in the march on Baghdad and the occupation of siege positions. In October the assault began.

It was to fail; and little purpose would be served by repeating each doubtful episode of the siege. Gun-fire was ceaseless on both sides. The Turkish artillery, and mines exploded under the bastions, made dangerous breaches; but by none could entry be forced. By night, torches lighted the walls. Ṣafi Quli had grown old in the tactics of defence. With him were Amir Jamal and Amir Fattaḥ, a former governor of Iṣfahan. Khasrau Pasha, with impatient folly, moved his camp nearer to the walls where it could barely be sheltered.

By mid-November, 1630, most of the Turkish ammunition had been used. A campaign of mere attrition must favour the besieged; and, seeing the walls now in many places reduced almost to ground-level, Khasrau ordered a general assault. On the fortieth day of the siege an advanced guard 500 strong attempted to rush the fosse. The main body crowded up behind. But the treacherous causeways of fallen brick-dust gave way beneath them, and a terrible fire rained from the walls. Among

[1] Gulshan even says that a royal order reached the Wazir at Darguzin, ordering him to Baghdad.

the slain were the highest officers of the army. Of the body-guard of Khasrau, whose furious courage kept him ever in front, not a man escaped.

Five days later a plenary council decided upon retirement. The retreat from Baghdad was made with all guns and stores in good order. The army reached Mosul in the early days of 1631 and halted for a week. While the Wazir still rested there, Khan Aḥmad of Ardalan invaded his transient conquests in Shahrizor. Five Turkish Pashas fled precipitately to Mosul. Received with smiles and gifts, they were escorted after investiture into another room where their executioners stood ready. None were left alive.

Before commencing the retreat, the Wazir had dispatched a column against Ḥillah. The idea—as useless and extravagant as the vain fortress at Gulanbar—was to secure a convenient base for the next campaign against Baghdad.[1] Khalil Pasha of Diyarbakr occupied Ḥillah with 20,000 Janissaries and others. The town was put ready for defence, of which it speedily had need. Rustam Khan, his work finished in restoring the position in southern Kurdistan, was at liberty to deal with the Ḥillah force. He camped before the town. The first skirmishes went against him. News was carried to Shah Ṣafi, who hastened to the spot.[2] For nearly four months Ḥillah withstood the siege. Khalil Pasha saw finally that such uneven forces could not long maintain the struggle. On a dark night, and alone, he galloped sword in hand through the Persian lines to freedom. His forces capitulated. For a night looting and slaughter proceeded; at dawn criers proclaimed a truce. A new citadel was designed and completed at great cost. The Shah returned, after pilgrimage, to his own country. Persian garrisons were restored at Fallujah and elsewhere.

The last effort of Khasrau Pasha at Mosul was a short cavalry campaign against Muṭlaq abu Rishah. The great Amir of the

[1] According to Na'imah, a strong column, based on Mosul and commanded by the Pasha of Tripoli, had made a raid on the middle Euphrates in the early spring of 1630, while Khasrau was still in Shahrizor. It had threatened the Holy Cities, rounded up small Persian garrisons, and been supported by Naṣir ul Muhanna. A raid so distant and detached shows curious strategy. Gulshan does not refer to it.

[2] So Gulshan. The Turkish historiographers do not mention it. It seems dubious if the Ḥillah campaign would bring the Shah from Iṣfahan.

desert ceased not to vacillate between Persian and Turkish sympathies, while robbing and defying both and serving neither. He was dethroned, and his Amirate conferred (as far as a Turkish Pasha had the power to confer) on Sa'd bin Fayyaḍh of the same family. Bakr Pasha retained the government of Mosul, placed now under the general charge of Ṭayyar Muḥammad Pasha of Diyarbakr. Its walls underwent thorough repair, workmen and masons from Diyarbakr and Urfah being brought for the purpose. Khasrau wintered at Mardin.

Before the last eddies of the Wazir's 'Iraq campaign had stilled, Baghdad lost by death its now veteran governor.[1] Ṣafi Quli, fanatical and rapacious by the accounts of his enemies, had well served his master. In appointing a successor, Shah Ṣafi trusted rather to the stars than to human judgment. The horoscopes of several candidates were examined. The choice fell upon Baktash Khan, an officer of Armenian birth, wild and dissolute, but brave and capable. His viceroyalty lasted as long as his country's dominion in Baghdad. In the whole fifteen years of Persian rule only two governors of Baghdad appeared; and they contrasted both in permanence and capacity with the short-lived Pashas of the Sultan. In 1635 'Iraq suffered great losses from a visitation of the plague.

§ 5. *Sultan Murad, 1638.*

Meanwhile Sultan Murad had grown to manhood. His youth had been spent in an atmosphere of intrigue, mutiny, and every visible corruption of the state. His earliest taste of effective reign was one of violence and humiliation. The veteran Ḥafidh Aḥmad was demanded by mutinous Sipahis in the Sarai itself: and the Sultan could not refuse to sacrifice him. From that day Murad entered upon the business of his reign. He proved himself strongly efficient, able, cultured, vigorous, the veritable restorer of his Empire to life and health; but, on the other hand,

[1] Tavernier (ed. cit., p. 84) has a pleasant but unhistorical account of the suicide of Ṣafi Quli, in disgust at supersession by a new governor. A similar example of the early currency of distorted but picturesque stories is in op. cit., p. 67, where he records the foundation of a great fortress at "Sharmely" on the upper Euphrates by the Grand Wazir, to protect himself from the Sultan's wrath at his failure to take Baghdad. For this story, cf. Parsons, p. 88.

almost inhumanly contemptuous of life, the murderer of his people by tens of thousands. To this disposition were soon added habits of intemperance. Yet

". . . with all his misdeeds, he saved his country. He tolerated no crime but his own. The worst of evils, the sway of petty local tyrants, ceased under his dominion . . . and the worst tyranny of the single despot was a less grievous curse to the Empire than had been the military anarchy he had quelled. Order and subordination were restored under his iron sway. There was discipline in the camps; there was pure justice on the tribunals. The revenues were fairly raised and honestly administered."[1]

While the Empire of 'Uthman groaned and prospered under this rule of terrible beneficence, it could not tolerate the continued loss of Baghdad. But seven years were to elapse between the failure of Khasrau and the final success of the Sovereign. In 1633 Murad first rode in person through the nearer parts of his Asiatic provinces. Two years later he marched from Scutari to Erivan, retook that great fortress from the Shah, and showed himself both a born leader of troops on service and a pitiless inspector of his provincial officers.

On the 9th of March 1638 the standard of the Sultan was again planted at Scutari. On the 8th of May, all preparations made and every resource and officer of the Empire mobilized and exactly directed, the army broke camp to begin the march on Baghdad. The route had been divided into 110 stages. Each day's march and each night's halt kept precisely to the arrangements made: and few stopping-places were unsignalized by some striking act of discipline, reform, or piety. At Aleppo, half-way, the army rested for sixteen days. A grand review was watched by the French traveller Tavernier. From Birijik raft-loads of heavy stores were dispatched downstream to meet Murad in central 'Iraq.[2] At Dulab died Bairam Pasha, the Grand Wazir. Ṭayyar Muḥammad succeeded him. Six days' halt was ordered at Diyarbakr, where the new Grand Wazir appeared in great pomp before his master. From here were dispatched the advance-guard troops to Mosul. They were formed of Aleppo and Tripoli contingents under Darwish Pasha, and the desert riders

[1] Creasy, pp. 251-3.

[2] Tavernier, p. 59.

of Abu Rishah. At Mosul an ambassador of India waited upon the Sultan with outlandish gifts. The bulk of the artillery was now embarked upon kallaks to descend the Tigris, twenty cannon being retained with the army. The troops were gratified by the distribution of largesse. The order of march was revised for the entry into hostile country. The Pasha of Mar'ash took the rear, of Diyarbakr the advance-guard, of Aleppo the guns. Still observing the time-table made months before, the army crossed the Greater and the Lesser Zabs, entered and passed Kirkuk, descended from the Jabal Hamrin upon the Khaliṣ, and camped before Baghdad on the 15th of November 1638.[1]

This was the last visit of an Ottoman Sultan to 'Iraq, the last exploit of the last of the great warrior-kings of his line. The great progress through his dominions now completed by Murad had already made upon his Empire an impression not, to this day, effaced. To many a peasant and tribesman, in many a half-legend of the ignorant, the name of Sultan Murad is familiar and terrible, while later monarchs of much longer reign are forgotten. The brief siege now to commence succeeded where three before it had failed, and settled the fate of 'Iraq for ensuing centuries.

The tent of the Sultan was placed upon a small eminence by the Tigris, close to the mosque of Abu Ḥanifah. He would not enter the shrine until victory had made him worthy to venerate the saint. The first hours after arrival were spent in arranging the disposition of the force, mixing with the common soldiery, and haranguing[2] the captains of the army. Siege-stores were distributed, the duties of each laid down. The camp and personal forces of the Sultan were opposite the Citadel and north-western face of the walls. On the north-eastern face the Agha of the Janissaries and the Beglerbegi of Rumelia were placed opposite the White Gate, later and long known as the Gate of the Talisman. Thence eastward to the Gate of Darkness at the south-easterly extremity were the Qaptan Pasha, two chief generals of the Janissaries, and the Pashas of Anatolia and Siwas. Within the walls were Baktash Khan, with Khalaf

[1] Additional to the authorities quoted for these campaigns, Creasy (ed. cit., pp. 254–6) quotes Hulme, and von Hammer (IX, p. 331) refers to the *Voyages* of du Loir (Paris, 1654).

[2] Thévenot, p. 570.

Khan and Mir Fattah. The guns, distributed between the commanders of each front, lost no time in opening fire, while a force, sent across the river to bombard the citadel from the right bank, greatly embarrassed the defenders by this unexpected fire.

The Sultan was constantly among his men in every trench and emplacement. Each phase of the siege was watched from the tower erected before his tent. To the wounded he gave consolation and presents. Frequent speeches heartened his officers, each a thousand times more terrified of their master than of all the armies of Persia. The details of blockade, of foraging, of rationing, of intelligence were his personal care. The spirit of victory and of fearful adoration for their leader heartened the troops erecting earthworks in ceaseless dust, and pressing the sap-heads ever nearer the moat. Pomegranates from the gardens of Shahroban, and great provisions brought on the 10,000 camels of Abu Rishah, cheered the work. The Persians, on their side, took heart from news of the Shah's advent. He had, indeed, reached the frontier at Khaniqin with a weak force of 12,000 men, but feared now or later to court certain annihilation by a nearer approach. To meet him the Sultan detached the Pashas of Tripoli and Aleppo, with irregulars of the desert. The Shah retired. Fresh cannon reached Murad's camp by the Tigris.

The bastion of the White Gate was the first to yield to the artillery of the Grand Wazir. Others upon the same face of the city were quickly levelled. A breach of many yards revealed the interior of the city; but the ground was scored with trench and barricade and the intended general assault was postponed. The work of destroying the walls went on from every battery. The great moat was gradually filled by the debris of the bastions, and by sand-bags flung in by the advance troops of the assailants.

The end was near. On the 23rd of December a fierce attack was delivered. It was repulsed; but the Sultan saw the moat now filled and no obstacle to general assault. He reproached his Wazir for postponing it. "Would God", replied Ṭayyar Muḥammad, with words memorable for their true spirit of devotion, "that to take Baghdad for thee were as easy as for thy slave Ṭayyar to give his life to serve thee!" The assault was ordered for the next day. A wakeful night passed. At dawn the attack was launched. A long breach lay open in the centre of the east face of the wall. The flower of the Turkish army followed the impetuous lead of the Grand Wazir. His scimitar laid low the first Persians he encountered, till a ball struck and instantly killed him. He was borne to his master, whose grief was sincere and bitter. Muṣṭafa Pasha received the seal of the Grand Wazarat, and the next moment took Ṭayyar's place at the head of the attack. Courtiers and high officers fell on his right and left: the charge swept on till the breach was held and the city lay open.

On Christmas Day 1638, the fortieth day of the siege and the centenary of Sulaiman Qanuni's conquest of Rhodes, Sultan Murad accepted the submission of the great frontier city of his Empire, the historic home of the Islamic prime, the object for fifteen years past of bitter and costly struggles. Baktash Khan sent messengers of capitulation. The Sultan dispatched high officers into Baghdad to lead the Khan to his presence. He was conducted between a double line of imposing guards from the tent of the Grand Wazir to the Diwan where Murad sat with every circumstance of splendour. His forehead touched the earth: he asked pardon for his long resistance. Chivalry in the Sultan was not quite dead. Pardon was freely given and costly presents bestowed; but the city must be instantly delivered. Baktash wrote to his officers within to abandon the defences and the city forthwith: each was free to go where he would. He warned the Wazir against further demolishing the defences, as many concealed mines lay ready to explode.

But the armistice intended to secure a bloodless occupation was broken by the ignorance and perverse loyalty of a remnant of the garrison. Turkish troops entered, but firing did not cease. At the Gate of Darkness, whence Persians streamed forth in hordes, confusion reigned. On the walls stray firing by the desperate and malicious provoked reprisals. The general amnesty intended by the Sultan, and all efforts of the Wazir, could not prevent the rapid spread of violence and looting. Street-fighting cost the lives of several high officers, and that in the very presence of the Wazir. Of the Turkish soldiery not a few were burning for revenge of a brother or a son. Mir Fattaḥ and captains with him refused to evacuate or yield. Guns were trained on their last redoubt. Slaughter grew general; and not till 20,000 of the garrison had been butchered was the town, quiet at last but drenched in blood, in the full control of the Grand Wazir.[1]

Pardon and amnesty were proclaimed by his orders to the whole civil population. Murad held in the mosque of A'dhamiyyah his diwan of victory, and sent off his messengers to Europe. Baktash Khan died suddenly by poison.[2] The government of the city was confided to Ḥasan Pasha (Kuchuk, the "Little"). A garrison of 8,000[3] was placed under Baktash Agha. The Mufti Yaḥya was instructed to restore the sacred shrine of 'Abdu 'l Qadir ul Gailani, and generous grants (largely from Shia' properties) were made for its upkeep. A sudden rise in the river swept Tigris water over the trenches outside the walls, obliterating the scars of four sieges. Murad held his court for six weeks in the northern suburb where he had first camped, and renovated the dome of its great mosque.

An unhappy accident renewed, in the camp and in the reviving city, the scenes of blood which had seemed complete. The powder magazine of Baghdad took fire and suddenly exploded. Of the lives lost by the shock and ruin some were Turkish. Murad ordered a general slaughter of Persians[4] wherever found. Refugees in the Ottoman camp were numerous. Three hundred pilgrims had just crossed the river to Kadhimiyyah. A thousand

[1] An exact inquiry at the time would not have easily revealed the course or the blame of this street-fighting and butchery after the capitulation. The eyewitness authorities agree on the pacific intentions of Murad. But the crisis of the campaign was followed by a break-up of discipline on both sides. In the bitterness of battle, of race, of religion, in the attraction of loot, in the size and narrow alleys of Baghdad, and in the mob-psychology of bloodshed, there were abundant materials for violence and confusion. Gulshan is definite in assigning as the cause the ill-timed resistance of Mir Fattaḥ.

[2] This is the event of which Tavernier has an echo (see foot-note, p. 68). Nuri, followed by von Hammer (IX, p. 342), makes the death due to poison administered by the Khan's wife. Gulshan makes it suicide.

[3] The more exact description of Gulshan reads: "He raised regular local troops in sufficient number to defend the province, and organized for the garrison of the town a picked army consisting of about seventy companies drawn from the (regular) sipahis, from the Janissaries of the Capital, and from the gunners and the jebechis." The distinction of imperial troops for town garrison, and local troops for out-station work, is important.

[4] Creasy (p. 256), in saying "a massacre of the inhabitants of the city", is misleading. All original sources specify that the order was directed against the Persians, though others may have suffered with them.

wretched captives were brought before the Sultan: a thousand heads fell from their shoulders in a single moment at his word. In the camp, the country around, and the city itself no Persian was left alive. It may be that the discrimination of Persian from Arab was imperfect; for, on the estimate of Court historians, the number of victims reached 30,000. These, with a handful of suspect notables of the city, satisfied the wrath and policy of the conqueror.

On the 17th of February 1639 Sultan Murad and a part of his army left Baghdad for Tabriz. The Gate of the Talisman whereby they marched from the city was instantly bricked up, and thus remained. From that day to the twentieth century none passed the portal honoured by a Sovereign.

IV

THE SEVENTEENTH CENTURY

§ 1. *Character of 'Iraq history, 1639 to 1704.*

From the usurpation of Baghdad by the Ṣu Bashi till its victorious relief by Sultan Murad, the name of Baghdad had been a watchword in Imperial politics. It was to retire now into comparative obscurity. A certain remarkable symmetry may indeed be noticed in the centuries covered by the present history. Once in each hundred years great events, or a striking scene in the struggle of Shah and Sultan, bring 'Iraq into prominence on the Turkish stage. The first conquest of the Qanuni in 1534 was followed by ninety years of provincial dullness: from 1639 to the Persian wars of the Afghan and Afshar period is similarly an age, eighty years long, of humbler history within 'Iraq: and from the last fighting with Nadir Shah until the close of the nineteenth century, 'Iraq emerges into a leading place in the Empire only when, in the second quarter of that century, it was dragged from its archaisms and seclusion to a place in the Reformed system. Sultan Sulaiman, the Ṣu Bashi and Murad IV, Nadir Shah and Aḥmad Pasha, Daud Pasha and 'Ali Riḍha, are the names marking the conspicuous stages in the present narrative.

We have seen Baghdad once more conquered. Every eye in Turkey and thousands in western Europe followed the army of the Sultan to 'Iraq. An historic march had been followed in forty days by completest victory. He had returned to a reception of triumphant brilliance in his own capital. The Grand Wazir stayed for a few more weeks in Baghdad to superintend the repairs of walls and buildings: then he, too, left the city and country to its own affairs. Its history for sixty years was to be unbrightened by incidents of international moment, or men of historic fame. We can reconstruct a few characteristic details of the rulers of Baghdad, the contumacy and migrations of the tribes, the secessions of Baṣrah: but the lack of a powerful foreign enemy or a strong usurper—of any circumstance, in fact, to hold the attention of the Empire or the world—has thinned our records to the meagrest.

The general historian may see in the period merely a dull epoch which confirmed in 'Iraq the tradition of Turkish misgovernment. The routine of the Pasha's court, the form and nomenclature of government, troops local and imperial, the small bureaucracy of Turks perfectly static in ideas and culture, for whom and by whom the whole administration ran—these phenomena in many decades of comparative peace became in 'Iraq so habitual as to exclude any other conception of government. These were the years when Turkish rule put down its roots, aided by its religious sanction and strengthened by deep conservatism. The Imperial government of the time saw in the 'Iraq provinces a possession distant and unproductive, a source occasionally of disturbing news. The pride of owning Baghdad was dulled by time. There was no Persian menace. The special difficulties of the province were not unknown, and the frequent infidelities of southern 'Iraq must remind of them. Yet it gave less trouble than Egypt, Syria, and half the provinces of Asia—far less than the Capital, shameless with mutiny and violence: and meanwhile the Pashaliqs and judgeships of 'Iraq remained to bestow for merit, favour, or cash.

The dweller in 'Iraq saw generation follow generation without a policy, because without ideals, of rule. Sonorous loyalty to faith and Sultan supplied, as a spring of government, what neither enlightenment, nor goodwill, nor skill were there to supply. He saw mosques founded, but never a road, school, or hospital; taxes increased or modified, but no principle of taxation conceived; dhabiṭ and qadhi appointed, but not controlled: expedient following expedient in the government of the tribes, from brutal violence to weak surrender, but no grappling with 'Iraq's basic problem, the incorporation of the tribes in the state. This and the squabbles of high officials with their military backing, the half-hearted fiscal or social reforms of a few, the various personalities of governors appointed under every condition of venal caprice in Stambul—these were the phenomena spread before the Sultan's subjects in 'Iraq.

Later chapters will deal with the long tenure of 'Iraq by a dynasty all but seceding from the Empire itself: with that before us, and behind us the usurpations of Muḥammad ul Aḥmad and of Bakr, it may be surprising that the country—so remote, ill held, and restive—did not drift sooner into secession or mutiny. But something more than merely favourable general conditions is necessary to produce a result in history: special opportunity is given by circumstances often petty and obscure, and always seized by personalities. Leaning towers take long to fall, the sick to die. In such generalities we must seek reason for 'Iraq's long cohesion with its Empire in a century when that Empire was feeble, distracted, remote, and 'Iraq the home of a distant, foreign, and unstable people, unanimously loyal to no government and by majority disloyal to Turkey.

§ 2. *The tribal map in the seventeenth century.*

Earlier pages attempted a brief review of 'Iraq geography in the first days of the Ṣafawis. They spoke generally of tribal conditions, but did not venture on detail of name and place. Between that century and the end of the seventeenth, a thousand changes of tribal dirah, of group and subsection, of dispersion and coalescence, were to modify the tribal map. Poor men or adventurers grouped round a Sayyid or the younger son of some tribal nobility, to form a tribe called by his name. Opportunity, war, peace-making, personality, these or any of them increased the tents, soon to divide into sections following each a son or brother of the eponymous founder. Legend stepped in to enhance the origin, faction and jealousy to form new enmities and fresh alliances. Discovered grazing-grounds, changed river-courses, pressure by neighbours, led to migration whose consequences were never complete, never at rest. Here a confederacy embraced mixed elements of marsh, desert, and sown-land, and there long separation or the clash of personalities came between sections originally of common origin and name. An obscure band of shepherds might bear the great name of Qaḥṭan or Tamim, a tribe of ten thousand tents might form a unit knit yesterday from a dozen tribes. Not a year passed but somewhat, and often in bold outline, modified the tribal landscape.

Yet in heart, culture, and interests they varied nothing; their civilization, politics, arms were universal and static: and this, more even than his lack of records, absolves the historian from a narrative of these myriad changes. The tribal body, like living matter, was ever building up and breaking down. We can but study examples of that process, assigning name and date to a few among countless cells.

In 'Arabistan we have seen the undisputed sway of the Walis of Ḥuwaizah. Late in this century a new force rose beside it. The Cha'ab[1] were a rice-growing, stock-breeding Arab tribe of lower 'Arabistan. Probably a change of dirah preceded their rise to power, but it cannot be said whether their earlier home was west or east of the Shaṭṭ ul 'Arab, whether originally they were Turkish or Persian subjects. Their earliest head-quarters, subsequent to their emergence from obscurity, was at Qubban. The weakening of the Wali, and the emergence of some powerful personality among themselves, led to rapid extension of their power. The two existed for many years side by side.

Somewhat earlier in the century, the lower Euphrates saw the formation of a powerful confederacy. The dominant tribes of the southern Gharraf, the main river below Samawah, and the Ḥammar Lake, were Bani Malik, 'Ajwad, and Bani Sa'id. With and under these were a hundred sections of camel-men and "people of the buffalo". The group had neither common name nor any bond save similarity and nearness. From the advent, as refugee from the Ḥijaz, of a Makkah noble—from his arbitration in the struggle of 'Ajwad and Bani Malik—from his murder and the flight of the Bani Malik with his infant son to the desert—from their return, with the boy grown up as their leader, to vanquish their rivals: from such history or legend[2] arose the ruling family of Al Shabib, for two centuries to govern the tribe-group now united with the famous name of the Muntafiq. Others can claim a purer origin, stricter keeping to desert codes; but no tribe of 'Iraq became so formidable to its rulers, so long

[1] Properly Ka'ab, but the K is always softened in speech. Notes on the Cha'ab history may be found in both works of Niebuhr (the *Voyage* and the *Description*), in various papers of Rawlinson, and in Layard, *Province of Khuzistan*.

[2] From local information, and from Mira'tu 'l Zaura.

patient of a single government of its own, so famous in the outer world.[1]

In the desert west of Euphrates, a great upheaval took place in the middle years of the century—a migration briefly told, but in itself gradual and prolonged. Desert conditions were those of all ages; but one acquainted with the threadbare guest-tents of to-day, when the lord of a thousand tents has no carpet but the cheapest mat and no cushion but a camel-saddle, may wonder at the luxurious properties described by Tavernier. The principal leaders of the desert bore the title of Amir or Sultan. "Cajavas ... covered with scarlet cloth fringed with silk," eunuchs, "a great number of lovely horses richly harnessed." "Tents of a very fine scarlet cloth, and a rich galoon-lace" seem to imply a standard of wealth in advance of later days. On the upper Euphrates, the unconquered princes of Arabia had gained ground since the days of Sulaiman Qanuni. 'Anah and Dair ul Zor were now theirs without dispute. But the event of the century was the coming of the Shammar. The history of the Arab world is the history of successive eruptions from central Arabia. To such was due the very presence of Arab tribes in 'Iraq; and yet another of the series was the northward march, about 1640, of a great company of the Shammar of Najd under their Shaikh Faris. To scare the scanty garrisons of the Euphrates towns, and claim their tribute, was an easy task. Tadmor was destroyed, the lesser tribes easily subdued. With the powerful Muwali, war continued for twenty years. The invaders ended as masters of the richer pastures. The defenders had incurred, by a slaughter of envoys of their Shammar enemies in the guest-tent itself, the greatest shame in the desert code. The Muwali, retiring to the Syrian border, ceased to be a leading tribe. The 'Anizah, who had been no better able at first to withstand the fresh blood from Najd, either recovered or were reinforced, and held their own for nearly a century of restless counter-raids. In the end they were to prevail and thrust the intruders across the Euphrates to the Jazirah. Many a legend still told in the guest-tents commemorates the great Shammar invasion.

On the middle and lower Tigris likewise the tribes were

[1] e.g. to an Englishman in Stambul in 1790 the "Montefiks" are "an Arab nation on the banks of the Euphrates" (Eton, 1801 ed., p. 280).

moving into their modern homes. In this century tradition records the foundation of the Albu Muḥammad by a visitor from other dirahs; and in this age, or near it, Ḥafidh—great-grandson of Lam—quarrelled with Barrak his overlord of the Ḥuwaizah dynasty (themselves of Rabi'ah stock) and founded the Bani Lam in their present lands, there to scorn cultivation, to quarrel with their Lurish neighbours, and to restrict the dirah of the Rabi'ah to the fork of the Tigris and Gharraf.

The last example of growth and change in the tribal world transcends the limits of a tribe, as it passes the boundaries of the 'Iraq plains; for it was the foundation of a Kurdish dynasty. Mention has been made of the old noble family of the Soran Begs in southern Kurdistan. They belonged loosely to the Mukri group and closely to the Pishdar tribe. Their country was in the valleys north and east of Keui Sanjaq. The connexion of Soran and Pishdar with the ancient name of Baban is not clear; but when early in the seventeenth century one Aḥmad ul Faqih arose in the Pishdar country, he bore and bequeathed the family name of Baban. In his lifetime he collected a following sufficient to distinguish him from his neighbours; and the varied claims of nobility, personality, and success enabled his son Mawand to extend his authority over the Shahribazar and neighbouring areas. But the real founder of the great fortunes of the Baban house was Sulaiman Beg, son of Mawand. In the second half of the century he was already an outstanding figure in the Shahrizor. A weak and dissolute Wali of Ardalan gave the occasion for a great extension of his rule. Sulaiman Beg, his ambition whetted by tales of folly and corruption at Sannah, and caring in his remote valleys neither for Sultan nor Shah, invaded the Ardalan in 1694 and occupied several districts. Two local governors were put to death. A force said to be 40,000 strong, sent by the Shah, assisted that of the Ardalan prince completely to defeat him next year with the loss of thousands killed and captured. Sulaiman Beg[1] repaired to Stambul,

[1] It is recorded by some that the defeat of Sulaiman Beg (or "Baba Sulaiman") was inflicted by combined forces of Persians and Turks. Others limit the Turkish part to the sending of an Elchi to the Kurdish prince, insisting upon his making terms with the Persians before they should be tempted to advance far into Ottoman territory.

His incursion into Persia was probably late in 1694, the defeat by Persian

where he was shown high favour, given the "Sanjaq" of Baban, and included officially in the Pashaliq of Kirkuk. His own head-quarters was at the village of Qara Cholan. To his time legend assigns the long-remembered incident of an encounter at Aḥmad Kulwan, where twelve of the Baban followers routed a force of Persians thousands strong.

At his death much of his province fell back beyond control into the hands of the Zanganah and other tribes, while part was bequeathed to his sons. After quarrels among these, Timur Khan was finally succeeded by Bakr Beg, but not before their dissensions had allowed some years of firm Turkish control by the Pasha of Shahrizor to be felt. This vanished with the emergence of Bakr successful. Under him the Baban power became paramount between the Diyalah (Sirwan) and the Lesser Zab, in all the hill-country east of the Kifri-Altun Kupri road. The Baban Beg could deal on equal terms with rulers of Ardalan, could welcome and protect as vassals the Jaf tribe when they fled from Juwanrud to his territory. The state maintained by the ruling Beg grew with his growing power; and there were doubtless signs already of the superior culture, with the rarer power of inspiring devotion, which marked his descendants.

§ 3. *Baghdad and its rulers, 1639 to 1704.*[1]

It was the first care of Ḥasan Pasha the Little, upon his appointment immediately after the city fell to Murad, to repair shrines and buildings, to attract back to Baghdad some of the

forces in 1695. Probably the expeditions of the Turks against him were subsequent to this, in 1698 and 1699. They were due, no doubt, to suspicion of his growing power and scant respect for his Turkish neighbours. The Wali of Baghdad was appointed "Sar'askar", and took with him the Pashas of Diyarbakr and Aleppo.

The course of events and its chronology are not evident; but the essential facts of his early self-made fortunes, aggression against Persia and its punishment, recognition by Turkey and subsequent flouting of its authority, are clear enough.

[1] Of the sources, Gulshan supplies seven-eighths of our information on Baghdad in these years. There are notes in Tavernier, Boullaye-le-Gouz, Auliya effendi, Godinho, Thévenot (vol. iv of 1727 edition), and Soares de Val. Baṣrah sources are given separately. The slight contributions of the Turkish historians may be found in von Hammer (Bk. X, pp. 24 and 141, and Bk. XII, pp. 396, 426, 430, and other places to be quoted). Niebuhr (*Voyage*, ii, p. 252) has a table of Pashas which agrees substantially with Gulshan.

terrified fugitives who had forsaken it for a tribal refuge, and to care for the gardens and amenities of the place. The Pasha was Albanian by race and famed for courage; but to the Grand Wazir, Qara Muṣṭafa, as he left Baghdad in early May, he seemed too little to possess the ruthlessness needed in such a province. Darwish Muḥammad replaced him in office—a man whose thrust and brutality could not be popular, even while the security induced by his rapid punishments was appreciated. He was a striking figure in his height and gait. Enormous moustaches fell nearly to his waist. His taste for luxury was gratified less by exactions than by large-scale speculation in grain and live stock, from which his position as Governor enabled him to make vast profits. In the earliest days, Muhanna of the Khaza'il rose in the Samawah area, claiming authority from the Shah and spreading disorder far across the Jaza'ir. Darwish Muḥammad sent his Kahya, 'Ali Agha, by whom the rebels were easily dispersed and largely butchered. Six hundred heads were sent to Baghdad. It is safe to assume that similar incidents were numerous during Darwish Muḥammad's three years in the Pashaliq, and that security stood relatively high.

The same Ḥasan Pasha—zealous, but lovable and compassionate—succeeded him. His two years of rule were troubled by no leading events, save a visit to Baghdad from Imam Quli, King of Turkistan, on his way to the Makkah pilgrimage. The defences of the Baghdad Citadel were improved by stronger bastions. Ḥasan the Little was followed by rulers known only by a brief remark on the qualities of each. Ḥusain Pasha, a boon-companion of Sultan Murad, and nicknamed "the Mad" from his singularity of character, reigned for five months. To posterity he was known as the founder of the Qamriyyah mosque, to his contemporaries for his disguised nocturnal wanderings in the streets, whereby to spy out every malefactor and dispatch them with his own hand. Fear spread abroad—but a fear that led to safe bazaars and crowded mosques. Muḥammad, his successor, was a staid Agha of Janissaries. He governed for a year. Of Musa Pasha, appointed in 1645 for the same period of rule, the zeal and justice were applauded. Of friction in his time with the Baṣrah prince we shall speak later.

Ibrahim Pasha, appointed in the autumn of 1646, had attrac-

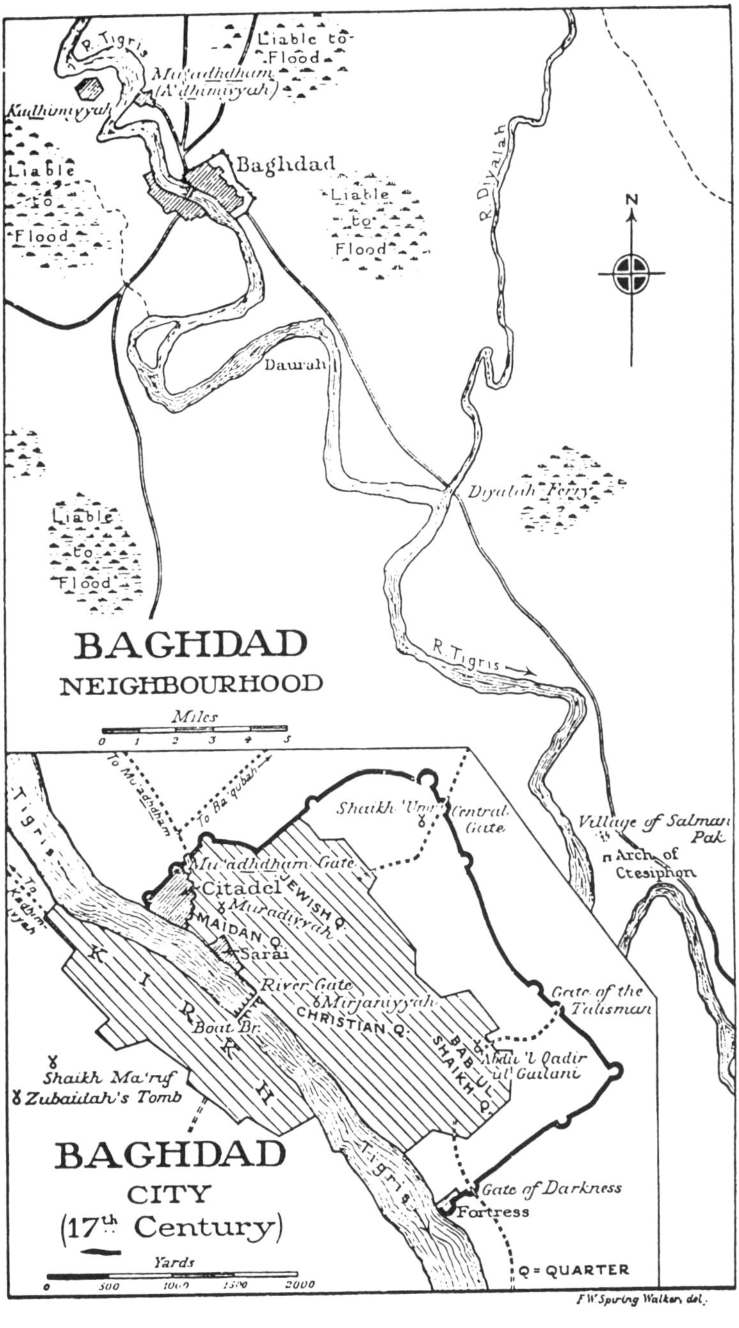
BAGHDAD
NEIGHBOURHOOD
R. Tigris
Liable to Flood
Mu'adhdham (A'dhamiyyah)
Kadhimiyyah
Baghdad
R. Diyalah
N
Daurah
Diyalah Ferry
Village of Salman Pak
Arch of Ctesiphon
Miles
0 1 2 3 4 5
BAGHDAD
CITY
(17th Century)
Tigris
To Mu'adhdham
To Ba'qubah
To Kadhimiyyah
Shaikh 'Umr
Central Gate
Mu'adhdham Gate
Citadel
JEWISH Q.
Muradiyyah
MAIDAN Q.
Sarai
River Gate
Mirjaniyyah
CHRISTIAN Q.
BAB UL SHAIKH Q.
K I R K H
Boat Br.
Gate of the Talisman
Abdu 'l Qadir ul Gailani
Shaikh Ma'ruf
Zubaidah's Tomb
Gate of Darkness
Fortress
Q = QUARTER
Yards
0 500 1000 1500 2000
F.W. Spring Walker del.

G 2

tions of youth and figure, but with a character vain and headstrong. These qualities brought trouble. Discord broke out with the Aghas of the garrison. A crisis was near, when news spread of the death of Saliḥ Pasha, Grand Wazir and the patron of the Baghdad Pasha. Ibrahim disbelieved the rumour, but made his peace with the Janissaries and continued his life of ease. Suddenly appeared[1] the advance-agent of a successor—the Mutasallim or deputy of Musa Pasha[2] the Fat. The local regiments ignored the supersession, and supported the Pasha who had enrolled and paid them. The imperial Janissaries preferred to follow the intentions of their royal master and prevent the strife of rivals in Baghdad. They met in the Maidan. Ibrahim, asked to be present, sent a deputy. They insisted on his personal attendance. The vain simpleton complied. They surrounded and closely arrested him. The local forces still refused to recognize his successor, and the deadlock, broken by street-fighting and lawlessness, lasted for three months. News of these conditions reached the Porte, and furnished the powerful ill wishers of Ibrahim with an excuse long sought. An equerry of the Sultan was dispatched to Baghdad with the death-sentence. Ibrahim was put to death, and a deputy filled his office till the new Pasha arrived. Musa Pasha, a confidential eunuch of the Court, was famed for an extraordinary obesity. Incapable of movement, and the victim of a violent temper, he surrounded himself with the lowest advisers. Acting on information half true, he decreed the death of the supposed supporters of Ibrahim, and drove many others from the city. Many, innocent and guilty, fled to a miserable exile in Persia before the wrath of the gross and choleric Governor should mark them down. At the same period steps were taken to increase the Baghdad garrison: neither quantity nor quality had shown well in the recent squabble. Three Pashas of neighbouring provinces received orders to contribute from their forces to 'Iraq. An event long remembered in Baghdad was the embassy of Muḥammad Quli, envoy of the Shah, who in 1648 passed through with a gift of elephants for the Sultan. The fat Pasha was

[1] The following episode is from Gulshan, supported in general terms by von Hammer (Bk. X, p. 140).
[2] Not to be confused with the predecessor of Ibrahim Pasha.

deposed in the first days of 1649, when his old enemy Murad Pasha gained the seal of the Grand Wazirate.

Thereafter the Pashaliq fell for a year to the saintly and beloved Aḥmad Pasha, surnamed "the Angel". He came to Baghdad from Diyarbakr, and left it to become Grand Wazir. It was in his later capacity that he chiefly contributed to 'Iraq history. While Governor of the province he had seen errors and abuses in the tax-system. As Grand Wazir he ordered that the method of fixed assessments[1] should be adopted, and the taxes farmed out. The first result was an increase in revenue which benefited the Imperial Treasury; but its collection—contrary to the benign hopes of the Wazir—was found to involve greater injustic and oppression than ever, at the hands of a hundred tyrannic tax-gatherers whom the royal authority must support. Malik Aḥmad governed Baghdad for less than a year (1649). His secretary, Ghannai Muḥammad, was a lawyer and accountant of high repute.

The firm and secure government of Arsalan Pasha was cut short after six months by his death of colic. He was buried beneath the dome of Abu Ḥanifah. Shaṭir Ḥusain Pasha resembled Malik Aḥmad in character. His observance of religion and charity gained him respect, and his pleasant personality made him everywhere popular with the city-folk. He died while still in the Pashaliq and still young, and was buried in the shrine of 'Abdu 'l Qadir ul Gailani. In each of these cases of sudden death in the province, a Mutasallim chosen by the Diwan of the Pashaliq directed the government until, two or three months later, a successor could arrive. In the summer of 1651 Qara Muṣṭafa Pasha was appointed. With his attractive person and character, modest, cultured, and intelligent, he was three times to hold the Pashaliq. In his first term, lasting for two years, he abolished the unhappy fiscal measures of Malik Aḥmad.

Martadḥa Pasha was a striking figure of the century. Appointed to Baghdad in 1653, he had already held the provinces of Damascus and Erzerum. The mainspring of his character was a vivid imagination. To the poor and ignorant he was a friend of extreme forbearance and lively sympathy; his violent

[1] The exact nature of the reforms cannot be appreciated.

temper, at other times, spared neither man nor beast. His passion for luxury and parade, unaccompanied by balance or morality, was gratified by religious ceremonials, spectacular distribution of largesse, and displays of shameless indecency. The security of the province was well kept. High officers lost their lives on the lightest suspicion; a hint of mutiny was picturesquely but brutally followed up: yet a tribesman from the wilds might walk past sleeping guards at the Palace, rouse the Pasha from his rest with the excited tale of some trivial wrong, and find the benign interest of a father. The Baṣrah campaign conducted by him, with partial success, belongs to another page. On his return he found lawlessness in possession of the city and all central 'Iraq. His own wish was to renew the campaign on Baṣrah; but to this the Porte did not agree, and Martaḍha spent days of brooding melancholy in Baghdad. After two years[1] he was removed from his Government under transfer to Aleppo.

Muḥammad Pasha the White, Governor for sixteen months, was gallant and athletic, but broken in health. A mutiny of the local troops gave him the opportunity to teach a salutary lesson. The dissolute ruffian who led them was induced by a ruse to appear in the Pasha's presence. His head did not remain a full minute upon his shoulders; but his confederates gathered to avenge him. The Pasha, brave and simple, thought to scatter them by a show of fearlessness. It was Friday. He passed on horseback through the streets to Mosque, and reached the open space where the malcontents were assembled. Bad characters lurking in the coffee-shops assailed the Governor and his suite with stones. Two troopers of the Lawand were killed. The trouble was easily suppressed; and the open courage of the Pasha was rewarded by his nickname of Aq, the White. One other incident of the day, illustrative of Turkish officialdom, is preserved—the advent of a new Agha of Janissaries followed closely by a missive from Court ordering his death. The congenial sentence was promptly executed and the former Agha restored.

[1] According to Gulshan, his rule ended on July 18, 1655 (Ramaḍhan 14, 1065). But Auliya effendi (p. 392 of vol. iv of the 1314 edition) reached Baghdad in Rabi'u 'l Awwal of 1066 and found Martaḍha Pasha.

Here we may break the record of successive Pashas to glance through other eyes at the capital of their province. Increasing numbers of Europeans passed through Baghdad, and some few have left records of their visit. French travellers were there in 1649, 1652, 1671, and 1695, the Turkish courtier Auliya effendi in 1666, a Jesuit of Portugal in 1663. European renegades were not unknown among the Aghas themselves; the French Catholic Bishopric of Babylon, founded in 1648, brought monks; while one or two merchants of the Italian states were commonly resident in Baghdad or frequent visitors from Baṣrah and Aleppo. The defences of the city in these mid-century years had fallen into the disrepair usual in peace time. The guns, many but small and already archaic, were little formidable. The right-bank portion was still unfortified. In the citadel

"The garrison", as one shrewd traveller[1] observed, "consists of three hundred Janissaries, commanded by an Aga. The city is governed by a Basha, who is generally a Vizier. His house is upon the side of the River, making a fair show; and he has always ready at command six or seven hundred horse. There is also an Aga who commands six or seven hundred Spahis. They have besides another sort of cavalry which is called Gingulili, that is to say, Men of Courage, commanded by two Agas: and usually there are about three thousand in the City and the towns adjoining. The keys of the gates of the City and the Bridge-Gate are in the custody of another Aga who has under him two hundred Janissaries. There are also six hundred foot-men, who have their particular Aga, and about sixty Cannoners who at that time (1652) were commanded by an expert artist that went by the name of Signor Michael, who passed for a Turk though he was born in Candy. He put himself into the Grand Signor's service, when he went to besiege Bagdat, in the year 1638." . . . "As to the civil government of Bagdat, there is none but a Cady who does all, acting even the Mufti,[2] with a Shiekelaslon or Tefterdar, who receive the revenues of the Grand Signor. There are in it five mosques,[3] of which two are indifferently well-built, and adorned with duomos covered with varnished Tiles of different colours. There are also ten inns, all ill-built, except two which are reasonably convenient. In general the city is ill-built; there being nothing of beauty in it except the Bazaars, which are all arched; else

[1] Tavernier (ed. cit.), p. 84.

[2] *Sic.*

[3] This omits many small ones.

the Merchants would not be able to endure the heats. They must also be watered three or four times a day; for which office several poor people are hired upon the public charge. The city is full of trade, but not so full as it was when in the hands of the King of Persia: for when the Turk took it, he killed most of the richest merchants.[1] However, there is a great confluence thither from all parts; whether for trade or Devotion's sake, I cannot tell. . . . Besides, all they that are desirous to go to Mecca by land, must pass through Bagdat, where every pilgrim is forced to pay four piastres to the Basha."

This was one of the commonest sources of friction with the Shah. Most travellers and traders, however, were little molested, and some praised the punctual methods of the customs-men.

Christian and Jew lived under a régime whose tolerance compared favourably with that of other provinces. Baghdad was too cosmopolitan (and the Islamic sects themselves too deeply divided) to encourage fanaticism. These minorities, moreover, were well behaved—not a matter of course in the Christian populations of Turkey—and familiar by long residence and unrestricted intercourse. It is likely enough that some minor distinctions against them were in force, as at Cairo and Damascus. They might not own white slaves or ride horses; negroes and asses were their portion. The greater humiliation of not riding at all, or of dismounting at sight of a Sayyid, was but little enforced. The same Christian sects were found then as later. The Nestorians had their own Church. Orders were represented by Capuchins and Carmelites. The Turks interfered with their church-going or feasting no more than to charge an admission-fee for entry to their own churches, and obligingly to purchase their children as slaves when the expenses of an elaborate funeral had impoverished a household to this extremity.[2] Their heaviest burden—shared indeed by Christian priest with Muslim shop-man, by Persian pilgrim with shepherd and porter—was their dependence upon the continual propitiation of governors heedless and ignorant though often good-natured, and easily inflamed by avarice or religion against communities always weak and often prosperous.

Muḥammad Pasha Khaṣki succeeded Muḥammad the White

[1] Persian merchants.
[2] Tavernier (ed. cit.), p. 86.

late in 1656. He had held the Governments of Egypt and Damascus. His generosity did not conceal a childish simplicity in affairs, and an insistence upon archaic forms and pomp. The discipline of local troops quickly degenerated ; women and wine possessed the barracks. In the autumn of 1657 a revolt of tribesmen in the Jaza'ir district called for the dispatch of a column. Mutiny stopped it before the scene of the campaign was reached. Veteran soldiers laboured to restore discipline ; they failed and died martyrs to their duty. Operations were abandoned, the army broke up and made its own way back to Baghdad. Khaṣki Muḥammad, alarmed at the news, called the older Aghas of his Janissaries, upon whom alone he could rely. They decided to close the city-gates against the returning rabble until they should deliver up the ringleaders. The gates were shut for three days while the mutineers camped without ; but, as the plan seemed likely to succeed, further sedition undid it. On a dark night malcontents among the Janissaries themselves stealthily roused all their confederates. By dawn their force was ready. The Sarai was stormed and three high officials demanded as the price of the rebels' withdrawal. Of these unfortunates the first was caught and done to death on the first day of street-fighting. For the blood of the second—a man entirely innocent—they clamoured on the following day. The Pasha could neither deliver nor protect him ; he bade them seek for themselves. He was found and butchered just as the cry of the mu'adhdhins fell from every minaret, calling to prayer. The third victim escaped from Baghdad to a tribal refuge. His house with many others was sacked by the mob-rulers.

The worst was now over. The older Janissaries had failed to prevent the disorder, but they now succeeded in calming it. The Pasha had fled outside the city. The objects of the mutineers' first demands had fallen to their hands. Public opinion hardened against them. The Janissary Aghas called a parade. All fell in and re-dressed their ranks as a loyal regiment. The local troops, anxious now to unite with them, were refused and driven from the parade ground. The Pasha outside, hearing of the improved position, approached Baghdad from Kadhimiyyah, and wrote in strong terms to the now loyal Janissaries for the surrender of the worst offenders. They were in the end delivered. Most were put to a death well deserved, others punished by loss of pay and privilege. So ended a miserable episode after a course of forty days.

The governorship of Khaṣki Muḥammad was remembered for other events less significant of misrule. The rich equipage of Ḥusain Agha, Ambassador of the Sultan to the Mughal court of India, passed through Baghdad. A Persian envoy with splendid presents from Shah 'Abbas II was escorted through 'Iraq to Stambul. Isma'il Agha, returning the visit by an embassy to Iṣfahan, returned thence to die at Baghdad. The year 1656 was remarkable for river floods. The waters, spread like a sea over the 'Iraq plains, almost levelled the banks of the few canals, silted their beds, and carried away whole settlements of reed and mud. The city walls suffered heavily as the moat filled and the water lapped at the foundations. The Pasha spared neither money nor effort. His restored bastions and well-made causeways along the sodden routes long redounded to his credit. To repair the Baghdad defences—where, with its stormy history, defencelessness could less than anywhere be tolerated—orders came from the Sultan to the Pashas of Diyarbakr, Mosul, and Kirkuk to send contingents. The camps of these surrounded the city until they were ordered away in haste to fight the famous robber Wazir of Anatolia, Abazah Ḥasan. Khaṣki Muḥammad, religious of the old school, sent gold to Madinah to improve a dome, added a minaret to the shrine at Najf, and gained greater applause by demolishing a Christian church to erect a mosque upon its site. His rule of three years ended at midsummer 1659. It was succeeded by the second appointment of Martaḍha Pasha.

Martadha had, since he left Baghdad, served with distinction against Abazah Ḥasan. He now paid Baghdad the compliment of preferring it to Diyarbakr, and obtained the Government upon set terms: to re-dig the silted Dujail canal, to collect outstanding revenues for the Treasury, and to remit yearly to Stambul two hundred "purses" of gold with some tons of gunpowder. At the camp of his predecessor, outside Baghdad, he examined the accounts of the ayalat. The debt of Muḥammad Khaṣki to the State was declared to be six hundred "purses", and Stambul confirmed the figure. The debtor's prayers gained its reduction to five hundred; but his ill favour with Muḥammad Kuprili—Grand Wazir at the time—prevented a greater indulgence. Paying something on account, he was then royally entertained by his successor. Martaḏha proceeded to his second duty—the repair of the Dujail. Well-organized labour completed it in three months. Important fiscal reforms followed. Some fixed assessments and many half-official perquisites of the finance officials were abolished. Permanent arrangements were made to meet the new obligations of Baghdad to the Throne, its yearly tribute of treasure and powder. Of outstanding debts little was collected: an ingenious interpretation of the calendar showed that none was due.[1] The Pasha secured his own position by generous presents to the powerful in Stambul.

The rule of this exceptional if faulty viceroy was blessed for its security, which he produced by prompt suppression of tribal restlessness and by unattended night-prowls in his capital. It was hated for the grinding exactions of his tax-collectors, for the general poverty due to rising prices, and for moral corruption which his own example encouraged. His wealth and display exceeded anything within living memory. The numbers and equipment of his body-guard recalled, to a simple public, the armies of famous conquerors. His claim to powers of clairvoyance was supported by incidents long passed from mouth to mouth. After three years he was transferred, in 1662, to Crete. His mind was perhaps affected: he saw in his new and smaller province a trap to snare him, and fled for refuge among the Kurdish mountaineers. Instead of asylum he found arrest; and by the Sultan's orders the Wali of Diyarbakr confined and beheaded the once gorgeous potentate.

His successor at Baghdad was well chosen—a venerable soldier[2] who had served there a generation before as a plain captain of Janissaries. His firm and tranquil government was doubly valuable after the hectic uncertainties of Martaḏha. Avengers and litigants found him cold and averse; peasants and householders acclaimed his abolition of vexatious imposts and suppression of official privilege. Stable and moderate in his

[1] By means (says Gulshan) of the difference between the Islamic lunar calendar and the Graeco-Roman solar. How this worked is not apparent to the writer.

[2] 'Abdu 'l Raḥman Pasha.

government, the old man was in private a drug-taker liable to wild outbursts of passion. He ruled for nearly two years. Every contrast was provided by his young, ill-guided, and rapacious successor. For six months the sedate of Baghdad shook their heads at the advisers, the pleasures, the heartless avarice of Muṣṭafa Pasha. Unregretted, death of a colic removed him to the burial-ground of 'Abdu 'l Qadir.

Qara Muṣṭafa Pasha followed, for his second period of office. A hazardous career of favour gained and lost, flight and promotion alternating, had finally brought him back to 'Iraq, where he was to appear yet a third time. The memory of later years recalled, of this tenure of the Pashaliq, only his lavish circumcision-feast for his son. The two years of Ibrahim Pasha the Long brought another Baṣrah campaign, of which more will appear elsewhere; and ended with the third appointment of Qara Muṣṭafa. Here again the disturbances of southern 'Iraq fill the chronicle, which preserves nothing else of a four-year reign. He died at Baṣrah a year later. The incoming Governor, Ḥusain, was for a time embarrassed by difficulties due to an inveterate enmity between his chief lieutenant and that of Qara Muṣṭafa. This only, with minor works of piety and improvement, is recorded. Several mosques and a bazaar were built or repaired by his directions. Flood-damage at A'dhamiyyah suburb was repaired by his care and by the help of funds from Stambul. He held the Pashaliq from 1671 to 1674.

His fall was due in part to the errors of subordinates weakly and blindly trusted, but still more to a false alarm in Stambul. A sudden rumour gained ground—due, if to anything, to some aggression of foothill Lurs—of a new Persian threat to Baghdad. It sufficed in 'Iraq to renew indiscipline in the garrisons, and in Europe to impel the rapid dispatch of an experienced Agha of Janissaries, 'Abdu 'l Raḥman Pasha. This moderate and prudent administrator restored order among his troops, and replied to the Persian scare by a thorough revision of his defences. Granaries and magazines were replenished, confidence was restored; and the viceroy followed this by reforms of the machinery of taxation and by acts of discipline against the worst of the local Governors. Among public works, he rebuilt the shrine of Ma'ruf ul Kirkhi, and continued work on the great flood-dyke begun before him; but in spite of much expense and the hardship of corvée labour the work did not survive. His government gave place at the end of twenty months to that—similar in its integrity, reason, and charities—of Qaplan Muṣṭafa Pasha. The new Governor survived with credit another rising of the tyrannical Janissaries, now shamelessly abusing their power in every province of the Empire. A great and costly jetty at A'dhamiyyah, repairs to the tomb of Muḥammad ul Quduri, and a pilgrimage to Karbala, showed the prudent piety of Qaplan.

'Umr Pasha, who succeeded, had held the provinces of Egypt and Diyarbakr, and now ruled Baghdad for nearly four years. Various enterprises recalled him to posterity—improvements in the tomb of Abu Ḥanifah, the dome of Abu Musif, a school attached to the Qamriyyah, the caravansarai and guard-house of Khan Azad. In his last year in Baghdad yet another mutiny of the Janissaries broke out, led by men of a draft fresh from Stambul. A successful campaign was led against the Bani Lam. In 1681 Ibrahim Pasha, an old military Agha, was transferred from Erzerum. He was applauded for checking the contumacy of his garrison, for punishing the oppressive and corrupt zeal of the town police. A jetty, a mosque, and a hand-rail on the boat-bridge were his contribution to public improvement. Three years and a half later 'Umr Pasha returned to the office for a second time for three years. Aḥmad Pasha held it for a year and was succeeded by the third appointment of 'Umr, which brings the record (left very meagre by our chronicler) to the year 1689.

The gentle rule of Ḥasan Pasha[1] was disturbed by a severe famine which had already gripped central 'Iraq when he assumed his government. The alleys of Baghdad were filled with dying. Kurds and Arab tribesmen sought from the rich of the city the bread which had failed them in their own fields. Plague as usual followed famine, and destroyed many thousands. The twin calamities ran their course, leaving Baghdad feeble and

[1] Niebuhr (*Voyage*, ii, p. 253), in his list of Pashas, identifies this Ḥasan with the Ḥasan Pasha who ruled from 1704 (or, as he says, 1702). Olivier (iv, p. 341) accepts it from Niebuhr. But it must definitely be rejected in view of our knowledge of the actual earlier career of Ḥasan Pasha (see p. 124 sub).

impoverished. An empty treasury distressed the Pasha not less than bad news from Kurdistan. In the Shahrizor, Mir Sulaiman [1] and Mir Ḥasan, Kurdish chiefs, had so far oppressed their natural subjects that Dilawir Pasha of Kirkuk was forced to interfere. The expedition cost him his life and achieved nothing. The Shahrizor province then took a significant step in addressing the Pasha of Baghdad with a request to send them a Governor. A Mutasallim was dispatched—the first time that Kirkuk or Mosul had admitted the authority of Baghdad as more than that of an equal neighbour. Ḥasan Pasha was relieved of his government by his own request; but questions arising from his accounts led to his detention in the citadel. His successor, Aḥmad Bazirgan, died of disease after a few months; and the people of Baghdad took their chance to set free Ḥasan Pasha, still detained. The Porte allowed this to pass, but conferred the province on Aḥmad, Kahya of ‘Umr Pasha the former Wali. He died early in 1694.

His successor,[2] a Ḥaji of the same name, was forced to notice the growing power of the Muntafiq under Mani‘. These troubles and others of central ‘Iraq are kept for a separate chapter. ‘Ali Pasha, appointed in 1696, showed vigour in tackling the larger tribes. He cut up a detachment of Shammar raiding across the Euphrates by Fallujah, dispatched the Muwali Shaikh on other punitive work, and himself chastised the Zubaid and Bani Lam. In 1698 Isma‘il Pasha, late Governor of Egypt, was appointed to Baghdad. His capacity for just and liberal rule was mixed, unhappily, with a hot and impulsive temper. He had held the high offices of Agha of Janissaries, Governor of Rumelia, and Deputy of the Grand Wazir. A mutiny of the garrison at Karbala was followed by the pillage of the Holy City, which the Shah, as Shia‘ champion, was swift to report to Stambul. Isma‘il was transferred to Van within two months of his appointment; but, seeing in this a menace to his own safety, he surprised all by his flight across the frontier to Persia, where he died in 1700. The new Governor of Baghdad, Daltaban Muṣṭafa,

[1] This can hardly be other than Sulaiman Beg Baban (p. 80).

[2] Baghdad was visited in 1695 by Soares Sieur du Val, who vividly describes the lawlessness of the Janissaries. ‘Il n'y a point de villes dans les États du Turc ou les Janissaires soient plus insolents que dans Babilone et ou la Justice se rend moins . . .’ (p. 118 of the MS.)

a vigorous and tyrannical Serbian, illiterate but thrusting, was promoted after his Baṣrah campaign[1] to be Grand Wazir in succession to the great Ḥasan Kuprili. Of the rule of his successors at Baghdad, Yusif Pasha and 'Ali Pasha, nothing significant is related.

In the fifth year of the new century,[2] Ḥasan Pasha was appointed to Baghdad ayalat. Since the conquest by Sultan Murad, thirty-seven Pashas had preceded him in Baghdad Sarai, in a space of sixty-five years. In central 'Iraq the period has shown us few striking characters or events worth the world's attention. A glance at northern and north-eastern 'Iraq will yield no more, so meagre are the records of the time. Only in the flatter and hotter regions north of the Gulf was being made a history of ambition, treachery, and reprisal.

§ 4. *Northern 'Iraq.*[3]

The northern Pashaliqs of Mosul and Shahrizor (with its capital at Kirkuk) were throughout this period independent of the Baghdad Pasha save when Imperial orders demanded co-operation. The dominating influence of Diyarbakr over Mosul, which some sixteenth-century evidence led to suspect, was no more; and the interference of Baghdad in Kirkuk affairs was limited to a single case in 1691. Once at least—in 1640—one Pasha held both the governments of upper 'Iraq. The later interrelations of the 'Iraq provinces show the status of each constantly modifying; and this would be so to a greater degree at a period when the personality or the rank of an individual Governor decided how far his sway should extend over his colleagues and neighbours. The military basis of the administration ensured that any Wazir or Beglerbegi could command any Mirmiran or mere Sanjaq in his vicinity. An accession to his existing province would be the regular reward for good service,

[1] p. 122 sub.

[2] So Gulshan. Niebuhr (ii, p. 253) says A.H. 1114 (A.D. 1702), making a reign of twenty-one years to end in 1723. Von Hammer follows this (Bk. XIV, p. 76). Olivier (iv, p. 341) copies Niebuhr. Ḥadiqatu'l Wuzara gives A.H. 1117 as the date, a year too late. Gulshan is the paramount authority.

[3] Authorities: Mosul Calendar; Tavernier; Auliya effendi (ed. cit., vol. iv); Sulaiman Sayigh. Behind the first and last named of these is Minhalu'l Auliya.

people and provinces alike existing for the enrichment and gratification of Pasha and Padishah.

Yet while the higher commands were still thus fluid, the smaller were crystallizing. As tribes gradually, by rise and fall, migration and settlement, took more and more their present locations, and the administrative value of natural boundaries became clearer, the ayalats split up as the charges of mutasallim, sanjaq begi, or ḍhabiṭ, into units agreeing more and more with those of the nineteenth century. The time-honoured limits of a tribal area or hereditary estate or natural valley or watershed became those of the future naḥiyyah or qaḍha, and even now were recognized by fief-holder and garrison Agha, by the Daftardar and his tax-farmers.

The area covered by the two ayalats included regions directly administered, as well as Kurdish city-states and tribes held with the lightest hand. Of the settled and governed parts of the Shahrizor province, nothing is left on record. Neither the pleasant city of Kirkuk, nor the string of Turkoman towns on the main route, nor the many villages of rain-cultivators, had changed character in the last two centuries. Turkish influence, where government found blood, tongue, and religion congenial, had deepened more than the Arab plains or the Kurdish mountains ever made possible. Of the successive Pashas and the incidents of their day, no record remains.

Mosul impressed its few European visitors unfavourably. Its mixed races and religious feuds offered constant fuel to the bitter and continual quarrels of factions in the town. The imposing walls, the shabby but pretentious buildings and filthy streets, had changed nothing since the raid of Salim the Grim had heralded Turkish conquest. The trade was still in Kurdish produce forwarded to Diyarbakr and Aleppo, in wheat and timber descending the Tigris to Baghdad, in feeding and partly clothing the Arab tribesmen. The famous "Muslin" had almost ceased to be made. Two ill-found khans accommodated travellers. Four Christian sects mixed and wrangled. A settlement of Capuchin friars had occupied a river-side building until, upon some pretext, the Pasha dislodged them. On the opposite bank and connected by the boat-bridge, the mosque of Nabi Yunis was a revered place of pilgrimage. The garrison in 1644 consisted of Janissaries and feudal cavalry to a number of about 3,000.

The main problems of Mosul government—malcontent Yazidis of Sinjar, Kurdish raiding parties from the foothills, locusts and drought and the changeless Bedouin—are easy to visualize, but the records are too meagre for continuous narrative. From the recorded names of the Pashas, of whom forty-eight fill the space from 1638 to the close of the century, little is to be learnt. Several are Wazirs, a majority held the lower rank of Mirmiran, some were transferred from other ayalats—Van, Qars, Baṣrah, Baghdad, Diyarbakr. The status of the Mosul ayalat therefore appears honourable, and its Pasha was able several times to lead a force to the assistance of his colleague in southern 'Iraq. Candidates of Mosul family at times secured the office. Such was Muḥammad Amin, son of the Bakr Pasha earlier mentioned. He held the ayalat for some months while Baghdad was still Persian. Such were Zaini Pasha in 1674, and in 1683 Kadum 'Ali of whose vicissitudes and picturesque brutalities the records have preserved a legend. With the other names at most a single fact is associated—the long captivity in Europe of Muṣṭafa Pasha "the Prisoner", the rapid vigour of 'Ali Pasha (lately Wali of Baghdad) against robber bands, the bitter quarrel of Ibrahim Pasha with the leading 'Umari of the moment, and its issue in the death of both. These three Walis held office in 1691, 1697, and 1712. About the last-mentioned year the revolt of one Rashwanzadah Khalil Pasha is recorded. He collected a force of desperadoes and terrorized the town and routes. The Wali of Raqqah, Ṭopal Yusif Pasha, was detailed to restore order, marched to Mosul, engaged and slew the rebel, and, to add vividness to his dispatch, sent his head to Stambul.

In the hill country north and east of the governed areas of the two ayalats, the peace of 1639 had finally divided the Kurds between the Shia' and Sunni powers. The Kalhur and Ardalan tribes looked definitely to Persia. The Mukri were divided, the Shahrizor valleys fell in Turkish territory. A number of points —Sakis, Zuhab, Darnah—were left for future generations to dispute. The migration of tribes still nomadic, the mutual raiding of frontier enemies, naturally ignored the boundary. Neither power lost a chance of gaining influence in its neighbour's affairs, nor did rivals within the Kurdish states and tribes scruple to invoke whomever seemed most likely to assist their private ambitions. But in general the seventeenth century saw the Turkish influence gaining ground in that fringe of Kurdistan with which 'Iraq history is concerned.

Farther north, Jazirah and 'Amadiyyah maintained their status of partial independence. The former, a small and ill-built town, was notable only as a meeting-place of merchants, a stage on the high road, and the site of a boat-bridge. Its Beg admitted no superior but his Turkish suzerain. The natural defensive position of 'Amadiyyah and its remoteness from main routes preserved it from Turkish interference. The Beg could, in 1660, raise 8,000 to 10,000 horse and a greater force of foot than any neighbour. His vassaldom included the condition of military service on demand. In 1701 his forces joined those of Mosul and Diyarbakr in extinguishing the rising in southern 'Iraq. The leader of that day was Rabbad Pasha. The rank of Mirmiran[1] was often if not habitually conferred upon the ruling prince of 'Amadiyyah, as later upon the Babans.

Keui had a similar independence under its Soran Begs. The smaller towns—Zakho, Dohuk, 'Aqrah, Raniyyah—gave some vague allegiance to the Begs of their greater neighbours. The bond included military support, some form of tribute or land-rights, and the obligation to submit disputes for settlement. Its efficiency depended on the personalities of the moment, the chances of a successful bid for greater independence, and the hope of help in such an enterprise from Turk or Kurdish neighbours.

Across the frontier in Ardalan, the great days of Khan Aḥmad Khan came to an end soon after the death of Shah 'Abbas. Shah Ṣafi, with his perverse insistence on butchering his best supporters, drove the prince into the arms of Turkey by an act of wanton cruelty.[2] By Sultan 'Uthman he was warmly welcomed. He settled, it seems, in Mosul.[3] His place in Ardalan was taken by Sulaiman Khan of the same family, but closely connected with the Persian Court. The further contact of Ardalan with the Sultan's dominions in the last years of the century has been mentioned in describing the rise of the Babans.[4]

[1] This carried the title of Pasha.
[2] p. 65, foot-note, *supra*.
[3] The Ardalan tradition runs that he "ruled" Mosul, Kirkuk, and Shahrizor for seven years.
[4] p. 80 *supra*.

V

THE PRINCE OF BAṢRAH

§ 1. *The line of Afrasiyab.*[1]

The name of Baṣrah has scarcely been mentioned in these pages since they referred (with a brevity enforced by lack of records) to its uneasy fortunes in the sixteenth century.[2] We saw the rule of a tribal vassal give place to the Pasha of an ayalat, and the Pasha in his turn distracted by lawlessness on land and river outside his city-gates, and resentment of a foreign government within. Elsewhere has been seen the ascendancy of Portugal in the waters beyond the Shaṭṭ ul 'Arab mouth, and the vain efforts of Turkey (but feebly assisted by its Baṣrah fleet) to replace that flag by its own. The history of Baṣrah in the seventeenth century reproduces, in different order, the same phenomena. We shall find it a spectator while the sea-power of the Gulf (which it is well placed to rule) was disputed by strangers. Again a local dynasty was replaced by Turkish government of the normal pattern, and again the governors found the problem of its administration too difficult for their solution. In an area never confessedly parted from the Turkish empire, it is remarkable to notice the completeness with which Baṣrah could stand aside from the struggles of Turkey and Persia for the possession of Baghdad—from the history of 'Iraq, indeed —for fifty years.

The opening years of the seventeenth century saw the hold of the Turkish Pashas of Baṣrah growing weaker and weaker. The rebellion of Muḥammad ul Aḥmad ul Ṭawil in Baghdad brought nearer the idea of local usurpation. There were old Baṣrah

[1] Authorities: Tavernier, especially loc. cit., p. 100, foot-note; Zadu'l Musafir of Shaikh Fatḥullah ul Ka'abi (cf. Mignon, p. 269); Malcolm; Pietro della Valle. For the Gulf, sources as before (Appendix I, § v (f)).

[2] pp. 31–3 *supra*.

nobles and powerful tribesmen with their own ambitions and scant respect for the Sultan's officers. About the middle of the second decade the government was secured by a native of the place, by name Afrasiyab. It is recorded that, after endless raiding and repression between the Turkish garrison and the tribes surrounding, the Pasha had agreed to leave them in peace. Later, however, the Arab inhabitants of Baṣrah town ceased even to tolerate the foreign garrison in its citadel.

> "So that the garrison being Turks, and the inhabitants Arabians, who could not endure to be curbed, they ofttimes quarreled with the Turks and came to blows. Thereupon the Arabians of the Desert came to the relief of the Citizens and besieged the Basha in the Fortress. At length because there could be no such agreement made but that one party or other took a decision presently to break it, there was one Basha whose name was Aiud who, after many contests and revolts which had almost tyr'd him, resolved to rid himself of the troubles and sold his government for forty thousand piastres to a rich lord in the country, who presently raised a sufficient number of soldiers to keep the people in awe. This great man took upon himself the name of Efrasias Basha . . ."

He "threw off the Turkish yoak, and took upon him the title of Prince of Balsara. As to the Pasha that sold his government, he no sooner arrived in Constantinople, but he was strangl'd". In this account[1] there is nothing improbable. Another source[2] accounts for the elevation of Afrasiyab with difference of detail only. By this version he had been

> "a writer in the office of military accounts at Baṣrah, at a period when the inhabitants united to expel their Turkish Pasha, named 'Ali, who finding his revenues daily decreasing, and with them the resources for maintaining his garrison, sold the government to Afrasiyab for eight hundred purses of three thousand Muḥammadis each : under the sole condition, that the Khuṭbah should continue to be delivered in the name of the Sultan . . ."

The information that would enable a better definition of the status of Afrasiyab is not forthcoming. His relations with the Sultan and with the Wazir at Baghdad ; his forces, Turkish or

[1] Tavernier, Bk. II, p. 89.
[2] Zadu'l Musafir.

local; his personal antecedents and backing: all are unascertained, It is said[1] that his father was of old Seljuk blood, his mother an Arab woman of Dair. His power to raise forces suggests a tribal backing; none, perhaps, but a powerful tribesman would have ventured to assume the position at all. His assumption of the title of Pasha, or its bestowal by a government anxious to retain his loyalty, argues a status less than independence. In dispatches to Stambul, doubtless, he declared his loyalty to the Khalif, who (as he later recognized Afrasiyab's son with farman and present) must have tolerated the half-secession of Baṣrah under the father. It is certain that Afrasiyab and his state paid neither tribute nor obedience to Baghdad or to Stambul. Baṣrah was beyond Turkish control, though not outside their suzerainty. The government of Afrasiyab was marked by security and content.

Beyond the city and suburbs of Baṣrah he extended rule and order over Qubban, Duraq, and other of the islands and mud-flats of the Shaṭṭ ul 'Arab. Elsewhere his outside relations were threefold. The Persian vassal of Ḥuwaizah, Manṣur bin Muṭlab, approached him for help or countenance in throwing off his own allegiance to the Shah. The desert and marsh tribes presented even to a local dynast most of the difficulties met by his predecessors and successors. And in the Gulf, great events marked his later years.

Since 1580, the paramount position of the Portuguese had started to decline. At home, Portugal was for sixty years to be subject to the greedy and fanatical government of Spain. In the Gulf, their cruelty and rapacity made them everywhere disliked; and, as fewer reinforcements reached their garrisons, Persian and Arab seamen could again venture on their voyages and dare to close their ports to the Dom. And other European eyes had now looked eastward. England, before the Armada, had sent Eldred, Newberrie, and Fitch to explore the Euphrates route; and, after it, formed in 1600 the first East India Company. The Dutch, in the last years of the century, had ventured into Indian but not Persian waters. The first twenty years of the seventeenth century saw the Portuguese still dominant but weakening. The strong monarch of Persia never acquiesced in their occupation and oppression of his ports and subjects. In 1602 his forces

[1] Zadu'l Musafir.

expelled them from Baḥrain, in 1608 he could bring formidable pressure upon the great market-fortress of Hormuz. Four years later the Portuguese occupied Bandar 'Abbas,[1] a station founded by the Shah as a counterpoise to Hormuz; but in 1614 Persian forces reft the place from the Portuguese, who never recovered it.

The death blow to their power was not, after all, to come from local rivals, but from Europe. The year 1616 saw an event which was to weaken the power of Hormuz more than any obstruction by Persian or 'Umani. The East India Company's ship *James* cast anchor at Jashk. Now established at Surat and in touch through embassies with the Shah, they had come to try their luck in the silk trade; and this mission to the Gulf achieved important results. A farman with every accommodating clause rewarded the efforts of Mr. Edward Connock, their ill-supported leader. A second Company's ship reached Jashk late in 1617. Negotiations with the Shah continued. Ground was gained in the share of the silk-trade diverted to British ships, in ceremonious correspondence between the Kings of England and Persia, and in the greater popularity which British methods acquired than Portuguese. Jashk, from 1618 to 1620, was used by increasing numbers of English trading-ships.

Hormuz was now doomed. The Shah was at his strongest. The trade rivalry had provided constant friction with the Portuguese, and the island-market was an old thorn in his side. But he lacked a fleet. Upon conditions carefully formulated, the Company was willing to supply it. At a meeting of the Company's Agent with the Governor of Fars, present and future privileges were settled. In January 1622 the strong Portuguese fort of Qishim fell to the British fleet, and early in February the assault on Hormuz began. A Persian force easily occupied the town, and began the blockade and mining of the fortress; but the defence was stout, the Shah's forces craven and ill found. In the harbour Portuguese ships were sunk one by one. Landing parties from the Company's ships assisted the land-besiegers. Though the siege continued far into April, it could have but one result. The Portuguese capitulated, marched out, and were shipped to Masqaṭ. The loot of the place, contrary to pre-

[1] Known to Europeans throughout the century as "Gombroon".

arranged terms, was snatched by the first-comer of the uncordial allies.

Portuguese power had sustained a crushing though not a totally fatal blow; the English had gained a market more convenient than Jashk, and the added favour of the Shah, who permitted them to settle at Bandar 'Abbas though not to fortify it. They were soon to find, however, that from the Persians there was neither justice nor redress to be had; nor could the Shah's demands for naval support against the remnant of the Portuguese, and against the Turks at Baṣrah, be easily refused. But these trials were slight compared with the appearance, in the guise of allies in a common cause, of a new European power. The Dutch had by now penetrated from the Indian Ocean into these narrower seas. They settled at Bandar 'Abbas at the same time as the British, building there a massive Factory, and joined their ships to the Company's in action against the Portuguese. These, now based on Masqaṭ and still strong enough for pirate-raids, were led by an Admiral of exceptional dash. Actions took place off Bandar 'Abbas in February 1625. All three combatants—Dutch, English, and Portuguese—lost heavily. A peace between Portugal and Persia was concluded in the same year, the former renouncing all claims to their old settlements on Persian soil.

With Afrasiyab in Baṣrah, the connexions of the Portuguese were slight until the fall of Hormuz. Thereafter they used it increasingly; and the shelter offered them by the Baṣrah ruler at last brought upon him the displeasure of the Shah. Baṣrah had not been threatened by the Persian armies that reft Baghdad from the Ṣu Bashi, nor by Karchghai Khan thereafter: it contained no Shia' shrines, and little cultivated land: but its vassaldom to the Sultan and its asylum for Portuguese trade must cease. In 1624 the Shah instructed the Khan of Shiraz, Imam Quli Khan, to remedy this nuisance which notably diminished the traffic of Bandar 'Abbas. Afrasiyab was bidden to renounce his Turkish and accept a Persian suzerain. He was to mint his money in the Shah's name, mention it in the public prayers (the crucial test of allegiance), and conform to Persian usage in dress. In return he should be a hereditary and a non-contributary Wali with the fullest local powers. Afrasiyab, supported by the

Portuguese, refused. An army was sent from Shiraz by way of Shushtar. At the Baṣrah dependency of Qubban, which it attacked, it was bombarded and repulsed by Portuguese ships. During the breathing-space that followed Afrasiyab died and was succeeded by 'Ali Pasha, his son.[1]

He informed Stambul of his accession, professed his loyalty, and asked for help. Of this, with the Persians astride of both Tigris and Euphrates, there could be little hope. He received, however, unexpected reinforcement in five hundred followers of the Wali of Ḥuwaizah, themselves refugees from Imam Quli. March 1625 found Baṣrah awaiting the Khan's attack; he was known to have left Ḥuwaizah. The force of 'Ali Pasha was small and amateur. The Portuguese, well paid to do so, lent five armed ships; conscription was proclaimed; city patriotism ran high. Notables of the town raised volunteer forces, even the peaceful Sabaeans marched to the Pasha's camp. The sea-force was divided. Three ships accompanied 'Ali Pasha to Qurnah, where the Persian forces were expected to try a crossing. Two sailed downstream to stop approach from that quarter. The fear and bustle of the short campaign ended in a mysterious anti-climax. The Persian force suddenly withdrew, abandoning even the furniture of their camp, before a shot was fired. Trouble in Shiraz, or an order from Iṣfahan, must be the reason; Baṣrah, at any rate, was saved. A few days later (May 1625) farman, robe, and scimitar reached 'Ali Pasha by the desert route from Stambul. His victory and popularity seated him firmly in his government. The defences of Qurnah, his natural outpost, were rebuilt. In 1629 Imam Quli made another attempt; and the miracle which had saved the town before could not be expected again. 'Ali Pasha invoked the aid of his tribesmen. A stratagem was adopted which history was to see repeated: the flood-dyke protecting the town was broken and the flat spaces for miles round inundated. The Persians, weak in water-transport and faced with these strange conditions, simultaneously heard of the death of Shah 'Abbas and retired. 'Ali Pasha was left free to

[1] Shaikh Fatḥullah gives 'Ali Pasha a reign of forty-five years commencing from 1603. It is, however, almost certain that Afrasiyab lived till 1624. Probably 'Ali, during his father's lifetime, transacted much business and was latterly Governor in all but name. Afrasiyab himself did not assume the government of Baṣrah till about 1612.

conduct his liberal and humane government. The powerful tribes of the Jaza'ir district, never for long obedient to Turkish rule, had formed a league against which Baṣrah and Baghdad alike were impotent. The lower Tigris and lower Euphrates were a defiant and truculent *imperium in imperio*. Afrasiyab had shrunk from embarking on hostilities against their savage bravery and inaccessibility; 'Ali Pasha now undertook the task. He marched and counter-marched through the marshy wastes, and "so broke the spirit of the population that, from that hour, the tameness of the people of Jaza'ir has become a trite proverb".[1] The fort of Mu'ammir was taken over from the Baghdad government. The court of 'Ali Pasha at Baṣrah was compared by its votaries to that of Harun ul Rashid himself. The arts and sciences were cherished, learned men found appreciative refuge, wise economy and secure justice gave a scarcely expected tranquillity. The laureate of the time and place was a celebrated poet, Shaikh 'Abdu 'l 'Ali ul Raḥmah.

A change, meanwhile, had been made at Ḥuwaizah, where the intrigues of Manṣur were not unknown to his Persian overlords. In his march from Shiraz to join the Shah at Baghdad in 1623, Imam Quli Khan had pointedly demanded the co-operation of the Ḥuwaizah forces, and waited for their arrival. None were forthcoming. The Shah several times required the Wali's presence at Iṣfahan, always in vain. His disobedience, not concealed by obsequious dispatches, was at last frankly expressed. Imam Quli, marching on Baṣrah in March 1625, paused at Ḥuwaizah to expel him. He fled with a large following to Baṣrah, while the Khan installed his nephew, Muḥammad son of Mubarak. Confident in his loyalty, Imam Quli left no garrison at Ḥuwaizah. Manṣur was welcomed by 'Ali Pasha in Baṣrah and allotted lands as near as possible to his old home.

§ 2. *The Gulf, 1622 to 1700.*[2]

For three generations following the fall of Hormuz, sea-power in the Persian Gulf was divided, suspicious, and mutually offensive. The elements concerned were the Dutch, the English, the

[1] Fatḥullah ul Ka'abi. Nothing else is known of such a proverb: and the tameness was short lived.

[2] Sources as before: the "Précis" now begins to be of value.

Portuguese, and the Arabs of 'Uman. No Turkish shipping issued from Baṣrah, and the Persians had no marine. Our sources enable us to trace some phases of Gulf life in great detail; but here no more can be attempted than an outline of the career of these competitors for the remainder of the century.

From 1630 the efforts of the Portuguese were confined to maintaining themselves in 'Uman and endeavouring to regain a footing at Hormuz. In the former they succeeded for a bare twenty years: in the latter they failed. Neither they nor the Persians were checked in the pursuit of their aims by their treaty of 1625. In 1632 the Shah's officers pressed for British assistance in an attack on Masqaṭ. It was not launched, however, and the Portuguese replied by further fortification. With a station at Baṣrah—where they had looked after the fall of Hormuz—and their post at Kung, Masqaṭ with Suhar was now their only *pied-à-terre* for Gulf enterprise. Their flag grew rarer and less respected, disliked as ever. In 1643 they lost Suhar to an 'Umani force. In 1650 Masqaṭ itself capitulated. Kung was dying, Baṣrah—always an outpost rather than a base—too distant and unsupported, and anyhow useless for Persian trade. Portuguese interests after 1650 were confined to Kung and to the half-piratical voyages of Goan fleets. With the Persians, their relations were as constantly estranged as the faithless avarice of Persian officialdom must make them. With the coasters and pirates of 'Uman, every contact was a scuffle. With the English, formal peace was indeed made in 1634, confirmed at Goa in 1636; but rivalry at Baṣrah and counter-intrigues with the Dutch remained. They professed to believe that the raids of Arabian pirates were British-inspired, if not British-led; and could point, in 1689, to the looting of their Kung Factory by a British privateer. Thus meanly and unregretted died the sea-power of Portugal in the Gulf.

The proceedings of the Company in that region can be learned with much fullness from their copious records. We are here not directly concerned, however, with their trade elsewhere than in 'Iraq. They maintained a Factory at Bandar 'Abbas, with branches at Shiraz and Iṣfahan. The death-roll among their officers was high. Convoys between the Gulf and Surat were frequent if small in scale. The difficulties under which the Company worked were such as inevitably to lessen their prestige and profits.[1] In collecting the stipulated half-share of the Bandar 'Abbas customs, every tuman was a labour, and large sums commonly in arrears. The privileges acquired there needed renewal by each succeeding Shah, and never for nothing. The demand for silk in England varied, and the supply in Persia was affected by the amounts exported through Tabriz or the Mosul route.

The Dutch showed greater commercial skill than the Portuguese, with methods no more laudable if less violent. They assailed the Persian market with every weapon of bribery, propaganda, and attractive speculation. They risked immediate losses for remote privileges. Their consignments were on a greater scale, their ships larger and better found than the Company's. At Bandar 'Abbas there were ceaseless causes of friction. In 1645 so dangerous was the atmosphere there that the British Factor dispatched his goods to Baṣrah, while the Dutch attacked Qishim and extorted fresh concessions from the Shah. In the years following their supremacy became more marked. Their convoys to Baṣrah captured the import trade of the Shaṭṭ ul 'Arab, and the expulsion of the Portuguese from Masqaṭ in 1650 gave them a still greater ascendancy. Not until the end of the ninth decade is it possible to trace a fall in Dutch and a rise in British prosperity.

At Baṣrah (the chief concern of the present history) the Portuguese had hastened after 1622 to found a Carmelite convent, (whose religious propaganda met with considerable success) and to assist the Pasha in his defence against Persian attacks. The first appearance of British trade there was that of a "pinace" with a small cargo in 1635, when Portuguese rivalry did not prevent moderate sales. Five years later, however, this competition proved too much for their second venture; a Portuguese fleet

[1] Within the ranks of the British traders there were dissensions visible to all the world. In the fifth decade, the monopoly of the Company was flouted by "Interlopers", or private traders, of their own country. These, forming an "Association", did not scruple to corrupt the Shah against the old Company and bid for separate favours at Bandar 'Abbas. Unity was restored in 1649. Again, from 1654 to 1657, the "Merchant Adventurers" gave similar trouble, until Cromwell himself ordered their suppression : and in the last years of the century a New Company, to supersede the Old, endeavoured to assume its whole privileges. After bitter struggles at home and in India, an amalgamation was concluded in 1700.

fresh from Masqaṭ had filled the bazaars just before a Company's ship came in. In 1643 a small stationary Factory was founded, and enjoyed a short term of prosperity before the long arm of the Dutch reached up the Shaṭṭ. In 1645, as has been seen, the Factor at "Gombroon" removed his stocks to Baṣrah: but later in the same year, open commercial war being now declared, a Dutch fleet of eight vessels appeared at Minawi,[1] ruining British credit in a day. Trade languished. Free at last from Portuguese interference, the Company was now discredited by feuds with its Interlopers as well as harried and undersold by the Dutch. In 1657 its Factory was closed by the Pasha, misled by malicious stories of its insolvency. Occasional British ships still appeared from Bandar 'Abbas and from Surat; but the Factory was not refounded in the present century. It is not clear whether the Dutch had a permanent settlement at Baṣrah in these years, nor how far they sought trade in 'Iraq.

The famous Capitulations were signed in Stambul in 1661, to be revised and confirmed fourteen years later. Sea customs at Baṣrah against British goods were thereby fixed at 3 per cent. But the Wazirs, elchis, and parchments of the Bosphorus were half a year's journey from the Gulf: by the end of the century neither in customs-rates nor in other relations had the Capitulations borne fruit. By presents, flattery, or whatever appeal most availed at the moment, foreign traders had to make their terms from day to day with rulers eager for gold and consequence, quickly inflamed and misled—rapacious or benevolent tyrants as the luck of the day would have it.

§ 3. *Decline of the House of Afrasiyab.*[2]

'Ali Pasha, prince of Baṣrah since 1624,[3] was rewarded for two successful resistances to the Persian threat by twenty-five years of flourishing rule. His position relative to the Sultan was variously assessed. He knew himself for an independent prince,

[1] The riverside suburb of Baṣrah, at the mouth of the 'Ashar creek.

[2] Sources: Zadu'l Musafir (cf. Mignon, pp. 272–90); Tavernier (ed. cit., esp. pp. 88–93); Boullaye-le-Gouz, Bk. II, pp. 290 ff.; Godinho (in Murray, *Asia*, i, pp. 395 ff.); Carré, i, pp. 100–30; Soares Sieur du Val (MS., p. 189 f.); Thévenot, iv, pp. 566 ff.; Gulshan is very full; von Hammer, x, p. 376, xi, pp. 242 ff., xii, pp. 396 and 420). The accounts in Basha'yan and in Ghayatu'l Muram seem to be derived from Gulshan.

[3] Probable date. See p. 104 *supra*.

content to receive formal recognition by the distant and almost legendary Khalif. The British traders hoped in Baṣrah for the protection of the Turkish flag, while travellers thither by land considered themselves to have passed out of Turkish territory. Actually, the Turks accepted the position as they accepted it in Kurdistan. Though Baṣrah under such a régime brought them nothing, it also cost nothing and had shown itself capable of self-defence. The local support available for Afrasiyab's line was, events proved, too slight to secure it the continuity of a Kurdish or Persian vassal-state. It had little tribal backing and no half-sacred tradition of nobility. It was a government of opportunity, securing for Baṣrah and its traders half a century of tolerable conditions, and for the Sultan, peace with honour.

The prince of Baṣrah sent no help[1] to the Turkish armies in their decade of struggle outside Baghdad. In the final campaign of Sultan Murad he took no part, neither did the Sovereign deign to look in his direction. Rumour at Baṣrah—through which passed a delegation from the Mughal emperor—had it that only the oncoming rains of midwinter had saved the port from Murad's legions: but more probably light terms of suzerainty were offered and accepted. Baṣrah, so remote and so tempting to the Shah, needed gentle treatment if the secession of a Ṣu Bashi was to be avoided.[2]

The reign of 'Ali Pasha thus continued without rival or question throughout the Persian occupation of Baghdad, and for twelve years after it. Friction with the neighbouring Pasha was not lacking. As early as 1640 a petition reached Baghdad from the inhabitants of 'Arjah, a town which had been occupied by an Amir of the desert Arabs and on his death seized by the prince of Baṣrah, near to whose admitted frontier it lay. But its citizens preferred the Baghdad Pashaliq; and Darwish Muḥammad Pasha thought it worth the dispatch of an imposing force, which garrisoned the place under a Governor of his own. In 1645 'Ali

[1] Gulshan (in its account of the siege of Baghdad by Ḥafidh Aḥmad) records that a giant siege-gun was ordered up from Baṣrah by the Wazir. This would accord with the suggestion of Na'imah that forces (under Qara Bakr) had been sent up (see p. 63, foot-note). But there is no other evidence of such assistance.

[2] Boullaye-le-Gouz in 1649 notes this as the key-note of Turkish policy to the line of Afrasiyab (Bk. II, p. 291).

Pasha seized the border fortress of Zakkiyyah.[1] Musa Pasha the Little sent a well-ordered expedition with guns and river-transport, scattered the Baṣrah garrison, and occupied the post and others across the frontier.[2]

The succession of Ḥusain Pasha, upon the death of his father in about 1650, was likely to complicate Baṣrah relations. Ḥusain Pasha lacked the graces which had endeared his father, but inherited a forceful and ambitious character. His violence and occasional injustice raised many enemies. Tolerant to foreign merchants and the weak Christian communities, he did not court the popularity of his countrymen. He flouted the Pasha of Baghdad, commenced collecting sheep and buffalo-tax from tribes admittedly under the Baghdad Government, and installed his nominees in their larger villages. The peaceful conditions preceding the campaigns thus induced by his ambitions are described by Tavernier.[3]

"The Prince of Balsara has entered into leagues with several strange nations, so that whencesoever you come you may be welcome. There is so much liberty and so good order in the City, that you may walk all night long in the streets without molestation. The Hollanders bring spices thither every year. The English carry pepper and some few cloves; but the Portugals have no trade at all thither. The Indians bring Calicuts, indigo, and all sorts of merchandise. In short there are merchants of all countries from Constantinople, Smyrna, Aleppo, Damascus, Cairo and other parts of Turkie, to buy such merchandizes as come from the Indies, with which they lade the young camels which they buy in that place: for thither the Arabians bring them to put them to sale. They that come from Diarbequir, Moussul, Bagdat, Mesopotamia, and Assyria send their Merchandizes up the Tigris by water, but with great trouble and expense. . . . The Customs at Balsara amount to five in the hundred, but generally you have some favour shown you, either by the Customs or the Prince himself, that the Merchant does not really pay above four in the hundred. The Prince of Balsara is so good a Husband, that he lays up three millions of livres in the year, His chiefest revenue is in four things, Money, Horses, Camels, and Date-trees; but in the last consists his chiefest wealth."

[1] So Zadu'l Musafir; Gulshan calls it Dakkah.

[2] "La fortresse solide de Qacr-Tabi, qui est du côte de Bassora", says Huart (p. 78), curiously mistranslating Gulshan بصره طرفنه تابع قصر نام قلعه, i. e. Qaṣr only is the proper name.

[3] Ed. cit., p. 89.

The date-tax was "three-fourths of a Larin, or nine Sous French". The profit from money was made by recoining the "Reals" of all foreign merchants in the Baṣrah mint to "larins", "which is worth to him eight in the hundred". Customs were collected on the land-frontiers, and on the Tigris at Qurnah, as well as at the Port. Civil justice was administered by a Qaḍhi, appointed not from Stambul but by the Pasha himself. Small Christian communities existed. A monastery of Italian Carmelites remained; that of the Portuguese "Austin-friars" left when their compatriot traders ceased to appear. The head of the Carmelites, though not of French nationality, was in 1679 appointed French Consul.

Ḥusain Pasha had ruled under these flourishing conditions for some four years when acts of internal oppression brought upon him troubles from without. He had ill treated Aḥmad Beg and Fatḥi Beg, brothers of 'Ali Pasha his father. They fled to Stambul,[1] and obtained farmans for the government of two Sanjaqs of the Baṣrah ayalat.[2] Armed with these, they returned to Baṣrah, and were received with every polite formality by their nephew. Hearing, however, that he intended their assassination, they stoutly defended themselves until he was contented with their exile to India. They embarked, but landed instead at Qaṭif to become the guests of an old acquaintance, Muḥammad Pasha the Mirmiran of Al Ḥasa.[3] From this asylum the two exiles wrote to the Pasha of Baghdad, explaining their hard case and this flouting of the Padishah.

Martadḥa Pasha, ruling Baghdad since 1653, called them to an audience. Their recitals did not flatter the character of their nephew. The opportunity appealed to Martadḥa. He rallied his army and, dispatching it under Ramaḍhan Agha the Kahya,

[1] The authorities used by von Hammer have not enabled him to recount the forthcoming campaign in correct proportions, e.g. "la tribu Arabe d'Efrasiab s'etait revoltée contre Mourteza Pasha, pascha de Baghdad", &c. (vol. x, p. 377).

[2] That the Sultan had in fact no power to make such appointments did not matter at Stambul, whose bureaucrats would not admit the separate status of Baṣrah. Thévenot (iv, p. 567) states that one of the uncles was appointed Pasha of Baṣrah, the other of Qaṭif and Ḥasa.

[3] On the status of Al Ḥasa see p. 38, foot-note. At the present time it was clearly considered part of the Baṣrah principality; but such attachment was nominal.

later followed in person and joined the force at ʻArjah. Neighbouring fortresses—Chaluchiyyah, ʻAqqarah—fell easily. The tribesmen favoured an army which was to deliver them from too strong a ruler. Transport, supplies, guides, spies, goodwill—all were forthcoming from the Jaza'ir tribes. Qurnah fell without a blow. Ḥusain Pasha fled to a refuge in ʻArabistan. Martaḍha entered Baṣrah, and declared Aḥmad Beg its ruler.

Thus a completely successful march had restored Baṣrah to the Empire after a virtual secession of half a century. A son of Afrasiyab had accepted office as the mere tool of the Baghdad Pasha. The days of the Baṣrah prince seemed complete. But, in fact, Ḥusain Pasha had fourteen more years to rule; and this by reason of his own determined character and the extravagant weaknesses of Martaḍha. The latter, once master of the town, accepted blandly the rich presents of the notables,[1] but was still unsatisfied. He ordered close guard and inventory of the goods of the ruling family. This was the first stage to pillage, which spared none of the rich in Baṣrah nor even the treasures of the Government: and execution of leading notables followed the confiscation of their goods. Baṣrah, from joy in welcoming a deliverer, was plunged in grief and apprehension. From loyal tranquillity it was roused, city and tribes alike, to mutinous rage by the sudden execution of Aḥmad and Fatḥi. The Jaza'ir tribes rose and attacked Qurnah. Turkish reinforcements were hurried thither from Martaḍha at Baṣrah. Disordered scuffles in marsh and date-garden showed the tribesmen more determined than the Pasha's army. The Baghdad troops suffered increasing loss. Steady desertion began; company after company headed for Baghdad; and Martaḍha Pasha himself found it impossible to maintain his position in Baṣrah. He left it suddenly and empty-handed,[2] rejoined part of his army at ʻArjah, and regained Baghdad through tribal territories now hostile and contemptuous. Ḥusain Pasha returned instantly to his Government, with a welcome of new warmth from his subjects who had now tasted an alternative régime. He resumed a rule generally humane and enlightened,

[1] اشراف not شرفاء: Huart wrongly translates as "des cherifs ou descendants du Prophete".

[2] Gulshan says that he left his loot and fled alone: von Hammer (x, p. 377) that he was "chasé de Baṣra"; Thévenot (iv, p. 568) that he left in consequence of a general rebellion, with all the riches he could carry.

rich in patronage of learning and wise in titular submission to the Sultan,[1] but sullied by his hard and ambitious character. A Portuguese Jesuit traveller in 1663[2] found Baṣrah "the greatest emporium of these seas", and admired "handsome country houses, orchards, gardens, and magnificent plains, watered by numerous streams".

But a further and fatal collision with the Suzerain Empire could not be many years postponed. The occasion was given by the ambitions of Ḥusain Pasha against his colleagues or half-dependants in the Gulf. He had already installed a nominee in Qaṭif. He now (1663-4) dispatched a tribal force—Bani Khalid under Amir Barrak—to occupy Al Ḥasa. Barrak had no difficulty in seizing the government from Muḥammad Pasha; but then, instead of retiring, he saw fit to retain Ḥasa for himself. Ḥusain, by a rapid sea-borne expedition, occupied the sub-province that he had coveted, while Muḥammad Pasha fled to Stambul.[3] The high-handedness of Ḥusain, and tales of violence in Al Ḥasa, combined to rouse the royal anger. Ibrahim "the Long", present Pasha of Baghdad and well respected in Stambul, could be trusted: all was favourable for the reduction of Baṣrah. Muḥammad Pasha was heard attentively and orders given for his restoration. This task was left to Ibrahim, who was instructed to assemble an army of his own and neighbours' contingents of Diyarbakr, of Aleppo, of Mosul, of Raqqah, of Shahrizor, and to chastise the house of Afrasiyab. The army gathered at Ḥillah. The Pasha's first step was to address a formal missive to Ḥusain, demanding obedience and reparation. It was met by an insolent reply.

The Prince of Baṣrah had long warning. He had strenghtened the fortifications of his capital and of Qurnah, and built an outpost at Qumait. For months past he had been expelling from Baṣrah all useless members of the population. This process provoked a resistance to which his threats and ferocity proved superior, and provided heart-rending scenes of hardship. His officers, slaves

[1] From whom (says Zadu'l Musafir) "by force of princely offerings he bought the Wazarat".

[2] Godinho (in Murray, i).

[3] This episode is referred to in all the sources. Both Zadu'l Musafir and Gulshan speak of outrages committed by Ḥusain's men in Al Ḥasa as the cause of the Sultan's wrath.

and free, were pitiless in the expulsion of the aged and weak. In the areas round the city, similar steps were taken to strip the country and render difficult the approach of the Long Pasha.

The Sultan's forces began their march on Baṣrah in November 1665. Though the standards of seven Pashas and a score of vassal Begs floated above it, organization and preparation had been neglected. The best defences of Ḥusain could not have withstood its siege artillery; but Ibrahim the Long, too confident and deceived by bad advice, expected a prompt surrender and daily watched for grovelling envoys to approach him. Rumaḥiyyah was reached, and no such overtures had been made; a last warning sent to Ḥusain was ignored; the army entered Baṣrah province and camped at Manṣuriyyah. A force of Ḥusain's irregulars and tribesmen here opposed it, but it scattered these without effort and made good its way. The river at Manṣuriyyah was bridged, and the army moved on Qurnah,[1] where Ḥusain in person directed the defence. Days lengthened to months, and the fortress still resisted assault.

In his absence, faction temporarily lost him his capital. Ibrahim Pasha had found means to corrupt the loyalty of powerful Baṣrawis. Late in the course of the Qurnah siege, Ḥusain was forced by shortage (or impelled by his besetting greed) to seize boat-loads of provisions from the Shaṭṭ ul 'Arab. To the owners nothing was given back save the battered and empty hulls; with shaking heads they joined the councils of the malcontents. These assembled, and dispatched a letter to the Long Pasha in his lines at Qurnah: Baṣrah, now ungoverned and exposed to disorder, begged him to send a governor to rescue the port for their Sovereign. Sulaq Ḥusain was sent as Deputy; but the Shaiks and merchants, now formed into a compact authority, preferred themselves to retain control rather than to deliver it to an unsupported stranger. In either case, Ḥusain Pasha lost the city.

His old dependant, Muḥammad bin Budaq, undertook to organize a counter-movement if support could be sent. Ḥusain's reply bade him proceed and promised the reinforcement of bedouin lances. Muḥammad collected the few but devoted

[1] Von Hammer speaks of "Kavarna", a misreading of قورنه. The court historiographers were not well informed of these distant events.

followers of his master, and attacked the buildings where the government of the moment was installed. A struggle ended in his rout and death, and the temporary masters of Baṣrah could survey with pleasure the now quiet but bloody streets; but they had forgotten an obvious precaution: through the open town-gates trooped in reinforcements from Ḥusain. These in a few hours reversed the position. The government of the city notables broke up. The houses of some were looted, two were put to death, others forced to concealment or flight. Baṣrah, as far as its scattered and terrified citizens had unity at all, again acknowledged the rule of its Prince.

The Qurnah siege dragged on. Tribal allies of Ibrahim were checked by those of the Baṣrah ruler. Janissary reinforcements from Baghdad fared no better. The resistance was never relaxed. Neither assault nor attrition availed the far superior attacking force. The besiegers in their turn were half besieged by loose guerrilla forces of marshmen, constantly harassing their lines. Supplies ran short, months of failure lowered morale. At last, independently of his Commander-in-Chief, the Pasha of Diyarbakr made overtures to the Prince. Terms were easily arranged. The Government of Baṣrah was to remain in the same family, but to pass from Ḥusain to his son Afrasiyab, Ḥusain himself retiring to Makkah. Formal apologies were to be offered to the Sovereign, Muḥammad Pasha restored to Al Ḥasa, loot returned to the citizens, tribute at once and annually to be paid to the Imperial Treasury. This complete confession of Turkish weakness fully satisfied Ḥusain. Ibrahim Pasha accepted the negotiations. Muḥammad was dispatched to Ḥasa. The armies of Ibrahim and his colleagues retired.

§ 4. *The end of Ḥusain Pasha.*

Ḥusain Pasha had been saved a second time by his wits and his tenacity. He returned to Baṣrah under the titular rule of his young son, but in effect to his third tenure of the principality. The recent settlement was unlikely to be lasting. There was still a strong core of opposition: the half-century's tradition of independent government had sustained heavy blows:

and the sincerity of his own submission to Stambul might well be doubted.

Yaḥya Agha—minister and relative of Ḥusain—was sent with letters and purses to Adrianople. His encounter there with another Baṣrah deputation was undesigned: he came in Ḥusain's interests, they to complain to the Padishah of his oppression; but confidential talks followed, and ambition was again the parent of treachery. Yaḥya accepted their offer to be himself a candidate for the province. The Sultan was moved by denouncements of Ḥusain and promises of greater tribute. Orders reached Qara Muṣṭafa Pasha—now a third time ruler of Baghdad—to break up the house of Afrasiyab, and to install Yaḥya. Forces similar to the previous were put at his disposal. His camp was joined by troops of Diyarbakr, Shahrizor, Mosul, Raqqah, and many feudal contingents. An advanced guard with baggage and ordnance was sent down by the Tigris. Qara Muṣṭafa left Baghdad with his main body on the 24th of November 1667. The slow march was broken by pilgrimage to Najf, and by a halt at 'Arjah. At Kut ul Mu'ammir a strong Muntafiq[1] contingent joined.

Qurnah was the first objective. To reach it, innumerable canals and marshes must be crossed. At Dar Bani Isad[2] five thousand well-armed auxiliaries of Ḥusain Pasha met the army, only to be routed with great loss after hours of fighting. The tribesmen scattered in their mashḥufs through the high reeds of the swamps; Qara Muṣṭafa heartened his men by the erection of a minaret of enemy heads. The difficult march was resumed. Late in January 1668 the army deployed before the Qurnah fortress, and made the dispositions of blockade.[3]

By Ḥusain Pasha news of this treachery and menace to his throne was received with fury. He vented his anger without restraint on his fickle subjects, chased from the town numbers of suspects, and did not spare venerable inmates of the Baṣrah harems. He dispatched his own women-folk to a refuge in 'Arbistan, and destroyed his palace.[4] All preparations made,

[1] In the previous campaign the Muntafiq had been with Ḥusain.
[2] Presumably the present location of that tribe, around Chubaish.
[3] Gulshan's account of this march is clearly that of an eyewitness.
[4] Carré (p. 113) adds that he offered Baṣrah to the Persians (perhaps to the Wali of Ḥuwaizah) in return for their help, but was refused.

he threw himself into the impregnable fort of Qurnah, which he had further strengthened.

But the successful resistance of the last campaign could not be repeated. The siege began early in February and lasted a month. It was pressed more keenly and skilfully than before. The best of siege artillery was operated by trained topchis from Stambul. Guns were brought nearer and nearer to the fortress. Their sudden fire terrified the defenders: and simultaneously a party under the Pasha of Diyarbakr had worked round to a face of the fortress inaccessible before. The double threat was decisive. Ḥusain Pasha fled by night to his prepared retreat in the Ḥuwaizah country. The defence broke up: the siemans and tribesmen of the garrison fled as they could, some to the marshes, some to rally to Ḥusain elsewhere. The fortress was entered and occupied, and pardon granted to the wretched remnant of the garrison. The Imperial army entered Baṣrah unopposed and welcome, though partial witnesses[1] speak of a severe punishment of the town for its long infidelity. Yaḥya was elevated to the Pashaliq, and bound by the strictest promises. Fifteen hundred Janissaries were left in garrison and 3,000 local mercenaries enrolled. Citadel and armoury were repaired and replenished. The official machinery of an ayalat was set up. Baṣrah renounced its special privileges and dangers, and entered the regular administration of the Empire.

Ḥusain Pasha was never to return to his country. At Shiraz he pleaded for the support of the Shah in vain.

"He then, with his son Ali Beg, journeyed to India, to the city of Oojain, by the monarch of which country he was entrusted with the charge of a district; and in defence of whose interests both of them fell in the field of battle not, however, before they had been joined by the females of their family from Duraq, whose descendents still exist there."[2]

So vanished from its throne and country the princely house of Afrasiyab.

[1] Shaikh Fatḥullah.

[2] Mignon, after Shaikh Fatḥullah; but no doubt partly legend.

§ 5. *A generation of vicissitude.*

Baṣrah, thus restored to the Sultan, had still a generation of uneasy fortune before it. It was to feel again the heavy hand of a local despot. Wasted by plague, it was to be the prey of a tribal usurper, and to be passed by him to the arms of a vassal of Persia. Only as the new century dawned was it to fall again —still precariously enough—to a Pasha regularly appointed. The government that permitted this repeated secession, and made no better use of this bridge-head of the land-route from Syria to the Indies, was distracted at the time by no struggle with Persia, no disloyalty of its governors in Baghdad. To explain its tolerance of these conditions we need look no farther than to the endemic difficulties of land-surface and distance, the wild tribal populace, the low standard of control attempted, the chronic maladministration and now general decline of the empire.

The incorporation of Baṣrah involved restraints which the selfish ambitions of Yaḥya were to find intolerable. Imperial troops and a Qadḥi from Stambul—these might be borne; but serious friction appeared with the Daftardar. The familiar bickering of high officials ended with the open insolence of Yaḥya: he forbade the Accountant to meddle, and withheld the pay of the Janissaries. They mutinied. Yaḥya fled the town. The Imperial officers had won—but for a moment; for Yaḥya, rapidly gathering an army of mercenaries and tribesmen, and skilfully fanning anti-Turkish excitement in the tribes, rushed the town, expelled the last of the Sultan's soldiers and scriveners, and assumed an absolute government.

A race followed for the possession of Qurnah. It was already held by Janissaries, whom the Baghdad Pasha rapidly reinforced with companies of siemans, with Kurds of Bajlan and Turkomans of Baiyat. These reached Qurnah and relieved their comrades, whom the desperate efforts of Yaḥya had failed to dislodge. The ruffians of his army took their revenge upon the defenceless townspeople of Baṣrah. The Sultan had meanwhile appointed a new ruler to Baṣrah, a chief of the chamberlains, Muṣṭafa Pasha, and bidden his namesake of Baghdad to set the Baṣrah house in order. Troops from the neighbouring ayalats were once more to mobilise. While these awaited the cool of autumn, the two Muṣṭafas marched alone, in the worst heats of June, with a few companies of levies. It was enough. Yaḥya fled by sea to India;[1] another great traitor passed from the scene. The contingents of the other ayalats returned to their homes. Advancing to Baṣrah, Qara Muṣṭafa Pasha installed his namesake into the governorship and left him the necessary troops and treasury.

The chamberlain, untried in government and faced with the task of revenue-collection in a province demoralized and unused to paying, resigned his office; whereat the Baghdad Wali, without losing his present province, was bidden to revisit the Port. He reached the Shaṭṭ ul 'Arab in 1670. His agents visited every Sanjaq and tribal dirah, compiling the Domesday Book of the ayalat. Sealed with his seal, a copy was placed in the Baṣrah treasury, another sent to Stambul. Baṣrah was added as a Mutasallimate to the Baghdad province, and soon afterwards Qara Muṣṭafa, replaced at Baghdad (as we saw elsewhere) by Ḥusain Pasha, was given it as a separate ayalat. He died there in 1672.

Twenty years of normal government followed. Pasha succeeded Pasha at intervals of a year or more.[2] In three cases the same Wali held the province for two terms. 'Abdu'l Raḥman Pasha, who had been at Baghdad in 1675, was appointed to Baṣrah in 1682. His learning, piety, and generous foundations[3] popularized and thereby enriched the government. He was interrupted after a year by an opposite character, Ḥusain Pasha. Complaints of the new-comer's rapacity led Stambul to restore 'Abdu'l Raḥman. His successor was a late daftardar of Baghdad, now promoted to the Wazarat.

In 1690 a disastrous outbreak of plague stilled the life and emptied the busy streets of Baṣrah. The death-roll was 500 a day. Corpses lay unburied in the bazaars. With the rich and poor of the city, the foreign garrison suffered as heavily. The tribes without, less afflicted by the plague, saw their chance.[4]

[1] For his later career see Carré (p. 125 f.): but Basha'yan makes him die suddenly on his expulsion from Baṣrah.

[2] The names and dates are in the Baṣrah Calendar.

[3] Described and praised by Basha'yan.

[4] For the period 1694–1700 at Baṣrah we have the short account (authentic in essentials for all its breezy inaccuracy) of Capt. Alex. Hamilton

The Muntafiq and Jaza'ir tribes collected some 3,000 horse, defied the government, and approached the city. The Pasha Aḥmad could muster but a bare 500 men. Few of these survived a long-drawn battle at Dair; the Pasha lay among the dead; nothing lay between the exultant Arabs and the bazaars of Baṣrah. But the hour produced a man. Ḥasan Agha the Kahya rallied all the able citizens, was unanimously declared Wali, and organized so strong a resistance that not a single tribesman entered. He himself was killed, and one Ḥusain Jamal elected. For another year Turkish government remained in being.

But the growing power of the Muntafiq under Mani' bin Mughamis had now assumed a scale terrifying to Baṣrah and serious enough to Baghdad. The port fell to Mani' in 1694. There was this time no royal consent to the usurpation. In the same year an avenging army left Baghdad under Khalil, brother of Aḥmad Pasha the Wali. Troops as usual were brought from Mosul and Kirkuk. The expedition[1] found touch with the tribal army in the Jaza'ir region. It was there defeated and scattered, and ragged tribesmen tore off the uniforms of the Janissaries. Mani' followed his victory by suggesting terms of armistice: he was forgiven all on promise of future allegiance. Khalil became Wali;[2] but Mani', powerless to withhold his hand from so easy a prey, again expelled him and was again proclaimed ruler by town and tribe alike. No foreign Pasha could have hoped for so wide a sway. He acquired part of 'Arabistan, and was paramount in the plains and marshes between the Tigris and Luristan. Badrah, Jaṣṣan, and Mandali obeyed him. His power for the moment overshadowed Ḥuwaizah. On the Euphrates he held 'Arjah, Samawah, Rumaḥiyyah.

The circumstances are obscure under which this rule of the

(i, pp. 82 ff.): he makes the Persian occupation to precede the Plague, and the Plague to occur in 1691: "in Anno 1691 a Pestilence raged so violently that above 80,000 People were carried off by it, and those that remained fled from it, so that for three years following it was a desert inhabited only by wild Beasts, who were at last driven out of the town by the circumjacent wild Arabs . . .".

[1] Von Hammer (xii, p. 396), followed by Huart (p. 137), speaks also of river-craft constructed by order of Sultan Muṣṭafa II, and of a commission given to Ḥusain Pasha of Raqqah to march on Baṣrah. But Ḥusain died, and apparently the river-borne expedition came to nothing.

[2] Omitted, however, in the list of Walis.

Baṣrah area gave place to its occupation by the Ḥuwaizah power. In 1697 their rivalry came to a head. Farajullah, Wali of Ḥuwaizah, defeated in battle a principal leader of the Muntafiq. The Baṣrah notables, weary of the caprices of a tribesman's rule, petitioned Baghdad for a regular Wali. Ḥasan Pasha, nominated for the duty by the Porte, was in Baghdad. He verified by special agents the favourable position in the port, and set forth. Qurnah was occupied, but for some reason he failed to advance to Baṣrah, and the expedition failed. An easier course then offered itself to the Pasha of Baghdad. Messengers from Farajullah Khan begged his permission to drive Mani' from Baṣrah. In whatever terms, the idea was approved. The Khan chased the Muntafiq forces from the town, occupied the citadel and the fort of Qurnah, and (contrary, it must be, to his Baghdad agreement) sent the keys to the Shah. Shah Ḥusain, new to the throne, passed them with magnificent presents to the Sultan—an embassy worthily acknowledged by a splendid deputation to Iṣfahan.

For many months the Ḥuwaizah rule in Baṣrah continued. The period was favourably remembered by local merchants.[1] With the Muntafiq Shaikh relations were those of strife and jealousy with intervals of alliance. In the first months of the new century fresh elements of confusion appeared with serious floods on the lower Euphrates. Towns were isolated, tribes swept from their own lands, and a dozen leaders sprang up to make what they could by the calamity. One ibn 'Abbas, perhaps of the Khaza'il, seized Rumaḥiyyah, Ḥiskah, and the outskirts of Najf. Mani' held the river from Samawah to Qurnah. To the north, Salman blockaded Ḥillah. 'Abbas of the bani 'Umair terrorized and stripped the Jaza'ir country. Dissensions among the Ḥuwaizah Khans increased the tangle. Farajullah, at war with the Muntafiq, had invited the Turks back; but, later himself deposed by the Shah, he became reconciled with Mani', and was succeeded at Baṣrah by Daud Khan.

The Sultan could not be ignorant that the conditions in southern 'Iraq were now worse than Ḥusain or Yaḥya had ever made them. To expel the Persians and chastise the tribesmen

1 "Bassora", says Capt. Hamilton (i, p. 82) "was many Years [*sic*] in the hands of the Persians, who gave it encouragement to trade, which drew many merchants from foreign parts to settle there, particularly from Surat in India."

was an urgent duty. The formidable task was given to Daltaban Muṣṭafa Pasha, the vigorous and intolerant new ruler of Baghdad. An impressive force assembled. A score of Kurdish contingents joined with timariots from half the ayalats of eastern Turkey. A flotilla of rafts was constructed at Birijik and placed under the command of 'Ali Pasha, the Governor-elect of Baṣrah. Heavy ordnance was sent down the Tigris on rafts. The army moved slowly by Ḥillah and Ḥiskah to Rumaḥiyyah.

So great a force had not been seen in lower 'Iraq for a generation. The robber-chiefs of yesterday hastened with a hundred protestations to kiss the hand of Daltaban. A large concentration of still hostile tribesmen was met below Rumaḥiyyah late in January 1701, and completely defeated. The severed heads of a thousand rebels formed a ghastly pyramid. Forty years later their grave-mound was still shown.[1]

The camp of Mani', where Farajullah was in refuge, heard with terror the size and ferocity of the oncoming army. A lesser shaikh was charged with negotiations for a safe submission. Fighting was over. Obsequious guides conducted the army to unresisting Qurnah. Farajullah made personal surrender: Mani' was pardoned or ignored: the Khan of Baṣrah gave up thoughts of resistance and fled. The dignitaries of Law and Religion in procession welcomed Daltaban into a Baṣrah exhausted by plague, disorder, and changes of master. Early in March 1701, 'Ali Pasha assumed the ayalat. A decade of strife and misery seemed to have closed.

[1] Otter (ii, p. 200); cf. Sestini, p. 235.

VI

BATTLES OF GIANTS[1]

§ 1. *Ḥasan Pasha.*

With the appointment of Ḥasan Pasha to the Pashaliq of Baghdad in 1704, its history enters upon a fresh era. After the little-known Pashas of the last century, it is relief to turn to a new ruler whose personality and achievements we can survey over twenty years. With the exception of Sulaiman the Great, no Governor mentioned in this history enjoyed so long a single tenure of office. His personal claim to honour in 'Iraq annals rests less upon the mere length of his strong and unquestioned rule, upon the pieties and reforms and comparative order which he introduced, than upon his successful invasion of Persian soil, and, far more, upon his foundation of a dynasty. The Pashaliq was to pass first to his son, then to the husbands of his grand-daughters; by whose time and in whose persons the Mamluk supremacy in 'Iraq was so well established that for a century no rulers of other race were conceivable. The course of the Pashaliq from Ḥasan Pasha to Daud Pasha is a dynastic course, first in his family, then in the close ranks of his slave dependants. From the view-point of Stambul, the appointment of Ḥasan Pasha was, for a hundred and thirty years, the last which the Sultan could

[1] Authorities for 1704-47: The oldest local account is that of Ḥadiqatu'l Wuzara, referred to as Ḥadiqat. It is largely used by Rasul Ḥawi effendi in Duḥatu'l Wuzara, and by Sulaiman Beg in Ḥurubu'l Iraniyyin. The latter two works are referred to as Duḥat and Ḥurub. Gulshan is of small value after 1700. For Mosul affairs the sources are mostly second-hand—the Calendar, the Ta'rikhu'l Mauṣal of Sulaiman Sayigh, and isolated documents quoted in foot-notes. Von Hammer for this period (vols. xiii-xv) uses Rashid (راشد) up to 1721, Chelebizadah 1722-8, Subḥi thereafter to 1744, and 'Izzi 1744-50. On the Persian side, Mirza Mahdi's Jihangusha i Nadiri is very full. William Jones's *Life of Nadir Shah* adds nothing to it. Hanway is invaluable, and behind him is Father Krusinski. Malcolm, Watson, and Sykes have been consulted. The important travellers are Hamilton and Otter.

enforce; for he and his son, redoubtable servants of the Khalif in their own province, laid down the clear line of schism from the Empire.

Muṣṭafa Beg, father of Ḥasan, was a Sipahi of Murad IV. The boy, born in Europe about the year 1657, received the education of the Sarai schools. He found favour with the Grand Wazir, and was early noticed for conspicuous courage in action. In 1683 he began a career of Palace appointments. Promoted Wazir in 1697, he held successively the ayalats of Konia, of Aleppo, and of Urfah. In each he left traces of a vigorous beneficence. In 1702 he was appointed to Diyarbakr, in 1704 to succeed 'Ali Pasha at Baghdad.

The records of his Pashaliq are typical of the widespread cares of a Wali of Baghdad. His tribal campaigns exemplified not only the unchanging remoteness of the tribes from acceptance of government; not only their perverse backsliding after successive punishments; but also the outside influences tampering with behaviour already enough unsettled. The Bani Lam had ceaseless relations of league and war with the adjoining power of Ḥuwaizah: the Jaf, Bilbas, and tribes of the Persian and Kurdish border were tempted by the threats and promises of the two Powers; and the half-settled Euphrates tribes were disturbed by their nomad brothers of the desert. We will pass his tribal campaigns in rapid review before noticing more personal features of the reign.

His first year was remembered for his vigorous punishment of robbers on the Lesser Zab. In the Mosul region a campaign ended in a stiff battle near Khan Nuqṭah, followed by the settlement of the repentant tribe. There was time in the same year for a first punitive expedition against the Bani Lam. In 1705 the chief campaign was against Salman, chief of the Khaza'il, who had been joined by parties of Shammar and 'Anizah, had looted Baghdad villages and threatened Ḥillah. His army was not a horde; the rudiments of an administration marked his rapid expansion. The Pasha advanced against him past Ḥillah to Ḥiskah. His forces scattered and he applied for pardon. The Pasha demanding his surrender, he escaped instead to the tents of Mani', Shaikh of the Muntafiq.

In 1706 the Shammar called for punishment. The Pasha

crossed the Euphrates below Fallujah, and after vigorous pursuit inflicted heavy losses and looted their belongings. The next campaign, against the middle Euphrates tribes of Al Ḥamid, Sa'adah, and the Al Rafi', was undertaken on the complaints of the Qash'am leader, Shabib, and with the aid of large tribal contingents. Operations ended in the submission of the enemy. The Zubaid were the next. At the Pasha's first approach they asked pardon and surrendered ringleaders. His back turned, their lawless defiance was resumed.

But the leading event of 1706—news of which was in the first dispatch handed to an incoming Grand Wazir[1] at Stambul—was the rebellion of Mughamis ul Mani' and the Muntafiq. The immediate causes of the rising were matters of cultivation-rights over Euphrates islands, disputes over taxation, and subsidies claimed by the tribe. Before the assumption of office by Khalil Pasha at Baṣrah in 1705, his deputy had quarrelled with the Muntafiq leaders. Khalil and his Kahya four times engaged the tribal forces with success; the rebel was deposed and Shaikh Naṣir made official shaikh; but Mughamis rallied the majority and delivered a successful surprise attack on Khalil. This threw the whole province of Baṣrah, to the very city-walls, into fresh confusion. Khalil, not for the first time, appealed to Baghdad. The Sultan ordered the usual rally of neighbouring Pashas—of Kutahiyyah, Diyarbakr, Kirkuk, and Mosul—with horsemen from the Kurdish Begs. In the last weeks of 1708 a large army assembled at Baghdad, advanced by Ḥillah to 'Arjah, and thence to Baṣrah without serious opposition. Touch was but lightly found with the enemy, and an indecisive battle fought. Mughamis withdrew into hiding, his forces to their inaccessible homes. Ḥasan Pasha installed a namesake as Governor of Baṣrah, and returned north through the Jaza'ir and Gharraf country. Mughamis emerged, took Rumaḥiyyah, and with 'Anizah help raided far into the Baghdad province. Ḥasan Pasha mobilized an army at Ḥillah. In the operations that followed, the agile tribesmen played with the regulars. Ever giving way before them, Mughamis finally disappeared without trace: the situation remained unsolved.

[1] 'Ali Pasha Chorli (von Hammer, vol. xiii, p. 174); he assumed duty on the 6th of May 1706.

Ḥasan Pasha, however—no doubt at his own suggestion—was given official charge of the Baṣrah ayalat, where a Mutasallim would act for him. This marked an important stage in a process later to develop.

In 1715 and the year following, punitive campaigns took the Pasha from top to bottom of his province, and outside it. The Bilbas, wild mountain Kurds east of Arbil, were taught a lesson. Bakr Beg, son or nephew of Sulaiman Beg Baban, had incurred the jealousy of the Kirkuk authorities. He was now with great difficulty dislodged, arrested, and put to death. The Baban territories fell back under Turkish sway from now until the emergence of Khanah Pasha in 1720; Ḥasan's operations in the Shahrizor ayalat, indeed, are significant of the same process of absorption as was visible in the case of Baṣrah. Order was restored in Ḥarir, where a feud in the Soran family had led to bloodshed. A nest of Yazidi robbers was eradicated from Sinjar by an expedition which cost the Pasha his Kahya and many men. In the same year the Bani Lam, invaded by large forces of 'Abdullah Khan, Wali of Ḥuwaizah, begged the reinforcement of Turkish troops. In 1717 an invasion of Bajlan territory by Persian Kurds took Ḥasan to the spot; but fear of trespassing on the Shah's soil prevented a pursuit. In 1718 a further Bani Lam campaign was needed. Their Shaikh, deposed and imprisoned, escaped and found asylum at Ḥuwaizah. At the approach of a Baghdad army, however, 'Abdullah Khan repented of sheltering the refugee, and sought favour by generous entertainment of all ranks. Trouble in the tribe continued; shaikh succeeded shaikh; and in 1719 'Abdullah Khan himself appeared as a suppliant in Baghdad. The same year was calamitous with an outbreak of plague, which took the heaviest toll in the crowded alleys of the Capital.

The peculiar conditions, the personalities of each tribe-group at the time, cannot be known: therefore the mere catalogue of tribal wars must be tedious and can be little profitable. Such, however, was the real life of the country; such are the surviving records; against this background, vivid and vital to a contemporary eye, must we view the foreign wars and the historical figures of the time. The immediate result of these many expeditions was a conspicuous raising of the standard of obedience to government from Sinjar to Fao. There was, for the first time, continuity of control, rough justice, and a firmness upon which men could count. The "Daulah", habitually ignored or despised by its tribal subjects, gained a moment's respect if little liking. The Pasha—himself a devout Ḥaji—linked religion with government by the foundation of mosques, the grant of lands and funds to pious uses. To this day he is remembered as Abu Khairat, the Charitable. He was punctilious in pilgrimage to the shrines of all sects. His tolerance was shown, in 1721, in permitting the foundation of a Carmelite mission-house. The repair of khans proved his zeal for the care of pilgrims and travellers. He multiplied canals to settle the bedouin. Bridges at Altun Kupri and elsewhere cost him money with which few Pashas would part. His good relations with Stambul[1] were not maintained without regular remission of revenue to the Capital; they were rewarded, as we have seen, by the accession of Baṣrah to his command, by an unwritten overlordship of Shahrizor, and (at an uncertain date) by the inclusion of Mardin, the independent government of a Waiwode, in the Baghdad Pashaliq. These important changes were personal to Ḥasan Pasha, and doubtless intended to be temporary.

His wife 'A'ishah Khanim, daughter of Muṣṭafa, a courtier of Sultan Muḥammad IV, was buried in 1717 in the tomb of Zubaidah, wife of Harun ul Rashid. 'Ali Beg, brother of the Pasha, was long employed by him in minor appointments. Of his daughters, Faṭimah was married to 'Abdu'l Raḥman Pasha (Governor of Kirkuk in 1722) and Ṣafiyyah to Qara Muṣṭafa Pasha of Trebizond.[2] Of Aḥmad, his only son, this history will have much to say. Born about 1685 at Chafalkah near Stambul, he accompanied his father to various commands. His education was neglected, but his intelligence, character, and athletic powers marked him for a career. After living for eleven years in Baghdad, he was appointed Pasha of Shahrizor in 1715, later transferred to Konia, and finally (perhaps in 1721) to Baṣrah.[3]

[1] There seems little justification for Hanway's remark (p. 251) that Aḥmad Pasha . . . "was the son of a man whose head the Porte had demanded several times to no purpose". Nor can we accept the suspicions of Niebuhr (vol. ii, p. 254) that Ḥasan Pasha kept the Pashaliq of Baṣrah in his own hands by raising tribal trouble against the successive nominees of the Porte.

[2] Khadijah Khanim, daughter of Ṣafiyyah Khanim, was in some way the patroness of the author of Ḥadiqatu'l Wuzara.

[3] Ghayatu'l Muram makes Urfah his first appointment, and records the

The culminating events of the long rule of Ḥasan Pasha will take us, in the autumn of 1723, beyond 'Iraq into Persia. For twenty years hence campaigns with Persia dominate the history of 'Iraq, while the son of Ḥasan Pasha led its armies. We turn now to those events in the Shah's empire which gave the signal for war.

§ 2. *The first campaigns:*[1] *Sunni against Sunni.*

A long peace between Shah and Sultan had begun with the treaty signed in 'Iraq by Qara Muṣṭafa, Grand Wazir of Murad IV, on the 20th of May 1639. For three generations Persia remained peaceful, wealthy, brilliant. Vice and luxury at Court seemed but the signs of secure plenty, art and architecture were the ornaments of culture and piety. Shah Ṣafi handed to 'Abbas II, he to Sulaiman, he to Ḥusain, the splendour and deadly weakness of the Ṣafawi throne.

Its fall came neither from the ever ready land hunger and religious rancour of the Turks, nor from the watchful ambition of a Russian monarch far to the north. It came by the hand of a savage conqueror from the mountain province of Afghanistan. Maḥmud Khan, son of a Ghilzai tribesman Mir Wais, had in

anecdote of his quarrel with the Wali of Mosul, whose pardon was more easily obtained than that of his father at Baghdad. Haji Muṣṭafa Pasha (hero of this story) was Pasha of Mosul from 1720. Aḥmad's appointment to Baṣrah must therefore be later than this. Duḥat dates it as 1718. The Baṣrah Calendar has a Mirmiran Aḥmad Pasha as Pasha of Baṣrah in 1715: this is either far too early or is another Aḥmad Pasha. The description by Captain Hamilton of Baṣrah in early 1721 is decisive. He tells (ii, p. 79) of such misgovernment as can scarcely have happened under Aḥmad Pasha. The Pasha of the moment had married a lady of the Sultan's family. To this was attributed a unique rapacity. Every appeal and complaint failing, fifty thousand townspeople marched out, headed by the Mufti. They camped by the Shaṭṭ ul 'Arab. No supplies entered the town. The language of Church and State was hotly exchanged between Mufti and Pasha. At length the cessation of all business inclined the Pasha to compromise. The demonstrators agreed to return if a dozen of the worst instruments of extortion were surrendered. All were pardoned by the Mufti, save one. Other anecdotes in Hamilton concern the destruction of a party of tax-collecting Janissaries (p. 87), the immoralities of the Carmelite Fathers (p. 84), and the iniquities under which he himself suffered as a dealer in pepper (p. 83). In all probability the appointment of Aḥmad to Baṣrah immediately followed (and doubtless corrected) this régime.

[1] The account here and later given of the Perso-Turkish campaigns of 1722–45 will be strictly from the 'Iraq view-point. They were fought on but one section of a front extending from Caspian to Gulf.

1720 invaded Karman and thrilled Persia with alarm. A few months later the storm broke.

Maḥmud left Qandahar in the earliest days of 1722. Marching by Karman and Yadz, he reached Gulnabad twelve miles from Iṣfahan. The fateful battle fought here shows too clearly the superior virility of the Afghans. Iṣfahan was invested and starved to surrender. Shah Ḥusain resigned to the Ghilzai Khan the throne of Persia, himself remaining in rich captivity: the tenth successor of Shah Isma'il gave up the Empire of Iran to barbarous invaders; Sultan and Pasha dealt henceforth with an Afghan and a Sunni Shah. A Ṣafawi pretender remained—Tahmasp son of Ḥusain, who escaped to rally supporters in the north. The first weeks of Afghan rule raised high hopes; but late in 1723 the ferocity of Maḥmud overcame the clemency which policy had bidden him show. From now until his death in 1725, his excesses of massacre revealed a madman.

In Europe the treaty of Passarowitz, freeing the Turks from many responsibilities, had left them able to deal with enemies or victims on the eastern frontier. The tottering Ṣafawis, the invading Afghans, roused cupidity and fear in Stambul; but these feelings were not instantly revealed. Peaceful and gorgeous embassies[1] still for a time passed between the courts of Shah Ḥusain and Aḥmad III, watched wide-eyed by the Baghdadis. News of the final threat of Mir Maḥmud reached Stambul by the fast messengers of Ḥasan Pasha before the fall of Iṣfahan. He received in return, but did not need, orders to put his own defences in order. The moat was cleared and improved, the crumbling walls made good. His agents plied between Iṣfahan and Baghdad, while with sardonic fluency he addressed letters of congratulation to the Afghan conqueror. Maḥmud replied with emphasis on his Sunni faith and his reverence for the true Khalif: and no line of diplomacy could have more embarrassed the aggressive ministers in Stambul.[2]

[1] Duri Effendi has left an account of his Mission, which twice passed through Baghdad (Appendix I, § 2). For that of Martadha Quli, see von Hammer (vol. xiv, pp. 79 ff.).

[2] Cf. Hanway, p. 177. The prevailing phases of the Turkish attitude to the Afghan usurpation were three: fear that a new Conquerer might be arising to threaten 'Iraq and the Empire; hope that by the internal confusion of Persia a chance of successful aggression might be offered; and annoyance that the new rulers of Persia were Sunni.

There is no place in these pages to trace the debates and diplomacies—Persian, Russian, Afghan, and Turkish—of these years 1722–3. Before the fall of Iṣfahan, and almost simultaneously with each other, Ottoman forces and the armies of Peter the Great invaded respectively Georgia and Daghistan. Ambassadors came and went between the frontier Pashas and Stambul, between Moscow and the Caspian provinces. The Turks early in 1723 declared war on their fallen neighbour and roused the courage and avarice of their forces by the ferocious fatwahs of their divines. The Russians, in the autumn of that year, agreed with Tahmasp the Ṣafawi to enthrone him at the price of half his kingdom. The two powers—Sunni and Christian—had three years before sworn eternal friendship and alliance, and now cemented it by a joint dismemberment of Persia.

The news reaching 'Iraq of the declaration of war on Persia was followed by word to rally the forces of every Pashaliq to Erzerum. The garrison and feudal troops of Mosul obeyed the summons; Ḥasan Pasha and his son at Baṣrah thought otherwise, and bade their Sovereign reflect that central 'Iraq, if not a likely prey of the Afghan, was at least the best of bases to attack him. In reply came orders for a separate invasion of Persia by way of Karmanshah. To Ḥasan Pasha was given the command. Seventy years old, and accustomed for the last twenty to look eastward,[1] this crowned his career. Joined by his son-in-law 'Abdu'l Raḥman with the Kirkuk forces, he marched in great pomp up the Persian road by Khaniqin, with guns, standards, and the forces he had spent many years in improving. The Begs of Kurdish tribes and city-states met him with their contingents. His army approached Karmanshah. The Persian governor 'Abdu'l Baqi Khan without a struggle surrendered the keys of the city. It was occupied and from that hour became a province of the Sultan.

Ḥasan had thus added one ayalat to the Empire. He was to add another and gain a proud title as conqueror of a third. The Wali of Ardalan, 'Ali Quli Khan,[2] had already corresponded

[1] The 'Iraqi authorities emphasize the fears that Ḥasan Pasha had since 1704 entertained of Persia, possibly owing to the tactless Shia' utterances of its sovereigns.

[2] Chelebizadah gives the name as 'Abbas Quli and differs slightly in his account of these relations

with Baghdad; the abdication of his own suzerain now led him to sound the Turks for support. Spies, however, informed Ḥasan Pasha of messages passing between Sannah and the Afghan: a double game was being played. Khanah Pasha Baban was sent to occupy Ardalan. 'Ali Quli submitted with most of his vassals, and Ardalan was the Sultan's. Another expedition was led against the Wali of Luristan, 'Ali Mardan Khan,[1] who had undertaken to support Tahmasp and refused now to bow to Turkish rule. 'Abdu'l Raḥman Pasha with 'Ali Beg, brother of the Commander-in-Chief, invaded his territory and heavily defeated him. He fled, but later surrendered to generous treatment.

The winter of 1723 was spent at Karmanshah. Ḥasan Pasha, old and tired, died before the spring.[2] Mourned by the whole army, his body was sent home for burial in the mosque of Abu Ḥanifah. The need of a successor was instant. The late Pasha and his family commanded the only influence which could be above rivalry. Urgent messengers to Stambul begged the appointment of Aḥmad Pasha. It was confirmed. Having hastily performed in Baghdad the ceremonies of mourning, he marched to Karmanshah, and by tact and generosity rapidly gained the obedience of his bickering vassals and quarrelsome soldiery. To reports of growing lawlessness in 'Iraq he could pay no attention for the moment.

In the spring of 1724 his forces[3] marched on Hamadan. Messengers rode on to demand its delivery. Many of the inhabitants would prefer a Turkish to an Afghan ruler, and all had seen the gentle treatment of Karmanshah: the Persian governor wrote to Iṣfahan for permission to surrender. None came, and the siege[4] began. The place was well stocked with military stores, skilfully fortified, and gallantly defended. The first Turkish assaults failed, though vigorously launched. They advanced by tunnelling, only to be met by counter-mines. Persian gallantry gained even their enemies' applause; but the superior artillery of the Turks was at last decisive. Three

[1] Hanway, p. 196.
[2] In spite of this Ḥasan Pasha was awarded the title of "Fatiḥ Hamadan".
[3] Given in full detail by Chelebizadah.
[4] Duḥat, Ḥurub, Chelebizadah.

breaches were made and rushed. Street-fighting and slaughter continued for three days and nights; the Feast of Sacrifice, greatest of Islamic festivals, was celebrated with human victims. An armistice concluded the massacre, the town and province of Hamadan became Turkish territory under Qara Muṣṭafa Pasha,[1] and public prayers included the name of the Khalif.[2] Columns, however, under various of the Turkish captains and vassals continued to operate, for opposition was not dead. Allah Werdi Khan, after initial success, was put to flight with heavy loss by the Wali of Mar'ash. Another counter-attack, led by Laṭif Mirza the Ṣafawi, was heavily repulsed by Ibrahim Pasha with Khanah Pasha Baban. Laṭif Mirza was captured, his force scattered.

Ashraf Khan the Afghan, successor of Maḥmud, continued to send envoys to the Sultan protesting with dignity against this war of Sunni on Sunni. The Afghan case was strong, opinion in Turkey by no means unanimous: Aḥmad Pasha among other high officials reported to Stambul that dangerous propaganda was busy in his army. Thenceforth his troops, and those of his colleagues in the far north, hourly deteriorated in spirit and loyalty. Meanwhile, late in 1725, his generals proceeded to the easy conquest of Luristan.[3] The Lurish Wali fled after a futile defence. The leading tribes of the Zagros accepted the titular suzerainty of the Khalif, and placated his representative with presents. During the winter a column from the army, commanded by the Wali of Mosul, penetrated far south into the Bakhtiari country. Advancing within three days of Iṣfahan, he there found touch with the Sunni Afghans of the garrison, learnt that the Lurs in his rear had crossed the 'Iraq frontier to make common cause with the Bani Lam and Zubaid, and withdrew his battered forces to Hamadan.[4]

[1] He had been brought to Shahrizor ayalat from Trebizond on the transfer of 'Abdu'l Raḥman from Kirkuk to Baṣrah late in 1723. He was now relieved at Kirkuk by 'Uthman Pasha, daftardar of Baghdad.

[2] Transports of joy in Stambul greeted the news, and an autograph letter of the Sultan thanked Aḥmad Pasha.

[3] Possibly Aḥmad himself (who had returned to 'Iraq late in 1724) was still busy with tribal campaigns there. Chelebizadah is certainly wrong in placing him among the forces before Tabriz in the summer of 1725.

[4] Fullest in Hanway (i, p. 232).

In the summer of 1726 urgent affairs called Aḥmad Pasha [1] to 'Iraq, hostilities died down, envoys of Ashraf passed through the camp, and news came eastward of debates and fatwahs in the Capital. The autumn brought on the most ambitious and least successful of the Hamadan campaigns; it was the Turkish policy to drown their religious doubts in success; and large reinforcements reached Aḥmad Pasha, confirmed in his appointment as sar'askar. From Diyarbakr to Hamadan and to Baṣrah, the full resources of eastern Turkey were mobilized and assigned to his command.[2] His armies, well equipped by the standards of the time, did not fall short of a hundred thousand men, while those of Ashraf were but a fifth of that number. The Afghan army contained few of the Qandahar veterans, their stores were inadequate, their artillery light; only in the munitions of diplomacy they were far superior. As the army of Aḥmad Pasha advanced from Hamadan towards the capital of Persia, Ashraf moved out twelve miles from Iṣfahan. By the 20th of November the Turks had left Hamadan eighty miles behind them, and only twelve miles separated the great and the feeble armies. A light force sent ahead by Aḥmad to tempt a battle was surrounded and cut up before his main body could relieve it. The offensive of Ashraf was with surer weapons. His agents moved among the Kurdish Begs, promising promotion, largesse, easy and profitable vassaldom to Iṣfahan. His written manifestoes passed from hand to hand, deploring a war between Sunni brethren. Bribes were placed in the right quarters. Finally four venerable 'alims of the Afghans appeared in the embarrassed presence of the Pasha. As they reasoned, the call to prayer sounded: the Afghan Shaikhs in silence rose and prayed among their intending enemies. The effect was profound. When the Shaikhs left to return to their own camp a large body of Kurds deserted with them.

An immediate battle was now the Pasha's only hope. His right wing was led by a Baban, the left by Muḥammad Pasha and two of the Kuprilis. Ashraf commanded his army from elephant-back. Ten rounds of gunshot at sunrise gave the

[1] Chelebizadah, Hanway (p. 247), von Hammer (xiv, p. 152) for full details of his army.

[2] Von Hammer twice (xiv, p. 135, and xiv, p. 150) refers to the Sar'askar of Hamadan as 'Arif Aḥmad Pasha, or merely 'Arif Pasha. This individual was never with the Hamadan army.

Turkish signal to advance. Now appeared, in full force, the result of the Afghan propaganda. Only the Pasha's right wing charged, each time to be repulsed: his main body never engaged the enemy. By afternoon a general retreat was ordered. Twelve thousand Turkish dead were left. Deserters, mutineers, and pacifists numbered far more. Nearly all the Kurds abandoned the army and scattered homewards. Aḥmad himself, abandoning his heavy baggage, retired on Karmanshah. Ashraf "accompanied rather than pursued them as far as the gate of this city";[1] there, with a stroke of genius, unasked he released the Turkish prisoners and their whole baggage.

The Afghan followed this moral and material advantage by confidential offers of peace. It was, from the first, a perverse and needless war: but a war party in Stambul, and Aḥmad Pasha himself eager to avenge his losses, were indisposed to peace. Fresh regiments reached Baghdad, to which Aḥmad Pasha had retreated from Karmanshah, and a fresh levy of the timariots increased his Janissaries and volunteers. In the late summer of 1727 he was able to review a new army of 60,000 men. But if in September he repassed Karmanshah and again drew near to Hamadan, it was rather to peace than to war that he advanced. Imperial orders reached him to open negotiations, and diplomats from Stambul arrived to assist. Before a blow was struck, ten days of parley sufficed to draft and confirm a peace. Hamadan, Karmanshah, Ardalan, Luristan were assigned to the Sultan. Ashraf was recognized as King of Persia subject to the spiritual supremacy of the Khalif. Aḥmad Pasha returned to troubled conditions in his own province; Turkish garrisons remained in their new territories; and Ashraf Khan hurried back to storms which he could not weather.

§ 3. *Nadir Quli and the siege of Baghdad.*

The Afghans had gained the crown by rapidity, tribal vigour, and the corruption of the Ṣafawis. They required, to hold it, a Persia incapable of producing rivals, and communications with their bases of man-power in Afghạnistan. Both were lacking. The end came, after less than a decade of usurpation, by

[1] Hanway, p. 249.

the hand of the last great Asiatic conqueror that the world has seen.

Nadir Quli, born in Khurasan in 1688, of birth "neither eminently high nor contemptibly low "[1] in the Afshar tribe, had passed a youth of adventure as shepherd, robber, and captain of irregulars. He had already, before joining his fortunes to those of Tahmasp, gained in his own tribe a body of devoted followers. In 1727 he had 5,000 veteran Afshars and Kurds to rally to the Ṣafawi pretender at Farraḥabad. Entrusted with the recovery of Khurasan, he brilliantly succeeded and in a few weeks gained the chief command of Tahmasp's armies with the new title of Tahmasp Quli Khan[2] and the great but congenial task of delivering his country from the Afghan usurpers. These were twice severely defeated in 1729.[3] Iṣfahan was recovered. Their last stand was near Shiraz. They were there entirely scattered, Ashraf captured and slain, and the Ghilzai dynasty in Persia banished for ever. The Ṣafawi was restored : but behind, ruthlessly ambitious, stood the Afshar tribesman.

Tahmasp followed his accession by the dispatch of an ambassador to Stambul demanding surrender of the western provinces. On the Bosphorus, the Grand Wazir conferred day by day with the Persian envoy. At Baghdad, news from both east and west confirmed the oncoming of war. In Persia, Nadir neither wished nor supposed that it could be avoided. In the spring of 1730 he rapidly engaged the Turkish armies based upon Hamadan. 'Uthman Pasha was driven back to the fortress, where he joined forces with his colleague Timur Pasha of Van. Nadir Quli "entirely despatched the two Bashas, seized their artillery together with an immense booty, and entered the city of Hamadan without obstruction. The inhabitants received him with tumultuous joy. . . ."[4] The Turkish garrison withdrew with the loss of its baggage to Karmanshah, and thence across the old frontier to Zuhab and Khaniqin.

To Aḥmad Pasha, perturbed at this sudden stroke, came

[1] Jones, *Life* (p. 1).

[2] He was long known in Europe as "Taemas Kouli", "Thomas Caun", &c.

[3] The statement in Jihangusha and in Jones that a formidable army of Turks, under the Governor of Hamadan, were with the Afghans is impossible to accept.

[4] Jones, p. 32.

almost simultaneously the declaration of war[1] by Sultan Aḥmad III. He found himself again Sar'askar.[2] Making Zuhab his base and rallying-point of his forces, he advanced on Karmanshah and reoccupied it without a blow. Ardalan likewise returned to its Turkish allegiance. Nadir was now far away in Khurasan:[3] to Tahmasp—feeble and jealous—fell the task of resisting the invading army. He hastened southward from Erivan to meet the threat. Aḥmad Pasha camped near Hamadan. Sonorous and futile correspondence passed between the opposing generals. The battle was fought at Korijan, a day's march from Hamadan, on the 16th of September 1731. The Shah lost the half of his whole army, the Turks barely 1,000 men. The whole Persian artillery and the entire territory reconquered by Nadir Quli were abandoned. The noble governors of Tabriz and Shiraz were among the slain. Hamadan was occupied without violence. The Beg of 'Amadiyyah and Waiwodah of Mardin took command of flying columns to collect stores, cut up stragglers, and reassert Turkish government. Tahmasp made no further attempt at resistance, nor Aḥmad Pasha at advance. The latter received a dispatch of emphatic thanks from the new Sultan, Maḥmud I.

But the crisis of sedition, mutiny, and dethronement through which the capital of the Empire had lately passed had decided the Grand Wazir to make peace before the strong arm of Nadir should again be felt. These instructions reached Aḥmad Pasha in the autumn of 1731 in his camp at Hamadan. Nadir Quli, to whom alone peace was now unwelcome, was not present to oppose it. The last months of 1731 and the first days of 1732 were spent in negotiation at Hamadan. On the 10th of January the Treaty was signed. The Ottoman demands had moderated. Tabriz, Ardalan, Karmanshah, Hamadan, Ḥuwaizah, and all Luristan were reincluded in the Shah's Empire. Discussed in full Diwan at the Capital, the diplomacy of the Pasha of Baghdad was approved, and he withdrew to the old frontier of Murad IV.

[1] See foot-note to heading of § 2 of this chapter.

[2] Von Hammer (xiv, p. 253), now following Subḥi, makes 'Ali Pasha Ḥakimzadah Sar'askar of the army. Neither Persian nor 'Iraqi sources confirm this, nor does it agree with his own account on p. 251 (op. cit.).

[3] Subḥi, followed by von Hammer (p. 253), incorrectly states that he was present at this time with the Shah.

If any hoped that such a treaty would bind the ambition of the Afshar, the error was short lived. His work was but begun.

> "Be it known to you, the Basha of Bagdat, that we claim an indubitable right of visiting the tombs of the Imams, Ali, Gherbellai, Mahallade, Mouza, and Husain. We demand the delivery of all the Persians who have been taken prisoner in the late war. . . . We are going soon at the head of our victorious army to breathe the sweet air of the plains of Bagdat, and to take our repose under the shadow of its walls."

In such terms [1] he addressed Aḥmad Pasha as the summer of 1732 turned to autumn. He signed as Regent of a new sovereign, and wrote in the true spirit of a conqueror. Tahmasp had now served his turn. The defeats of the 1731 campaign, the loss of Hamadan, and the conclusion of a feeble treaty gave Nadir his opportunity. He denounced the peace on grounds of religion and policy. The Sultan was curtly threatened with war if the remaining Persian provinces were not instantly restored; Tahmasp was thrust from the throne; and the infant 'Abbas Mirza was proclaimed Shah, with Nadir himself as Regent. A single step, to be taken at his discretion, now separated him from the throne of Persia.

Aḥmad Pasha, besides careful repair to his defences and granaries, had occupied the frontier passes of Darnah, Mandali, and Badrah, and reinforced his garrisons of Zuhab and Qaṣr i Shirin. Stambul was informed of the urgency of his danger. These steps taken, he could but await the rigours of a siege. The vassals, nobles, and forces of Nadir Quli assembled at Hamadan, 100,000 strong. At the head of these he moved on Karmanshah,[2] left his heavy guns and baggage at Mah i dasht, and advanced with rapid secrecy on the Zuhab outpost. Taking advantage of a dark night, he had the Turkish post by morning in his hands. Thence he proceeded with his whole force across the frontier to 'Iraq, where he learnt of the preparations of Aḥmad at Baghdad. Resistance in northern 'Iraq appearing less certain, a force

[1] Hanway (ii, p. 74). It is probably close to the original; cf. Jones, (p. 41). Von Hammer (xiv, p. 283).

[2] Karmanshah was restored to Persia by the 1732 treaty; but Hanway (ii, p. 76) assumes that it was still Turkish and speaks now of a siege and capitulation. Possibly the Turks had not, in fact, handed the city over.

was detached to deal with Kirkuk and Mosul, and cut these off from Baghdad. It advanced past Tuz Khormatu, ravaged the Kirkuk villages,[1] but failed to capture the fortress; and a small force sent to reconnoitre Mosul was easily repulsed by Ḥaji Ḥusain the Jalili Pasha. The whole then rejoined the main army in the south.

Nadir Quli crossed the Diyalah at Buhriz in the first week of January 1733. Minor encounters took place, weak Turkish parties being cut to pieces. A strong reconnoitring party under the Pasha of Keui, sent out from Baghdad to feel for the enemy, was completely defeated with the loss of its leader. The complete investment of Baghdad followed. Ten thousand Persians had already crossed to the right bank from far upstream, to ravage the western outskirts of the Capital and cut off the grain caravans from Ḥillah and the south. Against this force, whose later fortunes are uncertain, troops of Diyarbakr and Aleppo[2] were dispatched. While Nadir on the left bank occupied his siege positions, it was the constant effort of Aḥmad Pasha to prevent a crossing to the western suburb. On the 20th of January the first attempt was thwarted by musketeers under the Pasha's own command. In the night a few succeeded in crossing, only to be expelled when day broke. Nadir pressed on the work of cutting date-palms and weaving reed-ropes for a bridge, while to gain time he made overtures of peace. (These, passed on to Stambul, led after long debate to the mission of Ṭopal 'Uthman.) The European engineer entrusted with the bridging completed his operations some miles above Baghdad. A force crossed under Nadir's leadership; more were ferried over in boats; a strong column formed and marched on the Kirkh suburb. A party of Aḥmad Pasha's scouts barely escaped to bring news to their master. With the loss of the Euphrates caravans, prices must soar in Baghdad: and the Pasha dispatched a force of 30,000 to the right bank under his brother-in-law and the Wali of Urfah. The defenders had the advantage in artillery, of which Nadir had brought none to this quarter. Skirmishes

[1] Subḥi (von Hammer, vol. xiv, p. 284) errs in speaking of the capture of Arbil. His account of the operations shows his ignorance of the topography.

[2] These, if Subḥi is accepted, had reached Baghdad in response to Aḥmad Pasha's appeals during the summer.

followed, then a pitched battle. For a space the Regent feared for his own safety; but reinforcements crossed in desperate haste and turned the day. The Turkish force retired to the town with loss. Aḥmad Pasha now ordered a general withdrawal to the left bank. Nadir occupied the Kirkh bridge-head, enjoyed such accommodation as the town afforded, and sent officers to take possession of the Euphrates towns and to salute the Holy Cities. The Persian feast of the New Year—19 March, 1733[1]—was celebrated with great festivities in their camp. The Shaikh of the Bani Lam and a Ḥuwaizah noble arrived to pay dutiful respects to Nadir. Graciously received and bidden to attack Baṣrah, with a thousand protestations of devotion they withdrew to ignore their instructions.

Baghdad was now closely invested from every side. Within the walls, the Pasha was aware of many Persian inhabitants who must favour the enemy: rumour told, even, that principal citizens had been corrupted by the gold of Nadir. Spring passed into summer. Whispers of deliverance from without were faint. The garrison was too small for a sortie, too large for its limited food-stocks. The Persian weakness in artillery made capture by assault impossible, prolonged siege certain. Aḥmad Pasha had with him his son-in-law and Kahya, Sulaiman Pasha, his brother-in-law Qara Muṣṭafa, and other Pashas of the highest rank; but none shared his personal burden of leadership. From the walls of Baghdad could be seen a veritable city of buildings arising in the assailants' lines. Many Persian officers were accompanied by their families, for whom elaborate houses were erected. The camp bazaar was full and cheap. The contrast of this with the increasing famine within sorely tried the besieged. Their hopes were further reduced by the daily spectacle of reinforcements entering the camp of Nadir—columns which his cunning had dispatched by night from his own army, to depress the watchmen on the walls. Small wonder that the weaker of the citizens sought in desperation to creep from the gates, or even to throw themselves from the walls.

The energy of the Pasha was fully employed not in fighting

[1] The chronology of von Hammer is accepted throughout the siege. It represents a patient and exact co-ordination of Jihangusha, Hanway, and Subḥi.

but in maintaining resistance. Panting messengers—sent out by him for the purpose—would enter Baghdad with news of relief at hand. A deputation of Persian 'Ulama, allowed in to parley with the divines of Baghdad, were amazed to see large stocks of bread exposed for sale at prices suggesting plenteous abundance; the Pasha had commandeered all the bread in Baghdad for this display to deceive his enemies. When Nadir, mocking the hunger of the inhabitants, sent in a cartload of water-melons, Aḥmad returned a handsome present of the finest bread. But neither pleasantries nor half-meant offers of armistice or compromise could lessen the pangs of terrible hunger[1] nor postpone long the fate that, by midsummer, appeared inevitable.

As July opened, hope was almost dead. The Pasha alone did not flag in his determination; but even he could not know whether still to hope for, or despair of, the long-delayed armies of Ṭopal 'Uthman. If this great general had been a few days slower to appear or of weaker arm when he appeared: if Baghdad had looked to a commander less in character and repute than Aḥmad Pasha: if Nadir had shown in this campaign a judgement worthier of his other conquests: then the history of Baghdad and of 'Iraq and Turkey must infallibly have followed very different courses. Never can threatened city have more narrowly escaped its enemy, or deliverer better timed his saving approach.

§ 4. *The lame Deliverer.*

No more romantic figure crosses the stage of modern 'Iraq than that of 'Uthman Pasha the Lame. Born in Greece, educated in the "Seraglio" of Stambul and promoted rapidly to high rank, he became later Commander-in-Chief in Greece, and then Wali of Rumelia. Cruel wounds crippled and aged him. To one, whereby he walked with difficulty, he owed his name of Ṭopal, the Lame. To courage and devoted service he added far rarer gifts: a princely gratitude and generosity, untarnished honour, gentleness, and humility. He had no enemies; every private soldier was his friend. Soon after his retirement from the Grand Wazarat, the alarming threat to Baghdad became known in Stambul. He was sent as Sar'askar of Asia to repel the

[1] Cf. Joseph Emin (p. 5). The Christians were living well on the stores which their forethought had laid by, while the Muslim majority eat dogs and worse.

danger, with powers to take complete charge of the resources of the eastern ayalats. He marched out with a large but not overwhelming army.[1] The march to 'Iraq took nearly half a year; and such delay must argue ignorance of the critical need at Baghdad. He reached Mosul early in June. At Kirkuk he received a letter from Nadir written in a style of mocking contempt. The Regent bade him journey more quickly to his destruction, and threatened to capture him "as a child in his cradle"—an allusion to the litter in which his infirmities forced him to ride. In the country through which 'Uthman passed, there were abundant traces of the fire and sword of the enemy. The crossing of the two Zabs delayed his army. Near Kirkuk he captured two spies or deserters. Swearing them to loyalty, he made them bearers of a dispatch to Aḥmad Pasha, in which he hinted that Baghdad had still long to wait for relief. The traitorous Persians fulfilled the exact wish of the general by carrying the letter to Nadir Quli.[2]

From south of Kirkuk he followed the course of the 'Udhaim river. When the Tigris was reached, a letter from Nadir Quli bade him chose his ground and give battle. Messengers and spies from the Persians were detained, and released later to convey to their master information contrived to mislead. Ṭopal 'Uthman—cool, wise, and unhurried—gave confidence, if he invited criticism, by his very simplicity. Spies and light skirmishers from his own forces kept him fully informed. On the 17th of July they returned to report that Nadir had left his city-camp at Baghdad and advanced ten leagues upstream. Battle was expected on the 19th. Ṭopal 'Uthman called his officers, and gave the last detailed instructions. The army halted on the 18th, while the Persians toiled northward.

Ṭopal 'Uthman rose from a night of tranquil sleep, bade his physicians give him a draught to increase his strength on this day of days, and made his customary prayer.

[1] The component forces are given with great detail by Subḥi (von Hammer, xiv, p. 286). The force never exceeded one hundred thousand. It reached Mosul some 80,000 strong.

[2] A document of great interest and importance is the "lettre écrite à S. E. Mons. le Marquis de Villeneuve, le 10 août 1733, par le Sieur, Jean Nicodème, médecin de Topal Osman-Pascha" quoted in full by von Hammer (xiv, pp. 514–28). It is written from Tuz Khormatu prior to the last and fatal campaign of the lame hero.

"After he had prayed, he mounted on horse-back, which he had not done before throughout the campaign, having been carried in a litter since he left Diyarbakr. I could not attribute the strength he now showed to anything but his martial spirit, and the fire that glowed within him. . . . I saw him riding along like a young man, sword in hand with animated countenance and sparkling eyes, and giving his orders with admirable readiness and presence of mind."

So wrote his physician.

Battle began with the Turkish advance at eight in the morning of the 19th.[1] On either side discipline was equal. The tactics of the time and the flatness of the battle-field allowed little room for subtlety. The numbers of the armies showed but a slight advantage for the Turks. Only their cavalry gave ground to the main body of the Persians—fifty thousand under the personal command of Nadir; and behind the retiring horsemen were solid walls of Turkish infantry who stood firm. Three hundred Persian heads were thrown before the Sar'askar, and already it seemed that victory leant to his arms. The desertion of two thousand of his Kurds, however, turned the tide: guns were captured from Pulat and Ibrahim Pashas, and a breach was forced in the Turkish line beside the Tigris. Spurning councillors who bade him retire, Ṭopal 'Uthman called up his reserves of twenty thousand. The guns and lost ground were regained. The tide of Turkish victory set strongly in. The Janissaries in the centre advanced all along their line. Nadir, whose fearless exposure of his own person had cost him his standard-bearer and two chargers, could no longer rally his men. After nine hours of bloody and doubtful battle, the declining sun saw the Persians break, retire, and scatter. The lame Pasha had gained a complete victory.

Thousands of enemy slain and wounded littered the wide battle-field. The loot included the whole Persian artillery of all calibres, all their tentage and other baggage, all their provisions including fresh fruit and delicacies, their standards, musical instruments, and animals of transport. A generous share fell to the exhausted but joyous forces of the Pasha. He himself, in

[1] Further purely military details can be found in Hanway (ii, p. 86), and Nicodeme (von Hammer, xiv, 522 ff.). These accounts agree only in outline.

general council of his officers, wept for very joy and fatigue, thanking every commander for his efforts and Allah for the victory.[1] The Persians lost thirty thousand killed, and three thousand prisoners. The Turkish losses were little less. Two days were spent in clearing the field, burying the dead, and evacuating the wounded towards Mosul. The father-in-law and nephew of Nadir Quli, discovered among the Persian wounded captives, were generously treated and dispatched after the Regent. Letters of victory were sent from the scene to the Sultan, to Baghdad, and to many of the governments of the Empire. Deserters brought word that Nadir had crossed the border into Persia.

At the moment of victory Aḥmad Pasha ordered a sortie from his gates and fell upon the force—eight thousand strong—left by Nadir to hold the siege positions. Not a man escaped. On the 22nd of July the Daftardar of Baghdad reached Ṭopal 'Uthman with letters of congratulation. On the evening of the 23rd, as the relieving army drew within sight of the siege-buildings, Aḥmad Pasha rode into camp. The meeting—a moment as dramatic as any in the history of 'Iraq—was short and formal. On the day following, Ṭopal 'Uthman returned the visit. Deprecating ceremony after a victory due to other than human strength, he rode without pomp or entourage into the town of famine, pestilence, and death. From January to late July no food had reached the crowded city. More than a hundred thousand persons had died of starvation. Thousands had been thrown into the river, the bodies of the rest infected the air and brought disease in the wake of hunger. The few and feeble persons who watched the entry—impressive in its humility—of the noblest of his race, were too far gone in weakness to relish the sweets of deliverance and coming plenty.[2] The lame Pasha retired to his camp ten miles north of Baghdad and rested for eight days.

Thus far his campaign had been of complete and deserved

[1] Nicodeme (von Hammer, xiv, 523).

[2] It is preferred to follow the vivid eyewitness Nicodeme than accept the text of the dispatch given by Hanway (ii, p. 91) as that of Aḥmad to Stambul. According to it "... the great and mighty conqueror Topal Osman Pasha arrived with his victorious army at Iman Azem ... wither the people of all ranks, young and old, ran to lick the dust of his feet".

success. Already famous and revered, his rescue of Baghdad made him in a day the idol of relieved 'Iraq and of Stambul alike. Better for him to have died the death of a Nelson: for defeat and death, contrary to all that appeared, awaited him on 'Iraq soil. His work was done: Baghdad was veritably saved; and although Nadir Shah was twice more to camp before its walls, he was never to subdue it.

While Baghdad grew daily stronger in its convalescence, 'Uthman withdrew to the north. His army, reduced as it was to some fifty thousand, was further lessened by paying off such levies as belonged to the Arab or Kurdish provinces: but even the remainder could not be fed near Baghdad. Dispatches to Stambul called for every kind of reinforcement and supplies. At the Capital, extravagant joy had greeted the news of his victory. Honours and powers were heaped upon him; but nothing appeared of the supplies demanded, nor was he relieved, as he besought, of his command. Apprehensive and ill provided, he camped at Kirkuk. Aḥmad Pasha (to whom the veteran would have resigned his army) realized no less that the Regent must return. He repaired his walls, moat, and citadel, and stocked every granary with grain from wherever it had survived.

The recovery of Nadir well exemplifies his greatness.[1] He halted at Hamadan to reorganize and increase his army. Contingents poured in from every province in Persia. In a few weeks a routed handful of fugitives became a powerful and invigorated army. They advanced to Karmanshah. 'Uthman's force, rather than Baghdad, was his first objective, for no siege could succeed while a field army remained to cut the besiegers from their base. It was to Kirkuk, therefore, that he directed his march.

The appeals of Ṭopal 'Uthman for new men and new supplies were still unanswered. Not from Stambul but from the neighbouring provinces he had succeeded in raising small contingents—from Syria, from Mosul, from Diyarbakr, and from Arab shaikhs. Rumour, reaching his camp near Kirkuk, did not minimize the new and oncoming forces of the Regent. Pulat

[1] In the following campaign Hanway is far the fullest authority (ii, pp. 93-100). Jihangusha does not inspire confidence. Subḥi has a bare mention. The 'Iraqi authorities (Ḥadiqat, Duḥat, Ḥurub) add a few points.

Pasha, sent with six thousand men to hold a frontier, failed, abandoned it, and retired. The subsequent operations are obscure.[1] Ṭopal 'Uthman had fortified his camp: but he permitted detachments of his force to skirmish with the enemy now moving nearer, and a considerable success was gained. The plain of Lailan, spreading south-eastward from Kirkuk between low hills to the Tauq river, was the scene of the final battle. On the 26th of October 1733 the two armies were face to face. The army of Nadir was as great and fresher than that defeated three months before. He himself had lost his contemptuous over-confidence. Ṭopal 'Uthman was in worse case. His army, though rested, was by many thousands smaller than before. He was acting on the defensive, to preserve his army, not to deliver a great city. In the general battle that followed the Turkish army was completely defeated. Few saved themselves from the field. The lame Pasha could not, by every quality of skill and gallantry, rally his men. He himself was forced to leave his litter for a horse, wherefrom he was shot dead. His army ceased to exist. The entire baggage, artillery, and transport, as well as many prisoners, fell into Persian hands. The body of Ṭopal 'Uthman was brought before the Regent who "stood some time in silence and surveyed it with awful reverence", before sending it with escort to Baghdad.

Every contrast is presented by these two antagonists. In their service to their countries alone they may agree. One was to pass from popularity to hatred by his growing cruelties and avarice; the other was unfailingly gentle and generous. One led his men in the pride of "splendid physique, a fine appearance, a voice of thunder, dauntless courage and resolution . . . marvellous memory and abundant virility . . .":[2] the other benign, infirm, and advanced in years, could ride with difficulty. Nadir easily excelled in brilliance, dash, and ambition, 'Uthman Pasha in devotion to his country and his ideals, in an "anima naturaliter Christiana".

News of the great defeat was received with equal horror at Stambul and Baghdad. So great was the consternation that extra guards were placed about the Capital to prevent insurrec-

[1] The geography of Hanway and Jihangusha is altogether fanciful.
[2] Sykes, ii, p. 273.

tion. Leading members of the Diwan recommended any peace rather than further war against a general who was half-magician. Others urged the dispatch of further reinforcements; money and troops were voted; 'Abdullah Kuprili was appointed Sar'askar of Asia, and provincial governors ordered to rally to him.

Baghdad could expect nothing but renewed siege with the faintest hope of relief. Aḥmad Pasha refused to admit within his walls fugitive parties of the scattered army of 'Uthman; he had defenders enough, and too many "useless mouths". All who wished to leave Baghdad were allowed to do so; he himself sent his family to Baṣrah. He had little time to wait for the fulfilment of his fears. The expected enemy advanced by the Khaliṣ to Baghdad, and busied his army with repair of the elaborate siege-buildings; from Qara Tepe he had already sent a force across the Tigris to accept submission and supplies from the Euphrates districts. No relieving army was now hurrying south, no heats of summer were ahead to weary the unaccustomed Persians. The sole hope of the besieged was in their leader and his careful preparation. But the unexpected happened. Nadir Quli, for all his brilliance and magnetism, had been too long absent from a country barely subdued and ever restless with the ambition of vassals. News reached him of a dangerous rising in Fars in the Ṣafawi interest: he could not spare the weeks required to subdue Baghdad. To the Pasha, peace was a heaven-sent relief. Messages passed between them. The terms were those to which in successive ages the tired combatants of Turkey and Persia have returned: the boundaries of Sultan Murad, and general release of prisoners. Peace was signed, captives set free, presents exchanged. The text of the Treaty was sent to Stambul to be ratified. Nadir Quli, after visiting the Holy Places, returned to his urgent affairs in Persia.

§ 5. *The end of the struggle.*

The same messengers who brought this treaty to Stambul confirmed the complete retirement of Nadir Quli from 'Iraq. 'Abdullah Kuprili had still a very strong army in Armenia: his name inspired confidence, as the arrival in Stambul of the body of Ṭopal 'Uthman cried for vengeance. The war-party in the Diwan prevailed. The treaty made in the hour of need, and beyond the rosiest hopes, was set aside when danger receded. Turkish forces in the north remained east of the frontier: and Aḥmad Pasha, to mark the discredit of his treaty, was dismissed from Baghdad. Accepting, for mixed reasons, his Sovereign's orders, he assumed the government of Urfah.[1]

The year 1734 witnessed, after the suppression of the rebellion which had recalled Nadir from Baghdad, his new and successful offensive against the border fortresses still held by Turkey. Tiflis, Erivan, and Ganjah were besieged. By June 1735 the stage was set for his decisive meeting with the Turks' Sar'askar, now abundantly reinforced and long inactive. At Baghawand, near Qars, 'Abdullah Kuprili in a terrific battle lost his life and almost his whole army. Nadir occupied the cities he had besieged, and proceeded to the easy conquest of Daghistan and Georgia.

The Porte had now reason to repent their rejection of the treaty of December 1733. Aḥmad Pasha, now of Urfah, was appointed to the supreme rank in Asia[2] and charged with the conduct of peace negotiations. He moved to Erzerum. Plenipotentiaries passed to and fro. The demands of Nadir had stiffened since the treaty of Baghdad, and now included an indemnity. No conclusion was reached for many months. Nadir was content to leave open his relations with Turkey, while he completed the recovery of Caspian provinces from Russia and assumed, on the 11th of March 1736, the plume and diadem of Persia. At this ceremony he made explicit by proclamation the important reforms at which he had already hinted in letters to the Court of Turkey. He pronounced the adherence of all Shi'is to Orthodoxy as a fifth sect, the Ja'fari. His hope was to facilitate his dealings with Turkey, to add importance to his own (Sunni) family, and to unite—as a counterpoise to Shia' elements still loyal at heart to the Ṣafawis—the Turkoman, Kurdish, and Afghan elements in his army. The Sultan greeted with satisfaction this triumph of true religion.[3] Aḥmad Pasha was bidden

[1] His transfer was to Aleppo, for which Urfah was substituted at his request.

[2] So von Hammer (xiv, p. 338). Hanway (ii, p. 120) assigns the rank of Sar'askar to "Qara Achmad who had been for some time lieutenant to the governor of Bagdat".

[3] Dispatch dated April 1736. Hanway (ii, p. 133) gives apparently an authentic text.

to press for the conclusion of a treaty. Discussion continued. A separate Persian Amiru'l Ḥaj, free release of prisoners, recognition as orthodox of the new Ja'fari sect, were the Shah's final stipulations. Eight formal sessions of the Diwan discussed the religious and diplomatic issues. A treaty was at last evolved containing the necessary clauses. The frontiers should be those of 1639, and the Persian people should henceforth be considered as of the true Faith.

So ended, for a space, the destructive and costly war begun by Turkish greed and Persian distraction in 1723, closed by a brief peace in 1727, renewed by the restorer of Persian greatness in 1730, composed by the weakness of the last Ṣafawi in 1732. Repudiating that treaty, the Persians had waged aggressive war till the last days of 1733; and the peace then made was as quickly repudiated by the Sultan. At long last, on the 17th of October 1736 a peace descended which might hope to last. The religious difference was removed, frontiers were restored to the traditional line, and Nadir himself had gained the prize of his highest ambitions. He passed now to triumph after triumph in India, while the hero of Baghdad returned to the government which, after two years[1] of feeble misrule, welcomed him home.

The subsequent renewal of a war unwanted by Turkey, unneeded by Persia, was due to the perverse insistence of the Shah upon terms impossible for Stambul to accept—insistence in which one may suspect some elements of mental unbalance, the result of ambition too completely gratified and the companion of the insane cruelty and avarice of his last years. From Qandahar in 1738 he sent messages to the Sultan designed clearly to keep open the door for future hostilities. He claimed Diyarbakr and Armenia; he insisted that the Sultan should break off his Mughal alliance and demolish recent improvements in the walls of Baghdad. No reply was made. In 1741 a Persian embassy demanded formal acceptance of the Ja'fari sect. The claim was rejected, and the Ja'faris declared infidels and cannon-fodder for the sons of Tradition. Meanwhile Turkish envoys met Persian on the frontiers; garrisons at

[1] Ḥaji Isma'il Pasha governed for a year with little success, and was succeeded by Muḥammad Pasha the Lame (a former Grand Wazir) in 1735. Under him lawless tribes and oppressive garrisons had free rein.

Baghdad and Erzerum were increased; Turkey from end to end discussed the ambitions of Nadir and the dubious loyalty of Aḥmad[1] Pasha of Baghdad, than whom none had less wish for another war and siege.

Even before war was formally declared in June, Persian troops had crossed the 'Iraq frontier at Mandali and in the Shahrizor and alarmed Baghdad with an unfulfilled threat. Aḥmad Pasha made every effort to provision his capital, repair walls and bastions and breach-blocks, while temporizing with the confidential agents of the enemy. In the spring of 1743, while the harvest still stood high and green, arrived the envoys of the Shah in Baghdad. His hard-won respect for Aḥmad led him rather to artifice than to threats. "I wish you and Baghdad no ill; my quarrel is with the Sultan; deliver over your province, and you will not repent it," was the burden of his courtly messages. The Pasha reported his position to the Sultan, and prolonged his sessions with the ambassadors till the corn be gathered. Finally he returned a doubtful answer: "Take Mosul, and I will hand you Baghdad" was the substance, but time has not preserved the tone and point.

Nevertheless, the heaviest of the expected blows fell upon northern instead of central 'Iraq. Forces poured through the Shahrizor to Kirkuk, and laid siege to its fortress. The senior officers of the garrison, to whom the Persian forces were reported at 300,000, fled to Mosul and beyond. The regular troops followed.[2] The overwhelming army of the Shah ravaged the country-side, while the matchlocks of the Turkoman and Chaldaean townspeople held the high "Qal'ah" for three weeks. They capitulated finally upon terms of the security of life and property. The town was already heavily distressed, and five hundred of the defenders had been killed. The Persian army crossed the Lesser Zab, captured Arbil, and marched on their next objective, the city of the Jalilis.

Mosul was fully prepared. Ḥaji Ḥusain Pasha and his namesake the Muḥafidh by magnetic example had organized both a spirit and a system of defence. Trenches with deep "dug-outs" were ready, new stone built into the walls, new loop-holes

[1] p. 161 sub.
[2] Ives's *Voyage*, p. 311 (written in 1758).

cut. The last preparations for siege were pressed, every post allotted and every granary filled. Villagers flocked into the city.[1] Martial music and the ubiquitous presence of the Pasha cheered the incessant labour of trench diggers and masons. From Jalili to beggar, all joined in the toil. A Persian delegation demanding surrender was indignantly refused. The hot weather drew to a close.

In the latter days of September 1743, the enemy was sighted three miles away. The call to arms sounded, a strong sortie party of cavalry was paraded. These sallied forth, crossed the Tigris opposite the town, and with hopeless gallantry attacked the flank of the massed Persian army. Many fell at their onslaught; but they themselves were soon cut off and surrounded. Their leader showed inhuman courage; the force was extricated, rode clear of Persian bullets, recrossed and gained the shelter of the walls. The gates were now shut and a strict defensive adopted.

Nadir Shah remained for five days in camp at Yarinjah, then crossed and surrounded the city with ceremonial marches of his army. After reconnaissance he decided on twelve simultaneous points of assault, corresponding with the number of towers in the town walls. At each point he constructed earthworks to shelter his guns. Early in October a fierce bombardment from 200 guns began. The patriotism of local historians does full justice to the horror of the fusilade: the shells darkened the sky by day, lit it as with meteors by night. Life and property suffered heavily; but there was no loss of morale. The Ḥaji and his sons, Murad and Amin, showed themselves promptly and fearlessly at all points of special threat by day and night.

Nadir, whose head-quarters had remained at Yarinjah, came nearer to the town. Annoyed at the resistance, he ordered redoubled efforts. A breach was the result. The garrison could barely hold it; and while frantic efforts were made to block the gap and rally forces to the spot, the first signs of panic appeared. The fate of the city hung in the balance. Only the timely arrival of the Pasha availed, by his dauntless and inexhaustible

[1] Sources for the siege of Mosul are the Mosul Calendar (followed by Sulaiman Sayigh), Ṣubḥi in von Hammer (xv, p. 71), Duḥat and Ḥurub, and the two compositions mentioned first in section (*a*) of Appendix I (v).

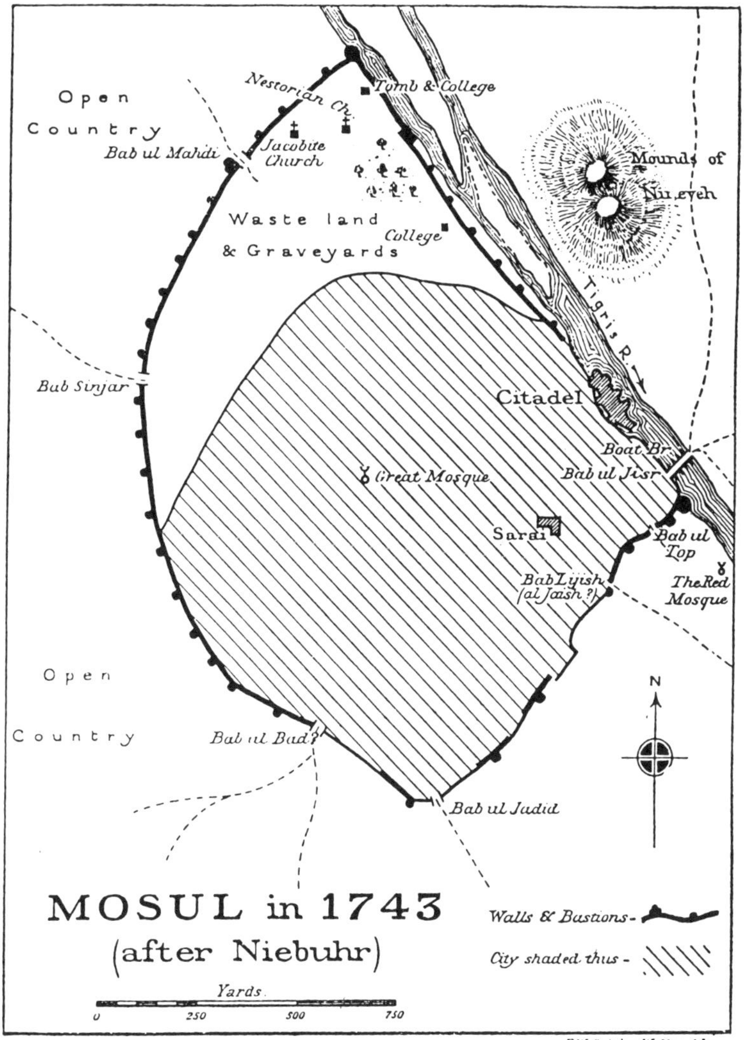
Open Country
Bab ul Mahdi
Nestorian Ch.
Tomb & College
Jacobite Church
Mounds of Nineveh
Waste land & Graveyards
College
Tigris R.
Bab Sinjar
Citadel
Boat Br.
Bab ul Jisr
Great Mosque
Sarai
Bab ul Top
Bab Lyish (al Jaish ?)
The Red Mosque
Open Country
N
Bab ul Bad?
Bab ul Judid
MOSUL in 1743
(after Niebuhr)
Walls & Bastions -
City shaded thus -
Yards
0
250
500
750

F. W. Spiring Walter, del.

vigour, to infuse new life into the panic-striken and close the breach. A second and yet narrower escape was to come. By laborious tunnelling the Persian infantry contrived to reach the very walls. Four great mines were exploded. The first three left the wall cracked and tottering; the fourth brought a great section crashing to the earth. An instant Persian assault was supported by strong forces from behind. The attack was well planned and its success seemed certain. Again fate, by a narrow margin, declared in favour of the garrison. A hail of missiles poured upon the assailants, who failed to widen the breach. Fire was brought and hurled upon the wooden gates—a breeze carried it back upon its authors. The walls were scaled—the heads of the scalers fell upon their comrades below. For some hours raged a conflict fierce with the desperate efforts of both sides. At last the breach, blocked with the dead and dying, was mended and re-manned.

Nadir Shah now judged that the defenders would not refuse generous terms. His first embassy gained nothing. A second reached the Pasha with offers too courteous and flattering to reject. Deputations were exchanged; the rich presents of the Shah were repaid with the finest of Arab mares; praises of the heroic Ḥaji were on every lip. The campaign, now become one of courtly phrase and generosity, was terminated by the departure of the Persian army. The defenders of Mosul, like those of Ilium, poured from the gates, tended the graves of their many dead, and gave thanks to the Compassionate.

While Mosul thus gallantly preserved itself, hostile armies had been seen in the south. A Persian force had threatened Baṣrah,[1] only to retire after three months' half-hearted siege. Around Baghdad 40,000 of the enemy had ravaged the country and undone the benefit of a score of tribal campaigns, while the main force of Nadir was at Mosul. The first effect was to raise prices in Baghdad—a process the more marked as the Shah in the north cut off the river grain-traffic. These uneasy conditions lasted until the failure of the Mosul siege. Nadir now withdrew his main army to Kirkuk, where it remained encamped.

[1] *Précis*, p. 24, § 57; Otter, ii, p. 380. The former speaks of 12,000, the latter of 30,000 Persians.

Aḥmad Pasha had already been named by the Porte as one of the three Sar'askars for the war. Nadir refused to treat with any other officer; and the Sultan's commission, conferring full powers upon him to negotiate, was accompanied by a present of money and a robe of honour. Conversations had already been opened. Though prisoners, pilgrim-taxes, and the status of Ḥuwaizah were among the subjects of discussion, the chief controversy was still religious. Nadir left his army, moved in person south to Mu'adhdham,[1] and thence on pilgrimage to the Holy Cities. At Najf long debates of the divines brought no conclusion. The Shah at last, alarmed by the growing course of discontent and rebellion in his own country and by Turkish preparations in the north, recrossed the frontier without a blow struck or a clause signed. Passing by Sannah and still leaving forces at Kirkuk, he was attacked and severely defeated near the former place by Turkish forces.[2]

The remaining campaigns and diplomacies, lasting for two full years, do not belong to 'Iraq history. The tide of war ran from 'Iraq northwards. Turk and Persian fought again on their annual battle-fields of Armenia and Adharbaijan. Three strong armies of Nadir Shah were opposed by three of the Sultan. The Persian siege of Qars was followed in the summer of 1745 by a crushing victory over Yahya Pasha. The Shah followed it by the proposal of impossible terms. The Ja'fari sect must be recognized; Van, Kurdistan, all 'Iraq and its holy sites must be ceded. Further conversations early in 1746 somewhat reduced his demands, but left him still claiming Karbala and Najf. Not until September did the glad news reach Stambul of peace signed in the Shah's camp near Kasvin. The religious claims were tacitly dropped, the traditional frontier accepted, ambassadors to be exchanged.

Death alone, it may be, preserved the two Empires from yet another disastrous breach of this reluctant treaty; but meanwhile it was hailed throughout Turkey with thanksgiving, and

[1] Jihangusha gives details of the gorgeous barge provided by Aḥmad Pasha for Nadir's use, and of the presents exchanged between them.

[2] Von Hammer (xv, p. 71, and foot-notes). This engagement, ignored by Hanway and Jihangusha, can scarcely have been of the magnitude suggested by von Hammer, nor can the Pasha of Baghdad have been present, as he says, with 100,000 men.

nowhere more than at Baghdad. Aḥmad Pasha was entrusted with details of the exchange of ambassadors. The selected envoy of the Sultan was Kaisariyyali Aḥmad Pasha, a courtier and diplomat of some renown. The retinue and presents on both sides exceeded those of every previous mission. But they were never to arrive. The gorgeous entourage of the ambassador, with his escort of 6,000 horse, had barely left Baghdad and crossed the frontier into Ardalan, when news met them of the assassination of the Shah. His bloodthirsty barbarity, which had changed the worship of his people into loathing and terror, met finally on the 23rd of June 1747 the end which it had too long escaped. Kaisariyyali returned by Sannah and Qara Cholan to Baghdad. Leaving Persia, he left a country to be plunged now into years of internal tumult, powerless for a full generation to trouble the Sultan's empire.

§ 6. *'Iraq in war-time, 1722 to 1747.*

From the first Persian campaign of Ḥasan Pasha to the death of Nadir Shah a quarter of a century had passed. The account of that momentous age would be incomplete without mention of its phases within 'Iraq, and some fuller notice of the great Pasha of the time.

'Iraq, for all that it was both battle-field and prize in the long struggle, was no "nation in arms". It was not in religion a unanimous partisan of either belligerent, nor racially concerned in the struggle of Aryan with Turk, nor uniformly moved by loyalty to its present rulers. Yet in the visible marches of foreign armies, the rapacity of patrols, the atrocities, councils, and stratagems seen and reported, there were lessons for it. An army and a national hero had marched to its defence. At no time since Sultan Murad had it thus seen itself in the light of Ottoman citizenship. Apart from the operations of war, some civil pride might witness the passage of gorgeous embassies to and fro. The Pasha himself—familiar in 'Iraq, eminent in Turkey—was a strong link between local and imperial sentiment. The greater permanence of Turkish officials, increasing recruitment locally of Imperial troops, more frequent intermarriage, all made for unity of interest. Such ground gained by the Sultan in the 'Iraq of war-time meant no assumption of the rights of citizenship, for such was foreign to all Turkish conception: it involved no closer subordination of province to Empire: less still did it produce obedient acceptance of the Sultan's rule. Indeed, while the ordinary misfortunes of war—famine, plague, and devastation—might inspire some rallying of loyalty to Government, other internal troubles worked wholly otherwise and reminded how weak, after all, was the Turkish hold, how little and precarious the ground gained. The tribes, far from rallying to their Sovereign, saw in the danger of his empire only a chance more boldly to flout him. The tedious succession of tribal contumacy and punishment—exaggerated in all times of stress—may be less interesting to a later age than the deeds of the famous, but is far more characteristic of 'Iraq annals and the weary task of its governors; and in these years foreign aggression, which knit the townsmen closer to their rulers, gave the tribesmen the better chance to withhold revenue, to raid, to attack or ignore a preoccupied Government.

Within a few weeks of the march of Ḥasan Pasha to Karmanshah central 'Iraq was in anarchy. Formulated ambition appeared amid the mere lawlessness of the tribes; a "tribal Government" should be formed from the Holy Cities to Diyarbakr. This was restored to order by Aḥmad Pasha in a rapid visit from the front in 1724. The Bani Jamil were hard smitten, then spared with a wise clemency; the Bani Lam routed and pursued from Tigris to Shamiyyah; and a last concentration on the middle Euphrates dispersed by a rapid and strong column based on Ḥillah. Loyal Shaikhs were appointed, dirahs re-marked, garrisons re-entered the towns. Early in 1726 the alarm came from the middle Tigris, where Lurish forces had joined the Bani Lam and raided to the walls of Baghdad. The Pasha of Baṣrah—husband of Faṭimah Khanim—was busy with the chastisement of the Muntafiq. These, pacified for the moment, needed yet harder blows in 1729, when Sulaiman Pasha (Kahya[1] and future son-in-law of Aḥmad) conducted large operations with good effect.

The appearance of Nadir Quli on 'Iraq soil, and the long siege of Baghdad, left behind it conditions of complete non-govern-

[1] Sulaiman's predecessor as Kahya was Muḥammad Pasha, husband of Khadijah the niece of Aḥmad. He seems to have succeeded 'Abdu'l Raḥman Pasha as Governor of Baṣrah (*Précis*, p. 15, § 38).

ment. The Shammar had furnished guides and allies to the Persians; they were punished by a swift column in 1736. Next year the Albu Ḥamdan (a strong tribe south-west of Mosul) were scattered with the loss of their Amir. The Zubaid south of Baghdad were attacked in successive years, before and after the removal of Aḥmad Pasha from the province. On his return, the need to punish the Bani Lam—open supporters of the Persian invader, and strong with Lurish alliances—took him to their dirah. The campaign was memorable for the reinforcements brought upstream from Baṣrah by the Qaptan, and for the Homeric single combats [1] of Aḥmad Pasha. A force stayed behind to collect revenue and was assisted by another visit of the Pasha—on a hunting expedition—in 1739. In the same months the Rabi'ah were visited; they had long withheld revenue, and now added to this the murder of a visiting Agha of high rank. Their defeat and payment of heavy reparations to the Kahya followed the usual course.

"Les Muntefiks et les Beni Lames", noted a French observer [2] in Baṣrah, "avoient donné plus de peine que les autres aux Pachas . . ." The former remained fairly quiet from 1729 until the emergence of their great leader Sa'dun.[3] His name is first met in 1738–9 at a meeting of shaikhs called by the Kahya at Ḥiskah. Presents and compliments were handed to each: Sa'dun instead was arrested and taken to close captivity in Baghdad citadel—the penalty of an offensive ambition which claimed even the "Sultanate of the Arabs". Munaikhir, a kinsman, was appointed Shaikh till Sa'dun, on many entreaties, was released and restored. Early in 1741 the Muntafiq rose again, surrounded and terrified Baṣrah, blockaded towns and looted villages from Qurnah to Najf. Yaḥya Agha, Mutasallim of Baṣrah, managed to hold the town till Aḥmad Pasha, returning in haste from a Kurdish campaign, relieved it in April. Instead of fighting, terms were made with Sa'dun,[4] who soon showed himself less

[1] Duḥat, year 1150.

[2] Otter, a leading authority (with the *Précis*) for southern 'Iraq in these years.

[3] Son of Muḥammad ul Mani' and founder of the Sa'dun family of Al Shabib.

[4] This and other suspicious manœuvres in southern 'Iraq led to a fairly general view (held by Otter) that Aḥmad was using Sa'dun to prove to the

chastened than encouraged. He blockaded Baṣrah, from whose walls none could issue in safety. Even the Agents of the French and British Companies were not safe from shameless demands and threats of violence. Sulaiman Pasha was sent with an army. Finding the Muntafiq forces fled to the high desert, and intent on revenging a private grievance, he followed them by forced marches. Sa'dun was defeated, captured, and beheaded. This cold-blooded murder of the gallant incorrigible Shaikh by a slave-born Agha was long remembered,[1] but its good effect lasted a bare five years. In 1747 the Muntafiq, again risen, cut the dykes and inundated to the walls of Baṣrah, where the horrors of plague, flood, and corvée labour distracted the townsfolk. On the middle Euphrates, conditions were no better. A column punished the Qash'am in 1733; in 1738 the Kahya marched through the area; and next year both he and his master were kept busy in the Shamiyyah and the western desert. In 1741 the outskirts of Karbala and Ḥillah were in anarchy, to be restored once more by Sulaiman Pasha, now an adept at such campaigns.

In the internal history of 'Iraq in these years, however, there was more of significance than these and a hundred similar rebellions raised and suppressed. In the south, a nation of Europe put down the roots of a long-lived trading connexion. In Kurdistan, a dynasty of the valleys grew formidably strong. In Mosul, a single family so far outstripped the rest as to hold the Pashaliq as its own for a century.

Baṣrah was revisited by agents of the Honourable East India Company early in the third decade of the century and its Factory opened as a permanent station. Its difficulties—apart from the vagaries and private ends of its own staff, and their heavy death-roll—all sprang from the caprice and prejudice of the local government, whose sole aim, first and last, was to make immediate profit from the foreigners. In 1727 a vexatious tax was levied on their Persian servants. In 1728 a Company's interpreter was arrested for no offence. Farmans were given and torn up by successive Governors, loans and presents demanded,

Sultan his own indispensability. Otter, followed by Hanway, is emphatic that there was no fighting; but Duḥat (year 1151) speaks of a battle under swamp conditions, after which the Pasha's pardon was obtained by the mission of Sa'dun's youngest boy to his camp.

[1] See Heude, p. 66.

claims unsatisfied, Capitulations unheeded, the customs rate altered at a whim. In a Persian threat on Baṣrah in 1735[1]—which came to nothing—the Agent could barely maintain neutrality, and the dilemma repeated itself in the blockade of Baṣrah in 1743. In a score of quay-side crises he invoked Aḥmad Pasha in Baghdad against the foolish rapacity of the Mutasallim, and rarely in vain. The Dutch Factory lasted until 1752.

In Mosul before the outbreak of war (and indeed habitually) fierce internal factions raged. In 1725 these centred round the figure of the famous Mufti, 'Ali Effendi ul 'Umari. The cause of friction was the Wali's jealousy of his special influence. Libellous stories gave place to blows and brawls. After six months exchange of robbery and murder, the restoration of peace was followed by outbreaks of disease and a visitation of locusts. From these sad conditions arose the bearer of a famous name. Late in the seventeenth century, a Mosul Christian[2] named 'Abdu'l Jalil was employed in the household of the Pasha. Subsequent admirers traced the Jalili lineage to an old ruling house, and brought it from Diyarbakr to Mosul about 1600. The high character and gifts of 'Abdu'l Jalil were praised without stint by posterity; and his sons meanwhile enjoyed—as the custom was—the same education as those of his employer. Some, if not all, grew up as Muslims. The eldest, Isma'il, rose rapidly to eminence. Wealth and popularity were united with abilities that became well known. In 1726 he assumed, ripe in years, the Pashaliq of Mosul; and a short tenure of office was remarkable for improvements and for his energy in the War. The Jalili family, without rival in Mosul for more than a century, was established. Ḥaji Ḥusain Pasha, the most famous of the name, succeeded in 1730 to the Pashaliq which he was to hold eight times.

The rise in power of the Baban family followed the emergence of two exceptional personalities, in times suitable to the quick growth of fortunes. Khanah Pasha, son of Bakr Beg, succeeded

[1] Known only from a reference in the dispatches of the Agent to "Gombroon".

[2] Sulaiman Sayigh (p. 273) singularly omits all reference to his religion. The grave of 'Abdu'l Jalil was long shown in a church.

to the government of Qara Cholan in 1721. Upon the occupation of Ardalan he was invested with its rule, his brother Khalid Pasha remaining behind to be confirmed in the government of the Baban Sanjaq. The influence of the family stretched now with varying force from Kirkuk to Hamadan. The government of Ardalan by Khanah seems to have lasted for four years, whereafter it descended to his son. Both were remembered as just and enlightened rulers. In 1730, however, the advance of Nadir Quli ended their sway in Persia. In the Shahrizor, at moments of Persian ascendancy—1730, 1733, 1743—alien governors appeared; and though these did not remain long enough to break the continuity of Baban rule, it is to such times that belongs the birth of a pro-Persian party within their own family. The Shah and his frontier vassals became the refuge and hope of pretenders to the Baban government. Nadir himself received the first of these, Salim Pasha, and installed him in Qara Cholan in 1743. For a year it became a Persian province. In the struggles of Salim with Sulaiman Pasha, son of Khalid, it is not surprising to find Aḥmad Pasha of Baghdad, in the last of all his campaigns, helping to suppress the Persian candidate.

In these years increasing touch was found by the Babans with their northern neighbours at Ruwanduz, which small principality had by 1600 extended its sway beyond its famous gorge over the Ḥarir plain. At Keui, the Soran Begs maintained their independence until 1730, when, during the long reign of Khalid Pasha, it became a Baban dependant. In the same period the relations of the Beg of 'Amadiyyah with the Turks were regularized. The Baḥdinan family, highly favoured by Sultan Murad, had long maintained its special position; but during these years, under circumstances of collision not recorded, Aḥmad Pasha dispatched his Kahya, besieged and took 'Amadiyyah, and granted terms after heavy punishment. Thereafter, a yearly farman and robe of investiture was granted from Baghdad. The great ruler of 'Amadiyyah was Bahram Pasha, a prince heaped with the eulogies of his descendants.

Of the ruler of 'Iraq throughout this long period of trial, of change, of uneasiness, much has perforce been said. He was not a man pre-eminently great; yet the biographies of smaller fill many shelves. To his subjects he appeared first as the son of an illustrious and familiar father, then as the life-long and indispensable ruler of the country. His enemies expressed the sense of a dangerous greatness by the change of his title to "Padishah".[1] His servants, guards, and entourage suggested little less. In frequent contact with Persian diplomats, he could maintain the Ottoman reputation for gorgeous ceremony. Illiterate as he was, his taste delighted in the recitation of poetry. Jealous of his dignity, and at times quick tempered, he was usually genial, tolerant, and merciful. No acts of brutality are recorded, many of clemency. He could fraternize with a huntsman, a divine, or a British trader.[2] His charities were scarcely less than those of his father the Charitable, if they fell short of the profuseness of Nadir at Najf. As horseman and hunter and hurler of the jarid, he was the first sportsman in his country.[3] His generosity was rare in a Pasha, popular in a country where it is more praised than practised, convincing in the desert where it is the chief of virtues.[4] In his use of unlimited power over a vast province Aḥmad Pasha showed qualities rare in eastern rulers: he was firm without crushing, reasonable without weakness. From his Imperial soldiery, dreaded bullies of his predecessors, he insisted upon discipline, maintaining his own ascendancy by the creation of a devoted local force, and by shrewd and rapid blows at sedition. He was without avarice, the greatest enemy of justice. Ambitious as he was of fame and triumph, and habituated to rule, his ambitions never took exaggerated form.

In his relations with Stambul he was not impeccable. Little or no revenue left Baghdad for the Capital; he refused at times to accept Imperial nominees to office; and the Porte was little pleased in recognizing, as it must, that he could not be replaced. 'Ali Ḥakimzadah, twice Grand Wazir and his inveterate enemy, was one of a large party in Stambul to whom

[1] Hanway, ii, p. 129; cf. Leandro di s. Cecilia, "Viaggi in Palestine," &c. in Murray's *Asia*, iii, pp. 75 ff.

[2] Joseph Emin (p. 6).

[3] Dr. Ives (p. 305), Duḥat (year 1145), Niebuhr (ii, p. 255).

[4] That such generosity had other sides is suggested by Otter (ii, p. 185) and Hanway (ii, p. 234). The money spent generously was public money and increased by fines on tribesmen and exactions (it was said) from Jews and other merchants.

his position seemed to transcend the proper limits of a subject a view shared in Persia and 'Iraq itself. Stories were told of Imperial envoys[1] sent to Baghdad and never again seen. By good observers it was suspected that tribal wars in southern 'Iraq were handled (if not organized) to keep the ayalat of Baṣrah[2] in his own hands. His ill wishers professed to fear, even more than insubordination within the Empire, an actual apostasy to Persia. Indeed the Viceroy of Baghdad, hero of assault and siege, famed from the Balkans to India, able at any moment to hand the Shah everything from Mardin to the Gulf, might have hoped for princely consideration had he changed allegiance: and a score of stories were current of the personal relations of Shah and Pasha, of the high regard of Nadir for his prowess.

Aḥmad devoted a long career to defending his province from Persia, and by no public act gave room for such suspicion of treachery. Yet it existed. In Persia it lived on hope, in Stambul on fear. It is imaginable that the Pasha would rather have changed sides than perished: but in recorded facts there is no justification for the odious nickname of "Nidhamu'l Mulk"—a famous traitor of Nadir's Indian campaigns—bestowed by his detractors: and in obedience to his own master he did not fail under the great trial of his transfer from Baghdad in 1736.

Within 'Iraq, he followed his father on lines leading to the unification of the country. Baṣrah, Mosul, and Kirkuk all at some time were the governments of his relations. The ayalat of Baṣrah was directly subordinate to him throughout, and in this the Porte, after efforts to the contrary, was forced to acquiesce. Mosul was never his; but he inherited Mardin from his father, dealt direct with 'Amadiyyah and central Kurdistan, kept order in Sinjar: the ayalat of Mosul shrank to a puny size and could scarcely, in practice, ignore his wishes. To Kirkuk little greater independence was left. His long tenure of the highest military command accustomed all to look to Baghdad for their orders, and to break down the old equality of status of the four ayalats.

He had time, when Nadir Shah for the last time turned his

[1] See especially Otter (ii, p. 260); Hanway (ii, p. 330).
[2] Otter (ii, pp. 144-7, 183 f.), &c.; cf. the *Précis*, p. 23, § 54.

back on the 'Iraq, to restore some order, to know rest and relief, to prepare for quiet years. These were not to be. He had survived Afghan, Ṣafawi, and Afshar: 'Iraq for thirty years need now fear nothing from the East. His work was done; and his long career outlasted but by sixty days the life of his greater rival, Nadir Shah. He died on campaign against Salim Baban, was carried to Baghdad, and buried beside his father under the dome of Abu Ḥanifah.

VII

THE SLAVES[1]

§ 1. *Abu Lailah.*

The sudden death of Aḥmad Pasha brought into instant prominence a feature of the Baghdad Court to which this history has so far but faintly referred. To Sultan Maḥmud and his advisers—Nadir dead, Persia distracted and unmenacing—the moment was ideal to restore the balance of provinces in 'Iraq: to cut off Mardin and Baṣrah, and install at each and in Baghdad loyal officers from the capital. To 'Iraq, where only men in late life could remember the days before the father of Aḥmad had assumed the government, such a fresh start would have been tolerable if strange; but to the small bureaucracy of the Mamluks it was unthinkable. Aḥmad Pasha had neither son nor grandson: but he had filled his palace with dark-eyed, white-skinned dependants to whom his family was master, father, and very creator.

Slaves[2] of Caucasian race were known in Turkey from the earliest times. In Egypt they had founded the remarkable dynasty overthrown by Salim I, and revived later at the cost of his successors. In the Sarais of Stambul and many lesser cities they had appeared at various periods. In Persia there

[1] Authorities for the period 1747–74: of local histories only Duḥat and Thabit are of primary, and Ghayatu'l Muram of secondary, importance. The first named is the basis of Jaudat Pasha (who is very brief for this period in 'Iraq) and of Thabit. Waṣif Effendi, himself using five previous historians, is the official historiographer for the period 1752–74, in succession to 'Izzi. He is used by von Hammer (xv and xvi) and by Huart (pp. 148–56). The Mosul authorities are as for the previous period. The principal travellers are Ives, Niebuhr, Parsons. Particulars of these and numerous others are in Appendix I. Niebuhr (later closely paraphrased by Heude) is the best 'Iraq traveller of any period.

[2] Known in Arabia as Mamluk (مملوك pl. مماليك), in Turkish as كول or كولمن (Kulaman), more commonly the latter. The 'Iraq historians in Turkish always so write of them.

were examples of their use even in high commands, and sometimes even without conversion to Islam. In race they were by majority natives of the Tiflis area of Georgia,[1] but other closely similar Caucasian breeds were included, with wild tribes—Laz, Abazah, and the like—who had migrated somewhat from the hills of their origin. All were of the vigorous and practical, rather than of the artistic and lethargic, branches of the Caucasian peoples; all were to show a striking aptitude for affairs; and most were disgraced by vices which prevented multiplication in their adopted country, and broke, in 'Iraq, the continuity of the dynasty they founded.

Ḥasan Pasha, bred in the Sarai and familiar with its innumerable grades of functionaries, bond and free, had during his long rule in Baghdad elaborated his own palace-life on that model. He found the usual public and private officials, with the usual faint line between them; he found, no doubt, a few slaves, Circassian as well as negro. He now instituted—rather by gradual changes than by a single organization—grades of servants arranged by "Chambers" or companies: such were the Khaṣṣ (confidential private servants), the Treasurers, the Storemen. By promotion and exchange between these departments (which recall by their archaic names the obsolete Gardeners, Houndsmen, Falconers, and Pantry-men of the Sultan, later merged in the Janissaries) a young man might make a career within the walls of the Sarai. Special training was needed, as it had long been given at the capital and undergone by Ḥasan Pasha himself. He arranged for the recruiting of boys to enter the various "Chambers"—a few from the sons of Turkish officials in 'Iraq, some from the leading 'Iraqis, but more and more from the Caucasian slaves of whom this new demand rapidly increased the supply.

The gradual elaboration of the "ich da'irasi" or Inner Court went on. The purchase and use of Georgians was not confined to the Pasha. Their privileged training and advantages

[1] Gurjistan (گرجستان). The natives of this country, called Gurj (گرج) by Turks, will be called Georgians in the present work. The term Cherkes (چرکس), properly covering all Circassians, is at times used as a name rather parallel to, than inclusive of, the Georgians.

in education made them as civil servants far superior to the common Turk or 'Iraqi. Many were the children of favoured and beautiful mothers; for both sexes were bought in the markets of Tiflis. Little by little they multiplied. Some, but a minority, were born in Baghdad. Both in the Pasha's service and in that of his captains, relationships grew up particularly favourable to slave or freedman. From domestic service with eminent masters, they rose to freedom and confidential offices—the equals, soon the superiors, of all save their old master. "'Tis no uncommon thing with them to give their daughters in marriage to their slaves, and who are often made governors of places. There is one piece of respect, however, which the master always requires when strangers are in company, and that is; for the slave to stand in his presence."[1]

To a European, usurpation by a slave majority, or the *coup d'état* of a devoted band of slave-mercenaries, is explicable enough; but the gradual absorption of all power in the state by imported slaves, before the eyes and almost with the consent of the citizens, must seem remarkable. To the Turk, however, pedigree counted less than in almost any country. Neither nobility nor office were hereditary. Many rose from the lowest obscurity to the highest place;[2] and all Muslims (as the Georgians speedily became) were equal before their Sultan. Among the 'Iraqis, at the same time, slavery had a different connotation from ours. Throughout the Arab world, and at all periods, the condition of slavery has been a tolerable and even an envied one. Where the system still survives to-day, the slave is more trusted and far more influential than the free dependant: as being part of the master himself, his authentic mouthpiece, and the devoted repository of his secrets.

Among Georgians bought and educated by Ḥasan Pasha was Sulaiman Agha. He had secured his freedom by conspicuous personal service to his old master's son, served gallantly through the siege, married 'Adilah Khanim (elder daughter of Aḥmad)

[1] Ives, in 1758. He adds: "It happened lately for the slave of a button-maker in Bassara to be raised to the government of that city; they never afterwards met, but the governor paid this point of respect to his old master."

[2] Bashir, a negro slave in the Sultan's palace, rose to be Qizlar Aghasi (Agha of the Women), and held despotic power for many years under Maḥmud I.

in 1732, and as Kahya of the province for many years acquired a fame only second to the Pasha's. The severity which made his name dreaded in every tribe secured him the goodwill of the citizens of Baghdad who welcomed tranquillity. When his master died in 1747, Sulaiman, now Pasha and Mirmiran, had been for fifteen years his right hand and, to all appearances, his chosen successor.

But Sultan Maḥmud and his advisers were fully informed of this intended succession. The moment had been long awaited: to many the death of Aḥmad Pasha was welcome news. The time was ripe to bring 'Iraq back to full subordination. The empire in Europe was enjoying a long peace since the treaty of Belgrade of 1739. Farmans were issued for the appointment of Ḥaji Aḥmad Pasha, Wali of Diyarbakr and former Grand Wazir, to Baghdad; and Kaisariyyali Aḥmad[1] (who still awaited orders in Baghdad) to Baṣrah. Sulaiman Pasha could not be passed over and had better be placated: awarded the ayalat of Adanah, he departed thither with many a backward glance.

The new Pasha of Baghdad assumed his duties under unpromising circumstances. The compact body of the Mamluks and the bulk of the public in Baghdad still hankered for Sulaiman; Kaisariyyali postponed his departure for Baṣrah.[2] Ḥaji Aḥmad, harassed by tribesmen on his march southwards, found a tepid public, a discipline relaxed, an empty treasury. To remedy this latter fault, he instituted taxes to which prompt exception was taken. The tribes felt that the long reign of obedience was over; the Janissaries began insolently to clamour for pay. The Pasha's excuses were rejected and street shooting began. He yielded, asking sixty days' grace to find the money. None came, and mutiny declared itself. His precautions did not prevent a sack of the Sarai and armoury, with an outburst of violence so alarming that he fled to the right bank.[3] The

[1] Called by Niebuhr " Altschi Pasha ", i.e. Elchi.

[2] Cf. *Précis*, p. 26, § 65. The Qaptan Pasha acted as deputy.

[3] So Duḥat and Waṣif. The Resident at Baṣrah had heard a different version: "the new Bashaw Cour Vizier's cutting off the heads of twelve of the principal Zanysarees, and ordering their bodies to be exposed in the public streets, which so incensed the several Chambers of them that they immediately rose in arms."

Janissaries declared him deposed. While the orders of the Sultan were awaited Rajab Pasha[1] assumed office as deputy-governor.

The Porte acquiesced in the expulsion of their nominee. He was transferred to Ichil, whose Mutasallim moved to Mosul, Ḥaji Ḥusain Jalili from Mosul to Baṣrah, and Kaisariyyali from Baṣrah to Baghdad. The Sultan further directed the dispatch of funds to pay the Baghdad Janissaries—part from Stambul, part from the estate[2] of Aḥmad Pasha. The storm in Baghdad died down. But the new governor, a courtier-diplomat, could do nothing with the bullies of the Citadel. By the end of 1748 his incapacity was patent,[3] and Tiryaki Muḥammad Pasha, an old Janissary officer, was substituted. He partially restored order during his few months of rule.

The position was now closely similar to that seen between the removal of Aḥmad Pasha in 1736 and his return two years later. Successive rulers, unversed in local affairs and unpopular as the successors of better men, tried for a space to stave off the inevitable surrender of 'Iraq to the dynasty now rooted there. Between the death of Aḥmad Pasha and the accession of his son-in-law, four tried and failed to maintain the Sultan's government. Even so had Isma'il and Ṭopal Muḥammad failed from 1736 to 1738. Sulaiman Pasha from Adanah pressed his claims to 'Iraq with a cogency made greater by the failure of substitutes. In 'Iraq his intrigues for the place had gravely embarrassed the Pashas. Kaisariyyali, before his removal, had severed the head of his own Kahya, condemned for intriguing with Sulaiman. The latter now offered to pay from his own pocket certain debts of government, and further to pacify the rebellious tribes of Muntafiq and Cha'ab, if the ayalat of Baṣrah were conferred upon him. The proposal was accepted. He was promoted Wazir, left Adanah, reached Baghdad and paid the debt. Rivalry between him and Tiryaki instantly declared itself, and before passing

[1] The "Radsjeb Pascha" of Niebuhr's list (ii, p. 253).

[2] A court equerry, Muṣṭafa Beg, had been sent to Baghdad as usual to confiscate it.

[3] See von Hammer (xv, p. 167): "Scarcely was the nomination of Kaisariyyali known, when the Amir of the Arabs, father-in-law of Aḥmad Pasha, came to blockade Baghdad in spite because the government. . . had not been given to Sulaiman . . ." From nowhere else does it appear that Aḥmad Pasha had married a tribesman's daughter.

downstream to Baṣrah he half-openly rallied his old supporters in Baghdad.

At the port he at once showed his superior qualities. He reduced the tribes, by rapid campaigns in his best manner, to an obedience unseen since he left 'Iraq. Muntafiq and Bani Lam, tribes of Ḥuwaizah and 'Arabistan, and Cha'ab pirates on the Shaṭṭ, felt his arm and obeyed. Swift and glowing dispatches of victory left Baṣrah for the Bosphorus: but these were as quickly countered by the jealous malevolence of Tiryaki Muḥammad, who informed the sovereign that Sulaiman was making common cause with rebellious Arabs. The days of Ḥusain and Yaḥya were not forgotten in Stambul; and orders went out to the Pashas of Siwas, Diyarbakr, Mosul, Aleppo, Raqqah, Mar'ash, and Mardin to rally for the reduction of a rebel. Sulaiman, however, urged his innocence; the formation of the punitive army was delayed; and a royal Equerry was sent to inquire into the case. He exonerated the Georgian. This could have but one consequence. Tiryaki determined to resist by force the entry of his rival into Baghdad.[1] Sulaiman moved from Baṣrah, and at Ḥiskah found strong support in men and money from 'Ali Agha, of whom more will be heard. Tiryaki marched with 14,000 men to Ḥillah. Sulaiman with 800 attacked them. There was little bloodshed,[2] for the Baghdad Janissaries changed sides in a body. Tiryaki himself bolted to Baghdad to find the gates shut against him. The Georgian freedman entered the city, which overflowed with welcome. Baghdad and Baṣrah, with Mardin and all the territories of Aḥmad Pasha, became his single command.

His tenure of this great office lasted for twelve years. From the first day, he was already well known and feared. Few rebellions were ventured under his strong government. In most of his rapid and decisive campaigns (whose midnight secrecy

[1] The ensuing campaign is shortly recorded in Duḥat (year 1162), Thabit, and Niebuhr (ii, p. 257). Waṣif passes over these operations, though he gives the farman appointing Sulaiman Pasha in full (Huart, xv, p. 150).

[2] That there was some slaughter appears in the stories that reached Baṣrah. "Our Bashaw", writes the Resident (*Précis*, p. 27, § 68) on the 12th of August 1749, "has gained an immense victory over the Bashaw of Baghdad, who attacked him unawares: however, he has killed and taken prisoner upwards of 12,000 people . . ."

gained him the name of Abu Lailah[1]—"he of the night") he was himself the aggressor. He never overlooked a tribal transgression, never failed instantly to chastise it, emerged successful from every quick tireless expedition. The back of his task was broken when as Kahya he had led campaign after campaign from 1733 to 1747; but during his own Pashaliq he rode again over every area of his province. Under him we may see Turkish rule at its best—a skilful, vigorous opportunism, well informed of conditions, well executed within limits, gaining limited and immediate ends, rather cunning than wise. It lacked ideals, save the vaguest that Islam and humanity could prompt; it lacked knowledge and theory; it abounded in follies, abuses, injustices: yet it met each immediate problem with a suitable expedient, and gained the applause of the moment without thought for the longer morrow. All this conceded, Sulaiman Abu Lailah was the strong, successful ruler of a large and uniquely difficult province. No hint of a rival disturbed his reign.

Reproached by some for a private life made disgraceful by the vices of his race,[2] he was the object of smiling or pitying looks for the domestic "rule within rule" which was said to give him second place in his own house. The dominance of 'Adilah Khanim his wife was no doubt the raciest topic of the Baghdad harems. She received callers of both sexes, extended her interference to state affairs, and organized a regular association of her favoured followers, distinguished by a silk badge. Upon points of personal precedence she was firm.[3] Her part in the murder of Salim Pasha Baban, and her bitter hostility to 'Ali Pasha, successor of her husband, are elsewhere described. The innocent husband of her sister 'A'ishah was put to death, it was believed, through her animosity.

With the Capital, the relations of Abu Lailah were outwardly correct: each year the procession of Qapuchis brought his farman of office, which successive Sultans saw no alternative to bestowing upon him; and in 1752, after the successful Sinjar expedition, he received a present of rich furs from his sovereign,

[1] Duhat mentions as alternative nicknames Abu Samrah and Dawwasu'l Lail. Niebuhr heard him called Sulaiman the Lion.

[2] Ives, *Voyage*, p. 284, gives sufficiently vivid details.

[3] Ives (p. 278) preserves a pleasant example.

and gifts for many of his tribal chiefs. But, in fact, he failed in many of the duties of a loyal viceroy. He was immovable, irreplacable. He sent no revenue to his master; on the contrary, his yearly accounts did not fail to show that his expenses on the army, fortifications, and other maintenance had exceeded the revenues of his province. As usual, stories were current of imperial intrigues against him. Successive messengers, it was whispered, had left Stambul with royal injunctions to remove his head—only instead to lose their own.

Under Abu Lailah the use of Georgian freedmen in important posts was much increased. The stream flowed more copiously from Tiflis to Baghdad since a Georgian held the government. The machinery of their education became more elaborate. Two hundred boys[1] were regularly under training. Different grades of teachers instructed in reading and writing, horsemanship and swimming. A young man graduated from this school became apprentice or esquire to one of the "Gediklis",[2] thereafter to be admitted as an Agha of the Household. Of the trained Georgians, Abu Lailah not only formed a small reliable fighting force, but used them widely in public offices—writers, collectors, garrison-commanders—as well as on his own staff. This debarred not only many Turkish officials, but the leading families of Baghdad, from the chief share in the affairs of government. What shaking of heads, what regrets or resignations this caused in the diwans of the Baghdadis, cannot be said; but it created a feeling to show itself eighty years later in the reaction from the Mamluks.

On first assuming the Baghdad Government, Sulaiman was forced to leave Baṣrah to the Qaptan. This officer was thought likely to resist supersession, but such fears[3] were unfulfilled: a Mutasallim was peacefully inducted early in 1750. A year later he (or the Qaptan) ventured to proclaim the independence of Baṣrah, secured the promised support of certain Muntafiq leaders, and fortified the suburb of Minawi. The bulk of Abu Lailah's forces were in Kurdistan. On their return the Kahya

[1] Two points are not clear to the writer—(1) Was there a single or were there several schools? Thabit suggests the latter. (2) Was this education confined to the Georgian slaves? Probably a small minority of Turks and Arabs participated.

[2] For these, see Huart, p. 152.

[3] Which were shared by the Resident (Dec. 1749).

was sent with a detachment towards Baṣrah. Not for nothing had Abu Lailah crushed the Muntafiq years before: at the first appearance of the force the tribesmen melted homewards. The Kahya marched on the port, gave Muṣṭafa Pasha one chance to repent, then chased him from the town and captured the whole of his river-fleet. The rebel bolted for Bushire. Baṣrah was placed under Ibrahim Pasha. The foolish and hopeless rising was over.

The Tigris tribes remained quiet, since their punishment in 1747. The Muntafiq under 'Abdullah—brother of Sa'dun—were in hand. Only the unpunished Cha'ab remained disturbed and menacing. Their allegiance to Turk and Persian was still dubious, while to neither did they pay tribute or respect. In the sixth decade of the century they had in Shaikh Sulaiman[1] a leader of energy and initiative. He commenced building a fleet in about 1757; by 1760 it was a match for the antiquated and immobile Turkish galleys; and by 1761 his aggression and impudence called urgently for a check. Abu Lailah ordered his Mutasallim to attack. Operations were begun but never pressed, and the Shaikh bought an easy peace.

Between the port and Ḥiskah, Turkish influence was slight, often flouted, but more than nothing. The high prestige of Abu Lailah, and the presence at Ḥiskah of an exceptional Agha, produced in these years a semblance of government on the Euphrates—slight and sketchy enough, but far more than the contempt and hatred normally shown by the marsh tribes for their Sultán's rule. No garrisons were maintained, direct government hardly attempted. The small towns and reed-villages managed their own affairs in the familiar atmosphere of tolls, blood-feuds, and general acquiescence in the code evolved by ages of desert and marsh-life uncontrolled. The shaikhs were accountable to the nearest Agha for the behaviour of their tribes to official and wayfarer, and themselves farmed the tithes and sheep-tax of the dirah. Such a régime depended upon the power of government to follow up a breach of faith or order with a prompt and heavy blow: and this, with Abu Lailah at Baghdad, was ever ready.

It is greatly to his credit, indeed, that in the twelve years of his rule so few large tribal expeditions were necessary. We shall

[1] Or Salman.

notice elsewhere important Kurdish and Sinjar campaigns in his first and third years, and early in 1756 the audacity of a Shammar raiding party was crushingly subdued—a long-remembered incident followed hard by the terrible famine[1] of that year. This was felt worst in the rain-lands of Assyria. Diyarbakr and Mosul harvests entirely failed not once but twice. The hand of famine stretched southwards, but never quite grasped Baghdad. Thousands of emaciated refugees brought misery, disease, and crime: twelve thousand Persians resident in Baghdad were ordered to leave it before scarcity should grow acute: but the order was not enforced and the need passed. Mosul was weak but partly restored in 1757: Diyarbakr was still in the worst of the agony.

§ 2. *'Ali and 'Umr.*

Sulaiman Abu Lailah died, aged sixty-eight, on the 14th of May 1762. He left no clear indication of a successor. Seven officers survived him who had at some time held the office of Kahya. Of these one was 'Umr Agha, husband of 'A'ishah Khanim, another was 'Ali Agha[2] who (Persian of birth) had greatly assisted Abu Lailah to the Pashaliq and subsequently held various Sanjaqs, including Baṣrah. The province was handed temporarily to the Daftardar, 'Uthman ul 'Umari, as Qa'immaqam while the Sultan's orders were awaited. Of these the first indication was the appointment of Amin Pasha ul Jalili (now at Kirkuk) as Muḥafiḏh of Baghdad; but scarcely had he reached the capital when (obtained whether by the influence ot the Grand Wazir Raghib Pasha[3] or by a wise expenditure) the rank of Wazir and farman for the united ayalats arrived for 'Ali Agha. The new Pasha left Baṣrah, camped near Ḥillah awaiting his farman, and entered Baghdad in state. Amin returned to Kirkuk. The property of the Daftardar, whose piety had not prevailed against the weaknesses of his profession, was confiscated with that of Abu Lailah, and himself imprisoned.

The reign which 'Ali had merited if not also bought began

[1] Ives, pp. 251, 324, 329.
[2] The authorities for his short reign are Waṣif Effendi (cf. von Hammer, xvi, p. 104, and Huart, p. 154, foot-note), Duḥat, and Niebuhr, ii, pp. 260–1. Ghayatu'l Muram and Thabit have brief accounts.
[3] The Sultan's first nominee was Sa'du'l Din of Raqqah.

characteristically. He put to death the worst of the Janissary Aghas and banished others. In the autumn of 1762 an angry rising of soldiery compelled him to leave Baghdad and camp on the right bank; but the rebels quarrelled among themselves, and after a few days he was able to re-enter the town and restore discipline. Despite his strong personality, he had not precisely the qualities required for the position. 'Adilah Khanim was still in Baghdad. She would tolerate the government of another of her father's servants, on condition that he would in all things seek her advice. This 'Ali Pasha—whom she had known as a charity-boy of obscure Persian birth—failed to do; and her jealous resentment increased the intrigues to which he was anyhow exposed. His generosity and charm gave him general popularity; but this did not survive the now flowing tide of indiscipline affecting tribe and garrison alike, the schemes of private ill wishers, and the insidious propaganda which hinted that a Persian could not but be a Shi'i and a traitor.

His short reign was full of incident. His first large expedition against the Baban is recorded elsewhere. In the autumn of 1763 he invaded the territory of the Bani Lam and received a large fine with their submission. Visiting Baṣrah, whose problems he had known as Mutasallim,[1] he found the Cha'ab under Shaikh Sulaiman still independent and predatory, and promised to the Resident the special favours of the Sultan, should the Company's ships help to cripple the Cha'ab fleet. The Englishman was encouraged to some such action by the interests of the Company itself, and two ships were sent. The Shaikh then sought terms without further fighting, intimidated by the nearness of the Pasha's army.

In the spring of 1746 the campaign was against the Khaza'il, where (as on the Tigris) the long calm of Abu Lailah had been broken. By this expedition 'Ali Pasha secured nothing and was even (it was said) substantially defeated. The triumph-songs of the marshmen reached Baghdad. The intriguing rival Kahyas and the disgusted Queen-Mother 'Adilah were quick to note that the arms of the Persian Pasha, deadly against Sunni Kurds, were faint and sparing against the Shia' Khaza'il. Rumour whispered the name of the Ṣu Bashi. A high officer died suddenly.

[1] *Précis*, p. 42, § 101.

"Poison!" pronounced the Khanim—"and he will not be content with but a single life!" Rivalry was heightened by fear and not allayed by the generous presents of the Pasha. A spirit of mutiny was abroad. 'Umr Pasha led the malcontents. Holding the Citadel, they bombarded the Sarai. The skill and charm of 'Ali gained a temporary victory: but amnesty and conciliation were too quickly followed by rigorous punishment of the Janissary leaders; and he paid for the error by a renewed rising more violent and more general. The Kahyas swore fidelity to 'Umr. Every street was barricaded, every gun levelled at the private rooms of the Palace. Seeing all lost, the Pasha crept from his quarters in disguise. A spy discovered him. He was dragged forth, imprisoned, and put to death—a brave, generous, and enlightened man, victim of jealous and selfish rancour.

As troops and citizens returned home through the quietening city, a grand Diwan sat to choose the successor. The claims of 'Umr were conclusive. He had led the successful rebellion: he was married to the daughter of the common master of all the rivals. The Diwan composed a letter to the Sovereign, false and lying in its traduction of the late Pasha, and begging the appointment of 'Umr. Sultan Muṣṭafa III saw no alternative. 'Umr Pasha assumed the government in the spring of 1764.

Sixteen years elapsed between his appointment and the elevation of Sulaiman the Great. This period consisted of ten years of feeble but peaceful government without more incident than tribal wars and sinking prestige: five years of strife among the worthless and quickly-changing rulers in Baghdad, while Baṣrah endured long siege and foreign occupation: and a year of deliverance from Persian and internal misrule alike, while the Great Pasha emerged from captivity to reign. By the increase in their numbers and the general acquiescence in their dominance, the position of the Circassian freedmen was by now the leading characteristic of the Baghdad government. Even in the enclaves not yet directly subject to Baghdad slaves were in use, and eyes could not but look to the Slave-Pasha of Baghdad. The attempt of the Sultan to suppress the dynasty (as he did by the supersession of 'Umr) failed as it had failed before, and led the greatest of all the Mamluks to the seat of Ḥasan Pasha.

'Umr reigned for ten years, with ever-lessening authority. In his first year of office he took up the task of tribal pacification. The Khaza'il Shaikh had continued defiant. 'Umr Pasha thither directed his first expedition. Lamlum, the principal settlement, was destroyed, a government-nominated shaikh appointed, a number of leaders decapitated; Shaikh Ḥamud escaped, reappeared, and was restored on worthless promises of improvement. The management of the Cha'ab was yet more difficult. Operations involved British and Persian co-operation. In 1765 the Regent of Persia, Karim Khan, arranged a joint expedition; but, the Turkish authorities being too late to join forces with him, he retired in dudgeon. The Mutasallim next led an independent column down the right bank. The offensive, however, was taken by Shaikh Sulaiman, who captured three vessels of the Qaptan, then purchased present and future impunity for a small sum. But the Cha'ab Shaikh was no savage. He turned to the third party, whom this understanding with the Turks did not cover. Capturing and boarding three British ships, he released the officers but retained the rest. The Bombay Government, whom the affair greatly impressed, sent out a fleet of six ships in January 1766. In the summer Maḥmud Agha, Kahya of 'Umr Pasha, arrived from Baghdad with reinforcements. The first of the joint operations was calamitous; two British ships were burnt, nine of the Turkish. An assault by land was repelled. Finally both forces were called off on receipt of a letter from Karim Khan bidding them withdraw from Persian territory. No compensation was obtained, now or later, for the Cha'ab assaults on shipping, but rancour gradually died down.

Save for a half-hearted campaign against 'Abdullah of the Muntafiq in 1769—due to the usual causes, but obscure in course and result—no further expeditions of 'Umr Pasha in southern 'Iraq are recorded: but the prestige of his government yearly declined. He lost the power even to depose and create official shaikhs through whom his predecessors were content to govern. His farman counted for less and less. From Qurnah by Euphrates to Ḥiskah, by Tigris to the Zubaid country, government became wholly inoperative. In the capital, intrigue real or suspected began to be directed at the Pasha. In the year of the Muntafiq campaign 'Abdullah Beg ul Shawi, of the great shaikhly family of the 'Ubaid and now a leading man in Baghdad, was suddenly arrested and hanged. The sons, Sulaiman and Sulṭan, raised a force of outlaws and cut every road round the city. 'Umr Pasha, marching twenty stages in eight days, moved a force from Baṣrah to Dujail. A short brush with the insurgents scattered them and made Sulaiman a fugitive. Sulṭan was captured and stabbed in the Pasha's presence. There were other executions. The Agha of the Janissaries was banished to Kirkuk and strangled. Sedition apart, a new influence in the Baghdad court partly explains the disintegration of 'Umr Pasha's later years. A man of low Persian origin—Muḥammad ul 'Ajami—had secured complete control over the feeble ruler. Wielding irresistibly the arts of a pander, and playing upon the lowest passions of his masters, he had gained entry into the highest circles. His influence over 'Umr was paramount.

So feeble as a man, so unsuccessful as a ruler was the freedman 'Umr. While government in lower and central 'Iraq degenerated, Mosul and the Kurdish states were making history after their kind. The heroic defence of Mosul had marked the fifth and longest tenure of that Pashaliq by Ḥaji Ḥusain Jalili. In 1747 he was transferred, a year later to reappear. His next successor was the Tiryaki Muḥammad who, later appointed to Baghdad, was expelled thence by Abu Lailah. In 1749 Ḥaji Ḥusain made his seventh entry. In the Kurdish expedition of Abu Lailah in 1750 Mosul forces co-operated with him. Three years later the raids and violence of the Yazidis of Jabal Sinjar called for an expedition upon a large scale. Abu Lailah brought a force to Mosul, and throughout the campaign (which ended in complete success) had the loyal and skilled help of Amin Pasha, son of Ḥaji Ḥusain.

Amin Pasha was appointed through his influence to Mosul, and subsequently to Kirkuk. In 1758 Ḥaji Ḥusain was posted again to Mosul, where several bold and successful robberies had indicated the weak rule and low resources of the Pashas who governed in the intervals of the Jalilis. Even the city, torn as usual by jealous and violent factions, was insecure. To restore order and prestige, the veteran Ḥaji was brought back; but, although he transacted business for some months, he had come home to die. Not without faults—avarice and an official conscience not always vigilant—he had immensely increased the prestige of his family, and is well remembered in Mosul to-day as the hero of the Siege.

Successive holders—not exclusively from the Jalili family—occupied the Pashaliq for a few months each. In their appointment, their own agents at Stambul were not more powerful than the wishes of the Baghdad Pasha. The distribution of power, indeed, in northern 'Iraq between the governors of Baghdad and Mosul was varying and irregular; but in the city, where alone government was fully operative, the pomp of the Jalili Pasha rivalled his colleague of Baghdad. During the reign of Muṣṭafa Pasha Shahsuwanzadah, in 1760, violent disturbances occurred. The Jalilis were divided for and against the governor. Intrigue grew to open sedition and insults to musket-fire. For four days the streets rang with bullets and hand-grenades: for three Fridays no public prayers were held. The situation cleared only with the return of Amin Pasha for the sixth time.

At Mardin the Mutasallim—or Waiwode, if he was still so called—was exposed in his mountain-city to factions not less violent, to the steppe and foothill politics of Ṭai and Milli, to the racial hatreds of Arab, Kurd, and Turkoman, to the religious acerbities of his Christians. The important sub-province, whose ill-recorded affairs fall scarcely within the range of the present history, still depended on the Baghdad Pashaliq—a relic of the empire-building of Ḥasan Pasha. Nisibin and Dairah were its dependants, Raqqah and Diyarbakr its powerful neighbouring ayalats.

The noble ruling families of Ḥasankif and Jazirah maintained governments of high local pride and continuity. Their relations to the Sultan's government were those, in miniature, of 'Amadiyyah and Qara Cholan. In the former of these, the long and peaceful reign of Bahram Pasha lasted till 1767. In the latter, Baban history will cause us to look again—as we have not looked since the death of Nadir—at 'Iraq's neighbour on the east.

§ 3. *Baban and Persian.*

The murder of the Afshar Shah had thrown Persia into years of anarchy. A dozen rivals fought for the throne. Coronation was followed by instant rebellion, victory by massacre, defeat by blinding. The present history has no concern with the multiform ambitions and barbarities of these princes and generals. The competitors narrowed at last to a chief of the Qajar Turkomans, an Afghan general of Nadir, and the Zand tribesman Karim Khan. To the last, of lowly origin but much charm of character, the prize was ultimately to fall. Many times defeated during the protracted fighting for the throne, he secured it finally by popularity and luck, and by 1757 remained unquestioned ruler. A puppet Ṣafawi, Isma'il, was made titular Shah: but the power and whole functions of royalty were exercised for twenty years by Karim Khan as Regent. He made his capital at Shiraz. A monarch who genuinely sought peace and the happiness of his people, he had no thought of war with the 'Iraq until the last years of his reign. Throughout the Pashaliq of Abu Lailah, there was no Persian question; on the contrary, the Khan delighted the Georgian with princely gifts. In the early years of 'Umr, as has been seen, there was abortive co-operation against the Cha'ab pirates.

But causes of friction were operating. For some years past the treatment of pilgrims to the Holy Cities of the Euphrates had excited the wrath of Persian Shi'is. At Darnah, on the frontier, the Beg—an Ottoman vassal—was allowed to take ruthless toll; at the shrines themselves the dangers of travel in 'Iraq found a climax in irksome and greedy impositions on the devout. The Regent first protested, then threatened: 'Umr Pasha replied nothing. The Shiraz government in vain demanded the repatriation of a hundred families of Persian sectaries resident in Baṣrah. For a further soreness, the Turks were scarcely answerable—the diversion of trade from Bushire and Bandar 'Abbas to Baṣrah.[1] At the same time the Regent observed in his own army a discontent best cured by active service: and the lure of Karbala and Najf were ever present to a Shi'i. Above all the principality of Qara Cholan was a stage for both Turkish and Persian actors, and could at any moment give pretexts for war.

Salim—the Persian candidate for the Baban government—had regained it from Sulaiman Pasha in 1747 and held it in spite of

[1] Parsons, p. 183.

Aḥmad Pasha's last and fatal expedition. For two years he treated the Baghdad government with scorn, and raided far into 'Iraq. In 1750 Abu Lailah marched out in person. The Turkish and Kurdish forces met four marches north of Baghdad; Salim Pasha was put to flight, his followers scattered. Sulaiman Pasha obtained his government, to hold it with interruptions for fourteen years. He was among the greatest of his line. His feudal army, as became a vassal, was at the disposal of the Baghdad Pasha; and he enjoyed the constant support of Abu Lailah, who rid him in 1758 of his most dangerous rival. Salim Pasha had never been forgiven his open adhesion to the Persians, his raids and robberies and elusiveness. To gratify the vengeance of 'Adilah Khanim he was bidden to Baghdad in flattering terms, where death by disgraceful treachery awaited him.[1] Of rivals remaining to endanger the position of Sulaiman at Qara Cholan, the chief was Muḥammad Pasha son of Khanah, who was able to usurp the government in 1760. An army sent from Baghdad defeated him on the Narin river, and he was later put to death by Sulaiman. Twice the latter's brother Aḥmad seized the government for a few months, but failed to retain it.

The death of Abu Lailah removed the restraint which had kept the Baban in good behaviour. Obedience to Baghdad ceased, raids began. 'Ali Pasha first vainly warned him, then led an expedition which the Baban marched to meet. Six thousand cavalry with guns and eight thousand footmen followed the lord of Qara Cholan. The battle was fought near Kifri. Sulaiman Pasha fled with eighty men from the field to Persia; whence, however (and possibly with the troops of the Karmanshah province), he regained his government. These vicissitudes did not rob his reign of remarkable successes. He extended the Baban sway beyond the Diyalah southward. He allowed no peace to the Ruwanduz government. Zuhab and Raniyyah were his, Keui itself, though its ruling family went on, was now but his dependency. Invading the Ardalan in 1763, he was heavily defeated by the Wali's forces: but the year following, having gained the signal favour of Karim Khan himself at Shiraz, he was installed in the government of Sannah. A year later he was assassinated. His son 'Ali succeeded in Ardalan by the grace of

[1] Ives, p. 283.

the Regent of Persia; and Muḥammad Pasha his brother, by the same influence, in Qara Cholan.

But bitter fraternal struggles in the Shahrizor went on: the three surviving sons of Khanah Pasha—Muḥammad, Aḥmad, and Maḥmud—rallied and rallied again their separate followings to seize the princely governments of Qara Cholan and Keui: and the connexion of these squabbles with the general relations of 'Iraq and Persia became yearly closer and more obvious. In 1774, after a lull in the Baban storm, Muḥammad Pasha seized his brother Aḥmad (then ruling Keui), and drove Maḥmud a refugee to Baghdad. He went on to excel his worst feats in provocation of the government of 'Iraq. Finally 'Umr Pasha dispatched his Kahya to install Maḥmud as ruler of Qara Cholan. The task was easy: Muḥammad fled to Sannah: Maḥmud released and enthroned his brother Aḥmad. To the watchful Regent at Shiraz—already resolved on war, launching ultimata at 'Umr Pasha,[1] and terrifying Baṣrah—this was the chance. An army of 14,000 Persians under 'Ali Mardan was dispatched to Kurdistan and across the frontier to restore Muḥammad Pasha who accompanied them. The troops of the Kahya and the now reigning Baban first quailed at the Persian numbers, then rallied and routed the enemy. The Shah's forces were driven from Shahrizor and 'Ali Mardan sent in captivity to Baghdad, whence 'Umr Pasha politely returned him to his master. Thus, without formal declaration, war with Persia began.

§ 4. *Homo homini lupus.*

The war was to involve no Turkish province save 'Iraq, and in 'Iraq but two battle-fields—the valleys of Shahrizor and the city of Baṣrah. The tribulations of the port are kept for a later page. While it groaned under siege and occupation, Baghdad endured five years of confusion and misery.

The year 1774, as we have seen, found 'Umr Pasha confronted with an empty Sarai, an emptier Treasury,[2] troops few and doubtful,[3] no assurance of his Sovereign's support, and a Persian

[1] Olivier (iv. 343).

[2] Nevertheless, in 1774 prices were again low: Parsons (p. 129).

[3] Indiscipline had followed the general demoralization of the Plague: "During the months of June, July and August there have been four officers

neighbour forcing a quarrel. The Pasha himself had deteriorated in character and lived in partial seclusion. Tales were told of his dependence on the worst advisers, and of base ingratitude for favours.[1] Every day brought appeals from threatened Baṣrah, and wild stories of Ardalan incursions into Shahrizor to enthrone this or that Baban. Kirkuk, it was said, was in danger. It was under such conditions—the sultry whispers before a storm which he could never hope to ride—that 'Umr failed to support Baṣrah,[2] and was blamed for his failure on the Shaṭṭ ul 'Arab and Bosphorus alike.

In 1775, after the humiliating Treaty of Qainarchi and three months since the siege had closed on Baṣrah, the Sultan could look eastward. At Stambul all realized the need to rid 'Iraq of the Slaves: the removal of 'Umr might ease the position in Kurdistan and in Baṣrah without a blow. The Wali of Raqqah, Ispinakchi Muṣṭafa Pasha, was appointed to command an expedition to 'Iraq. With him were the Wali of Shahrizor, Sulaiman Jalili,[3] and the Wali of Diyarbakr, 'Abdullah Pasha the Long. Imperial farmans appointed Muṣṭafa to Baghdad, and transferred 'Umr to Diyarbakr.

The three commanders arrived in Baghdad in good order, and pitched their separate camps outside the town. Feeling his way, Ispinakchi Muṣṭafa produced the two farmans. 'Umr accepted the order: with his household and personal followers he emptied the Treasury, left the city, and camped on the right bank. He had no force, and in honourable transfer there was little to deplore. But informers were not slow to work upon the fear and greed of his successor: 'Umr might yet show fight: meanwhile he was removing unhindered the treasures of his household. Ispinakchi ordered a sudden night-assault on 'Umr's defenceless camp.

and 27 privates of the corps of Janissaries put to death." Parsons (pp. 133–4).

[1] Parsons (p. 136 f.) who calls 'Umr "Hamet". Little can be made of his long anecdote of the "good old man" now ninety-five years old, who in his time had refused the Pashaliq in 'Umr's favour.

[2] He did in fact succeed in sending 200 Janissaries. Contingents demanded from the Kurdish Begs did not arrive. A force under the Kahya reached only the Khaza'il and Jaliḥah country on its southward march. Parsons (p. 165) is perhaps unjust in terming 'Umr's failure to relieve Baṣrah as "not only unaccountable but unpardonable".

[3] Son of Amin Pasha, who had died suddenly.

The fallen Wali rode for his life; but his horse stumbled and fell in the darkness, and the fall broke the neck of its rider.[1]

The supporters of ‘Umr Pasha fled from the city. Sulaiman Jalili returned to Kirkuk. Ispinakchi followed the confiscation of ‘Umr's property by exactions on the wealthy. ‘Ajam Muḥammad, the pandering courtier of his predecessor, was an assured favourite. Of a move on Baṣrah there was little sign. To Stambul Ispinakchi reported that the port was his, the Persians already in flight. The Mamluks, well knowing with what instructions he had come to ‘Iraq, gradually left the city and rallied to the side of ‘Abdullah Agha the late Kahya, whose rebellious forces, growing day by day, occupied villages and partially blockaded Baghdad. Ispinakchi's feeble attempts at suppression were unavailing. He informed the Sultan of the iniquities of ‘Abdullah. The Wazirs in Stambul had hoped for very different news: instead of Baṣrah relieved and Mamluks extirpated, their chosen agent was leading a life of pleasure in Baghdad, defied by the Slaves themselves. The choice of a successor fell upon the Wali of Kutahiyyah, ‘Abdi Pasha. Farman in hand he arrived at Baghdad. Muṣṭafa made no struggle. He fled to Mosul and on to Diyarbakr. Here waited the inevitable Qapuchi, in whose hands a few hours later his head was travelling to Stambul.

‘Abdi Pasha ruled for a single week. ‘Abdullah Pasha was already master of central ‘Iraq; and, Mamluk and rebel as he was, he had friends in Stambul. Baṣrah had just fallen. The Sultan bowed again to necessity, and the royal farman bestowed Baghdad upon him. As he entered upon his government, for which brighter days now seemed possible, a new appointment was made in northern ‘Iraq. The two ayalats of Mosul and Kirkuk were jointly given to Ḥasan Pasha, Governor of Mardin and an old Kahya of Abu Lailah. He found the position in Shahrizor sadly deteriorated. The defeat of ‘Ali Mardan in 1774 had been avenged by a general Persian incursion into Baban and other frontier territories. Darnah and Bajlan had suffered heavily, Shahrizor was overrun and Muḥammad Pasha Baban

[1] The author of Duḥat passes a surprisingly favourable judgement on ‘Umr—that he was brave, prudent, and loyal. For a different (but valueless) account of his death, cf. Irwin, p. 330.

restored, Kirkuk threatened, Badrah and Mandali occupied by border Khans. In the campaign which he now launched by imperial orders,[1] Ḥasan Pasha trusted much to the Baban brothers (Muḥammad at Qara Cholan, Aḥmad at Keui), though both had a dozen times changed sides. Aḥmad was to march by Zuhab to Karmanshah, and Muḥammad from Qara Cholan to Sannah. The latter entered Persia, routed an Ardalan force with heavy loss, and looted Banah. In a second battle the Wali of Sannah, Khasrau Khan, was bloodily defeated after a long struggle and barely escaped among his mountains.

The thanks and presents of the Sultan rewarded these victories: Muḥammad Pasha was now committed with the Turks. His brother, true to the politics of his family, took his old place as Persian protégé and joined the new and imposing army now dispatched by Karim Khan under Kalb 'Ali the Lur. Muḥammad fell back, while Ḥasan Pasha wrote in haste for support from Baghdad. The Persian forces entering Shahrizor seated Aḥmad upon the Baban throne. Here he maintained himself against the great efforts of his brother, whom the Pasha of Keui and the Wali of Kirkuk assisted in vain; until choosing a moment of victory to address Ḥasan with a humble letter of apology and protestation, he secured Turkish as well as Persian sanction to his tenure of the Baban Pashaliq. Ḥasan Pasha, for all his vigour and good intentions, had accomplished nothing.

Still less stood to the credit of 'Abdullah Pasha in Baghdad. His energy in rebellion entirely left him when he ruled. His only policy was to confirm the dominance of the Georgians, his only enjoyments to flaunt the pomp and power of his position and to extort the riches of the affluent. Ill health was added to intemperate vices. No help had been sent in the hour of need to Shahrizor; worse still the paramount duty—to relieve Baṣrah—had been forgotten.

The vexation at Stambul found vent against Salim Sirri, the prominent courtier who had urged his appointment. Salim offered himself for service in 'Iraq and promised to return with

[1] Formal declaration of war at Stambul closely followed the appointments of 'Abdullah and Ḥasan. Both were ordered to use every energy and resource to evict the Persians from 'Iraq. Jaudat (vol. i, Bk. II, p. 43) gives full detail of the great army whose assembly was ordered for the purpose. It does not appear that any considerable portion mobilized.

the keys of Baṣrah. By the people of Baghdad, disgusted with weak and worthless rulers, the advent of a high favourite from the Court was hailed with joy. Such hopes were doomed. Addicted already to pleasure, he was fair game for 'Ajam Muḥammad. The power of the Persian pander was now at its height. He had controlled successive Pashas, had gained a following, and (as treasurer to 'Abdullah Pasha) a comfortable fortune. He aimed first at the office of Kahya (now held by Isma'il Agha) and beyond that saw himself master of the Pashaliq itself. For some time past, it was whispered, he had corresponded secretly with Shiraz: led by his promises, the Regent was levying an army to march on Baghdad. Isma'il the Kahya did what he might to prepare the 'Iraq forces; but neither 'Abdullah nor Salim had stomach for war. They dispatched instead an envoy to the Persian capital, Muḥammad Beg ul Shawi. He found a friendly reception; but the release of Baṣrah was made dependent upon hard conditions. Karim Khan denied the threat to Baghdad: his army was intended only to punish refractory tribes of the frontier. A Persian delegate returned with Muḥammad ul Shawi to Baghdad, bearing a letter to the Pasha. News met them on the border of the death of 'Abdullah of dropsy.

This in the early winter of 1777 turned sloth and intrigue into open and violent dissension. Salim Effendi was elected Qa'immaqam pending an appointment from Stambul: but his orders ran unheeded. The last act of 'Abdullah had been to dismiss Isma'il Agha from his post in favour of 'Ajam Muḥammad. Parties now formed round the dismissed and the new Kahya, and street-fighting followed between the supporters of the two candidates. The Janissaries were divided; the local regiments followed the best payer. Each sought to attract the hooligans of the town. The Mamluks in general followed Isma'il; but 'Ajam Muḥammad had found means to corrupt many, and was strong in the open support of Salim Effendi. After some days of intolerable conditions Salim invoked Sulaiman ul Shawi to arbitrate and restore order. Accepted by both sides, he was successful: but his peace did not endure, and he himself joined the party of Isma'il. 'Ajam Muḥammad balanced the loss by the new-gained assistance of Aḥmad Agha ul Khalil, leader of a band of irregulars between mercenary soldiers and highwaymen. With him and the Persian were now the bulk of the Lawand. On the other side Isma'il controlled, through the Shawi influence, the mobile and ubiquitous 'Ugail. For five months in all the wretched and destructive civil war continued, while all waited for the Sultan's choice. Both rivals in Baghdad, and Ḥasan Pasha at Kirkuk, had urged their claims to the Pashaliq. Meanwhile, streets were barricaded, shots flying, collisions of roughs a daily event. Outside the city on the right bank were the 'Ugail camps: on the left, the formidable rabble of Aḥmad ul Khalil. No street was safe, no loyalty assured, no road passable. At last in April 1778 arrived the farman for Ḥasan Pasha. The storms died down. Isma'il Agha and the Shawi prepared to welcome the authentic ruler: and the Arab noble, while Ḥasan Pasha was still detained by struggles of the Baban brothers, became his Qa'immaqam in Baghdad.

Ḥasan Pasha entered Baghdad in state on the 4th of May 1778. Shops opened, the bazaar revived, visits were exchanged. Aḥmad ul Khalil made his submission and was appointed to an honourable post. 'Ajam Muḥammad first cowered and then insulted in the Citadel, which he still held in open rebellion. After a week he escaped by night from the fortress, joined his force outside, and was in turn joined by Aḥmad Khalil who, traitor again, accorded him the title of Pasha.

Ḥasan was to rule Baghdad for a period of two years disturbed wretchedness. The expenses of his splendid court and bodyguard[1] called for brutal exactions from Jew and Christian to support them. The city was quiet, the open country at its height of disordered anarchy. The rebel' forces of 'Ajam Muḥammad and his ally were never wholly suppressed. On the accession of Ḥasan, his first act was to recruit the 'Ubaid followers of the Shawi, to consolidate his own Janissaries and Lawand, and to tempt desertion from the enemy. In the first brush, Aḥmad ul Khalil defeated two columns of the Pasha's troops. Word was then sent to Aḥmad Pasha Baban—still ruling at Qara Cholan despite all efforts of his brother and the

[1] Vivid glimpses are found in *A Gentleman*, p. 53, &c. (Appendix I, § (ii)). The same observer calls him "an unworthy unhappy ruler, and a man of mean appearance".

Soran Pasha of Keui to dislodge him—to bring forces to the rescue. He marched, but died before Baghdad was reached. Maḥmud, the youngest brother, succeeded him and led the Baban army to join the Kahya, 'Uthman. With these reinforcements, Ḥasan Pasha routed a thousand of the rebel horde, captured or seduced some hundreds more. No longer formidable as pretender to the Pashaliq, 'Ajam Muḥammad and his bands of brigands remained—now under the walls of Baghdad, now in refuge in the Lurish hills—completely destructive of security on every route. Salim Effendi, disgusted at these brawls and miseries, left for Stambul where death awaited him.

So passed the summer and winter of 1778. The position of Ḥasan Pasha grew more and more precarious. No order was restored in central 'Iraq, his own backing was mixed and doubtful, rivals already appearing. A growing party rallied round Isma'il Agha, the former Kahya. In March 1779, Ḥasan dispatched Na'man Agha to govern Baṣrah, now suddenly released from the Persians. In October he was himself forced to leave Baghdad by the violence of demonstrations against him. He fled to Mosul, there to learn of his transfer to Diyarbakr, in which city he died.

The Sovereign had decided—rejecting the petitions of Isma'il, the protests of Haṣan—to reunite the three ayalats of Shahrizor, Baghdad, and Baṣrah under a strong rule certain to be acceptable and effective—that of the hero of Baṣrah now at last at liberty. While Isma'il was acclaimed Qa'immaqam by the Mamluks in Baghdad, the Sultan bade Sulaiman Jalili—thus a second time sent southward at crisis—hold the city as Muḥafidh; and the Mosul Pasha substituted the Shawi noble for Isma'il as Qa'immaqam. Nervous, delighted, or defiant, all classes awaited their new ruler. A true instinct foretold that a long reign lay ahead.

VIII

SULAIMAN THE GREAT

§ 1. *The siege and occupation of Baṣrah.*[1]

Among the Georgian freedmen whose boyish memories were of the household of Ḥasan Pasha, of the great siege of Baghdad in which they were too young to take their part, none was more distinguished for good looks and social charm and generous dignity than Sulaiman Agha. Under Abu Lailah his promise was confirmed; he found favour and promotion under successive Pashas of his race; and in 1765 he was appointed to the greatest office in the Pashaliq (save that of Kahya), the Mutasallimate of Baṣrah. Removed after three years, he regained the post in 1771, to the delight of a public groaning under the extortions of Mutasallims—'Abdu'l Raḥman, Ḥaji Sulaiman, Yusif—who had succeeded him.

Since the suppression by Abu Lailah of the abortive revolt of 1751, conditions at the port had been generally peaceful. Accepting as natural the insecurity of all inland routes and the common piracies of the Shaṭṭ, both populace and foreign merchants were content with urban security. Complaints of exaction, petty injustice, extorted presents, are indeed frequent in the dispatches of the time: but even these, less irksome under some governors than others, were subject to appeal to the Court of Baghdad. Year by year profitable trade was done. The French agent—first a priest, later a layman—kept permanent house in Baṣrah after 1755. The Portuguese had gone for ever. The Dutch moved to Kharaq Island in 1752. Several Italians had business at the port, Armenian and Jew bargained with Persian and Indian, Arab traders brought Yaman coffee and

[1] Sources: Olivier (iv, pp. 343 ff.); Joseph Emin (p. 450 f.); Parsons (pp. 154-62 ff.); Capper (p. 222); Irwin (p. 379). The *Précis* is valuable. 'Iraqi authorities as for the rest of the period.

returned with dates. The Honourable Company imported metal-ware and woollens, and bartered these for cash and for Persian silk. Its representative, promoted from Resident to Agent in 1763, was in 1764 strengthened by the grant of consular status—a step of great moment, long since taken by the French. The new rank brought no political ambitions: it was meant but to assist the head of the Factory in his self-defence against the rapacity of Aghas and the jealous bickering of the Frenchman. With similar objects a half-permanent Agent—first Armenian in 1755, then English ten years later—was now maintained at Baghdad.

The prosperity of the port was (though not prominently) among the causes of strained relations between Pasha and Regent. Had there been no other, Karim Khan might have been well content: for little prosperity survived the terrible plague of 1773. A reduced garrison, neglected buildings, increasing crime, cessation of trade, few and feeble surviving citizens: these were the legacy of the disease found by the Company's Agent on his return in October from Bombay, whither he had retired with his Factory in April.

As the plague subsided the menace of invasion grew. News of a threatened Persian attack was abroad. The Agent was dissuaded from instant evacuation of his stock only by the Muta-sallim's tactical arguments and promises. The Cha'ab, whose boats would be invaluable to either side, continued to flaunt a fickle treachery. Their promise to desert the Persians if need arose was followed by seizure of a Turkish ship. It was rescued by a British. They then with a threatening gesture withdrew all their tribesmen from Baṣrah. In this atmosphere of fear and doubt passed the year 1774.

At midwinter, raids of Cha'ab bandits showed clearly the open weakness of the town. With the new year, rumours of imminent danger revived, conferences were daily held between Sulaiman Agha and the Qaptan, notables and the Agent. The garrison mustered some fifteen thousand, but raw levies and tribesmen formed all but a tithe of these.[1] Guns were largely unserviceable, walls cracked and rotten, Intelligence service confined to casual informers. The protests of the Englishman were

[1] Olivier (iv, p. 344).

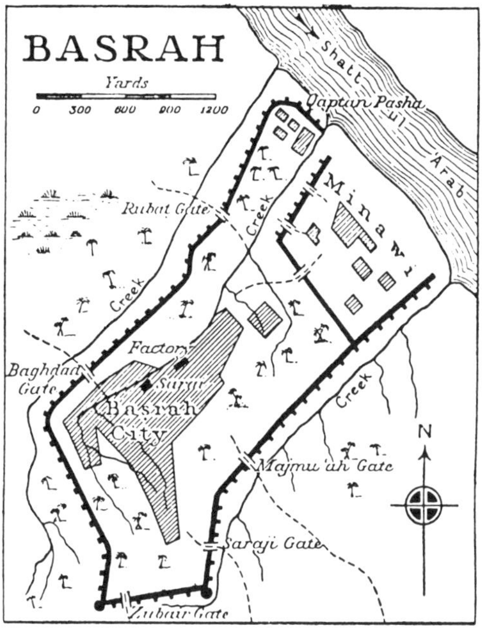

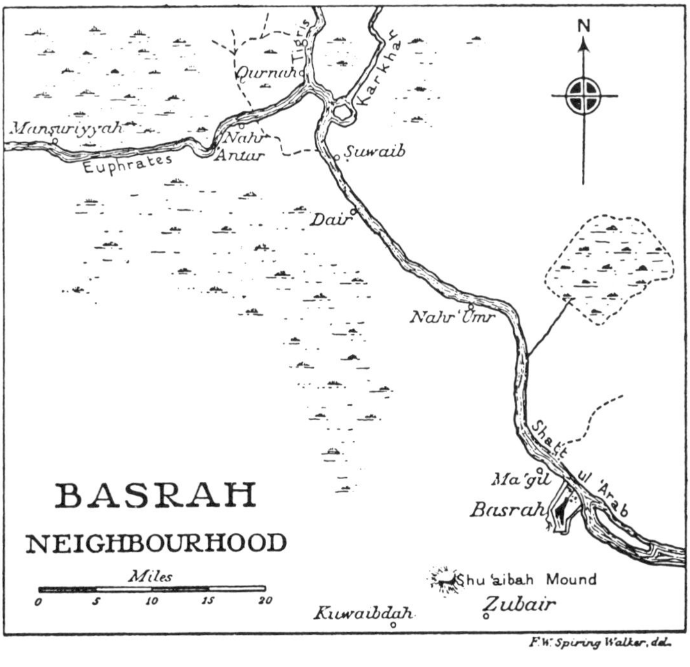

F. W. Spiring Walker, del.

unheeded until, as doubt changed into menacing certainty, the Mutasallim began vigorously to press on his preparations and to inspire a spirit of defence. Stores of provisions and munitions were collected and disposed, walls repaired, duties allotted. "The Musolem" writes an eyewitness "is not only very brave, but active and vigilant, and is almost the whole day on horseback, continually in action, overseeing the repairing of the walls, the gun carriages, and the mounting of the artillery. . . ." All blamed the Pasha of Baghdad for his delay in sending reinforcements.

On the 16th of March the long-expected enemy, some thirty thousand strong, reached the Shaṭṭ ul 'Arab near the mouth of the Ṣuwaib river. The Muntafiq contingent, posted on the right bank below Qurnah to resist a crossing, declined the task and retired incontinently: the Persians advanced unhindered to the western bank. Letters simultaneously reached the Turkish and British authorities from Ṣadiq Khan, brother of the Regent, requesting deputies to meet him and discuss suitable ransom. To these no reply was sent. A week later a second deputation from the Khan demanded two lakhs of rupees from Baṣrah as the price of its safety. Again no answer was given. The Cha'ab fleet meanwhile, sailing up the Shaṭṭ past Baṣrah, had joined the Persian and bestowed upon him the one facility he lacked. To meet it a boom of chained boats was undertaken above the mouth of the 'Ashar Creek; and the confidence given by it to the defenders increased with the arrival of two hundred Janissaries from Baghdad, with promises of further help, and with the return to service of the Muntafiq shaikhs—Thamir to Baṣrah, 'Abdullah to Zubair.

On the 16th of April the Persians formed their camp[1] three miles upstream of 'Ashar. Patrols ranged round the city. After three days, on a dark night, an assault was made upon the northern face. For two hours the Persians endeavoured to scale the walls. The resistance of the Basrawis (and notably the Muntafiq of Thamir) was encouraged by the shrill screams of their women.[2] The creek head was well held by the Qaptan. The attack failed, and daylight saw the heads of Persians

[1] The camp, as the siege went on, became more and more elaborate. Irwin (p. 379).
[2] Cf. Joseph Emin (p. 150).

exposed at the gates. The whole manhood of the town was in arms. Negro and Armenian rubbed shoulders with Janissary and marsh Arab. Carmelite monks were among the forces of Sulaiman. The energy and contagious spirit of the Mutasallim were the soul of the defence.

But the night attack cost the garrison two desertions. The Muntafiq tribesmen fled from Zubair, and the Agent and his staff retired with as little dignity.[1] Their part had been both inconsistent and inglorious since the correct policy of neutrality had been deserted. No sooner had the Persian army appeared than a British ship had sailed upstream and found touch with Ṣadiq Khan. The Agent and council were at all times to be seen riding round the walls, parleying with the Mutasallim, tendering warnings and advice. The Company's officers had tried vainly to prevent the Cha'ab fleet from joining the Persians, had helped to construct the 'Ashar boom, and, on the day before the night attack, given chase to a Persian fleet ascending the Shaṭṭ ul 'Arab from Bushire. After so complete an identification of the Company with the Turkish defenders, the stealthy embarkation of the Englishmen during the night attack was a sorry end.[2] Their descent[3] of the Shaṭṭ ul 'Arab was enlivened by a fierce cannonade with Persian ships.

The defection of the Company's fleet still did not give complete command of the river to the Persians. The boom prevented communication up and down stream; the Qaptan had a few craft that floated and might engage an equal number of the Cha'ab; the British at Bushire held considerable force[4] while treating with Karim Khan; and some four months later an arrangement was made by the Mutasallim with the Imam of 'Uman. A year before, Karim Khan had demanded Turkish co-operation against the Imam. None had been given, and to

[1] Olivier is wrong in placing the British evacuation before the siege. The Agent of the French company, and some Italians under his protection, stayed in Baṣrah throughout.

[2] Parsons (p. 186). The judgement of Mr. Moore, the Agent, in the matter was no doubt generally criticized.

[3] The Armenian adventurer Joseph Emin was in command of the *Success* (op. cit., pp. 451 ff.).

[4] Among craft at Bushire was H.M.S. *Seahorse*, in which Nelson was a midshipman. He seems at some time to have visited Baṣrah (Mahon, *Life of Nelson*, p. 4).

gratitude for this the ‘Uman ruler could now add the promise of generous pay. His mercenary ships held the Shaṭṭ for the late summer of 1775, and enabled supplies to be brought into Baṣrah.

This explains but partially the long resistance that the city was able to offer. The enemy blockade, indeed, was never complete; the familiar device of dyke-breaking was adopted in April 1775; and the co-operation of parties of Muntafiq and Bani Khalid outside enabled caravans to reach the city, though the attacking force had gained allies of similar value, the Khaza‘il. But the distress within was ever increasing. The determination of Sulaiman Agha barely sustained the defence through the winter of 1775. By early spring the poorer classes were in desperate straits. They had sold everything for bread. Work or wages there were none. Hope from Baghdad had been abandoned. Ṣadiq Khan, whose artillery had done little damage to the walls, waited patiently for surrender.[1]

This by the middle of April 1776 was inevitable. Provisions, ammunition, vitality were exhausted. Resistance must be futile, and could not but be fatal to hundreds of the starving. A letter, it was even said, had been received by the Agha from Baghdad advising surrender. He read it to the collected notables. The last straw had been placed: a deputation left for the Khan's camp to discuss conditions. The Persians under ‘Ali Naqi and ‘Ali Muḥammad Khan entered in good order the following morning. Beyond forcible billeting and minor incidents, no violence or disorder was allowed.[2] The state entry of the Regent's brother took place a week later. A garrison of some 6,000 troops was placed in the town. The Mutasallim and a party of notables were sent to honourable captivity in Shiraz.

First indications all pointed to a temperate rule. The Company hastened back to its Factory. But bad times were in store. The Persians were neither content with their present conquest nor ready to abandon their usual methods. The levy upon the

[1] Olivier (iv, p. 347) blames also the folly of Ṣadiq in postponing assault at the bidding of his astrologers. His gunners were under European commanders.

[2] This sets aside the rather conventional atrocities recorded by Muṭali‘u'l Su‘ud and Duḥat.

town of a large sum produced the inevitable results: the wealthiest citizens undertook the collection, while the poor found the money. Oppression and abuse spread upwards. More and more looked to the Agent[1] as their protector: the previous sorry exploits of the Company were forgotten. Ṣadiq Khan retained the governorship, and showed a tolerance and sense worthy of the Regent; but in his long absences the rule devolved upon ʿAli Muḥammad Khan,[2] a dissolute and brutal wretch.

The population of Baṣrah had now endured a terrible visitation of the plague, followed by intensive military service, the extremities of hunger, and the occupation of their homes by foreign soldiery. Had they been less broken and spiritless, a general rising might have ended the Persian rule. As it was, the sole hope was from the tribes. The Persian governor held little but the town and a few gardens; the Muntafiq were watching for a moment of sufficient weakness; even the Khazaʿil rather respected than obeyed the rare farmans of the Khan. Albu Muḥammad and Bani Lam were unaffected by Baṣrah sieges and occupations, while Bani Khalid withdrew to their oases far to the south.

Zubair[3] maintained a precarious freedom for some months. But early in 1778 ʿAli Muḥammad, wearied of the too easy rapes and robberies of the city, conducted a pitiless raid against it.[4] In the facile slaughter of defenceless townspeople a number of subjects of the Muntafiq Shaikh were lost; and to it may be ascribed (with other forays not recorded) the extreme bitterness of that tribe against the Persians. Reference is made[5] to an encounter where tribal generosity had been repaid by ferocious treachery. Not loyalty to the Ottoman, but hatred and disgust of Persia, led Shaikh Thamir to nurse schemes for the release of Baṣrah. The last collision between them was on a considerable scale.[6] The Persians had advanced some miles into Muntafiq country. The force of ʿAli Muḥammad was six thousand horse,

[1] Mr. Latouche.
[2] Nephew of Karim Khan. Duḥat wrongly says brother.
[3] For description of this place in 1771, see Carmichael, p. 48.
[4] Capper, *Observations* (p. 224).
[5] *A Gentleman* (p. 12).
[6] The incident is from Muṭaliʿu'l Saʿud, more briefly in Duḥat, copied by Jaudat Pasha; cf. Capper and *A Gentleman* (loc. cit.). A number of discrepancies in these accounts have been partly ignored, partly reconciled, in the text above.

as many foot, and eighteen river-boats bearing guns. Muḥammad Ḥusain Khan was left in Baṣrah with two thousand rifles as Muḥafidh. The Shaikh had picked his ground at Fuḍhailah not many miles from 'Arjah. Ever retreating, the Muntafiq drew their enemy into a trap. A space of level and humid ground was surrounded on two sides by a loop of the Euphrates, on another by impassable marsh; the fourth, through which the Persians were led to enter, was held by a section of Thamir's forces. The Persian charge carried them into marshy ground from which the tribesmen swerved aside. Extricated with difficulty and loss, they turned to find the outlet held. Hundreds were drowned in trying to escape by swimming, as many slaughtered. 'Ali Muḥammad was among the slain. So thorough was the massacre that but three men, it was said, reached Baṣrah. The stripping of the battle-field lasted for weeks. The bones of so many slain marked the site for a generation.

The Baṣrah garrison was hastily reinforced from Shiraz, but never to its original strength. Ṣadiq Khan opened negotiations with the Muntafiq for an honourable submission to Persian rule: his offers, which included religious clauses in the Shia' interest, were refused. Thamir was kept fully informed of affairs in Baṣrah, whose population was now reduced to the scale of a large village. Commercial life was dead. The removal of the Factory was imminent. Rumours of help from Baghdad and of peace with Persia were the sole springs of hope. In September 1776 news had arrived of great sums reaching Baghdad for a Persian war; in the following spring a relieving army from the north was daily expected; a year later Commissioners were said to have met at Shiraz. Meanwhile the occupation, costly and inglorious to the Regent, insulting if not threatening to the Turks, and disastrous to the people of Baṣrah, dragged on for four years.

Early in 1779 Ṣadiq Khan, returning from a visit to his brother in Shiraz, commenced to repair a commanding fort on the left bank opposite 'Ashar. This was the shadow of a coming event: the fort would cover his withdrawal when the end of his brother's now uncertain life necessitated his return with all his forces to Persia. In the middle of March the expected news arrived. Struggles for the throne of Persia were inevitable. Ṣadiq Khan could not delay. He summoned the notables, entrusted them with the temporary government of the city, and promised to release Sulaiman Agha. The cowed Baṣrawis accepted the new position without disturbance, while the Persians evacuated land and river without a backward glance.

§ 2. *Accession of the Great Pasha: the man and the times.*[1]

Sulaiman Agha had passed four years in Persia. He was kept in constant touch with Baṣrah by his friends, by Khoja Yaq'ub his indispensable Jewish banker, and by Aḥmad Agha, a promoted groom in his confidential service. At Shiraz his wit and wisdom made him many friends. In particular he gained the intimacy of Zaki Khan, half-brother of Karim, and now owed to him (and not after all to Ṣadiq) his restoration to 'Iraq and to his former government of Baṣrah. Ṣadiq Khan, an obvious claimant for the throne of Persia, was deserted by his own men and fled for safety.

The Agha made his way with his fellow captives to Ḥuwaizah, where he halted to appreciate his prospects. Shaikh Thamir, his enemy, held the city. Baghdad had already dispatched Na'man Agha as Mutasallim, in spite of representations from the port urging the appointment of their veteran Agha, to whom pressing invitations were also sent. He bade Na'man surrender the government, but could not advance to assume it as long as Muntafiq forces dominated Baṣrah. The Mutasallim refused. The position was resolved by the death of Thamir in tribal fighting, whereat the shaikhly rank fell to Thuwaini ul 'Abdullah, the friend (at this time) of Sulaiman. The Agha was bidden to enter the town. Simultaneously arrived the farman for his appointment to the ayalat with the rank of Mirmiran. In the few weeks of his stay, life was restored to the quays and bazaars of the depleted and impoverished town; but his heart was elsewhere. He knew himself for the first man in 'Iraq, and

[1] The period 1780–1802, and that succeeding it till 1826, is well served. The main vernacular source, Duḥat, is followed closely by Muṭali'u'l Sa'ud, and generally by Thabit Effendi. Mira'tu'l Zaura lightly touches this period. Ghayatu'l Muram embodies a separate (and predominately Mosul) tradition. Jaudat Pasha condenses Duḥat. Mosul authorities as before. The *Précis* continues of assistance. The most valuable travellers are Sestini (1781), Franklin (1787), Howel (1788), Olivier (1796), Jackson (1797), Abu Ṭalib (1802). Details of these and several less important are found in Appendix I (§ ii). Rich is invaluable on Baban affairs.

lost no means of urging the fact upon his Sovereign. In this he had a powerful helper in the British Agent, the kindly and popular Latouche.[1] The Agent supported his candidature as that of both a friend and a debtor, and further acted as his private go-between in dispatching large sums to Stambul for judicious disbursement. The Padishah was not deaf to such arguments. He had seen the succession of failures at Baghdad, and bowed to the need of another Mamluk. The Wazarat and the rule of the three ayalats[2] was conferred upon the generous candidate who alone could restore them.

Leaving the Qaptan as Mutasallim, he left Baṣrah in the spring of 1780 with a large force of Muntafiq under Thuwaini and a contingent from Zubair. Isma'il Agha had come south to 'Arjah to welcome him. Sulaiman interrupted his compliments by the removal, there and then, of his head. Three " treasurers " of the Agha's staff were summarily banished, the lesser folk treated with generous favour. At Karbala he made pilgrimage and dismissed Thuwaini. At Ḥillah, Sulaiman ul Shawi greeted the new Pasha in state. At the Mas'udi bridge was held the official reception by the whole body of notables and divines. Outside the city he camped for two days: then, refusing yet to enter upon his government, passed straight through Baghdad against the rebel force of 'Ajam Muḥammad and his confederates. Crossing the Diyalah, he won a complete victory. The forces of disorder were finally scattered. Aḥmad ul Khalil was killed, the detested Persian fled to Luristan. Not till July 1780 did the freedman Pasha occupy in state the capital of his now pacified province.

The place of Buyuk Sulaiman Pasha in history is not among the giants. He was neither conqueror nor legislator. His name is associated with no world-event nor with the rule of a mighty empire. He had admirable, but not the rarest, qualities of character. He did not far surpass his age and country in enlightenment. Yet his title is not ill earned. To no other Pasha of Baghdad, in three centuries and a half, did it fall to be

[1] The part played by British diplomacy in securing this post for Sulaiman Pasha was well known at the time; cf. Brydges, *Wahauby* (p. 187); Sestini (p. 161); Irwin (p. 339).

[2] The farman for the Shahrizor province followed the other by a few weeks.

known simply as "The Great". More homely and more convincing than the extravagancies of oriental praise is the considered account of an Englishman[1] who knew him in many relationships over many years:

"Suleiman was, perhaps, as fine a specimen of a Turkish Pasha as ever existed. Born a Georgian, he was possessed of great manly beauty—his stature and face were such as to give the greatest effect to the magnificence of the Turkish dress—his countenance had a strong expression of reflection and humanity—he was as expert in all military and field exercises and sports as those who made them their employment and profession—sincere and warm in the exercise and belief of his own religion, he was as tolerant as a Turk could be to those whom an article of his own faith bound him to consider as infidels—exact and economical in his own expenses, he was accused of avarice, but when he considered his country to be in danger he readily and freely parted with that which he had amassed slowly and by degrees. . . . His Court was splendid, and the establishment of his household was on the scale of that of a great sovereign. In the early part of his life he had received many favours and great assistance from the English, and to the very last moment he acknowledged this."

Of his geniality and humour the same witness has pleasant examples. Other European spectators do not differ in their estimate. To one,[2] the Pasha was "un bel homme, d'une physionomie gaie et ouverte, il passe pour très-brave"; to a critical observer[3] of his declining years, his government is strikingly contrasted with his predecessors:

"Il s'est appliqué à soulager la classe malheureuse, et empêcher que ces principaux officiers ne commissent des injustices, ou se permissent des actes de tyrannie. Il n'a pas souffert que les Arabes troublassent la navigation des deux fleuves. Il a favorisé le commerce en le protégant de tous ces moyens. . . . Sa bravoure lui a valu l'éstime de tous les gens de guerre: la tranquillité qu'il a maintenue à Baghdad, et la justice qu'il y a fait régner, ont fait aimer sa personne, ont fait bénir sa gouvernement. . . . Il avait, dans tous les circonstances, donné des preuves de courage, montré . . . de l'energie et de l'activité:—s'était

[1] Harford Jones (Brydges), *Wahauby* (pp. 190–1).
[2] Sestini (p. 163).
[3] Olivier (iv, pp. 350–2).

constamment occupé de tous les détails de l'administration, écoutant lui-même les plaintes des malheureux, se faisant rendre compte des affaires au tribunal de justice . . ."

With his entry of Baghdad opens the golden age of the Slave-government of 'Iraq. For over thirty years the phenomena of paramount power in the hands of imported Caucasian freedmen had been growing in clearness and reality. For fifty years more the rule of 'Iraq was to lie, with the helpless acquiescence of the Sultan, solely with Pashas of this alien blood. In the long reign of Sulaiman Pasha there was no hint of a rival: the struggles which followed his death were largely those of rival Georgians; and only the coincidence of a world reanimated by the French Revolution, a Turkey partially westernized, a reforming Sultan, and an 'Iraq laid low by abnormal blows of fortune, availed to remove the last of the slave-rulers from Baghdad.

In Mamluk Egypt, for a century before their final suppression the Caucasians ruled with bare tolerance of the Turkish flag and the powerless governor sent yearly from Stambul. In 'Iraq the slave-ruler was himself the Ottoman Pasha, appointed and yearly ratified by the Padishah. He governed in that Sovereign's name, however little to his profit; his staff and forces included Turks of Stambul; and it was not until the accession of Sulaiman the Great that the central government ceased to attempt the appointment of extraneous governors. The rise of Abu Lailah was forced upon it, and he survived its efforts to remove him. 'Umr Pasha was deposed not least because of his position as leader of the Slaves. But the special difficulties of governing the 'Iraq, the actual presence of the Slaves, in formidable force, and the preoccupation of the central power with a long and losing struggle in Europe, finally led to acquiescence in the rule of the local dynasty until new forces without and within changed all.

It is important correctly to conceive the singular relations now existing between the governments of 'Iraq and the Empire. Mere revolt was the commonest phenomenon at this period of Ottoman decline: the authority of the Sultan "was scarcely recognized, even in name, in many of the best provinces of which he styled himself the ruler". The historian of Turkey goes on to quote Wahhabi Arabia and Mamluk Egypt:

"In Syria, the Druses and the Mutualis of Mount Lebanon and the hill-country of Palestine were practically independent tribes and so were the Suliotes, and others in northern Greece and Epirus. So were the Montenegrins and dwellers in Hirzegovena, Moldavia, and Wallachia, though in form restored to Turkey, were in reality far more under Russian than Ottoman authority. . . . Revolt and civil war were the common practices of the chief Pashas. In Acre Djazzar Pasha refused tax and tribute, and put to death the Sultan's messengers . . . the same was the case with the Pashas of Trebizonde and Akhalzik. In Widdin, the celebrated Paswan Oglu for many years defied the whole force of the Sultan . . . like an independent and avowed foreign enemy. These are only some of the most conspicuous instances of vice-regal revolt."[1]

Of these many and melancholy phases of scism and revolt, that of 'Iraq is among the most curious. The Slave-Pashas at no time renounced their allegiance to the Sultan. In prayers, coinage, constant reports and rarer presents and yet less frequent tribute, in all the externals of public life, loyal vassaldom was complete. In the maintenance of public order, wherein Imperial troops marched side by side with the Georgian guards of the Pashaliq, the Slave-Pashas compare well with any ruler who ever bought the province in Stambul. They sought to protect it from Wahhabi and Persian: they waged no wars with neighbours within the Empire.[2] The dispatch of large contributions to the expenses of their master's wars was not unknown.[3] Yet whatever they showed of love and zeal for their nation and faith was that of proselytes. The majority were born Christians, none were Turks. Their power was based upon the close disciplined fraternity of their countrymen in a foreign land where, had they not ruled, they must have served. In the half-century now following, the power of the Georgian Pasha, supported by the only civil and military organization in the country, was that of an independent monarch. A half-hereditary dynasty, neither Turkish nor helped

[1] Creasy (pp. 447–8). Cf. Lane-Poole, "Lord Stratford de Redcliffe" (1890 ed.), p. 199 f.

[2] Niebuhr (ii, p. 258) cites an example from the Pashaliq of Abu Lailah—of which, however, there is no hint in any other authority: ". . . il est une fois allé à Damas et a pillé cette ville . . ."

[3] The outstanding example is Buyuk Sulaiman himself, who, says Brydges (p. 191), sent no less than half a million sterling to Yusif Pasha, the Grand Wazir, during his campaign in Egypt against the French.

to power by the government of Turkey, was now so firmly installed that for fifty years the Sultan could reckon 'Iraq but a respectful neighbour; and it so appeared to residents in Stambul.[1] The half-sacred farman of the Sultan was, however, as keenly sought by rival Georgians as it must have been indifferently bestowed by him on these usurping low-born foreigners whom he had never seen. This actual impotence over his own domains was accepted by the Sultan with less and less acquiescence as the spirit of reform grew in Europe and decade succeeded decade without restoring Baghdad to the fold. Yet the defection was never complete nor felt to be permanent, nor ceased to be sweetened by every outward respect. Many a province less remote than 'Iraq went far beyond it in dangerous faction and offensive disloyalty.

§ 3. *Tribes and vassals, 1780 to 1802.*

At the time of his accession, Sulaiman Pasha had already passed his sixtieth year. A reign of twenty-two years lay before him; and not until near its close did he show signs of failing strength. Yet, in a province stretching from the Milli Kurds beyond Mardin to the Karun river—a province lately weakened by plague, torn by civil war, invaded by foreign armies—a province replete always with every phase of division and disturbance—there was enough to weary the strongest. The old man was to see usurpation and dangerous intrigue in Baṣrah, an ally that was almost a rival in Shahrizor; the great tribe-confederations of the middle Euphrates rather gained than lost strength never loyally employed: factions in Mosul called for control, Mardin for frequent peacemaking; Sinjar and Cha'ab, 'Amadiyyah and the Holy Cities distracted the old ruler and his advisers even while new enemies threatened from Arabia. His own courtiers were to turn to rebels, blood to be shed before his eyes. Ceaseless effort was needed to maintain a minimum of respect for Pasha and Khalif. On another view, there was fair security in much of 'Iraq: trade was normally prosperous, city-life thriving and pleasant enough. A large and loyal force garrisoned Baghdad. The revenues, obtained without extortion, sufficed for the country's needs and for the mission of large sums

[1] Eton (p. 279).

to Stambul to assist the Sultan's arms in Egypt. We are dealing, in fact, with a Pashaliq great in length, wealth, and moderation, but disfigured, on a closer view, by the endemic diseases of the age and country.

In the city the new and promising régime was welcomed by slaves and citizens alike. The breach between these two remained: the old noblesse of Baghdad did not willingly see all the honourable governorships, all profitable farms, fall to the Georgian Aghas; but in their preference for an effective ruler over some oppressive voluptuary from the Capital they were united. Street-disorder melted before the appearance of firmness. Merchants returned from Persia or emerged from retirement. Fresh blood flowed through the city. Country areas round the Capital were not so quickly purged and revived. The victory and round-up of midsummer 1780 broke, indeed, all formidable resistance; but crime could be but gradually eradicated. The immediate difficulty of the Pasha was the absence of an adequate loyal force. The disorganized and dubious Janissaries were more danger than safeguard. The Slave-companies were thinned and scattered. But upon the latter his position must rest. He collected with all speed—locally and by fresh importation—a first instalment of a thousand Georgians, and set them to strenuous training. To the Janissaries he appointed officers of his own selection, and, at the risk of leaving himself perilously weak while the Georgian corps was yet untrained, divided them into posts on the middle Euphrates and the Khaliṣ area, rather than allow a concentration in Baghdad. Several of their leaders were put to death with public severity for trifling crimes: the loyal and useful were as generously rewarded. A few were banished from 'Iraq to join other units in Damascus and the Hijaz.

The chief tribal leaders of central 'Iraq made personal submission in the autumn of 1780. Some were detained in honourable employments, their spokesman with the Pasha being Ḥaji Sulaiman—chief of the 'Ubaid and head of the Shawi family—famous as councillor and diplomat. Of the tribes of the upper Euphrates, Diyalah, and middle Tigris, little is recorded in these years. For a long period no expeditions against them were necessary, and Baṣrah merchants (as the Agent reported) were glad to face the greater cost and delays of the Tigris route for the sake of its greater security. Not until 1797 did the Zubaid call for the mission of an army under the Kahya to punish robberies by road and river and to extract taxes overdue. The Rabi'ah were visited in the same year. In 1800 the shaikh of the Bani Lam was deposed, an interference which set the whole country from Tigris to Luristan ablaze. "The deposit shaikh has . . . attacked the shaikh appointed by the Pasha," the Agent wrote, "and the country from Coole [Kut?] to Gissar [Jaṣṣan] and from Gissar to the environs of Haviza [Ḥuwaizah] is in an actual state of confusion. The Shuma [Shammar] Arabs have on many occasions been . . . cruelly treated by this government . . . ." Mention of the Shammar shows that a leading tribal event of the time was now well advanced—their migration, under 'Anizah pressure, from west to east of the Euphrates. Sections spread themselves over the whole steppe from the Dujail and the Dulaim country northwards to Sinjar and beyond, while a branch, the Shammar Togah, crossed the Tigris and held its left bank from the Diyalah nearly to Kut. So great a movement affected the dirahs of a hundred tribes eased or displaced by it. It led, among others, to the 'Ubaid crossing the Tigris from Jazirah to Ḥawijah, when they bestrode the Jabal Ḥamrin.

In the middle Euphrates column after column was dispatched almost annually against the Khaza'il. A few months sufficed to show that hopes of better security in this region were vain. Ḥamad ul Ḥamud, the Khaza'il Shaikh, refused all control, scorned all orders. The sight of military preparations, and a final warning, did not avail: Sulaiman led out his forces, met and routed the tribal army. Shaikh Ḥamad replied by cutting the dykes; and the mud-islanded waste of reedy water that resulted was no possible theatre for a campaign. The Pasha countered with a remarkable feat, closed the breaches upstream and let the floods subside. Advance was now possible. Ḥamad fled west of the Euphrates. In the end, arrears of taxation were collected, indemnity levied, pardon and peace bestowed. The same history of disobedience and punishment, in the same difficult setting of the Shamiyyah country, was thereafter enacted in 1782 and 1784. The Euphrates route was scarcely used by such as valued life and property. In the Muntafiq troubles of 1787, the

Khaza'il were implicated. Five years later—and thereafter faithfully year by year—the wearisome succession of operations recommenced, and continued into the new century.

These were the worst but not the only offenders in central 'Iraq. Long-drawn hostilities with the 'Ubaid, which for five years made the very outskirts of Baghdad perilous, showed no less sadly the limits of the Pasha's power. They sprang in this instance less from the usual sources of tribal rebellion than from a clash of persons. Mention has been made of Aḥmad Agha, a confidential servant of Sulaiman. From the humblest duties he had become the agent and intimate of his master, with the high office of Muhurdar (Seal-bearer). He was both a champion of the Georgians (for whom he stood in the forthcoming struggle) and a striking personality destined for twelve years to be the second figure in the Pashaliq. Of singular attraction in face and figure, dignified, scholarly, and luxurious, and impressing all with his humanity and moderation, he was honoured in 1785 with the rank of Mirmiran and the position of Kahya. Among candidates of noble blood and more conspicuous record this appointment of the promoted menial caused deep resentment, and in none more than in Ḥaji Sulaiman ul Shawi. Between the freedman and the Arab aristocrat there had already been bitter jealousy. Both had the Pasha's ear; the Ḥaji was the more formidable, Aḥmad the more beloved. On his promotion he plied his master with stories of the Shawi's treasonable correspondence and dangerous ambition. Sulaiman Pasha, convinced, seized his property and bade him leave Baghdad. He fled to his tribe, which instantly rose in rebellion. Aḥmad was dispatched early in 1786 to quell the rebels. They retired before him, from the 'Ubaid country to Takrit, from Takrit to the Khabur. As the Kahya retired, Ḥaji Sulaiman returned; and to this menace a misfortune was added by natural causes. The spring flood of 1786 was abnormally low, no rain fell, the harvest entirely failed. Prices rose to famine level. The Pasha threw open his private granaries. Many fled the country, more died of hunger or consequent disease. These conditions produced a misery dangerous to the State. A crowd in Baghdad called curses on the Pasha as the cause of the famine; violence spread in the favourable atmosphere of desperation and superstition;

and finally the Pasha was forced to arrest ringleaders and scatter the crowd with troops. Order was thus restored until nature removed the cause.

The Shawi still hovered between the Khabur and the outskirts of Baghdad. His tribal army was joined by every rascal and outcast of the capital and villages. Roads and gardens around Baghdad were in constant fear. The Kahya, again dispatched against his rival, was heavily defeated; and the 'Ubaid with their motley allies, formidable in their triumph, drew nearer to the capital of which an organized siege seemed possible. Merchants and officials in Mosul and Baṣrah eagerly watched the course of the rebellion. Consternation, at this juncture, was caused by a sudden rumour that the rebel Ḥaji had been appointed Beglerbegi and Governor of the three provinces. Sulaiman Pasha himself believed it,[1] and begged the intercession of the Company's Agent. The story was untrue, but the wretched conditions of insecurity and half-blockade went on. Kadhimiyyah and Kirkh were harried and barely defended with 'Ugail help. Finally the Shawi rebel, deserted by his kinsmen and fearing again to face the troops of the Pashaliq, fled to Shaikh Thuwaini at Suq ul Shuyukh.

The great leader of the Muntafiq had kept his tribe loyal and tranquil for six years. In operations against the Cha'ab in 1784 he had effectively aided the Mutasallim. He had learnt from that campaign, however, the weakness of the Turks and the devotion of his own following. A swing of the pendulum was due, and the lure of Baṣrah could not be resisted. The Shawi outlaw sat at his councils: Ḥamad of the Khaza'il readily joined. His forces advanced on Zubair, where Ibrahim Beg, Mutasallim since 1785, was seized with his staff without ceremony or warning and detained in close arrest. The following day Thuwaini sent a body of Muntafiq horsemen into Baṣrah, seized the Sarai, and scattered or won over the scanty garrison. There was no disorder. On the third day he made his own entry, with another five thousand men. Arab tribal government began.[2] Heads of government offices and captains of the fleet

[1] Cf. the dispatch of Mr. Manesty, the Resident, dated the 20th of February 1787 (*Précis*, p. 69, § 162).

[2] Apart from the 'Iraqi authorities (especially Duḥat), particulars of Thuwaini's usurpation are in the *Précis* (p. 70, § 163); Franklin (pp. 263 ff.); Howel (pp. 23 ff.); Ferrieres-Sauvebœuf (ii, p. 86).

were arrested and their property confiscated. A "loan" of six thousand tumans was demanded from the townspeople.

While preparing the sword, the Shaikh was busy with the pen. It was easy to obtain from the frightened Baṣrawis a many-sealed petition that their dearest wish was his recognition by the Sultan as their ruler. This appeal was dispatched to Stambul, with strong yet humble representations of his own. Meantime he left the city with his forces and camped on the Euphrates to await the inevitable avenging army from Baghdad. His brother remained as his deputy in Baṣrah.

Sulaiman Pasha had sent as usual for his Kurds of Baban, Darnah and Bajlan, borrowed Janissaries from the Jalili, and written to the Cha'ab Shaikh for assistance. He was joined by Ḥamud ul Thamir, the eager rival of Thuwaini. The army entered the Khaza'il dirah and descended in late October 1787 to Umm ul 'Abbas in Muntafiq country, where a stern and bloody battle was fought. Thuwaini and his forces, repulsed and scattered, fled from the field. Baṣrah was entered without opposition. Ḥamud ul Thamir was appointed Shaikh of the Muntafiq, and Muṣṭafa Agha Mutasallim. The Pasha levied an indemnity upon the town, and doubled the customs duties for the rest of the year: then, leaving a garrison of Lawand irregulars, he returned to central 'Iraq. Some months later Ḥaji Sulaiman ul Shawi at last made overtures for terms, and received a conditional pardon, which forbade him residence in Baghdad.

But Baṣrah troubles were yet incomplete. After a year of tranquillity there followed a dangerous conspiracy involving the highest officers in southern 'Iraq and the rulers of Shahrizor. The new Kurdish Mutasallim of Baṣrah, fired possibly by some racial feeling besides ambition, seduced his Lawand garrison, wrote to 'Uthman Pasha Baban to synchronize a rising which should give independence to both, and by bribes and presents won over his Baṣrah officers. Sending for the outlaw Thuwaini, he wrote to Baghdad that Ḥamud ul Thamir was unequal to the rule of the Muntafiq, and the former Shaikh must be restored. Sulaiman Pasha was well informed. He consented indeed to the restoration of Thuwaini, but simultaneously transferred the commander of the Baṣrah cavalry to Baghdad and sent Muḥammad ul Shawi to the port bearing a public caution to the Mutasallim and a private request to the Qaptan Pasha. This was to remove the Mutasallim by a sudden blow. The Qaptan, Muṣṭafa ul Hijazi, mismanaged the affair, and paid with his own head an instant penalty for his maladroitness. The news flashed to Baghdad; a campaign was now inevitable.

The complicity of the Shahrizor was still unknown to the Baghdad Court, until intercepted documents revealed that the ambitions of the Baban Pasha were for the province of Baghdad itself. If Sulaiman Pasha left for Baṣrah with his army, what easier than for the Kurd to descend upon the defenceless city? Sulaiman hastened to address a dispatch in flattering terms to the Baban capital: 'Uthman Pasha was invited to Baghdad, where with a thousand courtesies his daughter was betrothed to the brother of the Kahya. By these means he was separated both from his own forces and from the influence of his ally at Baṣrah. In February 1789 the Baghdad force moved out. The campaign proved bloodless. As Baṣrah was approached, all opposition collapsed. Muṣṭafa Agha took ship to Kuwait, Thuwaini made for the desert.[1] Ḥamud was restored in the Muntafiq, and another of the Georgian Aghas—'Isa ul Mardini[2]—appointed to the Baṣrah Government. Of him and his successors nothing significant remains. Conditions at Baṣrah remained normal for the rest of the long reign. In 1791 ill relations with the Cha'ab led to the erection of riverain forts, increase of piracy, and indecisive contact of the Turkish and tribal fleets. Seven years later the unheeded demands of Sayyid Sulṭan, the ruler of Masqaṭ, for the settlement of old claims nearly led to an attack on Baṣrah by 'Uman forces. The British Agent was asked to mediate: but without his help some terms were arranged and the crisis passed. Ḥamud ul Thamir—hero of tribal legend for his eccentric personality—kept the headship of the Muntafiq for six years. The last exploit of Thuwaini (restored in 1796) belongs to a later page.

Many weeks' march from the Shaṭṭ ul 'Arab lay the hill

[1] Thuwaini took refuge at Kuwait ("Grain") whence Sulaiman Pasha was powerless to secure his extradition (Brydges, *Wahauby*, p. 176), and later journeyed to the Wahhabi capital Dar'iyyah. Thereafter he was pardoned in 1792 (the "year of pardons") and lived for five years in Baghdad.

[2] *Précis*, p. 70, § 163.

country of the Babans who had thought to join the Baṣrah Governor in a league of rebellion. No other case occurs of close relations between Shahrizor and the port; but with Baghdad they were now of the closest. The young Kurdish nobles lived habitually in Baghdad, and found there materials to deepen and widen their own feuds. Their wealth and retainers made them the observed of the Wali and his Ministers; and in intrigues with these each hoped to further his own or some kinsman's aims. Only with a son in high favour at Baghdad or Karmanshah could a reigning Baban feel secure. To the ruler of 'Iraq, distrusting his Janissaries and still drilling his new Georgians, the troops of Shahrizor were of the greatest service. Thousands strong, they came at his call to quell a rebel or ride down an outlaw. Well fed and mounted, led by the head of a royal house, their standard of outfit and their conception of campaigning were higher by far than those prevalent in 'Iraq, while in the city the silk and brocades and rich equipages of the Kurdish Begs were a high ornament to the court. Against this, their constant intestine quarrels and invocations of foreign arms rendered their vassalage fickle and dangerous.

The history of their empire has been traced up to the precarious rule of Maḥmud Pasha Baban, who in 1778 had succeeded his brother Muḥammad and brought forces to aid Ḥasan Pasha outside Baghdad. Under the new reign the high favour of his nephew Ibrahim surpassed his own, and he was marked down for a dismissal which his intrigues accelerated. The Governor of Kirkuk was 'Uthman Beg, formerly Kahya of Ḥasan Pasha and an old friend of the Babans. His namesake 'Uthman Beg Baban (son of Maḥmud) approached him for joint rebellion; he agreed; and the blessing of Maḥmud confirmed the plan. Buyuk Sulaiman marched to Kirkuk, where a Mosul contingent joined him. Rivals and aspirants ran to his side, and of these he selected Ḥasan Beg, son of Sulaiman Pasha, to succeed his uncle. Ḥasan held the throne for a few days: Maḥmud then made his submission, accepted terms, and was reinstated. Keui, although bestowed on Maḥmud Beg Soran, was now definitely of the Baban empire, which internal feuds had not prevented from growing also at the expense of its Ruwanduz neighbours.

The terms were quickly violated and Keui attacked. A second expedition from Baghdad was met by renewed submission and compromise. In 1783 the fickle Kurd again broke his agreement, threw off his allegiance, and pillaged his neighbours. Sulaiman Pasha in person marched from Baghdad, collected troops as he progressed, and was joined by Ibrahim Pasha from Keui. Maḥmud was deserted by many of his followers, driven from his defences, and met an inglorious death in Persia. His son 'Uthman found pardon in Baghdad, and his nephew Ibrahim assumed the Baban government.

Ibrahim Pasha is best remembered for his completion of the town of Sulaimaniyyah, begun by Maḥmud Pasha in 1781 and named in compliment to the Great Pasha. He strengthened his administration and added wide lands in the areas of Zuhab, Qaṣr i Shirin, and Khaniqin to the Sulaimaniyyah empire. But before long he forfeited popular support by his preference for city-dwelling, and a rival, as usual, was at hand. Summoned to southern 'Iraq in 1787, he was slow to comply. 'Uthman replaced him and fought with distinction at the battle of Umm ul 'Abbas. He, however, in his turn was discredited by his complicity in the Baṣrah rising of 1788, and did not survive his supersession (again in favour of Ibrahim). He died in prison. The see-saw at Sulaimaniyyah went on. Ibrahim maintained himself but for a year, to be succeeded by the brother of 'Uthman, 'Abdu'l Raḥman Pasha. The latter had fled to Persia on news of his brother's death; but his relationship to the all-powerful Kahya secured both amnesty and promotion. If 'Abdu'l Raḥman Pasha could not rise superior and invulnerable to the constant ambitions of rivals, the task was indeed impossible. He possessed every quality of a strong and successful ruler: yet three times between 1789 and 1811 his government was broken by the successful intrusion of a kinsman. His second tenure was afflicted by an outbreak of plague and alarmed by an earthquake. In 1792 his forces were used by the Pasha of Baghdad against the outlaw Shawi. In 1794 they raided Jabal Sinjar and almost to Urfah. In 1799 three hundred Baban horsemen joined in a raid on the Yazidis. Thereafter the prayers of Ibrahim at Baghdad found answer: 'Abdu 'l Raḥman saw himself deposed in his cousin's favour, and consoled with Keui and

Ḥarir.[1] Early in 1802 he was recalled from the latter government, and with his brother Salim sent to captivity at Ḥillah.

Of the other south and central Kurdish states little need be said. Keui Sanjaq had fallen finally under Baban dominion, though its own Soran family still sometimes governed it by grace of the Pasha of Baghdad; more often the chief Baban pretender of the moment used it as a stepping-stone to the greater government of Sulaimaniyyah. Ruwanduz maintained itself, but with shrinking territories, behind the gorge which was its defence and customs-barrier. At 'Amadiyyah, the long reign of Bahram Pasha closed with his death in 1767. His son Isma'il, who succeeded him, ruled for a full generation. Only at his accession, and once more in 1787, was his position assailed by rivals; but his death let loose the ambitions of several candidates of the Baḥdinan house, sons and nephews of his own. Fierce civil war ended with the induction of Murad Beg by the Baban, whose orders were from Baghdad. The dependencies of 'Amadiyyah—'Aqrah, Dohuk, and Zakho—were commonly assigned to members of the same Baḥdinan family, and admitted the overlordship of the paramount Beg. Jazirah ibn 'Umr was passing through days of prosperity, broken by violent strife in 1782. A year before it had held its own against the ruler of Bitlis.[2]

Kirkuk and its dependent towns made no history. The ayalat of Shahrizor, once the great counterpart of Baghdad, was now not the most prized or the wealthiest of its dependencies. Kifri fell directly under Baghdad, and the hill-states of the Kurds from Diyalah to Greater Zab dealt less with the Mutasallim of Kirkuk than with his master the Georgian. The same is true, and more strangely, of Mosul itself. This never lost its ayalat status, was bestowed always by the Sultan himself on a candidate of rank not lower than Mirmiran, and maintained a court not incomparable to that of the Great Pasha. Yet areas on every

[1] The frequency of change in the Baban rulers was natural under circumstances where the appointment fell to short-lived popularity, precarious strength, or capricious favour. Real or threatened intrigues with Persia, and the existence at Baghdad of a Kahya as powerful as the Pasha, were further reasons; but to keep the leading Babans ever hoping for favour, and ever fearing to lose what they had, was no doubt a conscious item of Baghdad policy.

[2] Olivier (iv, p. 251); Sestini (p. 128).

side of Mosul looked less thither than to Baghdad for punishment or privilege. Some might deal indifferently with either, but all, and the Jalili himself, must see in Baghdad their final arbitrator.

The house of 'Abdu'l Jalil[1] maintained its special position. Few Pashas—but still a few—from outside the family ventured to assume the Mosul government. From the death of old Ḥaji Ḥusain to that of Buyuk Sulaiman, twenty governors held the small ayalat, and of these thirteen were Jalilis. The crowded annals of the dynasty belong rather to local than to general 'Iraq history: it mattered little outside the walls of Mosul—though within it provoked repeatedly the most violent factions—whether this son or that nephew of Ḥaji Ḥusain had gained a short-lived farman. Far more than the Mamluks of Baghdad, the Jalilis played a part in the wider affairs of Turkey. They were frequently at Stambul. Amin Pasha—seven times governor of Mosul—spent years in a Russian prison, Fattaḥ his cousin died on special duty in Syria, Sulaiman held a score of high offices in the Empire. Their appointment to the Pashaliq might therefore reward good service abroad, or courtiership at the capital, or—and most often—the mere favour of the Georgian at Baghdad. Among the best remembered of the struggles in their city to which fraternal jealousy gave birth were those which followed the death of Fattaḥ in 1771, and the fierce street-fighting between partisans of 'Abdu'l Baqi and Sulaiman (sometime Muḥafidh at Baghdad) in 1784. In the latter case the strife was decided by the Court of Baghdad in favour of 'Abdu'l Baqi; whose rule, however, was cut short but a year later by his death in action against the Yazidis of Sinjar. Thereafter four quiet years led to a long peaceful reign of Muḥammad Pasha Jalili, a time praised by his subjects and applauded even by visitors from Europe.[2] He governed for eighteen years.

The inclusion of Mardin in the Baghdad Pashaliq, three generations back, had brought with it the problems of the northern Jazirah. Here foothill Kurd met nomad Arab, while camps of Turkomans precariously cultivated between the two. The Kurds, in such areas of mixed race, are always dominant:

[1] See their family tree, Appendix II.
[2] Olivier (iv, p. 256); Mirza abu Ṭalib (p. 289).

and these—though they had kept little purity of blood, and political unity was unknown—all knew themselves as members of the Milli branch of the Kurdish race, and all could crowd round a leader of the right type. This only was needed to turn robbers into a serious army, insecurity into active threat. Early in the ninth decade of the century such a leader had appeared. This was Timur Pasha, a Kurd of noble birth who had held high office in Stambul. Falling suddenly from favour, he fled the Capital for the wide spaces of his Milli kinsmen.

"He there invited to his tents adventurers and outcasts from every quarter, so that he soon had a numerous force about him, formed of excellent materials for his purpose. For the life he was to lead as an independent freebooter no man could have been more fit, and he soon succeeded in making himself acknowledged lord of these domains, and feared even by the established Pashas of Diyarbakr and Aleppo."[1]

To the traffic of Mosul he was a special menace. The first efforts of troops against him were a failure; Sulaiman the Great was then commissioned by the Sultan himself to remove the nuisance, and marched northward to Mosul early in 1791. Here he rallied thirty thousand horse and moved on Mardin. Timur could not stand before such an army. His forces melted, himself fled, and the Milli were heavily punished. The Waiwodah of Mardin himself had not escaped suspicion: he was fined and deposed. Two leading adherents of Timur were hung in Mardin and Ibrahim his brother appointed paramount head of the Milli.

The authorities are too jejune, nor is the present interest sufficient, to encourage a full record of Mardin affairs. The Waiwodah or Mutasallim ranked as third officer of the Baghdad Pashaliq, under which the sub-province was directly governed.[2] The violence of party and personal strife in the town exceeded that of Mosul itself. In 1794 the Mutasallim was forcibly deposed, and his successor fared no better. In 1796 a mutiny led to the flight of the chief of the Musketeers, and the dispatch of his head to Baghdad. The Waiwodah was then himself expelled, and another appointed from crowds of obstreperous

[1] Buckingham, *Mesopotamia* (i, p. 293).

[2] This surprised travellers who observed its greater nearness to Diyarbakr.

candidates for power. What tribal supports and cleavages, what presents to Mosul and Baghdad and balancing of Turk and Georgian with Milli, what street factions in Mardin, what rivalries, intrigues, assemblies, bribes, and murders played their part in the dim violent tangled politics of this extreme corner of the Pashaliq, can be better imagined than set down. The town was provided with walls by Sulaiman Pasha. Timur Pasha was restored to his country, and that as Wali of Urfah, in 1800.

§ 4. *The Wahhabis.*

Turning now from the ceaseless infidelities and factions of Euphrates, Jazirah, and Kurdistan, the historian of 'Iraq is faced with a new foreign enemy to the Pashaliq—an enemy constant in aim for all his mobility, menacing for all his poverty, and scarcely less alarming to-day to the settled lands of western 'Iraq than in the hour of his first appearance. Arabia, which had produced the Prophet and a hundred far-reaching emigrations, had made one more great religious eruption from the Najd oases.

In the early years of Aḥmad Pasha, the colleges of Baghdad contained a pupil, Muḥammad bin 'Abdu 'l Wahhab, destined to bring great dangers to this country of his sojourn. Before we find him in the cool libraries by the Tigris, he had studied in Makkah, in Damascus, and in Baṣrah. In trading journeys he had seen the cities of many men, and observed Islam from many angles. His life's task was Revival—return to the purity of Islamic teaching at its source, war on luxury, subtlety, and insidious wilful error. Leaving Baghdad, he made pilgrimage and settled for a time at Madinah. Thereafter, on the death of 'Abdu 'l Wahhab his father, he devoted his later life to preaching his doctrine of Simplicity and Return at his own village of 'Uwainah in Najd. Forced to flee, he took refuge with a neighbouring Amir, Muḥammad bin Sa'ud of Dar'iyyah. As he grew year by year in ascendancy over ibn Sa'ud, the union of their temporal and spiritual powers gave unity and spirit to the tiny state, and by its conquests spread its creed. The Amir died in 1765, leaving the rising kingdom to his son (by the Reformer's daughter) 'Abdu 'l 'Aziz bin Sa'ud. By 1775 ibn Sa'ud was a power in Arabia.

Henceforth the Najd empire of ibn Sa'ud was completely identified with the Wahhabi creed. The narrow and iconoclastic, but fierce and proselytizing, sect enlarged their state while warring on the debased Muslims of their frontiers. Every raid had its religious sanction. Their shocked contempt of the luxurious apostates on all sides of Najd led them not only to violence but to such expressions as soon created the belief that their assault was on Islam itself. The wilder of their subject tribes and troopers had, indeed, little knowledge of Qur'an or Tradition; their fury against the corrupted versions of their faith far exceeded their wrath against Jew or Christian; for the Khalif and all things Turkish they had intolerant contempt.

The earliest foreign wars of the Wahhabis were against the Bani Khalid in Al Ḥasa. Here they made little headway; but their crusading raids went ever farther afield. Before 1790 'Iraq had become conscious of a new uneasy neighbour: fanatic bands, with distinctive badges on their camels and strange tags of religion imported into the familiar sport of the Ghazu, were invading the Dhafir, Muntafiq, and Shamiyyah grazing-grounds. Slowly the actual character of the threat was realized. To the familiar elusiveness of desert forces the new enemy on the 'Iraq fringes had added an inspiration deeply alarming to the powers of 'Iraq. Wahhabi Mullas haranguing in the guest-tents of the Euphrates—fanning the ready fuel of scorn for Pasha and Sultan, playing on superstition and avarice —might be a powerful agency to detach tribe after tribe from the last vestiges of Ottoman allegiance. For long it remained doubtful how far the fever would spread into 'Iraq. The frontier tribes, already harried by raids, were as likely to succumb to fear or argument as to stand up for the province of which they formed an outpost. The Jazirah fell increasingly to Wahhabi arms and their persuasions; but in 'Iraq the creed made little headway. The Wahhabi armies, posing as forces of light and delivery, met the welcome rather of heretics and robbers. The tribes of 'Iraq, Shi'i or Sunni, had no taste for a conversion heralded by fire and sheep-driving.

The first 'Iraqi to strike back was Shaikh Thuwaini,[1] newly

[1] Brydges (p. 27), commenting on the truce which followed 'Ali Pasha's expedition of 1798–9, adds "the fault of its infraction was laid by the

restored in 1797 to his home and rank. Grazing tribes and open villages in south-western 'Iraq had now for ten years been exposed to swift pitiless raids; they had defended themselves by flight, arms, or conversion, with no sign of government support. Conditions had grown worse since in 1792–5 the Wahhabis subdued the Bani Khalid. The whole Islamic world heard of the new danger to the Ḥaj pilgrims. The Sharif of Makkah had hastened to report the peril to the Sultan. The Porte from 1795–7 repeatedly bade their Georgian vassal at Baghdad to protect the Empire and chasten the Wahhabi. Very aged, intermittently an invalid, and now largely in the hands of his officers, the Pasha had distractions and expenses in plenty without looking to his desert border.[1]

Thuwaini, arrived at his native region, spent three months in collecting at Jahra tribal contingents, in amassing lead and powder, and dispatching a fleet with stores to Qaṭif. It was accompanied by a number of Baghdad 'Ugail, and more than one regiment of the standing mercenaries. Columns from Kuwait, Baḥrain, Zubair poured in. Meanwhile 'Abdu 'l 'Aziz bin Sa'ud was camped with his armies at Al Ṭurf in Al Ḥasa. Operations on both sides were leisurely. Thuwaini's advance towards Ḥasa, difficult in waterless country, was unopposed; his arrival at the walls of Al Darrak, in Bani Khalid country, was ominous to the Najd commanders, before whose eyes their Ḥasa empire might turn against them. The last advance was towards Al Shibak, reached on the evening of July 1, 1797. Thuwaini was there assassinated by a negro slave. The army, possessed of no bond or discipline save in his personality, instantly dispersed into fifty contingents, each eager for the safety of their homes. Thus in treachery and panic flight ended the last and

Turks on Twiney": that is, he considers Thuwaini to have survived it. Vernacular sources make it certain that Thuwaini's expedition preceded 'Ali Pasha's; cf. Jackson's *Journey* (p. 51), in which "Twyney" late in June 1797 "had been sent to oppose the Waaby".

[1] Burckhardt gives as reasons for Sulaiman Pasha's inactivity that "he had so few pecuniary resources, and his authority is so imperfectly acknowledged within the limits of his own province". The former statement is refuted by Brydges with exact knowledge (*Wahauby*, pp. 17–18); the latter is true, but did not preclude frequent expeditions in all directions. Truer reasons are, that the danger was not fully recognized in Baghdad (though it might be in Najf and Samawah) and that the Pasha was in his dotage.

better-deserving effort of the great Muntafiq Shaikh,[1] and the first counter-stroke of 'Iraq against the Wahhabi power.

A few weeks more than a year elapsed before the Pasha of 'Iraq, stirred by this defeat of his tribes and exhorted by his sovereign, had prepared a counter-stroke.[2] Throughout the summer of 1798 the new Kahya 'Ali Pasha was busied with the collection of an expedition on an unusual scale. It contained five thousand Janissaries, mercenary regulars, artillery rather plentiful than deadly, and contingents of the 'Ugail, 'Ubaid, Shammar, and other tribes. Muḥammad Beg ul Shawi accompanied the Kahya as adviser on desert affairs. Baṣrah was reached on December 2. Here parties of Dhafir, Muntafiq, and Bani Khalid were contributed, bringing the total of tribal forces to more than ten thousand.[3] Leaving Zubair, 'Ali Pasha directed his march southward to Jahra. Stores were conveyed in deep-sea muḥailahs. Ten thousand camels carried water and necessaries, but their number rapidly diminished. The rigours of the march involved frequent rests of many days. Finally, the first objective,[4] the twin fortresses of Ḥufuf and Mubarriz, was reached. The Pasha's artillery was brought to bear on the mud defences: but the attack was neither skilful nor whole-hearted. Every day of camp under these conditions entailed great hardship. Wastage among the camels threatened to leave none alive. The force of the expedition had been spent before it had reached its prize. Outcry arose among the army for return; and this became entirely necessary as the news arrived that the son of ibn Sa'ud had cut the line of march north of Ḥufuf, and was salting the wells. 'Ali Pasha, destroying much of his heavy baggage, started to return as he had come; ibn Sa'ud's forces (fearing his artillery) retired before him. At Shibak, death-scene of

[1] Mira'tu'l Zaura makes Thuwaini advance far into Najd and besiege Dar'iyyah. This cannot be accepted.

[2] This expedition of 'Ali Pasha is to be found in Burckhardt, in Brydges (*Wahauby*), and in Duḥat and 'Inwanu'l Majd.

[3] The two British eyewitnesses differ remarkably in their estimate of 'Ali Pasha. Harford Jones speaks (*Wahauby*, p. 19) of his "ignorance of military affairs, and haughty and absurd manner", and elsewhere of him as "ignorant, bigoted, irascible, obstinate, ill-mannered and brutal". Mr. Manesty at Baṣrah found him "a brave and enterprising young man". *Précis*, p. 79, § 184.

Both Burckhardt and the author of Duḥat blame 'Ali Pasha for not making Dar'iyyah his first objective.

Thuwaini, a hurricane added to the damage and misery of the army. At Wataj the two camps were in sight. For three days they surveyed each other. Messengers passed to and fro. 'Ali Pasha demanded evacuation of Ḥasa, good treatment of 'Iraqi pilgrims, return of captured guns, and indemnity. Sa'ud, master of desert diplomacy and in secret touch with the tribesmen[1] of the 'Iraq army, vaguely referred these conditions to his father. The Turkish forces reached Baṣrah intact, and the expedition had ended with nothing accomplished. Baghdad was reached in July 1799. There remained the ceremony of ratification, for which the Baghdad Sarai was decked and garnished. To impress the wildling envoy of ibn Sa'ud, great efforts were made to surround the palace and person of the Pasha with all the appurtenances of majesty and wealth. As every guardsman and flunkey, gorgeous and solemn, awaited a no less dignity in the desert ambassador, there appeared instead a quick-stepping tattered Arab who brushed aside Pashas who would escort him, squatted before Sulaiman, proffered him a dirty scrap of paper, and declaimed in the Arabic of Najd a speech curt and insulting.[2]

With offensive fanaticism on one side, and the provocations of desert custom on both, such a peace could not hope to last. A year later pilgrims of the Khaza'il were attacked near Najd. On another occasion, Persian travellers were attacked and plundered in the same locality. In the summer of 1801 'Abdu'l 'Aziz ul Shawi was sent on embassy to Najd: he returned to report that peace was not desired. As Wahhabi forces were reported from Shifathah, the Kahya stationed himself close to Karbala. Muḥammad ul Shawi with the Shammar leader Faris ul Jarba engaged the enemy, and an indecisive battle was broken off by the thirst of the combatants.

The crowning tragedy was at hand—an act of cruel and brutal avarice draped, like so many horrors, in the weeds of religion. Early in 1801 plague had driven the Pasha and his court from Baghdad to the healthier Khaliṣ. News came from the Muntafiq of Wahhabi armies moving up for the spring ghazu. The Kahya was bidden to proceed to Hindiyyah: he

[1] Especially Muḥammad Beg ul Shawi.
[2] Brydges, *Wahauby* (pp. 23–7).

had not left Baghdad when news was brought of the entry and sack of Karbala, richest and holiest city of the Shia' faith.

On the evening of April 2 the alarm had spread in Karbala that Wahhabi forces were in sight. Most of the inhabitants were on pilgrimage at Najf; the remainder hastened to the gates. The Wahhabis, judged to number some six thousand camel-riders and four hundred horsemen, dismounted, pitched tents, and divided their forces into three parts. From the shelter of a khan they assaulted the nearest gate, and forced an easy entrance while the inhabitants, unled[1] and panic-stricken, ran as terror directed. Forcing their way into the court of the shrine, the ferocious Purists began their task in the very Tomb. The rails, then the casings, then the huge mirrors of the shrine were torn down. Offerings of Pashas, Princes, and Kings of Persia, walls and roofing plated with gold, candlesticks, rich carpets and hangings, bricks of copper, doors studded with precious stones —all were seized and dragged forth. Within the Tomb nearly fifty persons were massacred, in the courtyard five hundred more. In the town the raiders murdered without restraint, looted every home, spared neither age nor sex from brutal ill treatment or captivity. The sum of the dead was computed by some at a thousand, by others at five times the number.

In vain the Kahya moved to the spot, garrisoned Ḥillah and Kifl, removed the Najf treasures to Baghdad, fortified Karbala itself with a wall: no revenge was to be had from an intangible enemy. To the Pasha, in extreme age and illness, the blow was a death-blow; throughout Turkey, throughout Shia' Persia, ran a thrill of horror; unpunished and exultant, the savages of Najd shambled homeward on their camels heavy laden with unappreciated treasures.

§ 5. *End of the Great Pasha.*

Of the long Pashaliq of Sulaiman little remains to record but a single vivid incident. Earlier mention has been made of Aḥmad, the Pasha's confidential man of thirty years' standing. His preferment had caused the rebellion of Sulaiman ul Shawi; his

[1] Mirza abu Ṭalib (p. 326) blames 'Umr Agha the Governor, a fanatical Sunni, who did nothing to protect the town. He was, in fact, put to death by Sulaiman Pasha.

energy as Kahya had been used in the command of every campaign for a decade; and his economy and devotion had supported nearly the whole burden of the State while his master grew in age and weakness. Refusing high office in Stambul, he had preferred to serve in Baghdad until the Pashaliq must in time fall to his patience. Attractive and widely popular, he was for years the second man in 'Iraq for rank, for power almost the first. Enemies, however, had been made: his low birth, the offensive satire of his speeches, his burning jealousy, his great riches[1] had gathered forces of envy and resentment against him. These indeed were not inconsistent with his continued safety and succession: but his ambition, too little patient, was to defeat its own aim.

In 1793 the Pasha had offered his resignation to the Porte in favour of Aḥmad.[2] It was refused; but the Kahya did not cease to press the delights of retirement, and to absorb power into his hands. By 1795 parties were taking shape against him. Rumours of his ambition, if they reached the Pasha, were not believed: Sulaiman had, on the contrary, planned a further honour for his favourite—the hand of his daughter Khadijah Khanim. Aḥmad, for private reasons,[3] postponed acceptance of the match; whereupon the lady threw her considerable influence into the scales against him, and selected for herself another suitor—none but 'Ali Agha, now Treasurer and later leader of the unhappy expedition to Al Ḥasa. At this moment the Pasha, approaching his eightieth year, was afflicted by a serious illness. High fever with alarming symptoms reduced him to the verge of death, whither Persian doctors and astrologers were assisting him; cool Kurdish air benefited him nothing; and only the timely skill of a French physician (long resident in Baghdad) restored him to feeble health. Over the old intimacy of Pasha and Kahya no shadow of the coming blow was cast. So passed April 1796.

But the plans of 'Ali Agha, now leader of the party resolved on the removal of Aḥmad, were matured. The personal attendants of Sulaiman Pasha had been secured by the conspirators. The occasion selected for the murder was a morning audience-

[1] Olivier (iv, p. 262); Jackson (p. 97).

[2] Ghayatu 'l Muram (year 1258). Olivier (p. 355) says that Aḥmad pressed the old man to resign and was refused.

[3] His objection was due to the charms (and possibly the protests) of his existing wife.

session of the Pasha, who, true to custom, left his private apartments, entered, and was seated. As the attendant Kahya mounted the steps, a score of daggers struck him down. Hacked with brutal blows and thrown into the courtyard below, his body was left for hours to feast the eyes of the populace. Sulaiman Pasha with a feeble gesture of horror rose and fled to his private chambers. His councillors, Muḥammad ul Shawi and 'Abdullah, the Jewish banker, were instantly called: and whether (as some thought and think) the deed had from the first the sanction of the old man—convinced at last of a treacherous ambition in his servant—or whether his apparent horror and alarm were sincere, the Agha of Janissaries was now bidden to ride through the streets announcing the just death of a proved traitor. The wedding of 'Ali Agha to Khadijah followed no later than the same night, and his promotion to Mirmiran and Kahya was as prompt. The hoarded possessions of Aḥmad enriched his old master, but could never console him for the loss, deserved or not, of a minister loved and valued.[1]

In the closing years of the reign the customary expeditions against Zubaid, Khaza'il, and 'Afak tribes spoke of outland conditions normally insecure; revenue and rich presents sent to Stambul showed a vassal still loyal if (with declining powers) sinking somewhat in the estimation of the Padishah; and the humiliating blows of the Wahhabis provoked against the Pashaliq the frowns of the Muslim world.

There remains but the last phase. The Pasha recovered from the alarming illness of 1796, assisted by the prayers of Jews, Christians, and the Faithful. But his remarkable vitality, used to the full for eighty years, must in time grow faint. Early in 1802 he became a permanent and soon a helpless invalid. The possibility of a successor[2] from outside was not considered in Baghdad or in Stambul. The Pasha's sons were still in boyhood. Of his daughters, Khadijah was the wife of 'Ali Pasha the Kahya; another had been given to Salim Agha, lately Mutasallim of Baṣrah; the remaining two were affianced to Daud Effendi and to Naṣif Agha, the Chief Chamberlain. All these

[1] Brydges (p. 182).
[2] See the full dispatch of Brydges (then Harford Jones) to Lord Wellesley dated 9th May 1802, quoted in the *Précis of Turkish Arabia Affairs*, p. 30.

must be considered candidates for the succession. The heads of the Shawi family, the Mutasallims of Baṣrah and of Mardin, the Daftardar and the Agha of the Janissaries might all cherish more or less serious ambitions. By such was the flickering life of the Great Pasha watched with sentiment and avarice. All were Georgians save the Shawi Arabs and the Janissary Agha. As August opened Sulaiman was a dying man. Alarm at the plague which had driven him from Baghdad, and helpless horror at the tragedy of Karbala, were the last blows beneath which he sank. The end came before noon on the 7th of August 1802.[1]

[1] Duḥat thus summarizes his good works: he had repaired the walls of Baghdad, and fortified Kirkh with wall and moat. He added to the Sarai, built the Sulaimaniyyah school "with all its branches", restored the Qabbaniyyah, Faḍhil, and Khulafa mosques, and maintained teachers. He gilded the dome of Abu Ḥanifah, built the bazaar and khan of Sarrajin. He rebuilt Dali 'Abbas and Charman, made or restored the walls of Mandali, Ḥillah, and Baṣrah, constructed the Narin bridge and arsenals at Kut (?), Baṣrah and Jaṣṣan. He fortified Zubair, Mardin, and Aski Mosul. Khans at Iskandariyyah and Karbala were his work. Another task performed not by but under him was the digging of the Hindiyyah canal from below Musayyib to water Najf.

IX

THE LATER MAMLUKS

§ 1. *Three short reigns.*

Buyuk Sulaiman had not ceased to breathe when violent factions, long meditated, broke out.[1] The lesser of the candidates for the succession withdrew and temporized as the crisis came. 'Ali Pasha the Kahya, Aḥmad Agha of the Janissaries,[2] and Salim Agha alone maintained their ambitions. Aḥmad had already, a few days before the end, called the British Resident to his councils and begged him for a letter to the Ambassador at Stambul; he now (perhaps an hour before the Pasha died) collected whatever rabble was to hand, seized the Citadel and bombarded the Sarai. Meanwhile the Pasha's death was confirmed and 'Ali assumed office as Qa'immaqam. Naṣif played a double game, keeping secret touch with both Sarai and Citadel. The firing of guns shut every shop and filled the streets with frightened citizens mostly armed. Parties formed. The bulk leaned to 'Ali Pasha, the legitimist candidate and *de facto* ruler of the town; but the Janissary in the Qal'ah could neither be dislodged nor silenced. Day followed day and the issue remained doubtful.

To resolve the deadlock, 'Ali Pasha at last withdrew as Qa'immaqam in favour of the Janissary and retired to his own house. Firing ceased. Aḥmad Agha however was unconvinced that such withdrawal could be sincere: and he was right. 'Ali, crossing by night to Kirkh side, rallied the citizens, the 'Ugail, and some detached bodies of the Janissaries. His supporters, cutting

[1] Brydges (pp. 204 ff.), as an impartial eyewitness, has been followed rather than Duḥat. They agree in parts.

[2] Brydges (p. 205). It was through Aḥmad Agha that the Porte hoped to obtain the treasures of the old Pasha.

the bridge, swarmed over in boats, brushed by the first opposition offered and, joined by hundreds more, occupied the Sarai and Maidan. The Janissary Agha still held the Citadel; but the game was lost. 'Ali, again in charge of the all-powerful gold bags, melted the rebels in a few hours. Aḥmad Agha fled to hiding in Baghdad, while Sa'dullah Agha took command of the now docile Janissaries. Order was everywhere restored. Aḥmad was dragged from his refuge and dispatched by the daggers of the Georgian guards, fourteen of his lieutenants were seized and strangled. Salim Agha was given the government of Takrit.

"The fighting and confusion in the city from beginning to end lasted between a fortnight and three weeks; the expense of powder, balls and shells was enormous, from all which the list of killed and wounded did not amount to more than five: but, to make up for it, when Aley Kiah became completely triumphant the bow-string and gallows had their full share of victims."

So summarizes an eyewitness.[1] A petition, bearing the seals of all Baghdad, besought the Sultan to confirm the appointment of 'Ali Pasha. Sums equivalent to £60,000 were dispatched to Stambul for the same object, with some small part of the rich possessions of Sulaiman. Of the remainder, the Georgian officers and 'Ali himself secured the bulk. Four months later a royal decree promoted him to the rank of Wazir and to the whole government of the Great Pasha.

The period of one complete generation,[2] which elapsed between the accession of 'Ali Pasha and the fall of the Mamluks, is made up of the Pashaliqs of himself and four successors. To none was a peaceful end allowed: and the five years of 'Ali was the longest of the reigns save for that of Daud Pasha, the last. Throughout the period 'Iraq resembled many provinces of the Empire in its virtual independence, its abuses, its local tyrants never incorporated even in the provincial government; and

[1] Brydges (p. 209).

[2] Authorities to 1830: Duḥat (up to 1825 only), both works of Sulaiman Beg and both of Yasin ul 'Umari, and Muṭali'u'l Sa'ud. Ghayatu'l Muram stops at 1803 and Ghura'ibu'l Athr at 1811. The most important travellers are Dupré (1807), Buckingham (1816), Heude (1817), Porter (1818), Rich (1811–20), Wellsted (1830–1). The authorities for 1830–1 are given later (pp. 263 ff., foot-notes). The Turkish historiographer [illegible] contains some references.

throughout it worked in Stambul those forces and that personality ultimately to demand its surrender. The interest of its own history during the period lies in the personalities and intrigues of Baghdad, in the continued normal lawlessness of the tribes, in the last menaces of Najd, and in Kurdish politics involving more and more delicate relations with the Persian neighbours. These aspects will be treated successively.

The first act of 'Ali Pasha was to march against the Bilbas Kurds, the powerful tribe chastised a century before by Ḥasan Pasha. Ibrahim Pasha Baban by his instructions led the offensive, and 'Ali joined his vassal forces at Arbil. The Bilbas surrendered without more ado and paid a large fine in live stock. 'Ali Pasha crossed to Mosul, where he found the long reign of Muḥammad Pasha Jalili drawing to a close. Thence, reinforced by troops of that Pashaliq, he moved against the robbers of Jabal Sinjar, where tactics of blockade and ever-increasing pressure drove the Yazidis from their caves to accept harsh terms of surrender. The more accessible Jazirah tribes were visited and punished. During the campaign Ibrahim Pasha Baban died and was succeeded by 'Abdu 'l Raḥman, who owed his release from Ḥillah and subsequent pardon to the disorders of 'Ali's accession. From Sinjar the army moved to Tel 'Afar. Here sentence of death awaited Muḥammad Beg ul Shawi and his brother, that of captivity their young cousin Aḥmad. Muḥammad Beg, greatest of the Arab subjects of the Pashaliq, owed his death to jealousy, to fear, and to the memory of suspected treachery when, on the Najd campaign of 1799, he had corresponded with the enemy. Jasim, his son, fled to the 'Ubaid. Fighting followed between these and the Milli of Timur Pasha, willing perhaps to please Baghdad by the capture of a fugitive. Timur failed: a column of 'Ali Pasha was no more successful, and a mutiny in Baghdad compelled his instant return thither. A severe attack of plague had subsided before 'Ali re-entered the city in the autumn.

Of the remaining events of the Pashaliq little is unconnected with either the Wahhabis or the Kurds, for both of whom separate pages are reserved. A number of prominent Aghas (including Daud Effendi) could find no place in the uncongenial court of 'Ali Pasha, and left for Baṣrah or elsewhere. Suspicion of intrigue with the Baban led to the fall and death of Khalid Agha the Kahya, whereat the place was given to Sulaiman Beg, the son of 'Ali's sister. The tribal campaigns are of little interest. Another attempt to capture Jasim ul Shawi in 1804 was forestalled by greater emergency in Kurdistan. Tribe was used against tribe when the 'Ubaid, Ghurair, and Ḥamdan were pursued by Faris ul Jarba with his Shammar and severely punished at the Euphrates crossing. Again in 1805 the 'Ubaid were the objective. Early in the spring of 1806 the young Kahya led a force to Bani Lam territory and visited the Rabi'ah and Maqaṣiṣ. For the rest, the country was secure and peaceful by the standards of the time. But the reign was to be short. The Pasha's sudden and violent death was connected with old private jealousies. Madad Beg, of Abazah race like himself and son of a Caucasian whose slave 'Ali had been in childhood, had come to Baghdad three years before. The opportunity he sought came when, on the 18th of August 1807, 'Ali was at prayers. Madad and his servants stabbed him to instant death; then, rushing out, dashed from place to place for support or sanctuary. Eluding the Kahya's troops, they crossed by night to the right bank. Naṣif Agha alone attempted to create a rising in their or in his own favour. None responded: and a few hours later their corpses and his were exhibited at the bridge-head.

The succession was not in doubt. After the dour and fanatical, vigorous and unpopular 'Ali, the attractive character of his nephew was generally welcome. Sulaiman Pasha, still in his twenty-second year, was intolerant, impetuous, and not free from avarice, but of pure life, cultivated mind, and good intentions and instincts in public life.[1] As Kahya, as descendant of the Great Pasha, as actual master of Baghdad, he had every claim. He remained as Deputy-Governor for many months while the Porte abortively appointed Yusif Pasha (a late Grand Wazir) to a command which he could not in fact approach. After long delay the farman for the appointment of Sulaiman—known as Kuchuk "the Little"—arrived in the late spring of 1808.

During his reign of three years, security was generally above the average. Baṣrah and Mosul, indeed, were torn by faction;

[1] Rich; cf. Rousseau (*Description*, p. 25).

but tribal campaigns were few, and Baghdad untroubled by violence. The summer of 1808 was devoted to a Kurdish and a Wahhabi expedition. In 1809 a yet more exhausting campaign took the young Pasha to the extreme limits of the province against tribes of the Urfah ayalat. His success is doubtful; and before operations were complete an urgent call took him from Ras ul 'Ain to Mardin. The timely aid of Timur Pasha, Shaikh Faris, and other vassals restored the position, but not without serious trespass into the Diyarbakr ayalat.[1] Returning from Mardin to Mosul Sulaiman found civil war there in progress.

The death of Muḥammad Pasha Jalili after an eighteen-year reign had left the government to his son Maḥmud; but violent opposition[2] was led by As'ad Beg, a son of old Ḥaji Ḥusain Pasha. From the struggles of these two, the rule fell to their kinsman Na'man Pasha, a man feeble in health and oppressive as a ruler. This could be borne; but the subsequent appointment of Aḥmad Effendi, the mere secretary of Na'man, roused a storm of Jalili protests. Sulaiman the Little tried in vain to support his nominee: but the fierce resistance of the Jalilis under As'ad finally drove the parvenu from the town, and Mosul and its neighbours attained for a time that condition of complete non-government which suited, and suits, so many of its sons. Help was ultimately sent from Baghdad to the fugitive Aḥmad—still titular Wali—who organized a formidable force and struck hard for his rights. At the very point of victory he was killed; the Jalilis regained control; and the situation was resolved only by concession to necessity. Maḥmud Pasha became Wali, to be succeeded by eight more governors of the same family.

In Baṣrah, Salim Agha (son-in-law of Sulaiman the Great) was Mutasallim in the spring of 1810. He had long cherished ambitions for the Pashaliq; and news of the arrival of an Imperial envoy in Baghdad led him to think the time ripe for action. Orders reached him from Sulaiman to relinquish[3] his office. Relying on his own persuasiveness and on Muntafiq support, he refused. To the same Muntafiq, however, his superior entrusted the duty of suppressing him; and they preferred the latter role. On their

[1] The offence thereby given was considered one of the causes of Kuchuk Sulaiman's early fall. [2] Cf. Abu Ṭalib (p. 290), Dupré (p. 118).
[3] *Précis* (p. 105, § 231) and Duḥat.

slow approach from the north and that of Turkish forces by the Tigris, Salim shut the town-gates and stowed his belongings on ship-board; then, realizing that his confederates were enemies, sailed for Bushire. The rebellion, unworthy of the name, was over. Aḥmad Beg, foster-brother of Sulaiman the Little, entered the port as Mutasallim.

Thus some sort of peace had fallen upon both extremities of the Pashaliq. But the present ruler was not long to enjoy it. A new and determined monarch now sat upon the throne of 'Uthman. He had heard of an ominous invasion of Diyarbakr, and could learn from his treasurers, in a single word, the extent of his revenues from 'Iraq. At the moment, indeed, no drastic stroke was possible; but a representative of high rank, the "Ra'is Effendi", Ḥalat Muḥammad Sa'id [1] was dispatched to Baghdad. This delegate confronted the Little Pasha with the suave alternatives of remitting a regular revenue or vacating his position. Still empty-handed, he left Baghdad for Mosul, where he contrived to rally such parties as must together be invincible. Maḥmud Pasha Jalili, 'Abdu 'l Raḥman the reigning Baban, many of the greater shaikhs, and banished or disgraced officers of the Slaves themselves, rallied to the Imperial messenger. He proclaimed to them the deposition of Kuchuk Sulaiman. A force of fifteen thousand men advanced southwards upon Baghdad. A single engagement was enough. It was fought in the afternoon and evening of the 5th of October 1810. It ended in the desertion of Sulaiman by most of his force, his complete defeat, his flight almost alone across the Diyalah southwards, and his murder by tribesmen of the Shammar Togah.[2]

The question of a successor at once arose. The last word must rest with Ḥalat Effendi, bearer of a blank farman on which he could write any name; but the greatest immediate force was that of the Baban, whom ambition as well as loyalty had brought to Baghdad as king-maker.[3] It was he who had put to summary

[1] Minister for Foreign Affairs. For his career, see Ta'rikh Jaudat (xi, p. 5).

[2] *Précis* (p. 106, § 232). Rich agrees closely with the oriental authorities.

[3] The tradition friendly to the Babans represents that 'Abdu 'l Raḥman refused the offer which Ḥalat Effendi made him: the other, that he begged the post and was refused. The latter is probable; such an appointment must have been a complete and dangerous failure, nor could Sultan Maḥmud have accepted it.

death suspected Aghas, he who appointed a new Kahya and other officers, and he who, securing the agreement of Ḥalat finally to the promotion to the Pashaliq of ‘Abdullah Agha the Tutunchi,[1] stamped out some feeble opposition. The Tutunchi was confirmed as Pasha of the three ayalats. The farman was read, the state entry made, and Ḥalat Effendi retired full-handed to Stambul.

‘Abdullah Agha (now Pasha) was of exceptional type. He had been a slave [2] bought by Sulaiman the Great at Baṣrah. During his master's lifetime he had joined ‘Ali Agha in the murder of Aḥmad, and had held various offices besides the governments of Baṣrah and of Mardin.[3] His chances of succeeding the old Pasha had been favoured by the British Resident. ‘Ali Pasha banished him to Baṣrah, where he remained until Sulaiman the Little ordered his execution; but Salim Agha, a kinsman and old colleague, permitted his escape to Kurdistan, whence he joined Ḥalat Effendi at Mosul. Tahir Agha, his companion in these adventures, became the tried friend and later the Kahya of the new Pasha. ‘Abdullah had industry, an active mind, and an education fitting him to converse with Europeans on equal terms. He was liberal in religion, attractive and inquisitive in conversation, at home in literature as in affairs. In previous offices he had won a rare reputation: revenues had grown without extortion, discipline without repression. He was generous without extravagance, just in magistracy, and accessible to all. But little, unhappily, was to come of these exceptional parts. The party of Sa‘id—eighteen-year-old son of Sulaiman the Great—and smaller cliques, each supporting a powerful Agha, were persistent in opposition, and numerous changes among the high officials suggested a jealous restlessness within the Sarai.

With ‘Abdu ’l Raḥman Pasha, whom the revolution had left dangerously powerful, his relations soon deteriorated: indeed, the expedition against the Baban early in 1812 was his chief campaign. The victory of Kifri greatly strengthened his position. It was at the same time a personal triumph for his Daftardar, Daud Effendi, of whom much more will be heard.

[1] Tobacconist. It is not known to what he owed this nickname.
[2] Mr. Harford Jones (dispatch of 9th May 1802) errs in stating that he came from "one of the most respectable families of the city".
[3] Cf. Mirza abu Ṭalib (p. 276).

After the Kifri battle the Tutunchi proceeded to Kirkuk and Mosul to punish disloyal townsmen who had favoured the Baban, weed out the worst officials, and punish tribesmen *en route*. At Mosul Sa'dullah Pasha Jalili averted the wrath of his old colleague by a royal reception. 'Abdullah retired to Baghdad in the autumn of 1812.

The winter was occupied in preparing for another Kurdish expedition. From this the attention of the Pasha was diverted by ominous news: Sa'id Pasha had bolted to the Muntafiq and been warmly welcomed by Ḥamud ul Thamir, whom 'Abdullah Pasha had tried in vain to depose. Busy diplomatists sped between Baghdad and Suq ul Shuyukh. Ḥamud urged that no more harm was intended than an asylum for the son of "our old Effendi". Many dissuaded 'Abdullah from embarking on a course which must force the Georgians to choose between the son and the mere servant of their old master. Tahir Agha the Kahya urged war, which indeed could only be postponed; and in January 1813 the Baghdad forces left for the Muntafiq country. Ḥamud with the bulk of his tribe, the personal followers of Sa'id, and the crowd of adventurers and outlaws who had at various times found a refuge in the marshes lay a few miles from Baṣrah. He was outnumbered: but desertions from the enemy soon began to swell his forces. In the first skirmishing Barghash son of Ḥamud was terribly wounded. Fortune, it yet seemed possible, might favour the Pasha, until wholesale desertion from his army forbade it. Tribal allies and Georgian guards alike ranged themselves with Sa'id and his uncouth protector.

'Abdullah Pasha with Tahir and a few followers were left alone and fugitive. Ḥamud, the almost bloodless victor, sent his brother to offer them personal safety. They could not but accept. Sent in close captivity to Suq, their lives hung in the balance while Barghash fought for life against his wounds. He died, and their fate was sealed. The Pasha and his party were strangled, buried, dug up again and decapitated. Thus sordidly, after unmerited failure and humiliation, died a ruler of rare parts and promise, to make way for a successor a hundred-fold inferior.

§ 2. *The Wahhabis, 1802 to 1810.*

Turning for a moment from the busy and violent politics of the capital, we must glance at later phases of the Wahhabi menace. Raids upon the villages and grazing-parties of western 'Iraq continued yearly, at times venturing across the Euphrates into the Shamiyyah, even into the Zubaid country. But mud walls now protected the villages and increased garrisons the towns; the shepherds had learnt at short notice to drive their flocks from danger and to call upon the nearest Agha and his Lawand; and converts in 'Iraq did not increase.

The assassination of the aged 'Abdu 'l 'Aziz bin Sa'ud late in 1803 was thought by some to have been inspired by the Pasha of Baghdad: its author was an Aghan Mulla resident in Baghdad, avenging his sons slain in the sack of Karbala. The Wahhabi raid on Najf in the last days of that year was in stronger than the usual force; but the Shrine of 'Ali stood firm inside its now formidable walls. 'Ali Pasha hurriedly mobilized his troops (newly returned from the Sinjar) and invoked tribal assistance the more eager since the recent show of force. Faris of the Shammar was ally and counsellor. The force advanced to Ḥillah and beyond, when the raiders vanished. In the spring of 1804—the grazing-season as usual attracting the Shamiyyah tribes to the desert—Wahhabi tribes fell upon them, rode unchecked to the walls of Baṣrah, brushed aside Muntafiq opposition, and captured members of the Sa'dun family. For the city defences they were no match; and even at Zubair, which they could isolate and starve, they made no headway until an accident delivered the place into their hands. A stronghold on the walls, now crowded with townspeople, was used also as a magazine; and an explosion destroyed not only the tower, but practically the whole of the garrison. The general retirement of the Najdis followed the appearance of Ḥamud ul Thamir with reinforcements of Muntafiq, who joined forces with Ibrahim Agha the Mutasallim. 'Ali Pasha meanwhile had received the Sultan's order to lead a counter-attack, and late in 1804 assembled his forces at Ḥillah. His main body advanced little from their base. A small detached company penetrated far into the enemy's dominions, but was forced by thirst to retire,[1] bringing with it

[1] Their leader was Aḥmad Effendi, Secretary (and future Pasha) of Mosul.

a booty of four hundred camels. The forces of ibn Sa'ud remained on the outskirts of 'Iraq. The garrison of Baṣrah was increased.

In the spring of 1806 the Wahhabis made their annual excursion northwards from Najd. Their raiding parties against frontier towns were persistent but generally unsuccessful: from Zubair and Samawah their camel-men were easily driven by the townsmen and their tribal allies: at Najf they almost succeeded in gaining the town by surprise, only to be routed by the Najfis from the very walls. Zubair was threatened a second time, and fears felt in the port itself. But the flooded country prevented the movement of camels, and the Wahhabis, exhausted with weeks of riding and burdened with wounded, did not press the attack. Seeing them weak and wavering, Cha'ab and Muntafiq horse drove them back with loss, and cleared the villages they had occupied.

In the last year of 'Ali Pasha the usual alarmist rumours reached Baghdad. The Pasha moved his camp to Ḥillah, but no raiders appeared. The threat materialized next year, during the reign of Kuchuk Sulaiman, when a large force of Wahhabis was reported within sight of Karbala. Exaggerated stories of their strength caused terror in Baghdad itself:[1] shopkeepers and merchants were forced to arms. The Wahhabis, however, never crossed the Euphrates. A party, indeed, took Shifathah and raided rice-fields and villages towards Ḥillah, across the little Hindiyyah canal, but retired on the arrival of the Pasha at Ḥillah. This was not the last of the Wahhabi offensives. But from now their efforts grew feebler and less feared. Not until their power was broken from the Egyptian side[2] did the shepherds and drovers of the Euphrates feel safe; in 1810 a plundering party of 'Abdullah bin Sa'ud reached a point not far from Baghdad; and for a few years thereafter Wahhabi agents could still take toll from 'Iraq subjects in the Karbala marshes. Gradually a state of flickering hostility, half-sanctioned raids, occasional

[1] Cf. Anon., *Journal d'un Voyage dans la Turkie, etc.*: "on ne parle à Baghdad que des Vahabites" (in 1808).

[2] The Ḥijaz was recovered by Muḥammad 'Ali from the Wahhabis in 1812–13. Early in 1815 he defeated them in the critical battle of Bisah; in the same year Tusun, his son, invaded Qasim. Operations in Najd in 1817–18 ended after a hard and doubtful campaign in the surrender of 'Abdullah bin Sa'ud.

panics, conversions and alliances was reached and has endured on a frontier impossible of agreement. Najd became to 'Iraq an uneasy incalculable neighbour, its terrors varying with the personality of its ruler. The passage of caravans from Turkish territory to the Najd oases, and the use there of Turkish currency, was gradually permitted by the Wahhabi Amirs after 1810. But, as neither the intolerance nor the ferocity of the desert sectarians grew less (and are little less to-day) this source of fear and danger for the Euphrates became permanent, and incidents occurring in the twentieth century repeat faithfully those of the Mamluk period.

§ 3. *The Shahrizor, 1802 to 1813.*

The role of 'Abdu 'l Raḥman Pasha Baban as kingmaker in Baghdad has been described. It was to be repeated a few years later by his son: and this power to make and unmake rulers in a great Turkish province is one claim of the Baban state on our attention. Another is the effect of their constant intrigues and factions on the relations of Persia and 'Iraq, and in the blurring of a frontier which thereafter a century was insufficient to define.

For a time the Baban vassal—re-succeeding to his Government in 1802—loyally assisted his overlord of Baghdad. His forces suppressed trouble at 'Amadiyyah and were found among Turkish garrisons on the Euphrates. But his obedience did not last: in 1805 he brutally murdered his colleague and rival, Muḥammad Pasha of Keui—mobilized with himself for a campaign against the outlaw Shawi—and thereafter by a score of robberies and outrages showed that his allegiance to Baghdad was thrown off. His deposition was entrusted by 'Ali Pasha to the Jalili, whose Mosul forces and auxiliaries were completely defeated by the rebel Kurd at Altun Kupri. 'Abdu 'l Raḥman looted the town, surveyed the corpses of a dozen Turkish commanders, and retired to fortify a position on the Darband pass in readiness for the inevitable army from Baghdad. It came, and he failed to withstand it: rapid flight to Sannah alone saved his life, his following was scattered, and his throne given to his kinsman Khalid.[1]

[1] See genealogical tree of the Babans (Appendix II) for Khalid and other Babans subsequently mentioned.

The Persians neither had abandoned their claims to Shahrizor nor were indifferent to Baban sympathies. Instructed from Sannah, the Shah conferred a fief upon 'Abdu 'l Raḥman and wrote to the Pasha of Baghdad requesting his reinstatement. To this and to a second messenger no favourable answer was given; but the rumour spread in Baghdad that massed Persian armies waited on the very frontier, ready to invade the province and work their will on 'Iraq at large. 'Ali Pasha decided to be first in the field. He left Baghdad at midsummer 1806 and met his Kurdish allies at Shahroban. Despite his officers' protests that an invasion of Persia needed Imperial sanction, he crossed the frontier and advanced on Karmanshah. Not until several villages had been looted came the Sultan's peremptory orders to desist. The Shah ordered his eldest son, Muḥammad 'Ali Mirza governor[1] of Karmanshah, to guard the frontier, and the Wali of Ardalan to support the fugitive Baban. 'Ali Pasha abandoned the campaign, but left his Kahya (Sulaiman the Little) to support Khalid. The Kahya foolishly entered Ardalan, engaged Persian forces with his tired army, and was himself captured. Meanwhile Muḥammad 'Ali Mirza crossed the frontier above Khaniqin, and raided for some miles into the Baghdad ayalat. Simultaneously 'Abdu 'l Raḥman with Persian forces entered Sulaimaniyyah.

The accession of Sulaiman to the Baghdad Pashaliq was the signal for further enormities of the Baban. He attacked Keui, and led a raid by Kifri to the Khaliṣ. Again he was declared deposed, again Kuchuk Sulaiman, in early summer of 1808, led an army against him, again the Darband was successfully turned and 'Abdu 'l Raḥman a fugitive in Persia. Sulaiman Pasha was installed in Sulaimaniyyah, while Khalid first sulked in Kirkuk, then with six hundred followers crossed into Persia and joined forces with 'Abdu 'l Raḥman. Such a defection left to the Pasha of Baghdad no choice: he permitted the return of 'Abdu 'l Raḥman and compensated Sulaiman with estates elsewhere. At this stage, while 'Abdu 'l Raḥman was still in highest authority in Shahrizor, occurred the mission of Ḥalat Effendi and the priceless help he secured from the Baban. Eloquent and cordial, we may be sure, were the protestations of devotion of the Kurdish prince, who for years past had been now an outlaw,

[1] For his vigorous character and large resources see Porter (ii, pp. 202 ff.).

now independent, and now openly allied with Persian troops against the Sultan.

Conceit and over confidence in his new friendship with the bureaucrats of Turkey cost him his Persian alliance: in frontier politics—a squabble at Sauj Bulaq, rivalry at Zuhab—the Wali of Ardalan found the Tutunchi at Baghdad more accommodating than the Baban at Sulaimaniyyah: and thus while his better relations with Baghdad fast deteriorated, with Sannah they were embittered by his obstinacy. He forfeited the support of both, and both were willing to substitute Khalid. The operations and intrigues that followed ended in the installation of Khalid at Sulaimaniyyah, 'Abdu 'l Raḥman at Keui: but no sooner had Persian troops withdrawn than their work was undone, and 'Abdu 'l Raḥman entered Sulaimaniyyah to flaunt his scorn of the 'Iraq government by raids on the Arbil and Kirkuk villages. In the winter of 1811 his deposition was again decreed in Baghdad; and in June 1812 a formidable army under 'Abdullah Pasha met his forces at Kifri. The day at first favoured the Kurd, whose horsemen rushed the guns and brushed aside the first line of the enemy. But the Mamluks, bravely led by Daud Effendi the Daftardar, counter-attacked and carried all before them. 'Abdu 'l Raḥman rode from the field, while the victors erected a minaret of Kurdish heads. The victory made a great and joyful impression in Baghdad. At last, it seemed, the Pashaliq had asserted its rights over the wayward and unprofitable Kurds, and should now taste the wealth of their cool and fertile valleys.

While Khalid, however, for the third time commenced to reorganize his province, 'Abdu 'l Raḥman had once more invoked the Persians. For him they had no love; but they welcomed this further chance to assert their claim to the Shahrizor. Muḥammad 'Ali Mirza bade Baghdad restore the fugitive. War must follow a refusal, while compliance would surrender the whole fruits of the Kifri battle: nothing remained but to oppose the restoration by force. The Mirza had already crossed the border with 7,000 men, and 'Abdullah Pasha was ready for the road, when the flight of Sa'id Beg to the Muntafiq forbade him to leave Baghdad. 'Abdu 'l Raḥman was easily restored to the governments of Sulaimaniyyah, Keui, and Ḥarir. After a year of peace, he died in 1813 and was succeeded by Maḥmud his son.

§ 4. *Sa'id Pasha.*

On news of the result of the Muntafiq campaign, the Qaḍhi of Baghdad announced the accession of Sa'id and wrote for the usual confirmation from Stambul. Accompanied by Ḥamud ul Thamir, Sa'id entered Baghdad in state on the 16th of March 1813. Late in June his farman arrived. Now in his twenty-second year, he had taken hitherto no part in public affairs; but it was hoped that a pleasing person and manners might be backed by abilities worthy of his father.

The learned Daftardar, Daud Effendi, assumed the office of Kahya. His relations to his old master's son were at once those of a brother-in-law, a dependant, a tutor, and a Prime Minister. Though he shortly ceased to be Kahya, he retained the post of Daftardar and conducted in 1813 and 1814 a series of successful tribal campaigns on Tigris and Euphrates. In the Zubaid he restored Shafullah ul Shallal. The Khaza'il were visited. In Karbala a partial blockade of tribesmen—embarrassing at the season of pilgrimage—was broken up. In a campaign against the 'Afak tribes in 1814, his prestige and the rare discipline of his troops secured its object without a blow. In 1815 the Khaza'il were firmly disciplined. A year later great tribal confederations of western 'Iraq came to blows. The deposed Khaza'il Shaikh called in Shammar and Zubaid to help: the Pasha replied by sending for the Muntafiq, the Dhafir, and the 'Ubaid. But although the party of authority was victorious in this campaign and in others, yet everywhere restlessness and insurgence were increasing. The age-long quarrel of the town-sects in Najf—Zugurt and Shumurd—grew to open fighting; governors sent by Sa'id were expelled by citizens of the small townships; serious disorders broke out at Kirkuk, and lasted for several months.

In Baghdad, the scene was gradually taking shape for a revolution of type common in Eastern history. The Pasha's advisers, during the absences and after the fall of Daud Effendi, were a foolish mother, a worthless friend, and a buffoon. His early distribution of offices had caused head-shaking among many whose sentiment had welcomed him, and these doubts were increased by an extravagant generosity. But his popularity was not instantly dissipated. Trade flourished, exactions were rare. The tastes of a voluptuary were unaccompanied by those of a tyrant: his very mildness was a main cause of his fall. The royal state of the Court was maintained. For this, and to find pay for the Georgian guards, loans were taken from private persons and punctiliously repaid by drafts upon the Customs. But the daily-growing weakness of the country in wealth, in force, and even in internal order was apparent. The policing of Baghdad itself sadly deteriorated. Violent brawls had become common among the 'Ugail. Unpunished robberies by organized bands were more and more frequent. Leading men were among the promoters of such outrages and the purchasers of the spoils.

Daud Effendi was now the second man in the Pashaliq. He began, and serving a worthier master might have ended, a loyal and efficient minister; but causes of estrangement were at work. The jealousy of rivals frightened the effeminate ruler with stories of intended assassination. The idea of reprisals was quickly mooted, and as quickly reached the ears of Daud. The breach was widened by the doting folly of Nabi Khanim, the Pasha's mother, with whom—and a still worse influence—was his bosom friend Ḥamadi Agha. Daud, on his side, did not fail to keep touch with an old friend, Ḥalat Effendi in Stambul. To his ears were carried full details of the deterioration in 'Iraq. Incidents were related—sometimes imagined—which showed Sa'id in the worst of lights. High circles at the Capital, if not the highest, determined to displace Sa'id by Daud.

The immediate occasion was given by the young Pasha's mishandling of the Baban position. His predecessor had left Maḥmud in Sulaimaniyyah, and Sulaiman Pasha (eldest son of Ibrahim) in Keui. So they continued for two quiet years. Two principal pretenders, however, frequented Baghdad. Of these the veteran Khalid Pasha gained the governorship first of Arbil, then of Keui. Sulaiman Pasha fled as usual to the Mirza at Karmanshah. In 1816 Sa'id foolishly appointed his other favourite, 'Abdullah Pasha brother of 'Abdu 'l Raḥman, to Sulaimaniyyah. Maḥmud appealed to Persia: Sa'id prepared to support his nominee with arms: and at this moment arrived an envoy from Stambul to report to the Sovereign on the whole frontier question. He stayed to see the powerlessness of Sa'id.

the extent of Persian penetration, and the wretched maladministration of 'Iraq. A few weeks later it became known that Sa'id was deposed.

'Abdullah Pasha Baban stayed at Kirkuk. In Baghdad several leading Aghas left the sinking ship and rallied at Karmanshah. Leading persons waited upon Daud Effendi (now ousted from his office of Daftardar) and represented, to no unwilling ears, his claims to the highest office. Leaving Baghdad in September 1816,[1] he was followed by many leading past and present officials by Zangabad to Sulaimaniyyah, where he met a flattering welcome from Maḥmud Pasha Baban and was acclaimed as the future ruler of 'Iraq. Maḥmud Pasha declared his final breach with Persia if he might serve a Pasha of Baghdad worthy of his devotion. A general rally of exiles took place. Sulaiman Pasha (late of Keui) accompanied the *emigrés* from Karmanshah. From Sulaimaniyyah was sent the formal petition of Daud to Stambul for appointment to the Pashaliq of 'Iraq. After forty days he moved to Kirkuk and camped at a village two miles distant. Already he made appointments to the offices of the Pashaliq: to each Agha of his staff some plum was allotted.

The Sultan's order for Sa'id's dismissal was followed by a nomination little expected: the three ayalats were bestowed on Aḥmad Beg who—foster-brother of Sulaiman the Little and lately Mutasallim of Baṣrah—had been promoted by Daud to the post of Kahya. The order was cancelled a few days later, but not until a copy had reached Kirkuk. Aḥmad at once left Daud's camp, entered Kirkuk, showed his credentials, and was accepted by the greater part of the town and garrison, who had previously acclaimed Daud. The latter, incredulous and alarmed, bade them adhere to their first loyalty: the reply was an attack on his camp by Aḥmad. The Kirkuk notables doubted which side to join, and joined neither. Daud awaited his fate, with which a Qapuchi from Stambul must at any moment acquaint him. After agonies of suspense, royal chamberlains bearing the parchment of his appointment as Beglerbegi of Baghdad, Baṣrah, and Shahrizor, entered the camp at Toqmaqlu village in

[1] 12th Shawwal 1231 A.H. (Duḥat).

November. A fortnight later the Pasha-designate advanced by Tuz and Kifri on Baghdad.

The hapless Sa'id had shown, since the flight of his brother-in-law from Baghdad, every phase of irresolution. He made and remade appointments to every office, sought the favour of all, endeavoured, for a moment, to govern. Urgent messages brought Ḥamud ul Thamir with a Muntafiq force, while 'Abdullah Pasha from Kirkuk, and later Khalid Pasha from Keui, contributed contingents. These, with the head-quarter Lawand, the Janissary garrison, the 'Ugail, and the regular foot-soldiers of the Tufenkchis, Baratlis, and Qalpaqlis, formed an army which could defy Daud and his Kurds who now approached within sight of the walls of Baghdad. Not his rival, however, but the deadlier enemies of famine and poverty, most terrified Sa'id. Prices of food rushed up. The Kurd and Arab forces had all to be fed. The Treasury was long since empty. The regular and mercenary troops demanded their pay, present and arrears. The tribesmen were restless at each day of absence from their homes.

Nevertheless, the initial success was theirs.[1] The first brush occurred on the 7th of January 1817. The advance guard of Daud's forces bivouacked within reach of the Citadel guns. A sudden attack by 1,500 of the Muntafiq horse completely surprised and scattered it. Daud himself barely escaped, and his whole force withdrew to a distance to rest, reorganize, and recruit. The elated Sa'id felt justified in releasing forces he could not support, and dismissed his Muntafiq. Ḥamud retired with the high spirits of a victor. In Baghdad, for these days of grace[2]

"a very unusual degree of tranquillity prevailed. The gates of the city which had been built up were again thrown open" . . . and "the chiefs in general, uncertain of the course they should pursue . . . appeared sufficiently inclined to pay their court to the brighter hopes of the youthful Sayud [Sa'id]. The Pasha himself . . . made no further use of the success attained. . . . Nothing in fact remained to remind one of those bloody frays that had been fought the week before under

[1] Heude (p. 174); *Précis* (p. 100, § 240). Duḥat (always favourable to Daud) ignores the incident.

[2] For the whole incident we have the eyewitness account of Heude as well as a full narrative in Duḥat and others.

the walls except uncertain rumours of impending harm, and quicker succession of removals and appointments among the officers of state, and, now and then, a cautious whisper of Daood effendi's increasing strength and near return."

These whispers became louder and more articulate. Leading men began quietly withdrawing from the town: Sa'id's call for a levy was resisted. Daud's agents were not idle, the Georgian regiments already half-corrupted, desertion increasing. Open rebellion broke out in the notorious Bab ul Shaikh quarter. Sa'id remained feeble and irresolute. His efforts to overcome insurgence and crime were unorganized, fitful, and half-hearted. For five days fruitless and confused conflict, with constant rattle of musketry and thunder of guns, the war-cry of the 'Ugail, the company-songs of the Janissaries, the groans of martyrs in this most sordid and hopeless strife, filled the narrow dark alleys of Baghdad. When the swollen and confident army of Daud was at last seen from the walls, Sa'id retired with some hundreds of the 'Ugail to the Citadel.

Invited by the chief persons of the city, Daud Effendi entered in state on the 20th of February. The bazaars rang with his name; his farman was read in the Sarai. Daily he summoned the Citadel to surrender, while strengthening his hold on the town: a rough order was restored, all offices filled, and the main body of his forces entered the city. By his affectionate references to his brother-in-law, and his pacific attitude, Sa'id was partially reassured. His 'Ugail [1] were ordered to leave the Citadel. Then

"on the very night of their retreat . . . the new Janissary Agha . . . silently presented the signet of authority at the gates of the Citadel. . . . It was understood, and the guards withdrew. . . . On demanding admittance at the door of the private apartment, into which the unfortunate youth had retired, his anxious mother (foreboding ill) fearfully unbarred the entrance. . . . The hour and the presence of the revengeful Sayyid, however,[2] had already told her the fatal truth. Whilst the mother clung around her devoted son, in distracted agony shrieking and imploring mercy . . . their victim was struck down with a battle-axe and a headless trunk alone remained in the parent's arms." [3]

[1] Duḥat is doubtless guided by partisanship in accusing Sa'id of instigating a counter-revolution at this stage.
[2] Sayyid 'Ulaiwi.
[3] Heude (pp. 169–70). Sulaiman Beg agrees closely.

§ 5. *The Last Mamluk.*

On no character met in these pages is it more difficult to pass sentence than on Daud. Born in Tiflis about 1767, brought to Baghdad in 1780, sold and resold and converted to Islam, he fell finally to the household of Sulaiman the Great. To skill in arms he was soon seen to add literary gifts, with a taste for formal religion: he became first a confidential writer—master alike of Arabic, Persian and Turkish composition—then Keeper of the Keys, then Seal-bearer. His marriage to the daughter of Sulaiman raised the suspicious jealousy of 'Ali Pasha, during whose reign he lived, a studious Mulla, in the shrine of 'Abdu 'l Qadir. Daftardar under 'Abdullah the Tutunchi, Kahya and again Daftardar under Sa'id, his fortunes thereafter have been traced.

At the time of his accession he was fifty years of age. His manners were courteous and unaffected, his charm was such as to captivate his most determined opponent. His appearance was that of a handsome bearded man of medium height and the carriage of dignity, his face placid but intellectual. His Court was the most elaborate and princely of which Baghdad had memory. He showed cowardice and irresolution on striking occasions, on others distinguished himself by bravery. He welcomed progress and enlightenment with one hand, and repelled it with another. His generosity accompanied a grinding avarice. His undoubted intelligence did not preclude the narrowest folly, the sorriest judgement. In treating individuals, he was inconstant and disloyal. He had the touch of higher quality, the spark of rarer personality which raised him from slave to Pasha while others (closely similar in type) were among the ruck of sanctimonious Mullas: nevertheless, it was with these that he had most in common. Yet, while in no essential a great man, he is a striking figure in more than the externals of extended rule and gorgeous setting; and wiser and stronger rulers than he must have fallen before the combination of circumstances which, after fifteen years of wealth and power, removed him abject and penniless from Baghdad.

His assumption of the Pashaliq was marked by great initial moderation and the fairest promises. The rebels of Kirkuk and the Baban family were pardoned, the followers of Sa'id could save their lives by payment of large fines. But a policy of uniform mildness was inconsistent with the times: the Qapuchi who had brought the farman could not return empty-handed: the Treasury was empty, revenue-paying at a standstill, and troops of all descriptions long unpaid. The punishment of some of the officers of the late Court was a necessary discipline, of others a gratification of revenge, and of a few a mere means of present extortion.[1] Only when the capital had been purged of dangerous persons, the Treasury partially replenished, the troops paid, and the Pasha proclaimed throughout the land, could he address himself to the task of government.

The half-generation of Daud's Pashaliq is marked by no first-class events. Internal disturbances conformed to the familiar type. Relations with Persia were inglorious but indecisive. His administration—bitterly criticized by European observers—enjoyed a prestige sufficient to ensure an obedience not obtained by better rulers, a security long remembered. The autumn and winter of 1817 were occupied by short vigorous tribal campaigns, the first of many to be conducted by the able but unscrupulous Kahya, Muḥammad Agha. Whether the objective was Bani Tamin, Shammar, Albu Musa, Bani 'Umair or Ghurair—whether the Kahya or a lesser officer was leading the Pasha's forces—the victories were easy and bloodless. The loot of live stock was followed in each case by a change of shaikh and a few months of good behaviour. In the early campaigns of 1818, the Dulaim were mulcted of revenue arrears, the Shammar Jarba brought strictly to book, the Yisar near Ḥillah stripped of their flocks. A rapid blow from Baghdad crippled the Shammar Togah. Later in the same year a dangerous position was created by the flight of Ṣadiq Beg—eldest surviving son of Buyuk Sulaiman—to the Zubaid: Jasim ul Shawi was already a fugitive with the Khaza'il: the two joined forces and a host of malcontents rallied to them. Daud, preoccupied with Baban affairs, might well fear that the history of 1813 was to be repeated, a son of the

[1] It was believed at Baghdad at the time that imprisonment and torture were common in these early days of the reign: nor can we entirely discredit the version of Heude (op. cit., p. 211). Keppel in 1824 heard that 1,500 had been put to death: Groves in 1831 calls Ṣaliḥ Beg "almost the only male relation he (Daud) had allowed to live". These are vast exaggerations: Duḥat limits the victims to two.

Great Pasha to enter Baghdad on tribal shoulders. He dethroned Shafullah, the Zubaid shaikh, and simultaneously made friendly overtures to Ṣadiq. A few weeks later a column was sent to chastise the outlaws, whose forces scattered while they sought safety in remoter tribes.[1] In other campaigns belonging to 1818, the Sugur, an 'Anizah section west of Musayyib, completely defeated the Agha sent against them; a second expedition against a rebel chief of the Shammar gained easy victory and abundant loot; a third operated with success in the Najf neighbourhood against desert tribes. Elsewhere, in October 1818, a reverse was suffered: picked companies of the Georgian guards were roughly handled by an inferior force of tribesmen. Many were killed, three hundred captured. A large force under the Kahya was immediately mustered.

In the expedition which ensued the objectives are not clear, but the operations (of which a vivid glimpse is given by an English writer[2] who visited Muḥammad Agha in camp) afforded choice examples of the "strange impolicy and savage oppression of the Turks towards their peasantry".[3] Not by force of arms, still less by wise settlement, did the Kahya gain his ends. He succeeded instead in trapping by the grossest treachery a dozen of the rebel shaikhs, and dispatched them to an abject captivity in Baghdad. Even this coup did not pacify the middle Euphrates: the men of the desert, furious at the outrage to honour and decency, raided to the Euphrates and across it. The Kahya's counter-raid by friendly tribes was successful. The battle-field shifted from Ḥiskah to 'Afak, thence towards the Tigris at Bughailah, and back to the Shamiyyah marshes. In the end resistance was broken, great fines collected, and Muḥammad Agha returned to a grateful welcome in Baghdad.

Of the tribal campaigns of 1819 the chief was directed at the Dulaim, in a stampede of whose tribesmen many were drowned swimming the Euphrates. Accounts were settled with other elements—Zauba', Jumailah, and Abu 'Isa. Finally a visit was paid to Shifathah. Arrears of taxation were everywhere collected, robes of investiture bestowed on the deserving. Much remained undone, however, in tribal and urban pacification. In Mandali

[1] Ṣadiq Beg was later pardoned.
[2] Porter. [3] Rich.

district a notorious outlaw, Sayyid Ṣaliḥ, terrorized the frontier. In the north the inveterate robbers of the Sinjar infested the roads to Mosul and Mardin in parties several hundreds strong: Tartar dispatch-riders were among the looted, and European travellers despaired of passing by that route. The Pasha of Mosul, himself insecure,[1] could not restore order. At Baṣrah crime and terrorism prevailed. A strong party of Najdi tribesmen broke into the town in July 1820, attacked and almost captured the Sarai, and wrought havoc and murder in the bazaars.

§ 6. *The raids from Karmanshah.*

The alarming invasion of 'Iraq by the prince of Karmanshah is the central event of Daud's Pashaliq. It was followed by a second invasion as formidable, and by a dangerous civil war. It calls for a glance at general 'Iraq-Persian relations for some years back and at Baban politics since the accession of Daud.

Persia, in the twenty distracted years of strife during which it substituted the Qajar for the Zand dynasty, had no attention to spare for 'Iraq. Agha Muḥammad, the fiendish eunuch who established the Qajar line, cast curious eyes, indeed, at the Holy Places of 'Iraq, but could not move to acquire them. Fatḥ 'Ali Shah, who succeeded in 1791 and outlasted many a Pasha of 'Iraq, was thought more willing to profit by the potential causes of war annually produced in Kurdistan: nervousness in 'Iraq increased as men heard of the splendour of the Persian Court and its reception of European diplomats. Wahhabi aggression was watched as keenly from Teheran as from Stambul; echoes of the sack of Karbala, of Ḥusain's own tomb, rang through Persia. To none was the religious horror deeper, the chance to intervene in 'Iraq more favourable. The abstinence of the Shah is best explained by his receipt of heavy money-bags from Baghdad, for avarice was his passion.

This crisis past, an event yet graver in its consequences for 'Iraq was the appointment of Muḥammad 'Ali Mirza to Karmanshah in 1805. Fierce, capable, ambitious, his province soon came to include a great part of Persia, and his army regiments

[1] Aḥmad Pasha Jalili succeeded Sa'dullah in 1813 and rebuilt the walls. He was removed in 1817 but restored in 1819, Ḥasan Pasha having ruled meanwhile.

trained on the European model. Earlier pages have traced his constant efforts of sword and pen to make the Baban province Persian soil. In the feeble days of Sa'id, Persian acquisition of all 'Iraq was freely discussed. The Mirza was restrained, perhaps, by the reluctance of his father to break the peace, by the pressure of foreign diplomats[1] in Teheran, and by large sums sent as hush-money to Karmanshah.[2] But none of these restraints prevailed for long: once again the Baban family threw open the door to the Persian prince.

The relations of Daud Pasha with Maḥmud Baban rapidly deteriorated from sworn friendship to open breach. At Sulaimaniyyah the talk was of Daud's jealous and restless intrigues against Baban unity; at Baghdad all blamed Maḥmud's perversity in guilty correspondence with Karmanshah, his flouting of Daud's fatherly advice. By 1818 the quarrel had no issue but in arms. The advance of Baghdad forces and the treachery of his own relations drove Maḥmud—now if not earlier—to address the Mirza. Ten thousand Persians crossed the frontier to support him, others raided Mandali, Badrah, and Jaṣṣan. Against the latter Daud at once dispatched his Kahya, who drove them back. Against the main body he sent 'Abdullah Pasha, uncle of Maḥmud, who reached Kirkuk to find all the valleys to eastward in possession of the Persians. Once again serious fighting was postponed. The Mirza demanded the restoration of Maḥmud. Daud, who had written for reinforcements to Stambul, could not refuse, and the Persian forces retired to their own country.

But this had removed but one of a hundred pretexts. In the following months other Baban pretenders—then living in half-retirement at Kirkuk—quarrelled with the local Aghas and fled as usual to Karmanshah. High officials in Baghdad were found to be involved in their ambitions, the Kahya himself among them. Malcontents and refugees gathered at the Court of Muḥammad 'Ali. Elsewhere and for other reasons Turkey and Persia were at this moment on the point of war. The Pasha of Erzerum had protected two nomad tribes claimed as Persian subjects. The Governor of Adharbaijan, to which the tribes

[1] The British Ambassador in Persia persuaded the Shah to respect the 1639 frontier.

[2] See Porter (ii, p. 202). His assertion that the Pasha paid a regular tribute to Karmanshah cannot be accepted.

belonged, was 'Abbas Mirza, heir of the Shah, who was further incited by a Russian emissary urging him to invade. Muḥammad 'Ali Mirza saw in the asylum of the Baban princes a similar pretext. He had, moreover, the standing complaint of Persian pilgrims' ill treatment in 'Iraq. From his father, whom he visited to consult, he now gained full permission. The Baban exiles were first dispatched on a roving commission. They crossed at Zuhab, looted Khaniqin, and raised the cry "To Baghdad!"; but their advance stopped as troops moved out to meet them.

Daud Pasha had hastened to inform his sovereign of the threat. His dispatch arrived just after news of the invasion of 'Abbas Mirza in the north. The Sultan replied in terms of war. Baghdad was to be strengthened, the army prepared, and Persia invaded as fast and far as might be. Immediate reinforcements of 5,000 Albanian "Haitahs" were ordered out, of whom some portion reached Baghdad. Maḥmud meanwhile was confirmed in the Baban government, while the Mirza bestowed the same prize on 'Abdullah Pasha, his uncle. Daud, adding the Haitah to his own forces, dispatched the whole and forty guns under the Kahya Muḥammad Agha to Zangabad, where they arrived in September 1821. After forty days' wait the Kahya moved by Kirkuk to the Bazyan pass, to find that 'Abdullah with 5,000 Persians had already entered the Shahrizor. The two armies moved from their different directions on Sulaimaniyyah. The resulting deadlock was solved in a way doubtful even to contemporary observers. The Kahya's army was dispirited by a Kurdish winter and by disease. Supplies were short and would be shorter. Muḥammad Agha attacked, was totally defeated, and himself left his scattered army to join the enemy. To many the attack was but a blind, his treachery flagrant: to others he appeared a gallant general whom fear after disaster had driven to refuge in the enemy's lines. His beaten forces retired on Kirkuk, towards which the Persian army (after installing 'Abdullah at Sulaimaniyyah) followed them. But the dour Turkoman peasantry of Kirkuk had little fancy for a Persian ruler; several were put to death for refusal to obey; the Qal'ah had no intention of surrender, and the Prince could not stay for a siege.[1] Moving by Tauq to Kifri, he occupied the line of

[1] Southgate (ii, p. 209).

townships and presented Muḥammad Agha, the renegade Kahya, to all as their Pasha-elect. The army halted on the Khaliṣ.

Daud Pasha had stocked and fortified his capital for a siege. Volunteer companies had been raised, the household guards prepared for a service rougher than palace-duties. Help from Stambul was asked. The city remained calm until news came that the Persians were at Hibhib, a bare day's march from Baghdad. Hundreds then fled from Baghdad to Ḥillah, prices rose, and a blockade appeared inevitable. Its issue would have been doubtful. Daud had a full treasury, copious stores, adequate man-power, and little fear of treachery within. The attacking forces were ample for an extended raid, but scarcely formidable in the siege of a great walled city. The trial was not made. Cholera was raging in the Persian army, possibly also in Baghdad: the Prince himself was seriously ill. For some weeks his army rested near Ba'qubah with an outpost at Khan Bani Sa'd, fifteen miles out of Baghdad. His foraging parties visited all parts, and one, in an encounter with Sufuk ul Faris, newly Shaikh of the Shammar, was severely handled. No sortie was made from Baghdad.

His illness and the wish to avoid a long and indeterminate campaign induced the Mirza to suggest terms. A Shi'i 'alim was sent in to negotiate. Daud Pasha replied by the mission of two ambassadors not less reverend. Settlement was quickly reached: Sulaimaniyyah was to be given to 'Abdullah Pasha, the Khaliṣ loot made good, and Turkish territory forthwith evacuated. The Persian army retired, recrossed the border, and marched for Karmanshah. Muḥammad 'Ali Mirza died at Karind. The retirement was a profound relief to Baghdad, news of the Mirza's death a greater. Fugitives to Ḥillah or Fallujah returned to the city. Squadrons sallied from Baghdad to punish tribesmen who had helped the Persians with guides or stores, and to restore control. An expedition visited tribes on the Dujail. The Persian garrison left at Khaniqin was entirely destroyed. An edict announced the remission of all revenue for a year from villages stripped by the enemy.

A state of war, however, between Sultan and Shah continued. 'Abbas Mirza was still invading Ottoman soil in northern Kurdistan, and the Shah himself was reported at Hamadan with a large army. On the Turkish side, the Walis of Diyarbakr,

Mosul, and Baghdad were instructed to counter-attack. Among the Sovereign's orders was a specific command to Daud to lay Muḥammad Agha by the heels. Accordingly, an army of 10,000 men was marshalled at Baghdad under the new Kahya, Ḥaji Ṭalib Agha,[1] and moved with its horse and guns by the Khurasan road to the frontier.

Muḥammad 'Ali Mirza was succeeded by his son Muḥammad Ḥusain, whom revenge and ambition led to contemplate an invasion of 'Iraq on a large scale. Ḥaji Ṭalib had barely reached Zuhab when the Persian general, who had levied an army of 40,000, crossed the frontier at numerous points. At Mandali his forces massacred five hundred Turks. Moving on Qizil Rubaṭ, he compelled the Kahya to give way. A conference of Turkish captains resolved on retreat; but the Persians, advancing into Shahroban and the Khaliṣ areas, were simultaneously harassed by tribesmen, who cut up their scouts and burnt all crops on their line of march. A Shammar force eight hundred strong under Sufuk decoyed and then engaged and roundly defeated a large force of Persians—a feat soon copied by other tribal contingents. Cholera was again rife among the Persian troops. They retired, looting as they went. The frontier was crossed, the second invasion was finished and had failed.

Meanwhile in Shahrizor the death of Muḥammad 'Ali Mirza had restarted the tedious rivalries of the Baban family. Maḥmud Pasha, by a bold march and a costly battle, regained Sulaimaniyyah. Persian and Ardalan troops drove him from it. 'Abdullah, accepted for the moment by both Baghdad and Karmanshah, held the throne until Maḥmud, abandoning Turkish for Persian allegiance, replaced him with the consent of both. The mission of Aḥmad Beg, brother of Daud, to assume the direct government of the State sent Maḥmud hot-foot to Persia, and brought Baghdad troops to Kirkuk. That they were accompanied by 'Abdullah Pasha—time after time the Persian candidate—cannot surprise students of these intrigues remarkable for the absence of any consistent loyalty, any humane principle, any end but the crudest self-interest. Peace descended only when, by arrangement of the two powers, Maḥmud was

[1] Father of Sulaiman Beg the historian. He was a freedman of Buyuk Sulaiman.

restored to Sulaimaniyyah and 'Abdullah to Keui. The first Treaty of Erzerum, signed on the 18th of July 1823, was an important document in frontier history, but it held little promise of settlement. The old frontier of Murad IV (which for two centuries the arms of both parties had sought to define) was reaffirmed no more exactly, and every scope and pretext for border restlessness remained.

Little remains to record of the Pashaliq of Daud. A dangerous but abortive rebellion was followed by the usual course of tribal chastisements and politics, and by some years' rule of the type long familiar in 'Iraq.

The appearance of Muḥammad Agha—the rebel Kahya of the Shahrizor campaign—as leader of a formidable rising on the middle Euphrates caused the liveliest fears in Baghdad. 'Abdullah Agha in 1778 had gained the Pashaliq by determined rebellion and the support of the Georgians: Muḥammad in 1824 was a stronger character, a more notable leader of the Mamluks, and thereby the more alarming outlaw. His following grew quickly from the rallying of adventurers, outlaws, and tribesmen ever ready to throw off the present yoke. The country was still demoralized from the Persian raids, and Baghdad indignant at new taxes levied by Daud. Ḥaji Ṭalib had been replaced as Kahya by the feeble and foolish Aḥmad, brother of the Pasha. Meanwhile the army at Ḥillah grew, oaths of allegiance were taken in the Holy Cities, and an attack on Baghdad contemplated. The rebel forces defeated without difficulty two weak columns sent from Baghdad against them. But this success was turned to no profit, and a new determination appeared at the Court in Baghdad. Ḥaji Ṭalib resumed the office of Kahya and was empowered to make sweeping changes in the staff of his frightened master. He mustered a force, while the Pasha exercised his gifts in diplomacy. Georgian renegades were attracted back by pardon and promises; tribes were broken by the advancement of rivals. Ḥaji Ṭalib, advancing on Ḥillah, met an army 4,000 strong. But propaganda had done its work. The desertion of much of his forces, and too little tenacity among the rest, left Muḥammad Agha a beaten fugitive.

The collapse of this rebellion was followed by some improvement in tribal conditions. Zubaid and Shammar contingents aided the Pasha in his chastisement of ill doers, while his own forces were led by a brilliant officer, Sulaiman Agha Mir Akhor, Master of the Horse. The largest expedition was in southern 'Iraq. A combined movement was organized to restore the prestige of government in the Muntafiq, where old blind Ḥamud ul Thamir had now for years paid neither tribute nor respect to his Pasha. Rival Sa'dun candidates were made welcome at Court, and accompanied the Mir Akhor towards the dirah of the Muntafiq. Ḥamud summoned the Cha'ab to his aid, sent agents to recruit in 'Arabistan, and a messenger to the Imam of Masqaṭ, Sayyid Sa'id. Many elements contributed to his force. His sons, Faiṣal and Mâjid, led it to the walls of Baṣrah, which suffered the rigours of a blockade. From the water the fleet of Masqaṭ pressed no less dangerously until bought off by the Mutasallim. The Mir Akhor's march on Baṣrah was purposely slow: the port could defend itself against a gunless enemy, and time was the best solvent for Ḥamud's army. He had judged well. The followers, then the allied tribes, then the very sons of Ḥamud realized the hopelessness of the attack on Baṣrah, keenly as they had pressed it for a few days. Section after section went over to 'Ajil, the young and brilliant Sa'dun on whom the rule of the Muntafiq had been bestowed. 'Ajil, distributing largesse and favours, came into his own; Ḥamud fled; and the Mir Akhor retired to Baghdad. Baṣrah and its tribes relapsed to normal conditions, broken only by fierce quarrels at Zubair. The State of Ḥuwaizah was declining but still powerful. The relations of the Cha'ab with Baṣrah were still undefined, the boundary between the Shushtar and the Baṣrah provinces still doubtful within wide limits. The Treaty of Erzerum did not solve the problems of this frontier, which was the more disputed after the foundation of Muḥammarah at the Karun mouth in 1812. Its founder, of the Muḥaisin tribe, was a Cha'ab vassal; but Ḥaji Jabir, his son, went far to throw off their suzerainty, and Muḥammarah by 1830 was rather a rival than a support to the Cha'ab power.

The last years of Daud Pasha were marked (apart from certain phenomena of progress reserved for a later page) throughout the Pashaliq by little of significance. Agha followed Agha at Baṣrah, at Mardin, at Kirkuk. The leading tribesmen kept their place—'Ajil in the Muntafiq, Ḍhirb in the Khaza'il, Wadi ul Shafullah in the Zubaid. In the Milli, Aiyub Beg had succeeded Timur his father, and Faris of the Shammar Jarba given way to Sufuk. The latter, high in favour from his feats against the Persian invaders, lost it and became the worst enemy of the Pasha. In the Baban kingdom the settlement of 1823 did not endure. It was followed by the first phase of a long struggle between the brothers Maḥmud and Sulaiman Pashas. A Persian garrison remained in Sulaimaniyyah until the death of Fath 'Ali Shah in 1834. The Baban State, indeed, was already in decline. It was now more dominated by Persia than at any time by Turkey. The struggle of the brothers led to lawlessness and poverty, and the plague was to complete its ruin. Its northern neighbour Ruwanduz was gaining rapid ground under the Blind Pasha. In the Mosul Pashaliq, Jalili followed Jalili without more incident than the mutiny and violence long habitual in the city, and a devastating famine in 1827.

X

THE END OF AN EPOCH

§ 1. *A last glance at Mamluk 'Iraq.*

'Iraq a century later remembers Daud Pasha for his learning and Muslim piety, for the magnificence of his slave-guards and domestic army, his generosity, and his frank independence of Stambul. Of the first we cannot judge, though tales of mullas and professors silent in his presence are still told. Of his religion, we may borrow a phrase from the historian of a more famous monarch: he was "pious without effort", and almost without effect on conduct; this philosopher-king of the East had all the picturesqueness, a touch of the benignity, none of the spirituality of an Aurelius. We pass to safer ground in his entourage. In the courtyard of his Sarai stood Janissary guards and scores of Georgian attendants in brilliant uniform. By the door of the audience-chamber appeared the three horse-tails of the Wazirate with the Imperial Crescent and Star. In the Diwan within, nothing was lacking of gaudy splendour. The furniture of the ante-rooms, the royal reception of visitors, the detail of ceremony, the bearing of every courtier and attendant, impressed visitors from Europe as "a state . . . perfectly that of a royal prince".[1] Sober and critical observers[2] were astonished at the signs of profuse wealth, of a culture consistent if limited, of a finished luxury thought to exceed that of the Sultan's court.

The principal officers of the Pashaliq—apart from the major governorships of Baṣrah, Kirkuk, and Mardin—were the Kahya, counterpart of the Grand Wazir at Stambul, several Muṣaḥibs (courtiers or councillors) among whom was the "Babu'l 'Arab",[3] and the regular members of the Diwan: Daftardar, Secretary

[1] Porter (ii, p. 249). [2] Heude (p. 172); Aucher-Eloy (p. 235).
[3] Official spokesman of the Arab tribes.

of the Diwan, Chief Chamberlain, Master of Ceremonies, Chief Equerry, Head of the Bailiffs, and Warden of the Private Apartments. Among the Aghas of the Interior, whose number and equipment were the glory of the Court, were the personal retainers of the Pasha, each with the title of his office—of the Wardrobe, the Coffee, the Sweetmeats, the Harness, the Carpets, the Laving-Water, the Drinking-Water, the Pipe, the Standard. Riding abroad, the Pasha was accompanied by a score of these personal Aghas led by the Treasurer, the Sword-bearer, and Chief of the Watchmen. The transition is easy from these to the military forces of the Pashaliq; for since the days of Abu Lailah the Georgian bodyguard had grown into a brigade of the choicest troops.[1] Sulaiman the Great had greatly increased their numbers and organized them as a military force. Daud gave them foreign instructors and modern arms. Tradition still speaks of three Mamluk regiments each named after a son of the Pasha, and each a thousand strong. To other military resources—Lawand and 'Ugail mercenaries, Tufenkchi and Baratli regular infantry, Janissary and Topchi still faintly Imperial in character, tribal rabble, Kurdish princes' contingents, and the few surviving feudal horsemen—the foregoing narrative has at times referred.

The revenue of the Pashaliq was collected by expedients of varying age and origin, some survivals of feudal usage and some devised newly by the latest Pasha. His Customs, varying at his whim, were a source of gain less vexatious to trade and travel than the wayside tolls of every shaikh and village headman: the farms of Sanjaq, canal, or tribal territory brought to the Treasury but a fraction of what was squeezed from the ultimate payers, who suffered the more as they were weak and accessible. The poll-tax of Jew and Christian was collected, with many abuses, by the highest bidder. Further sums accrued by taxes on goods in transit, by state-monopoly in the commonest trades, by falsified exchange-rates and corrupted coinage. Sheer plunder was known to drive leading citizens to seek redress in Stambul itself, and not without effect. The duties of Police

[1] Compare Niebuhr (ii, p. 256), dealing with 1765, with Thabit dealing with the last period: the former gives 800 Ich Aghalari, the latter 1,800: the Aghas of the Outside (Kahya, officials, and their households and retainers) were in 1765 200, in 1830 1,700.

were performed in the chief towns by Janissary posts and by the bailiffs of the Pasha and his officers. For justice, there was the yearly Qadhi in Baghdad and his lesser counterparts elsewhere: life was cheap, the Shara' rigid, and all was for sale.

Of government in general, a true picture would indeed give prominence to the endemic tribal disobedience with which it was every year's task to deal—to robber bands unsuppressed, travellers impoverished by wayside blackmail—to ruthless taxation of the few accessible, powerlessness to touch the rest. Towns and lands were still sold to be governed by this or that favourite slave or genial courtier, Aghas still bullied, troopers still raped and robbed: the Court, far richer than the country could rightly support, harboured many a foolish, ignorant, and fanatical adviser: and to the faults of a low conception, a lamentable system, of government were added sad weaknesses in the present ruler. But the picture must show more than this. Civil war was an end. Adequate forces were supported to punish recalcitrant bedouin and to parade the Capital. In the Pasha's steady fostering of disunion in every tribe was the embryo of a policy to detribalize. In his constant bestowal of lands, consciousness of the need of securer tenure may have blended with mere generosity, for which quality he was famous. If many suffered exactions in his name, not a few were delighted by bounty at his own hands. Schools and a printing press were founded. Baghdad was beautified by new mosques and the triple-arched bazaar which to-day shelters its busiest exchanges. Private enterprise erected many fine dwelling-houses in the fashion of the period, work more pretentious and more durable than anything built since.

Such in outline was the 'Iraq of the third decade of the nineteenth century, such its ruler, its luxury at Court, its groaning misgovernment abroad. Of its fortunes under the long Mamluk dispensation nothing remains to record but the catastrophe which for ever removed them. Many violent changes witnessed in these pages have seemed to follow no rule or cause but caprice or accident, to involve no process of evolution or principle. In the fall of the slave-government it is otherwise. Remarkable calamities of nature, indeed, assisted its collapse and saved a death-struggle, but the conditions, the causes, the instruments which forbade its longer continuance in the nineteenth century, had now long been working. The fall of Daud Pasha and his whole dynasty and régime came with a dramatic suddenness and finality; but for a full generation before 1830 the fall had been inevitable. The general processes of history had demanded the removal of an anachronism: great changes in the government of Turkey had made the demand more clear and urgent: in its dealings with other powers of Europe the Mamluk rule had shown too little modernity: and by the person of its Governor it was to give, as the issue proved, the final provocation.

§ 2. *The change of times.*

The connexions of 'Iraq with the powers of western Europe had increased since the later eighteenth century in scale and closeness. We have the memoirs of thirty travellers, and these were but a fraction of 'Iraq's visitors from Europe and India. By 1800 French Carmelites and a Greek banker and sometimes a Venetian merchant at Mosul entertained subalterns of the East India Company passing to and from furlough. Tartar riders carried to the Bosphorus the dispatches of European consuls with those of the Pasha. From Baghdad to Aleppo, by the desert route, ran the regular camel-mail of the Company. The labouring river-craft from Baṣrah brought the satins and velvets of France, English cloth, metal goods from Germany, glass of Vienna and Bohemia, sugar of America. French and Italian religious orders had settlements, and the Bishop of Babylon often combined the charge of his see with the post of Consul of France. Both at Baṣrah and Baghdad French consular officers had been first in the field: but at neither did they assume a consequence worthy of their nation. The choice of agents was at times unhappy, and no great volume of French interests lay in their hands. Ill paid and ill found, they lacked address in dealing with the local government. In 1796 a French political mission[1] passed through 'Iraq; but two years later their representatives in 'Iraq were arrested, their papers confiscated, and their premises occupied. After release, their operations remained upon a scale humble if not obscure. Their Agent's claim for formal precedence over British diplomats was put aside by the Pasha himself with

[1] To which is due the *Voyage* of M. Olivier.

little ceremony. The chosen instructor of Daud's troops was a Frenchman, as had been the physician of Buyuk Sulaiman; their consul at Baṣrah had some acquaintance among the notables of tribe and city; but the superior consequence and prosperity of the Company's staff was ever a source of jealous indignation.[1]

In the position of the Honourable Company great improvement had been made since 1780. It had earned the personal gratitude of Sulaiman Pasha for its aid at his accession, and he repaid the debt by twenty years of complete favour and by frank utilization of its services. In 1782 he placed orders through it for arms and ammunition from Bombay, in 1798 and 1799 demanded a further consignment of munitions with European instructors from India. In 1802 another such shipment lay on the Tigris by Ctesiphon just as the struggles for the Pashaliq were at their height. The meditation of the Resident was more than once gratefully employed: on the rumoured appointment of the Shawi to the Pashaliq[2] in 1787 the Pasha begged instant communication through him with the Ambassador in Stambul: and in 1798 it was through Mr. Manesty at the Baṣrah Agency that accounts with the Sultan of Masqaṭ were to be settled. To the gradual but open increase of the Resident's influence in tribe and town the Mamluk government offered no objection, though moments of its most striking favour might be preceded by, and never for long precluded, acute differences with the local authority. In 1793 (among many such) broke out a quarrel with local Jews of Baṣrah and with the Mutasallim so severe as to lead to the Residency removing for nearly two years to Kuwait.

Baghdad had become the permanent station of a native Agent of the Company in 1783. Thereafter it was frequently visited by the Resident from Baṣrah: and in 1798—an inevitable development, but designed especially to meet supposed Napoleonic intrigues in the Middle East—a permanent British Resident was appointed there also. The powers of a Consulate were conferred in 1802. Thereafter Baghdad became the chief centre of British influence, of which the character as well as the degree could not fail to be gradually modified. Of acquisition or penetration there was no sign or question. The immense

[1] Cf. Fontanier (i, pp. 171 ff.); Sauvebœuf (p. 88).

[2] P. [illegible] supra.

services which a wise and progressive government might render to 'Iraq could not but occur to British traveller and 'Iraqi citizen alike; but such imaginings were remote, unformulated, unwarranted. Nevertheless the increase in British prestige up to and after Daud Pasha was very marked. The Pashas became aware of India as a great neighbour with whom to exchange courtly messages and occasional protests. Military stores continued to be ordered thence. The state visits to 'Iraq of General Malcolm (journeying from missions in Persia to Bombay) showed to all the pomp and wealth of an English elchi. The establishments of the Residents[1] both at Baghdad and Baṣrah—the large premises, prosperous staff, uniformed flunkeys, stables, river-craft, and guard of Sepoys—were those of a specially favoured nation. From 1807 to 1809, though war had broken out in Europe between Great Britain and Turkey, the British representatives in 'Iraq continued honoured and unmolested, and the Pasha to correspond amicably with Calcutta. More and more, since the first intimacy of Harford Jones with Buyuk Sulaiman, the "Baleos" became a figure of importance in the Pashaliq. The appointment of Claudius James Rich to the Residency in 1808 was an important milestone. Possessed of every advantage of breeding, attainments, and temperament, in thirteen years he added immensely to the dignity of his Residency, which became an acknowledged centre of the best local society, the rendezvous of the highest officials and notables, an open guest-house, and a home of antiquarian research. Rich maintained himself through the stormy last days of Sulaiman the Little, enjoyed the high favour of 'Abdullah Pasha, and congratulated Daud on his accession.

His relations with the latter, after a first period of cordiality, were those inevitable between a vigorous, disinterested, and scrupulous Englishman and an Oriental despot surrounded by ignorant and fanatical counsellors. Daud and his ministers could not but be nettled by constant criticism of their invasions of European rights, their inflation and deflation of coinage-values, their perverse hindrance of European trade. In 1820 the Pasha did not scruple to declare that "no European rights existed in

[1] From 1798 to 1810 there were Residencies at both. In 1810 Baghdad became the Political Agency in Turkish Arabia, with Baṣrah as its subordinate. In 1822 Baṣrah was further degraded to be a Native Agency, held by an Armenian.

Baghdad". This preposterous verdict—contrary to reason, to history, and to the specific orders of the Sultan—was accompanied by a customs duty doubled against British goods, and by every description of incivility and obstruction. Rich determined to leave Baghdad for Bombay: the Pasha forbade it. The operations which followed are unique in the history of diplomacy. Rich, supported by his Sepoy guard, the Residency servants, and some chance visitors, determined to resist arrest. The building was surrounded by infantry, camel-men, and artillery, whom barricades and rifle-muzzles confronted. Cowardice, however, extricated the Pasha from the absurd position to which avarice and folly had brought him. His officers were deterred by their respect for the Baleos and by the gravity of the position, while many quarters of Baghdad were prepared to rise against a hated ruler. The troops were called off, but Rich remained a prisoner. Not until the Governor of Bombay had addressed strong missives both to Baghdad and to Stambul was Daud finally (in May 1821) induced to permit Rich's departure to India. Good relations were restored between the Pasha and the incoming Resident, nor were they subsequently broken to the same extent.

Thus British diplomatic annals in Mamluk 'Iraq (in themselves vivid and interesting) demonstrate from a fresh angle the contention of the present pages—that the government of the dynasty founded by Ḥasan Pasha in 1704, and now in moral though not material decline under Daud, was an offensive anachronism and as such condemned. A nation of Europe, which in two centuries had built up its trade and attained patiently a legitimate (but not less remarkable) social and diplomatic position, could not see these advantages demolished at the capricious word of the venal and backward Government of Baghdad. The Resident in 'Iraq was proportionately a more eminent figure than the Ambassador at Stambul: insults to the one must attract the grave notice of the other and through him of the Government of Turkey. In permitting the British Resident to become (as many now acclaimed him) the second man in 'Iraq, the Mamluk Pashas had shown some recognition of the means of progress, some willingness to be guided, some lightening of prejudice, occasional friendship and courtesy; but they had thereby admitted to their midst standards to which they could not conform, a phase of modernity wholly discrepant with their methods, and simultaneously critics at close quarters whose reports would reach the Capital. The Sultan could not but learn that the Government of Baghdad, which had failed to protect the province from Wahhabi raiders and failed to keep peace with Persia, was even providing cause of estrangement with the Powers of Europe.

On such lines lay one of the reasons for which the central government would gladly replace the 'Iraq dynasty by its own rule, as for a century it had been powerless to do. And the Turkey which finally undertook the task was not the Turkey which had appointed Kaisariyyali, removed 'Umr, and sought peace by the appointment of Buyuk Sulaiman: it was an Empire reanimated and yearly more intolerant of the schism and many delinquencies of the 'Iraq Mamluks.

The Treaty of Qainarchi was by many regarded as the death-blow of Ottoman greatness; yet even in that age a spirit of reforming optimism was not dead in the disheartened, backward, and largely apathetic empire. Little came, indeed, of the military and naval improvements of the Admiral, Ghazi Ḥasan Pasha: but they indicated both the lines of future reform and the reluctance of Turkish opinion to accept it. Sultan Salim III ascended the throne in 1789 by temperament, training, and conviction a reformer. During a reign of twenty years he advanced far towards destroying the anachronisms whereby his country was weak and mutinous and ever less able to maintain its place. Three years after his accession he began a series of fundamental reforms: feudal abuses were to end with the gradual absorption of feudal lands into the domains of the State; provincial governors were to serve for a fixed term of three years only; tax farming and its oppressive abuses were to vanish. Schools were founded, printing encouraged, foreign works translated into Turkish, missions dispatched to the capitals of Europe. Of this ambitious programme, some part took effect in the more amenable localities; to 'Iraq, it need not be said, there was no question of attempting its application. In military reform Sultan Salim proceeded slowly, yet too fast for the times. He allowed the creation of a single regiment on modern lines, but a hint to the Diwan of extending new methods to Janissaries produced instant mutiny. The seed of a new army was sown by the personal enthusiasm of the Sultan in soil rich with the superb military virtues of the race, but stifled by the deep roots and poisonous herbage of bullying, shameless, and obsolete Janissaries, and reactionary obscurantist 'Ulama, to whom the drill and gunnery of Europe were the antics of infidels, Ḥaji Baktash a better strategist than Suwarrow or Napoleon. The constant tale of mutiny and oppression by the Janissaries in every part of the Empire proclaimed the grossness of the present abuses, yet the difficulty of reform; and in 1807 Salim was deposed by the ruffians whom he had failed to exterminate or to modernize. Reform took fresh life with the accession in 1808 of a young prince of vigour and principle, Maḥmud II. But again reaction triumphed; and the young Sultan with bitter helplessness was forced publicly to ban the reforms nearest to his heart, while the glaring abuses of the Janissaries were confirmed and blessed. For another half generation the old companies, supported by the Divines and the whole of conservative opinion, showed in a dozen battles their hundredfold inferiority to Greeks and Egyptians, and in a score of mutinies their shameless sacrifice of all to their own privileges.

Not until 1826 did Sultan Maḥmud venture to exact from his Diwan a decree insisting that a proportion of each company should submit to the new training. The usual mutiny followed, and on an alarming scale; but the issue was otherwise. The whole body of Janissaries in Stambul was destroyed to the last man. Many thousands more were put to death in the various cities of Turkey. Near and far, the time-honoured Companies were dispersed or annihilated, their name proscribed, their standards destroyed: and the assemblage of new troops, on a new system, was ordered.

This great day of deliverance for the Turkish Empire, owed to qualities of a single man, had direct results in 'Iraq which will be seen. With the partial failure of its due harvest of benefits—the result of Russian aggression pressed on before the new Ottoman arms should develop full power—this history is not concerned, nor with the difficulties in Europe, Asia, and Africa to which the youthful Nidham Jadid could not prove fully adequate. The other principal reforms of Maḥmud II showed no less the spirit of a new Turkey to which the Mamluks of 'Iraq must be anathema. While Daud Pasha in Baghdad was bestowing and entailing most of 'Iraq soil to favourites and dependants, the Sultan was placing the great body of Religious Endowments under State control. A single imperial decree called back to the State all the feudal grants (now long abused) of several centuries; the ruler of 'Iraq was daily granting fresh and irregular privileges. His weak opportunist policy to tribal Shaikh and Kurdish prince was far removed from his nominal master's decision to put down each and all of the petty tyrannous "Valley Begs", to whom, indeed, the Mamluk Pasha might himself be likened on a greater scale. In Stambul efforts were being made—efforts which an ensuing century has not seen fully fruitful—to stop abuses of taxation and official oppression; in 'Iraq caprice, swayed by fanaticism and avarice, was the sole arbiter of taxation and procedure.

Of these great changes in the Empire, indeed, the rulers of 'Iraq were ill informed. Few of the Mamluk Aghas had visited Stambul, few knew the very geography of their Empire: they knew the remoteness of the Capital and the proved powerlessness of the Sovereign to impose his wishes in 'Iraq. The Pasha, with his limitation of outlook, his old-school education, his unwise and ignorant advisers, did not and could not know the extent of the reforms in Turkey nor the iron character of its ruler.[1] Yet, as we have seen the Mamluk Pashas extend and then reverse a half-welcome to the European pioneers of progress in their country, so the last of their line did not wholly reject (yet did not in spirit half fulfil) some part of the reforms which he was bidden to apply. The character of the Janissaries in 'Iraq had changed much in the preceding century. Fewer and fewer, and finally none, of their officers came from Stambul. Drafts of recruits ceased to arrive from abroad, and the lack was made good by local enlistment. Their last appearance, perhaps, as a force with any pretence of imperial character was in the succession struggles of 1802. Thereafter—and indeed before—

[1] The contrast is remarkable between the characters of Pasha and Padishah: the former suave, learned, courteous, picturesque, but weak, cowardly, and misled; the latter clear-sighted, vigorous, determined, sacrificing ease and peace for reform, and helped by few or none in battling against the gigantic evils of his Empire.

the Janissaries were but a corps locally raised, locally paid, and similar in all essentials to the Baratli or Tufenkchi, though still ready with the phrases into which tradition had crystallized, and differing somewhat in dress and function. Elsewhere in Turkey their bullying oppression increased as they neared their end: in 'Iraq it diminished as local forces overshadowed them. In the middle eighteenth century, not the Pasha himself dared to remain unregistered in a Janissary Company: enrolment was a social necessity, involving not duties but self-protection. Under the later Slave Pashas this ceased with the monopoly of privilege for which it stood, though non-combatant membership was still common.

Sultan Maḥmud, immediately upon his destruction of the Stambul Janissaries, demanded similar action from the provincial governors. The order reached Baghdad in the late summer of 1826. The Pasha kept it secret, hoping by a loyal obedience at once to improve relations with his Sovereign, and remove the only power in the Pashaliq not wholly his own. Forces were brought from out-stations to Baghdad, when, on an appointed day, the Sarai was packed with chosen Mamluk troops. Two batteries commanded the courtyard. In the midst stood the Janissaries, of whom eighteen companies were at the time stationed in Baghdad. Such a gathering was unique; the hush of expectation was poignant. The royal decree, read aloud, was received with incredulous amazement. The Pasha, with tears at the fate of the Janissaries—ancient and familiar bulwark of Islam—bade all be enrolled in the new forces which were to take their place. Without violence or rancour, without change of commander, every soldier of the companies doffed his qalpaq for a head-dress of the new pattern, registered his name in the Nidhamiyyah regiment, and heard joyous salvoes of the guns prepared, if need had been, for another duty. Similar scenes, as bloodless and as remote from the prototype in Stambul, followed in Ḥillah, Baṣrah, and elsewhere. It remained to equip the new army. The direction of its training was put in the hands of M. Deveaux, a French officer[1] who had served Muḥammad 'Ali Mirza at Karmanshah. Advice was given also by Major Taylor, the

[1] Huart (p. 175, foot-note)

Resident, whose son was undertaking in 1830 to raise cavalry regiments on the same model.[1] As early as 1824 the Pasha had asked Bombay for a British doctor and equipment for a thousand men; but these, intended for the Mamluk guards, had been refused. After the formation of the Nidham Jadid (and specifically for it) he applied for assistance on a greater scale—for officers and instructors and artisans, for three large armed vessels, for large quantities of munitions. Again he was refused —not least, it may be, from fear that these very arms might serve the uses of rebellion. But the New System grew: by 1830 several thousand men were under arms and training, regularly paid and heartened by early successes in tribal war. With the enrolment and use of these forces went the institution of factories for their clothing and other military requirements.

"Everything", writes an English missionary[2] in Baghdad in the same month, "is tending to the settlement of a European influence. . . . This tendency to adopt European manners and improvements is not only manifested in the military department, but in others more important. The Pasha has a great desire to introduce steam navigation on these two beautiful rivers. . . . In fact I feel that the Lord is preparing great changes in the heart of this nation."

For such a view there was indeed some show of justification—factories opening, a mechanic from Geneva, a gardener from Greece: talk of quicker traffic from Europe to India by the Euphrates route, and the sight of British officers—Ormsby and Elliot—busy with the surveys of the rivers. To the criticism of the last phase of the Mamluk régime that it was static, even reactionary, so much defence[3] could be offered: signs of material progress, modern arms, hope of improved transport, increasing consequence of European representatives. The door to progress was not wholly shut: rather it was opened fitfully, slammed capriciously. There was desire for the phenomena, none for the

[1] Fontanier (i, p. 192) characteristically but absurdly says that Taylor tried to oust Deveaux from his duties and to bring a regiment of Sepoys from India as a model.

[2] Mr. A. N. Groves, *Journal.* His account, being written from day to day, is extremely vivid and authentic within its limits.

[3] Materials for such defence are in Mira'tu 'l Zaura and in Groves (especially pp. 1-17), and Stoqueler (pp. 44 ff.).

spirit, of advance; and not a yard was gained on the path of righteous government.[1]

§ 3. *Act of man and act of God.*

By 1830 the person, the household, the dynasty, and whole order of Daud Pasha was doomed for reasons to which some justice has now been done. To the self-respect of the parent Empire, the century-long independence of Baghdad was intolerable. In the sole particular of his substitution of Ni<u>dh</u>am for Janissary forces had Daud Pasha obeyed his Sovereign—and in the Mamluk guards he still retained an instrument more dangerous to his overlord, and no easier to control, than the Janissaries had been in other provinces. Every other of the abuses at which the Sultan was at inexorable war flourished in 'Iraq and would flourish again: the vagaries of the Pasha were offending the diplomats of powerful nations: the anachronisms of the Mamluk régime were now absurd, now humiliating, and now dangerous. When the Pasha of Baghdad—richest of provinces save only Egypt—forbore to help his Sovereign with suitable remissions in the desperate need of the Russian war, the last straw was placed which broke imperial forbearance. It was resolved to unite the 'Iraq province to the reformed Empire. The first step must be the mission of a solemn envoy to demand the relinquishment of power by the Mamluk Pasha. For this duty was selected Ṣadiq Effendi, a noted diplomat. He was entrusted, ostensibly, with the collection in Baghdad and elsewhere of contributions to the new armies; and with his departure from Stambul rises the curtain upon the last act of the Mamluks of 'Iraq.

Annual processions of Qapuchis bringing farman and Khila' were familiar; but instinct warned Daud that the present embassy was more significant. He made ready large sums collected by years of avarice wherewith to buy security if need be. A high official was dispatched as far as Tuz Khormatu to meet Ṣadiq Effendi with a four-horse carriage (unique rarity in 'Iraq) and with gifts of welcome. But the envoy had already determined

[1] The description of Daud Pasha by Stoqueler (p. 44) as "a successful innovator on the Turkish system of rule" in the same sentence as mentions "his long resistance to the Porte" may confirm or explain the fears of the Bombay Government when asked for munitions.

upon his policy: fresh from blood-curdling accounts of Daud Pasha told him at Mosul by the Jalili, he treated the reception committee with the greatest haughtiness. On arrival at the suburb of A'dhamiyyah he refused (contrary to all precedent) to halt by the shrine of the Grand Imam before entering the city. Approaching Baghdad forthwith, he passed between lines of the Pasha's guards and sought his allotted quarters without a glance at the pageant of reception or a visit to Daud who awaited him in full splendour in the Sarai. Scared faces in Baghdad grew longer.

His first visit to the palace was paid on the morrow, when, by delaying his rising to the latest moment, Daud Pasha repaid pointedly, if unwisely, the discourtesy of his guest. Formal compliments were exchanged, coffee and sweetmeats offered. No word was uttered of the objects of the mission. Next day,[1] a second call was as formal and as barren. At the third, Ṣadiq at last showed his hand: the Pasha was deposed, must instantly deliver his government. Delay, compromise, was refused. The Pasha's protestations gave way to threats; and before Ṣadiq departed a violent issue was certain. Returned in rage and apprehension to his quarters, the Qapuchi demanded Mir Akhor Sulaiman Agha, bade him obey the Padishah by slaying this shameless rebel, and promised him the Pashaliq as a reward. The Mir Akhor asked for time, and sped hot-foot to his master in the Sarai. Gravely disturbed, Daud Pasha called Muḥammad Maṣraf and the Jew banker Isḥaq to his councils. Within an hour all had agreed: danger was balanced against danger, fear with fear: without haste or panic the formal ambassador of the Sultan was sentenced to death by murder. On the evening of the 19th of October 1830, after the hour of prayer, companies of the Regulars filed silently into their places around the envoy's lodging. Quietly each room was filled with trusted Mamluks. The servants were made fast: the chosen murderer, Khalid Agha, with Ramadhan Agha a chamberlain of the Pasha, broke without ceremony into the presence of the doomed and now horrified ambassador. At his scarce-articulate question they told their orders, short and simple. His prayers for respite, for

[1] According to Thabit. Mir'at implies rather that the critical interview (of which he ventures to give the *ipsissima verba*) took place on the first day.

a last interview with Daud, his entreaties and promises availed nothing. Khalid's huge hands closed on his throat, and strangled life with his sword-knot.

The Pasha, disguised and surrounded by his bodyguard, had waited near the Mu'a<u>dh</u><u>dh</u>am Gate for news of a successful issue. When it was brought, he entered the death chamber, himself verified that life was extinct, and bade them bury the body. His expressions of regret were not wholly insincere: his weak character reacted from its unusual resolution, and the future, inevitably to follow this desperate crime, was menacing enough. Another Qapuchi yet awaited at Mosul for the results of Ṣadiq's mission: another lay behind at Diyarbakr. Meanwhile the news spread rapidly through Baghdad. One party feared already that the Pasha would find safety only in surrender to the Shah: to another, his forces seemed adequate to face anything that a distant and preoccupied Sovereign could send: some hoped that Stambul would, after a century of precedent, close its eyes to the Mamluk peccadilloes. The Pasha, reporting the Qapuchi's death of cholera to Stambul, attempted for a time similarly to deceive the public in Baghdad.[1] But the truth was known; already prices rose as all sought to buy food against whatever troubles might ensue: and these, to judge by intercepted letters, would be neither slight nor slow.

To the general causes which called for the excision of this Mamluk enclave from the Sultan's Empire, a definite and heinous occasion had now been added. The Sultan, faced in Africa with the intolerable successes of Muḥammad 'Ali, could not brook a second rebel on this scale. The suave dispatches of Daud he was well able to assess. It remained to choose a successor. Baghdad was offered first to Yusif Pasha, a Rumelian adventurer who had held the ayalat of Aleppo: but his demands in cash and troops for the task precluded the appointment. A second candidate, Ḥaji Muḥammad 'Ali Riḍha Pasha, consulted with 'Iraq émigrés in the capital and offered himself for the service for a mere six thousand purses and a brigade of troops.

[1] Aucher-Eloy (loc. cit.) suggests that the Resident was forced to condone the crime by his interest in the permanence of the present régime. Stoqueler (p. 51) gives the version wherewith Daud tried to exonerate himself to Taylor—that Ṣadiq was the aggressor, &c. Fraser (ii, p. 260) supports Aucher-Eloy.

A junior Wazir with a good record,[1] he was promoted to the joint provinces of Aleppo and of all 'Iraq save Mosul. Mustering his forces at Aleppo in January 1831, he left it in early February with nine guns, a small force of the Aleppo Nidham, two regiments of feudal cavalry, and a crowd of irregulars, who were shortly increased by the Shammar of Sufuk. Letters constantly left his camp to possible malcontent elements in 'Iraq by the hand of willing intermediaries and deserters from the Mamluk regiments. His generosity at Mosul won all hearts; its governor, Qasim Pasha ul 'Umari, was appointed his second-in-command. Then, as all was ready for advance, news from lower 'Iraq stopped the avenger, whose task after all had fallen, it seemed, to hands mightier than of men.

As early as July 1830 rumours had reached Baghdad of plague in Tabriz. Two months later its terrible effects were confirmed, and there had been cases in Kirkuk. While Baghdad was horrified at the murder of the Qapuchi, varying news came in of the plague's progress. It had left Kirkuk—it had returned—it was ravaging Sulaimaniyyah. In response to the Pasha's own inquiry, full instructions for quarantine were drafted by the Residency surgeon: but conservative influences, which pronounced all prophylaxis to be impiety, prevented the adoption of any precaution whatsoever, and caravans from the plague-stricken cities of Persia and Kurdistan freely entered Baghdad. On the 21st of February it was learnt that the Sultan had pronounced Daud Pasha a rebel and an outlaw;[2] on the 24th, that 'Ali Pasha had left Aleppo; and a month later, the first cases of plague occurred. The outbreak was in the poorer houses of the Jewish quarter. In the first days of April, all who could fled from the city: but whither? Tribesmen held every land approach, the river-boats were few and crowded and already plague-ridden. By the 4th of April a hundred and fifty a day were dying. The Christians[3] and the few Europeans strictly blockaded their houses to allow no contact. The Pasha and his

[1] As Mutasallim he had suppressed trouble at 'Aintab. He was by race a Laz, of the Circassian people of that name on the south-eastern coast of the Black Sea.

[2] Mira'tu 'l Zaura speaks of an unfulfilled conspiracy among the Baghdad Mamluks to secure imperial pardon and their own immunity by the murder of Daud.

[3] Both Sulaiman Beg and Wellsted emphasize this. Mr. Groves took similar steps, but even so he lost his wife (op. cit., pp. 140 ff.).

household longed to flee the infection, yet dared neither take nor leave their hoarded wealth: all discipline was relaxed, robbers without ranged unchecked, and the enemy themselves were reported ever nearer the city. The Resident and his party left by boat for Baṣrah.

All accounts[1] of this appalling visitation agree in the details of its terrible course. The population passed from indifference to panic, from noisy grief to the silence of death and despair. By the 10th of April, seven thousand had died in fifteen days. On the 11th, twelve hundred perished. From that day until the 27th the daily roll of dead stood at fifteen hundred to three thousand. Not one patient in twenty recovered. Food was almost unobtainable, no water-carriers worked, all city-life was suspended, no thought was but of the dead and dying. Every function of government was stilled, the troops, officials, and servants of the Court were attacked and destroyed with the rest. The terrified Pasha could find none to take his orders: he bade them bring boats, not a boatman was alive. All efforts of the living to keep pace with the rate of burial could not avail. Finally the dead lay unburied in the streets, little children and the infirm wandered helpless and starving, brutal and heartless crime looted and exulted for a brief hour till the same death laid low the violent and the meek together.

From the 21st of April a fresh source of terror appeared. The Tigris was in high flood somewhat later than its wont. Already the waters round Baghdad had prevented thousands from escaping, and allowed no food-stuffs to come in. Inch by inch it now crept to the tops of the neglected flood-banks on the riverside, until cellars began to fill and a single foot of crumbling dyke kept the river from the city. In the night of the 26th a section of the wall subsided on the north face of the town, and part of the citadel collapsed. Two hundred houses fell in the first few hours. Within twenty-four, part of the Sarai and seven thousand houses were in fallen ruins, burying the sick, the dead, and the few still healthy in a common grave. The priceless horses of the Pasha's stable ran wild in the streets, his vast granaries lay open. The

[1] Mira'tu 'l Zaura is full and vivid. Wellsted (i, pp. 280 ff.) is an independent eyewitness, Groves (*passim*) an exact diarist. Aucher-Eloy (p. 328 f.) is short but comprehensive. Stoqueler (p. 57) covers Baṣrah. Fraser (ii, p. 234) is from Groves.

water began to sink after two days. By the 30th it had subsided a yard, and by the end of the first week of May not only the flood but the intensity of the plague had passed its worst. Although the population, now crowded in the few dry quarters, offered a fair field for its ravages, yet a weakening in the virulence of the attacks (sure sign of the passing of an epidemic) gave hope that Baghdad would not after all entirely perish. Many, however, continued to sicken, and the toll of the unburied dead, torn by dogs in the slush of the flood-water, was not yet complete. Only when the month was two-thirds through did a term seem set to the unparalleled agonies of the city.

Gradually the bodies were taken to burial or to the river, strayed animals made fast, a little food offered for sale, and the voice of the call to prayer sounded from such mosques as remained. Much of the city was ruined past repair, but ample still stood for the cowed remnant of population and the few hundreds who regained the city from outside. The bazaars, largely collapsed and wholly looted, began a feeble traffic; but many crafts had vanished for ever with the hands that had practised them.

§ 4. *The fall of Baghdad.*

No more miserable eyes than the Pasha's surveyed the wreckage of Baghdad. Four haggard wretches attended his person in place of the scores of proud Georgian Aghas. Of his glittering regiments, a few dozen souls remained. The palace lay half in ruins. The treasury was full to no purpose, every bond of loyalty weakened or snapped. In the last days of the plague Daud himself sickened of the disease, and lay alone in the gilt rooms of his palace, served by an old woman, and crushed with weakness and apprehension of the future: for, besides the present horrors of Baghdad, his every plan for self-defence was miscarrying. In his first fears of retribution, before the plague, he had sent a tribal force to hold the Euphrates line at Dair ul Zor and regulars to Mardin. Recalling these with a false confidence (born of lying dispatches from Stambul), he later sent Yusif Agha and regiments of the Nidham to strengthen Kirkuk, where plague destroyed most and the townspeople expelled the rest. In the early days of his own illness he dispatched the Mir Akhor to recruit mercenaries in the

Khaliṣ; but Death removed the veteran captain, and the new levies dispersed. The next to leave Baghdad—half-blockaded now by the light forces of Sufuk, and approached ever nearer by the vanguard of 'Ali Riḍha's army under Qasim Pasha of Mosul—were Muḥammad Maṣraf and Muḥammad Pasha Baban. Their object was to collect fragments of Yusif's regiments and to raise more by generous pay. Reaching the Khaliṣ, they learnt of the destruction of Yusif and the near presence of Sufuk, turned south and east into Shammar Togah country, and fell, with their whole following and treasury, victims to the greed and ferocity of the tribesmen. Another heavy blow had fallen upon the Mamluk Pasha, whose feeble form was now borne for some hours daily from his bed to the audience-room, and seen by the few callers whom curiosity or habit brought to his side.

The next news brought in was of the arrival of Qasim Pasha at Kadhimiyyah with Sulaiman Ghannam the 'Ugaili (who had accompanied 'Ali Riḍha from Stambul), and with Shaikh Sufuk. The farman of Daud's dismissal was read aloud, every knee bowed to the Padishah, and a score of agents were sent on to Baghdad. Of these the first result was a rising by some scores of ruffians of the Bab ul Shaikh quarter, who marched on the Sarai, set fire to a gate, and fled at the first shot fired by a slave of the cowering Pasha. For him there was no rally, no friend appeared. At dead of night, with a single Abyssinian slave who held him as he rode, he left his palace and took refuge in the house of a private friend. But the determination was now general to yield to the new powers: and a deputation of notables and 'Ulama, to whom his hiding-place was known, led him with every outward respect to the house[1] of Ṣaliḥ Beg, from whom a solemn bond was taken to hand him in due time to 'Ali Riḍha. Qasim Pasha entering the city was greeted by the same committee as had placed Daud in captivity, and escorted to the Sarai. All seemed over, and without strife: the chief lieutenant of the Sultan's governor sat in the seat of power, and his superior had but to advance from Mosul and be welcomed.

But the tactless violence of Qasim (given, men said, to wine)

[1] This house subsequently became the British Residency.

and the ill behaviour of his Shammar and 'Ugail allies, soon moved the Baghdadis, in whom fickleness alone is constant, towards opposite councils. It was freely whispered that Qasim Pasha intended to play false to his master and hold Baghdad for himself: to do this he must remove Turks and Mamluks together and rely on his Arabs alone. When the farman deposing Daud Pasha was read in public, Qasim demanded his instant production; but of this his own council—officials and notables of the city—insisted upon postponement. It appeared indeed—and the news spread broadcast—that of the few troops and officials who had survived the plague, more than half must risk their very lives by the elevation of Qasim. They rallied hot-foot to the house of Ṣaliḥ Beg. The debate was not of politics but of self-preservation, the issue that Qasim must be removed.

On the morning of the 13th of June, Qasim in council awaited the promised production of Daud. The party dispatched to bring him returned, but returned alone; and simultaneously was heard tumult from without. A force of Mamluks, 'Ugail, and citizens had surrounded the building: the new governor was a prisoner. As his followers within, and the various supporters of the old régime without, rallied their forces to defence and attack, the confusion grew and firing increased. Guns were dragged from the Citadel, bombs and munitions seized from the arsenal by the besiegers. From within, many deserted a cause clearly without hope. In the afternoon Qasim and the Waiwodah of Mardin surrendered.[1] Sulaiman Ghannam still held a wing of the Sarai till sunset; then, in the darkness, looted all that could be removed, set fire to the audience-hall, and sword in hand fled through the empty streets. The fire he had kindled gained ground from room to room of the Sarai till a great part of the still standing structure was destroyed, and with it the priceless treasures of the Pasha's household. Jewels and jewelled objects, gold and rare carpets, silks and cloths from a dozen countries, scores of articles of eastern art perished in these flames lighted by desperation amid resentful misery;

[1] Sulaiman Beg nowhere mentions the fate of Qasim Pasha after surrender. Groves heard that he was put to death; Fraser (i, p. 262) that he was thrown into a well. The Mosul Calendar states that "he was slain by Daud Pasha".

the rest fell to the firstcomer of the 'Ugail or the riff-raff of Baghdad.

But these disorders united every party. A general reaction set in in favour of Daud, not least because the looting of the Sarai was a crime for which 'Ali Riḍha must hold all equally to blame. The common interest was now to maintain a governor who could protect them. Ṣaliḥ was forced to accept the post of Qa'immaqam. He assumed it as the mere puppet of Daud, whose own nomination would be too frank an insult to the Sultan. At the same time letters left the city[1] for Stambul: in return for the conferment of united 'Iraq on Ṣaliḥ or Daud, the notables of Baghdad offered greatly to increase, and faithfully to pay, the annual tribute, besides indemnity for all the expenses of 'Ali Pasha's army. To 'Ali they wrote that his advance would meet barred gates and their stoutest resistance: let him, like themselves, await the orders of their common Sovereign.

'Ali Pasha had left Mosul on receipt of news of Qasim's entry into Baghdad. The messenger of the Baghdadis found him camped on the Greater Zab, whence he now ordered instant advance. Pausing nowhere, he reached Baghdad by the beginning of June, camped at Mu'adhdham, and disposed his guns so as loosely to blockade the city. The citizens replied by a few rounds expressive of their intention to resist. In the ten weeks that succeeded, every day brought its rumours of intrigue within and without, its tale of violent crime in every quarter of Baghdad, its bloodshed at the gates and beyond them. 'Ali Pasha, moved by character and policy alike, preferred inglorious and surer patience to an assault which must cost life and bitterness. The defenders had in all some five hundred regular troops of the Nidham or Mamluk guards, and as many 'Ugail. 'Ali Pasha without had two regiments of horse, two of infantry, and some 12,000 irregulars. Using freely the weapon of his gracious manner, he hinted at high posts for whatever renegade joined his force; tribesmen were flattered and enriched, lands prodigally bestowed. Of the ultimate issue there could be little doubt. The defenders based hopes now on the advent of Arab allies, now on a favourable answer

[1] Thabit says "by means of the British consul Taylor".

from Stambul, now on rumours of weakness in the enemy. Their own divided councils and demoralization were shown in violent collisions in the streets, in barricades of quarter from quarter, in gangs of hooligans. Discipline outside was little better. Arabs of 'Ali Pasha's force attacked the Kirkh suburb without authority and were hurled back; a company of his Albanians changed sides for higher pay; and the Arabs of Sulaiman Ghannam, blockading the approach from Ḥillah, were scattered by a force which cleared this entrance and captured the tents and baggage of the ruffian 'Ugaili.[1] Encouraged by this success, the defenders attempted another sortie, but broken and flooded ground prevented them. An ill-organized sally against the enemy's position at Mu'a<u>dh</u><u>dh</u>am gained command of two redoubts of 'Ali Pasha's camp until a small force of his cavalry put it to rout. More ambitious schemes[2] were first hailed with delight, then discredited as premature or unwise. Both sides continued a futile long-range bombardment.

Although these sorties produced some momentary gain in unity and morale, the position could not but soon relapse to its original hopelessness. Ṣaliḥ, a weak voluptuary, could not even in these desperate straits forgo his pleasures and assume a firm command; Daud Pasha was ill and seen by none; funds were not inexhaustible, and scarcity soon became deadly famine. 'Ali Pasha himself was scarcely less embarrassed by shortage of cash to pay his forces, by whom, after a summer intolerably hot, the rains and cold of winter might yet have to be endured. Ignoring perforce the murmurs of discontent, he ceased not, meanwhile, to extend his hold on all parts of the Pashaliq save its capital. His representative was received in Baṣrah, where the influx of refugees from Baghdad, the consequent spread of the plague, and the ceaseless attacks of Zubair and other outlying Arabs, had necessitated the withdrawal of the Mutasallim and his return with Cha'ab help after weeks of siege.[3] Ḥillah was occupied by

[1] It is clear that the 'Ugail—fickle by character and mercenaries by trade—were divided throughout. Some had followed Sulaiman Ghannam, some stood by Daud, many lost themselves among the gangs who terrorized the town.

[2] Evolved by M. Deveaux, who had survived.

[3] Groves, 174, 213, 232; Stoqueler, 42, 57, 67–8: 'Aziz Agha, who had been Daud Pasha's Mutasallim in Baṣrah and now with difficulty regained his post, was induced to declare for 'Ali Riḍha. (Mira't.)

a Mamluk deserter, the Khaliṣ and Diyalah regions were already held. Mamluk renegades in the camp used every argument and device to induce those within to accept the new Pasha: even Daud's personal retainers were led to believe that 'Ali Pasha's mission was to restore Mamluk greatness under new auspices. By hope and fear, by hunger and jealousy, by threats and promises, the attacking army gained a steady increase by desertions from within.

As September opened, the end was plainly at hand. Conditions in Baghdad became intolerable. The proceeds of robbery were exposed for sale without fear or shame. Food ceased to be obtainable. Meat was never seen. Funds were exhausted, the Pasha's own jewels hawked for sale. Hunger, secret intrigue, and very wretchedness brought the citizens to breaking-point. On the twelfth, many decided to wait but five days more for Shaikh 'Ajil (who in fact had approached Baghdad and been turned back) and then to placate the enemy with the heads of Daud and Ṣaliḥ. To 'Ali Riḏha, desperate from want of money for his troops, at this moment came dispatches from Stambul bidding him abandon his own campaign (if it were still in progress) and return to Stambul as best he might.[1] Powerless to obey (since the lure of Baghdad alone kept his army together), he determined at last to force an issue.

A few hours later, knocking at the Mu'a<u>dhdh</u>am Gate proclaimed his messenger to those within. He bade their representatives meet his outside the walls. At the conference, held in a garden near by, his spokesman urged the Baghdad delegates to choose, and choose at once, between generous pardon and the bitterest punishment. The agents of Ṣaliḥ Beg returned to urgent and secret conclave with him and with Daud. A night of agonized indecision brought no solution; it remained instead for treachery to act where prudence had failed. The intrigues of traitors and deserters within the walls had detached many from the side of the old régime: and certainty that it was now doomed rallied these in a few hours into a party ready for any action to save themselves. In the uneasy night of the 14th of

[1] So Thabit. Such instructions appear remote from the known policy of the Sultan, and from the actual issue; but Sulaiman Beg is highly authoritative.

September, they rushed the pickets of the Gate of Darkness and possessed themselves of the means to admit the Imperial troops. Messages passed before dawn. Soon after it, companies of 'Ali's army entered unopposed. The city had painlessly changed hands.

'Ali Pasha remained in his camp outside; Daud arose from troubled rest. Before dawn the chief of the 'Ugail reported to him the fall of the city, and urged him to seek instant safety by flight to the Muntafiq. Daud pondered long, then answered that his feebleness forbade flight: the will of Allah must be done. Having prayed the early prayer he rode fearfully the short distance to the citadel, and sought refuge in the chambers from which, fourteen years before, Sa'id had been dragged to death. Refused admission, he entered a house[1] near by, and sat in dignity and silence alone to await that which must in an hour declare itself. At mid-morning, officers of 'Ali Pasha were directed to the place. Coming with humility and respect to the presence of Daud they escorted him without the city to the tent of his successor. 'Ali Riḍha rose from his place while the cavalcade was yet distant: greater reverence had never been paid to the Mamluk in the old glory of his court than he now found as an abject captive. Together the Pashas sat at coffee, exchanging cups as the familiar sign of respect and intimacy, and murmuring the customary questions. Safe-conduct was sent to Ṣaliḥ Beg; Darwish Agha, nicknamed the "Qa'immaqam", was appointed to that office in the city; and town criers proclaimed general amnesty. Full freedom was allowed to visit Daud Pasha in the camp, where his liberty was unrestricted.[2]

While security and trade reappeared hour by hour in the streets and all were impressed (not least by the moderation of the victor) that great changes were at hand, preparations went on for the dispatch of Daud to Europe. The letter of 'Ali Pasha announcing his own success begged also on grounds of policy for the Mamluk's pardon. The orders of the escort were instantly to put their prisoner to death if rescue or escape should be

[1] Thabit says the house of Juwad Beg, one of his old servants: Mira't, the house of his own son Nuh.

[2] Mira't says that the renegade Mamluks with 'Ali Riḍha (Rustam, Sa'dun, and Abu Bakr) urged him to put his prisoner to death, but that 'Ali preferred to leave the decision to his Sultan.

attempted. Stories are still told of incidents of the journey and of the doubtful reception at Stambul. Daud had indeed given bitter offence to a monarch stern in punishment. That he was spared is due perhaps to the recommendations of 'Ali Riḍha, perhaps to some hope of using him in negotiations with Egypt,[1] but more probably to his own striking qualities, his eloquent personality, his learning in the Law and the Faith;[2] all of which considerations would have availed him nothing in the Turkey of fifty years before. He was sent now to honourable exile in Brusah, accompanied by his family and supported by remnants of his private estate. After the alarming victory of the Egyptians at Konia in October 1832 it was decided again to employ him. He became Wali of Bosnia and later President of the Council of State in Stambul. In 1839 he was appointed to the Wilayat of Angora, but recalled on some suspicion to his old retreat at Brusah. In 1845, having attracted the particular favour of Sultan 'Abdu 'l Majid, he chose an appointment suitable to his bearing and attainments—the Guardianship of the Holy Shrine at Madinah. Here the gifts of tongue and mien and a romantic past brought him a regard scarcely less than his old throne in 'Iraq. He died in 1851. So, venerated as expounder of Islam by word and piety, he passed who, as a Christian slave-boy, had left Tiflis for Baghdad nearly seventy years before; had won in his new home and changed religion first freedom, then office, and finally a viceregal throne for half a generation; had exchanged, in a few weeks, pomp and power for disease, beggary, and fear of death. Spared and promoted contrary to all expectation, he had enjoyed high offices in the Empire for twenty years more, and died lamented by the great and good in the death-place of the Prophet.

§ 5. *'Ali Riḍha.*

"From the great body of the citizens", writes an eyewitness[3] on the day of the fall, "all fear is removed, and both animals and inhabitants alike rejoice in returning abundance." Prices

[1] This is urged by Sulaiman Beg (Mira't): the cogency does not otherwise appear.

[2] Stoqueler (p. 51) speaks with ignorant facility of "a judicious distribution of gold"—but of such he had little enough, nor would it have bought Sultan Maḥmud.

[3] Groves.

dropped a hundredfold and stores appeared for sale which for weeks had been unknown. Crime stopped in an instant: the streets cleared and refilled, caravans entered and the bazaars opened.

Remaining in camp outside the walls until Daud Pasha had safely started, 'Ali Riḍha was visited by all the notables of Baghdad and charmed each by his felicitous manner. To the Mamluks he promised a score of appointments and estates. His entry into Baghdad lacked nothing in solemnity, though it had little splendour. On the third day, true to custom, all were invited to the formal reading of the farman. The house chosen—for the Sarai was a burnt ruin—was filled with chosen troops. In the courtyard stood the surviving Mamluks, of whom but a few had fled the city in alarm. Ṣaliḥ Beg was indisposed and absent. The farman proclaimed, the Pasha retired to an inner room. This was the signal: a party of Albanians turned suddenly on the Mamluk Aghas, shot the most part with their muskets, smote and slew the rest to the last man. A few were arrested and dispatched elsewhere in the city. Ṣaliḥ was thrown from his horse and murdered in front of the house from which, for a few uneasy weeks, he had governed Baghdad.[1] Thereafter the official orders from Stambul for these savage but prudent acts were read out in justification. Every Mamluk was sought from within and without the city. The traitorous Georgians who had accompanied the Pasha to Baghdad—the spies and agents who had assisted him during the siege—the grateful recipients of his special favour—all bit the dust. A mere handful contrived by prolonged hiding in distant parts of the Pashaliq to gain a belated pardon. The goods of the murdered Aghas were distributed, a portion sold and paid into the Treasury.

The farman of 'Ali Riḍha Pasha was for the rule of "Baghdad, Aleppo, Diyarbakr, and Mosul"—a group of provinces never otherwise bestowed on a single governor; but he did not in fact govern more than 'Iraq itself. The old title of Khalif[2] was revived. Within a few days of his entry into Baghdad, the

[1] Fraser (i, p. 266) differs in detail.

[2] This had always clung, faintly and unofficially, to the rulers of Baghdad, to whom it could be applied in a *local* sense devoid of competition with the Sultan's pretensions. This is equally true of its use by 'Ali Riḍha, though in his case the authorities specifically record it.

farman of his appointment had been read in every city in 'Iraq. The new régime was accepted and operative. The pardon of his predecessor, the modern dress of the Pasha and his staff, the Europeans by whom he was surrounded, the expected relaxing of Islamic social custom, all spoke of a new era. The past privileges of the East India Company were cordially and specifically renewed.

The long schism was ended. The provinces of 'Iraq, so long half-severed from their empire, were to take their place anew as parts of the reformed and progressive whole. The Georgian dynasty was gone for ever. As Daud Pasha was borne to Stambul, his servants and guardsmen to their graves, 'Iraq in that hour became a province of modern Turkey.

XI

FROM THE MAMLUKS TO MIDḤAT PASHA

§ 1. *Imperial and foreign relations.*

In completing to the close of the nineteenth century the history thus far brought to the year 1831, the same scale of presentation cannot be followed. A bare two chapters will be allotted to these seventy years.[1] This decision is forced upon the writer by powerful considerations. His written oriental sources almost cease. To find others would involve researches into Turkish archives and newspapers from which he is entirely prevented. Diplomatic records are still unpublished. Travellers' accounts exist, but must rather illustrate than direct the narrative. Thus forced to curtail his narrative, the historian may feel a hint of relief: with the change of turban to fez, of flowing beard to the stubble of the half-shaven, of careless medieval rule to corrupt sophistication, too much vanishes which unfamiliarity made attractive, too much of shabby ugliness appears.

The present chapter will record main features of the period from the accession of 'Ali Riḏha Pasha in 1831 to the appointment of Midḥat Pasha in 1869. First will be considered the position of the 'Iraq provinces in the Turkish Empire, and their foreign relations; then constitutional and administrative changes within them; thereafter, lines of attempted progress in the suppression of rival or unfriendly enclaves, and in the treatment of the tribes; and finally the development (by foreign agency) of modern means of communication.

The 'Iraq ayalats after 1831 remained unquestioning parts of the Turkish Empire. The interest of large-scale apostasy, foreign wars, ambitious dynasts, does not illumine this period. Unwilling contributions yearly left the 'Iraq pashas for Stambul. Military and civil officials were all on the Imperial strength, none

[1] The writer has abstained from quoting authorities: much of his materials is unwritten, while of the documents ultimately necessary he has seen but a small part.

dared to resist the wishes of their superiors. All posts might still be secured by the old means of purchase and favour; many were indistinguishable from the old tax-farm governorships; but none might be retained contrary to the Sovereign's wishes. On the contrary, the degree of centralization ordained by Maḥmud II, and in force from 1834 to 1869, was later modified as excessive. Largely nominal in the remoter provinces, it was galling and impracticable when applied.

Viewed in world-politics, 'Iraq had its share of the increasing attention paid to Turkey by the statesmen of Europe. It lay on a suggested route to India, it contained an important British diplomatic agent. International commissions on the 'Iraq-Persian frontier—the mission of high inspecting officials from the Capital—the growth of foreign trade, a river-marine, and the telegraph—archaeological research—such were external means tending to bring 'Iraq into the modern world. Examining its foreign relations more closely, we find that in the Gulf these were slight, while with Arabia they were but the familiar restlessness of border tribes; but with Persia there were successive stages of suspicion and acrimony.

On the Kurdish frontier, Baban rivalries gave constant causes of friction with the Shah till the fall of that house in 1850. The depredations and infidelities of the nomad tribes, crossing and recrossing the border, led to constant protest and denial; Jaf and Pishdar grazed on both sides, the Hamawand raided from Kirkuk to Hamadan. In lower 'Iraq, the close association of Persians with the turbulent Holy Cities involved them in punishments aimed at the criminals and rebels whom they sheltered, while the treatment of their pilgrims was subject of bitter complaint against chauvinist Pashas of the day. Persian traders had little sympathy from governors to whom they were heretics and outcasts; the Shah in turn was suspicious of the sheltering of Persian princes in Baghdad. Under such conditions it was inevitable that the points of difference could hardly be adjusted. Muḥammarah, founded by the doubtful vassal of a tribe claimed by both powers, was attacked and looted by 'Ali Riḍha in 1837.[1]

[1] The surviving but now weak Ḥuwaizah state received its death-blow when, in 1833, the Karkhah changed its course and left the town riverless in a single day.

This was followed by huge Persian demands for compensation, and the town was soon reoccupied by a Muḥaisin shaikh who, obedient neither to the Cha'ab nor to Baṣrah, relied on Persian backing. Sultan and Shah continued to claim the town and to agree upon no line of frontier. Constant incidents of threatened aggression, sheltered fugitives, tribal time-serving, kept the situation delicate. The outcome was the second Treaty of Erzerum of 1847. Its terms assigned Muḥammarah to the Persians and dealt generally with border tribes, pilgrims, and navigation. In 1850 a Frontier Commission of British and Russian, Turkish and Persian, representatives started work from Muḥammarah; but its operations were stultified by the claims and antics of Darwish Pasha, and resulted in a vague *status quo.* Surveying and inquiry were continued along the frontier by British officers, and the preparation of maps dragged on in Moscow. Conditions remained similar until the Crimean War, by causing Turkey to fear a Persian alliance with Russia, aggravated the mutual suspicions. When in 1869 the Anglo-Russian maps were complete, a Convention was adopted repeating the *status quo.* This convenient phrase, however, covered conditions still hopelessly fluid with grazing nomads and asylum-seeking marauders; and a settlement based on consent and on permanent features seemed as remote as ever.

Within 'Iraq, the passage of the country from a medieval to a modern international plane increased its points of co-operation and friction with foreign representatives. On the one hand, British enterprise was performing invaluable services for 'Iraq, and asking nothing but security for its growing trade: and on the other, the bigoted 'Iraq rulers resented but could not prevent the presence, the privileges, the tribal friendships of these foreigners whose Resident could break careers by a word in Stambul, was irritatingly right, embarrassingly honest, inconveniently vigilant. Where the eighteenth-century trader-consul had humbly asked nothing but the Capitulations and to be left alone, the nineteenth-century Resident [1] was the spokesman of steamship companies, telegraph construction parties, archaeologists, and charitable

[1] These included some exceptional men—Sir H. C. Rawlinson (1843-55), Sir A. B. Kemball (1855-68), Colonel Herbert (1868-74).

funds;[1] nor did the occasional application of tribesmen for British protection fail to annoy the Pasha. The idea indeed was not wholly absent either from shaikhs, Effendis, or some British officers, that the future of Great Britain in 'Iraq was likely to be important and possibly paramount.

§ 2. *The phenomena of Reform.*

These external relations have told nothing of the transforming modernization which, proceeding within 'Iraq fitfully, half-heartedly, unwisely, forms the leading feature of the period.

The changes in administrative grouping in these years show an inconstant but general tendency to approach the "Wilayat System" which Midhat Pasha was to apply. The far-flung command of 'Ali Ridha[2] soon narrowed to 'Iraq proper. Kirkuk, which the Sultan may have wished to separate from Baghdad,[3] remained connected with it. Mardin was detached from 'Iraq to Diyarbakr in 1835. The Kurdish states, as they successively fell into direct Turkish rule, were grouped under Mosul and Kirkuk. Mosul in 1850 became a sanjaq of Baghdad, while Basrah in the same year became a separate ayalat. After twelve years, it was reduced as suddenly to be the office of a Mutasarrif, and raised once again in 1875.

The history of the administration itself is the record of a partial application of the various comparatively liberal ordinances of the contemporary central government. The radical (but too often nominal) reforms of Mahmud II continued till his death in 1839. In that year the new Sultan, 'Abdu 'l Majid, published in the famous Khatt i Sharif of Gulkhanah the fundamental institutes of civilized government, and bound himself to observe them. These—known in Turkey as the Tandhimat—were the pattern for provincial governors, and were reaffirmed with additions in the Khatt i Humayun of 1856. The reforms, which really substituted a Western for a Turkish conception of government, penetrated but slowly into 'Iraq and produced there results unworthy of their principles. Military reorganization had

[1] Notably the "Oudh Bequest"—a large fund left by the (Shia') King of Oudh. Its distribution to the Mujtahids of Karbala and Najaf was among the most delicate duties of the Resident, and so continued till the Great War.

[2] p. 275 *supra*.

[3] Mira'tu 'l Zaura suggests this.

already well begun, but long remained incomplete: the various and grotesque equipment of the New troops was for years the amusement of travellers, while their drill had modified almost to vanishing in its transplantation from Paris to 'Iraq. Conscription, applied with ruthless but momentary firmness to Mosul in 1835, was not attempted in lower 'Iraq before 1870. The old irregular Haitahs, continued under the new régime, remained a curse from which relief was vainly hoped from the Tandhimat. Of the body of the Reforms there was no sign in Baghdad and none in Mosul until the age of Najib Pasha, from 1842. It became clear, thereafter, that every abuse of lawlessness and insecurity, with forces wholly inadequate to suppress it—of tribes ill treated with haughty feebleness—of a populace ruined by the exactions of tax-farmers on lines heedless of economic reason—was easily consistent with the Reformed government. While certain ancient malpractices waned, and historic appointments—the Kahya's itself—grew obsolete, yet, if government be judged by the freedom and happiness of subjects, the new era showed no great advance upon the old: security was as low, justice as rare, exaction as cruel, policy as foolish. In certain aspects, indeed, there was progress. A standard, however remote, had been set. Increasingly officials appointed to high office had something of modern education. There was greater specialization of function. There were, in fact, the bones of reasonable government into which the rare ability and goodwill of a governor might yet infuse life. Advance was marked also by the limitation of local powers—a needful measure even though, in half-savage 'Iraq, it too often deprived government of its readiest weapons.

The same period made explicit in 'Iraq the various phenomena of provincial government to which other provinces were accustomed. In it grew up the numerous class of regular officials—the Effendis—who stepped into the place of the old arbitrary pashas as those for whom the provinces existed. Literate but not otherwise educated, backward but decorous in social habit, uniform in a travesty of European dress, exact and over-refined in the letter of officialdom, completely remote from a spirit of public service, identifying the body public with their own class, contemptuous of tribe and cultivator, persistent speakers of Turkish among

Arabs, and, finally, almost universally corrupt and venal—such were the public servants in whose sole hands lay the functions of government. With them came more of the nomenclature which Gladstone mocked, of the naïve, ill-drafted laws applauded in Europe, smiled at in Baghdad, of the Councils, the seals, the registers, the processes whereby any number of ill-paid officials could be employed, any question be indefinitely delayed.

For all this failure of the Reforms, and the unhealthy features which the age perpetuated, it was yet marked by real progress in other directions. Considerable success was met in applying a main line of Sultan Maḥmud's policy—the destruction of the Dere Begs. In Mosul and Kurdistan important results were gained, and some anachronisms put down in the towns of 'Iraq; in the tribes, however, the task proved too great, and the disease was but aggravated by the treatment.

§ 3. *Personalities of the Period.*

'Ali Riḍha Pasha held the government of Baghdad, with its dependencies of Kirkuk and Baṣrah, for eleven years. He showed some liberality of mind; his generosity was proverbial; and his mildness half concealed his ineptitude. To foreign pioneers of progress he was accommodating. He had no fanaticism, no exclusiveness. He possessed genial manners, genuine benevolence, some literary and scientific pretensions. But as a ruler he was a total failure. His only tribal manœuvre was the setting of tribe against tribe. His indolence and obesity forbade personal effort, and placed him at the mercy of bad advisers. He could control neither town nor tribe nor his own irregular forces. A formidable mutiny, led by 'Abdu 'l Ghani the Mufti, marked his first year in Baghdad. In 1833 an abortive rising of 'Abdu 'l 'Aziz, the former Mutasallim of Baṣrah, came to nothing. Further outbreaks of plague showed that no lessons in quarantine had been learnt. In fiscal matters was seen the familiar co-existence of rapacious tax-farmers and an empty Treasury. The considerable later reputation of 'Ali Riḍha rests on his replacement of Daud and on his broadcast bestowal of lands. He married in Baghdad. In 1842 he was transferred to Syria.

A far more considerable figure was the adventurer captain of irregulars whose appointment as Pasha first of Kirkuk, then of

Mosul, was secured by 'Ali Riḍha—Muḥammad Pasha, nicknamed the "Injah Bairaqdar".[1] This relentless character ruled Mosul from 1835. His chief work was in the destruction of the ring of Kurdish states—an important achievement reserved for separate description. He gave to Mosul and the surrounding roads an unprecedented security, enforced conscription against tremendous opposition, built new streets, an arsenal, a barrack, a hospital, and by pitiless methods secured peace and justice for subjects who had never heard of Tandhimat. He died, to the immediate relief and subsequent long regret of his province, in 1843. Of his successors, many glimpses may be had in the pages of Layard.

Baghdad fell in 1842 to Najib Pasha, a man of high Stambul family and intimate with the Sultan. He had intelligence, courage, and exceptional vigour; but his nationalism had become an alarmist hatred of foreigners; to obtain money, too often for his private use, he resorted to exactions the most short-sighted and devastating; his haughtiness offended the tribes, where his forces were powerless to control situations he had himself induced; his very violence was not proof against bribery, nor his reason against fanatical prejudice. Other parts of this chapter cover the chief incidents of his reign. He was succeeded, after two short and undistinguished Pashaliqs,[2] by the first appointment of Namiq Pasha in 1852.

A year later arrived a figure still honourably remembered—Muḥammad Rashid Pasha, nicknamed Geuzliki "the spectacled". He was to die in Baghdad after five years of honest, vigorous, and liberal rule. None assisted him in his sincere efforts to govern, nor could his problems be soluble in so short a time and with his puny resources; but under him the reformed government was seen to be possible of reasonable application in 'Iraq. He insisted on honest work from his officials, tried to combat corruption, increased revenue by decreasing the plunder of tax-farmers, secured a constant channel of export by supplying the Ḥijaz with grain, and opened a score of irrigation canals. He was, however, hard pressed to find money for Stambul when the Crimean War called for funds. His successor 'Umr Pasha,

[1] The اینجه بیراقدار . . . "lean standard-bearer".
[2] 'Abdu 'l Karim Nadir ("'Abdi") in 1849, Wujaihi in 1851.

known as Sardar i Akram, left the name of a good soldier and vigorous upholder of government on the old lines; 'Amarah was founded in his time. The next two pashas[1] were of no mark. Namiq Pasha returned to a seven-year tenure of office in 1861. He had the vigour and narrowness of Najib, and showed extreme perseverance in a policy of tribe-breaking for which—however laudable an aim—he had not a tithe of the means; and the resentful confusion, approaching anarchy, left in the wake of his campaigns did much to desolate the country and offend the powerful. Shibli Pasha—a former captain of bandits—was his well-known lieutenant. Namiq, however, is to-day remembered not for his follies and failures but for the tangible achievement of public buildings in Baghdad which he began and Midḥat Pasha was to finish; and stories are told of his careful finance which remitted to Stambul large sums for Sultan 'Abdu 'l 'Aziz to squander on palaces. After him Taqi 'l Din, lately governor of Kirkuk, ruled Baghdad for a few months and was followed by Midḥat Pasha, who entered on the last day of April, 1869.

§ 4. *The extension of direct rule.*

This history has in general taken such a view of Turkish government as to restrain applause at its wider spread: and if the displacement of blue-blooded Kurdish Begs from their long independent or vassal thrones is hailed as progress, it is progress only from the Turkish viewpoint; since the rule of the incoming Effendis with their Haitahs and Ḍhabṭiyyah was no improvement, for peasant and shepherd, on the sway of Baḥdinan or Badr Khan. Yet no imperial government could endure, after the inspiring lessons of Sultan Maḥmud, the half-hostile, half-contemptuous presence of hereditary princes within its frontiers: though in truth powerless to govern them, and distracted with problems enough without them, the Turks cannot be blamed for their suppression of the Mosul and the Kurdish dynasties. The ease with which these collapsed shows the decadence of their old rulers.

In the moment when the reforming Sultan glanced south and east at 'Iraq, the Jalili family was doomed. Its hold on Mosul

[1] Muṣṭafa Nuri 1859, Aḥmad Taufiq 1860.

was already weakened by opposition of other elements. 'Ali Riḍha in 1831 had found an 'Umari Pasha, who was succeeded by a native of Aleppo. Yaḥya, the last[1] Jalili, took the Pashaliq by force in 1833; he lost it by force in 1834; and these bloody struggles gave sure sign that a change was possible and easy. The Injah Bairaqdar was appointed in 1835, and Mosul in a day became a normal province. The proud Jalilis sank into the ruck of land-owning notables.

The appearance of Rashid Pasha, former Grand Wazir and Wali of Siwas, at Diyarbakr with an army in 1835 presaged the fall of many Kurdish thrones. He suppressed trouble at mutinous Mardin, detached that area permanently from Mosul to Diyarbakr, seized the great Sufuk and sent him to Stambul. Punishing Tel 'Afar, he moved across the Tigris against a greater objective. The Bairaqdar from Mosul and 'Ali Riḍha from Baghdad supported his expedition with simultaneous columns.

The small Ruwanduz state had passed about 1810 from Aughuz Beg to Muṣṭafa Beg, the latter of whom, at incessant war with the Babans till a marriage alliance pacified them, then solidified and wisely ruled his kingdom. Before his death his son Muḥammad Beg—or Mir Muḥammad—took over the government from his weakening hands. In 1826 Muṣṭafa died;[2] Muḥammad (known as Kor "the Blind" from an affection of one eye) succeeded, and put his two uncles instantly to death. The remarkable qualities of the Blind Beg showed themselves in an unbroken series of conquests. He subdued the strong Shirwan and Baradost tribes to the north, reduced the Surchi, expelled the Baban governor from Ḥarir, took Arbil and Altun Kupri, and installed his own relations in these places. Keui and Raniyyah were wrested from the Babans, the lesser Zab becoming their frontier. 'Ali Riḍha was forced to recognize this new power, and raised him to the grade of Pasha. Early in 1833 Muḥammad moved on 'Aqrah, took the place by siege, and expelled Isma'il Pasha its governor. Easily deposing Sa'id Pasha of 'Amadiyyah,[3] he made the Baḥdinan territories the government

[1] i.e. the last to rule. Numerous members of the family are still at Mosul.

[2] Inevitably, there was suspicion of foul play.

[3] At this time Dr. Ross, of the Baghdad Residency, visited him. Fraser (i, p. 68 ff.).

of his brother Rasul. Dohuk and Zakho became dependencies of his empire, in which from the first impeccable discipline was kept by his just severity. Such security had been never known; all contrasted it with the lawless confusion in 'Iraq. He next raided across to Jabal Sinjar, destroyed villages close to Mosul, occupied Jazirah ibn 'Umr, and terrified the Badr Khans of Ḥasankif; Nisibin, Mardin itself, were threatened. But this was his term; the appearance of Rashid, the chosen instrument for his suppression, instantly checked his menaces, loosened the bonds of his ephemeral empire, and delighted his enemies and rivals. The blind Kurd, always more feared than loved, retired towards his capital. Deserted by many, he failed even to profit from the jealous bickering of Rashid and 'Ali Riḍha, and finally surrendered on the strongest guarantees of good treatment. He was sent to Stambul, whence many expected his return as a Turkish vassal; instead he vanished mysteriously, victim of Turkish caution and treachery.

In Arbil and Altun Kupri Turkish officers reappeared. 'Amadiyyah for a moment revived, but the Babans did not regain their ground. Ruwanduz was still governed by the brother of the blind Pasha. In Jazirah a Mutasallim replaced the Beg. In 1837 troops from outside 'Iraq, under Ḥafidh Pasha, again crushed the Sinjar Yazidis; and in 1838 the Injah Bairaqdar took up the unfinished work in Kurdistan. 'Amadiyyah was finally annexed after a siege, 'Aqrah and Dohuk followed: the Kurdish rulers and their families became harmless pensioners in Mosul or Baghdad. Turkish officials and Haitah appeared in the mountain villages, first concurrently with, but later instead of, the last signs of indigenous rule. The new régime was precarious, nominal, barely operative in the tribes and remoter mountains; but, at least, most of the rallying points of the Kurdish nation had been destroyed.

Others lingered a few more years. In the composite tribal empire of the Milli (bequeathed by Timur to Aiyub) Timawi Beg, grandson of the founder, survived the suppression of his father by Rashid Pasha in 1834 and regained power when the Turks were weakened by Egyptian victories in Syria. His son Maḥmud outlived the hostility of the Wali of Diyarbakr, and left to his famous heir Ibrahim Pasha a formidable confederacy in the early days of Sultan 'Abdu 'l Hamid. South of the Lesser Zab, the Babans endured until 1850. We have seen elsewhere the beginning of the disastrous struggle between the sons of 'Abdu 'l Raḥman Pasha. In the last weeks of Daud Pasha, Sulaiman regained the rule. In 1832 he was expelled by Persian forces, only to reappear and rule for seven more years the valleys of Shahrizor which the plague, the weakness and disorder following dynastic quarrels, and the rise and fall of Ruwanduz had enfeebled and depopulated. Till 1834 a Persian garrison remained in Sulaimaniyyah. Thereafter, in an Indian summer of the Babans (which shone, however, on little outside their capital), imposing regiments were raised on the new model. This belated yet remarkable attempt at a modern army was continued by Aḥmad Pasha, whose rule was broken for a year in 1840 by a return of Maḥmud Pasha, his uncle. The Persian army which restored this veteran raised a diplomatic storm by its invasion of soil claimed as Ottoman; the Shah himself was said to be party to it, with designs on more than Kurdistan; and, with the retirement of the Persians, Aḥmad again assumed the Baban government. In 1842 his deep and doubtful commitment in frontier quarrels led to his removal to Baghdad. Qadir Pasha, grandson of the founder of Sulaimaniyyah, was to succeed; 'Abdullah, brother of Aḥmad, disputed his entry; and a Persian invasion, designed to restore Maḥmud, failed by the opposition of 'Abdullah, who remained as ruler till Aḥmad returned on a change of pashas in Baghdad. Najib Pasha hoped by encouraging feuds finally to unseat the dynasty. He succeeded. 'Abdullah was again preferred to his brother, and given Sulaimaniyyah with the significant rank of Qa'immaqam. For years past the Baban had been tributary to Baghdad, and Sulaimaniyyah contained Turkish troops; the tribute was now raised, the imperial garrison increased. The end came in 1850, when Isma'il Pasha, a Turkish general, replaced the last Baban. So vanished from Kurdistan the house which, for a century and a half, had ruled wide territories with fame and power. It made way for the paper Regulations, the timorous venal officials, the weak opportunism, the foreign language of the Turkish government.

Elsewhere than in Kurdistan, simultaneously, the Turks were showing their decision to rule. In Baghdad itself 'Ali Riḍha in

1833 struggled to expel the 'Ugail from the western suburb into which they had penetrated as residents and masters, and Najib Pasha in 1847 purged the Bab ul Shaikh quarter of elements long known for their seditious resistance to government. In 1843 occurred the still famous chastisement of Karbala. For years past the town, half Persian in population and a shelter for every runaway malefactor from Mardin to Muḥammarah, had been virtually excluded from Turkish government. Neither Daud Pasha nor 'Ali Riḍha were allowed to enter it. In 1842 its internal government was vested in the gang-leaders of the Yaramaz,[1] to whose hooligan terrorism bowed Mujtahid and governor alike. Najib Pasha, late in 1842, insisted on the town's reception of a Turkish garrison. It was refused. Military operations followed. The town was hotly defended; fighting in the gardens was followed by regular siege; and the final fall of the city to the Turkish soldiery was accompanied by atrocities (quickly and manifold exaggerated by rumour) which horrified both Persia and the *corps diplomatique* in Stambul. In Najf conditions were not dissimilar. The two city-clans of Shumurd and Zugurt cared nothing for Pasha or Sultan, everything for controlling the all-powerful fatwahs of the Mujtahids and for pursuing their own vendettas. Contemptuous disaffection became revolt in 1852, when Turkish troops in a day's bitter street-fighting inflicted on the town a punishment on the Karbala model but less ferocious, and again in 1854 when an officer sent by Namiq Pasha forced his entrance against the united forces of the two clans.

§ 5. *Tribal Policy, 1838 to 1869.*

The reader of these pages will know better than to suppose that the dissolution of the Kurdish states and the hard blows struck to reclaim the Holy Cities were enough to incorporate these places in an effective system of Turkish rule. Yet as a result of the operations of these thirty years the Sultan's writ did in fact run farther than it had, and opposition, if still present in

[1] Yaramaz (يارماز) in Turkish means "good-for-nothing". These were the deserters, criminals, or mere adventurers who had found refuge and livelihood in Karbala. They were many hundreds strong, and organized under regular leaders.

all its elements, was the less focused and less blatant since the passing of Dere Beg and Yaramaz.

The tribal policy of this period was similar in aim. Of all the difficulties confronting its rulers, the tribes were the head and front. The nature of this difficulty has long since fully appeared. To the remarks made at an earlier period on the tribal character there is nothing to add here. Still (throughout lower 'Iraq) urged by their Mujtahids against the Turks, still fundamentally opposed in interest to organized government, asking nothing of the state which for ever pressed them for taxes, preferring the tribal code to any court of justice, completely conservative, so hungry as never to miss a chance of gain, so wild and unmoral as to keep no bargain, observe no compromise, still masters, returning unchanged after a hundred punishments, of road and river and all the country save narrow areas: their continuance in this form and scale was rightly seen by the Pashas of these years to be inconsistent with the existence of any government worth the name. The problem was of extreme difficulty. Three centuries of misrule had aggravated it. To Turks, of all governing peoples, it would be the hardest to solve.

Various lines of solution might have presented themselves. To the Turkish mind, the tribesmen were but savages maliciously opposing government. In fact, they were primitive communities still living a life (remote from everything postulated or intended by civilized governments) than which they could visualize no other, and to which none had shown them an alternative. A thousand times, as they followed the promptings of the tribal mind, they had collided with this foreign hostile thing, government; but no government had bidden them "Cease to live thus, and live in the better way that we shall make possible for you". The true solution of the abiding tribal problem was to break the tribes not by occasional bludgeon-blows, but by providing an alternative life which they could accept and prefer. The true answer to the riddle presented to Najib and Namiq Pashas was "Settle your tribes on the land: help them to irrigate by canals: give them security of hold: tax lightly and justly: allow no trespass against those you have settled: reward generously, punish constructively".

This solution was not adopted. The Pashas of the period

—nationalist, intolerant—strove to crush life from the tribes by weight of arms. They rejected indeed the old policy of slide and opportunism. They aimed at forcible conversion of the tribesmen from wild outlaws into obedient citizens, without showing them how to live as these and without inspiring a hint of the respect which would evoke obedience. The tribal leaders still saw the Turkish rulers now perfidious, now weak, now brutal; they saw the oppressive treatment of the settled folk whom every tax-farmer robbed and every Dhabtiyyah bullied; they saw the contempt for themselves, the haughtiness, the scornful insolence of the Turk; and they recoiled from the threat to rob their freedom and give the horrors of government in exchange. The policy of merely destructive tribe-smashing must always have failed. It failed in this period for special as well as general reasons. It was attempted with forces far too small to accomplish it, without consistency, without strategy. The result was to inflame tribal 'Iraq to worse conditions than any remembered, to drive cultivators back to the desert, and, at the moment when modern communications were appearing, to reduce the country to the last weakness and misery.

'Ali Ridha was content to see the ancient methods continued. He frequently changed the Shaikh of the Muntafiq, set up a rival to Sufuk, employed Wadi as lieutenant and tax-gatherer. His mishandling of the tribal elements brought Baghdad more than once to a state of blockade. 'Anizah, Shammar, and Zubaid ranged outside its walls, disgusted at the Pasha's inconstancy and eager for all that his weakness might yield them. Sufuk, caught and sent to Stambul by Rashid Pasha in 1836, returned to dominate 'Iraq from Mardin to Baghdad. Only in 1847, after assassinating his rival Nijris, was he finally (and then by treachery) murdered by order of Najib Pasha. The latter was the first exponent of forcible unconstructive detribalizing. His Pashaliq was distracted by incessant tribal campaigns.[1] In 1843 the Khaza'il and Shammar were the objective, in 1844 the

[1] To the period of his Pashaliq also belong the notorious massacres of Tayari Christians in 'Amadiyyah district by a Badr Khan (of the Jazirah ibn 'Umr family) and the fanatic Nurullah in 1843. These—the subject of protest by Sir Stratford Canning in Stambul—were repeated scarcely more mildly in 1846. Meanwhile Shaikh 'Abdu'l Qadir was emulating them in Sulaimaniyyah district.

Khaza'il and 'Anizah. In 1845 he visited southern Kurdistan, suppressed trouble at Najf, and dealt with the 'Ubaid. The bedouins of the Euphrates border gave trouble in that year and the next, when 'Afak and the Muntafiq were also unsettled. Confusion in the Jazirah followed the murder of Sufuk in 1847. In 1849 the Bani Lam rose against the appointment of a Muntafiq shaikh to farm the taxes of their area—an arrangement of incredible folly. The Shammar raided around the city of Baghdad. The Hindiyyah tribes, whose official extortioner of the moment was Wadi of the Zubaid, revolted against his pitiless collections. The suppression of this rising caused bitter enmity between Najib and his military colleague, who finally replaced him and conciliated the Hindiyyah group. The reign of Najib closed in melancholy and hopeless tribal disorders from end to end of 'Iraq. His policy, applied with extreme vigour, had gained nothing.

These conditions and these hopeless remedies continued. Under 'Abdi Pasha there were large operations on the Euphrates when tribesmen, among other excesses, butchered the whole garrison of Kifl. Namiq Pasha in his first tenure of office was faced with a general rebellion of Euphrates tribes under Wadi. Under Geuzlikli a comparative lull appears, showing how far the blind haughty intolerance of a Najib and a Namiq were responsible for the exaggerated troubles of their day. In Geuzlikli's persistent clearance of canals there was perhaps a hint of wiser policy—to extend the settled districts, increase revenue by increasing the area of its incidence, reclaim the tribes gradually to a life reasonably alternative to their defiant outlawry. Under the Sardar i Akram there were further risings of the Hindiyyah and Shamiyyah tribes, further 'Anizah raids, and a strong punishment of the Hamawand.[1]

In Namiq Pasha's second reign, tribal revenue-demands were steadily increased,[2] constantly resented, fitfully with futile violence enforced. Bani Lam passive resistance was punished. In the Muntafiq two years of war—its aim the conversion of the Shaikh

[1] These, the most famous robber-tribe of south Kurdistan, were perhaps Jaf by origin and appeared in the Bazyan area (after earlier sojourning in Persia) about 1830.

[2] Notably in the Muntafiq.

ul Masha'ikh into a Qa'immaqam[1]—resulted after widespread misery and lawlessness in the mere substitution of one Sa'dun for another, Fahad for Manṣur.[2] Though torn by internal feuds, and rivals now not only for tribal rule but for official title, all shaikhs of the Muntafiq were still resolved to resist the absorption of their old privileges into Turkish hands. The long Muntafiq war was followed by Khaza'il operations as protracted and as barren of result. The Hamawand raided with more than usual boldness and impunity.

§ 6. *The new communications.*

In 1831 the navigation of the 'Iraq rivers was confined to craft which were time-honoured before Herodotus saw them. Skin-borne rafts of the Zabs and upper Tigris, flat wooden rafts from Birijik to Fallujah, pitched coracles at every ferry and fishery, reed and wooden skiffs in the marshes, sailing and rope-drawn craft on lower Tigris and Shaṭṭ ul 'Arab, and the hundred-ton sea-going muhailahs of Fao—these would still have held the field had not invention and opportunity gone hand in hand. The steamship was new to the world; and Great Britain was eagerly seeking a faster route to her growing commitments in India.

The appearance in 'Iraq of the scout-screen of modern transport—the surveyors—occurred under Daud. Two officers of the Indian navy were busy in 'Iraq in 1830. Captain Chesney descended the Euphrates from Al Qa'im to Fallujah in the last days of that year. Thereafter all three spent some months in initial survey of almost the whole river-system, and all were impressed with its navigability. Chesney, encouraged by the personal interest of King William IV, gave such evidence before the "Steam Committee" of the House of Commons in 1834 as led to an expedition, financed partly by government and partly by the Honourable Company, under his own command. Meanwhile the Slave Government had vanished from Baghdad, and 'Ali Ridha had in 1833 advocated steam enterprise on his rivers. In the early days of 1835 he received the farman issued—in grudging terms—to permit the Chesney expedition.

[1] Simultaneously the Sa'dun territories were to be decreased by detachment of large tracts to Hai and Qurnah.

[2] The Sa'dun family tree (in which all paramount shaikhs are underlined) should be consulted.

The voyage of the *Tigris* and *Euphrates* started from Birijik in April 1836. The *Tigris* was lost in a blizzard a month later. The voyage of the *Euphrates* is of unique interest, and should be studied in the pages of its narrators.[1] By the cultivators of Ḥadithah the explorers were urged to stay and hoist the Union Jack in Baghdad. At Ḥillah they were booed as heretics. The wild Khaza'il of Lamlum marshes showed themselves fierce, cunning, and treacherous. At Suq was encountered the trap laid by the French consul, intended to upset their plans and their steamer by a date-log bar. At Qurnah civilities were exchanged with a Turkish gunboat, and at Baṣrah were inspected the rotting and immobile hulks (regularly reported to Stambul as ocean greyhounds in leash) of the Qaptan Pasha. Thereafter for five years the *Euphrates* continued to cruise in 'Iraq waters.

In 1839 the component parts of four iron steamers were disembarked at Baṣrah.[2] For over a year the flotilla navigated and surveyed the rivers unquestioned, though no farman appeared till 1841. Authority was then given to Lynch (by name) to maintain two steamers. In 1842 three were removed to India. The *Nitocris* alone remained, attached to the Residency, and was later replaced by the *Comet*. The period was one of great activity in mapping. To the surveys of those days, the work of Lynch, Felix Jones, Selby, Collingwood, Bewsher, are owed the accurate maps which held the field till 1914. Herein was no mean service to the country.

The Euphrates line as the mail-route to India had been abandoned, when it appeared from the loss of the *Tigris* and other accidents that, for fast and regular sailings, the river would never be adequate. British government enterprise after 1842, therefore, was limited to surveying, while in other fields the Turkish government took its place. Rashid Pasha Geuzlikli was quick to see the great possibilities of the steamboat. In 1855 he called a meeting of merchants and formed a Company, wherein half the capital was to be found by government, half by the

[1] Chesney, Ainsworth, Helfer.

[2] The intention of this flotilla is not evident. They were useless for merchandise, and never used regularly for mails. It would seem that their function was to be no more definite than a general throwing open of the country. Lieut. Lynch was placed in command.

public. An order was placed at Antwerp for two steamers, the *Baghdad* and the *Basrah*. The former was assembled in 'Iraq just before the death of Geuzlikli, the latter after. In spite of the public's half-interest, the two succeeding Walis would not accept private freights.[1] In 1867 Namiq Pasha organized the service as the 'Uman-Ottoman Administration, placed his Director of Medical Services in charge, and built a repair-shop. But he had no monopoly. In 1861 the Lynch Company, whose place on 'Iraq waters had been nobly earned by that family,[2] obtained a farman for the use of the *City of London*. Namiq Pasha offered strong opposition, but the farman was confirmed. Objection was renewed in 1864 when the *Dajlah* appeared. But the Pasha was powerless to prevent this further invasion of 'Iraq by modern craft, far superior to his own and destructive of 'Uman-Ottoman profits. He retaliated by the greatest local opposition and by increasing his own fleet, for which the *Mosul*, *Frat*, and *Rasafa* arrived in 1867. From the earliest days, however in spite of good profits, the repairing and fueling of this fleet, with corrupt officials and unpaid crews, presented difficulties which remained unsurmounted. The two Lynch boats were well kept and profitable.[3]

Turning to land transport, we shall find surprising the long absence of wheeled vehicles from 'Iraq. The flat open country, the greater economy, might well have led to adoption of a form of conveyance elsewhere evolved by and for similar conditions. A closer view shows that this lack of enterprise is to be explained if not excused. General stagnation, fear of the social results of innovation, small funds at the disposal of small ideas, need not be emphasized. There are more particular reasons. The transport must be able to deliver at a destination in towns, and these had no streets for carts: Baghdad itself, to the end, had but a single street where wheels could move. The merchant, from whose khan the transport-cart must stop at a great distance,

[1] It may be that their activity as transports in the constant tribal wars of 1856–61 left little chance for trading voyages.

[2] Lieutenant H. B. Lynch had served for years in 'Iraq, losing one brother in the *Tigris* accident, another by illness.

[3] By-products of the river-boats were the rise of 'Amarah and Kut, a perceptible educational effect on riverain tribes, and the denudation of the banks of willow and tamarisk, with increased degeneracy in the régime of the river.

will prefer the ubiquitous donkey and the Kurdish porter. Outside, on the main routes, the obstacles were other. In upper 'Iraq and the Kurdish fringes firm gravelly soil can everywhere support wheels; south of Hit and Samarra stone ceases, and roads are differentiated from desert or plough land solely by their deeper dust or mud. Only by constant care can a passable surface be maintained. Countless irrigation cuts, capriciously and ever freshly crossing the tracks, stop carts but not pack-animals. Culvert materials are scarce, and none but a firm public authority can force cultivators to bridge canals, to abstain from flooding the highway, and from ignoring its existence with the plough. And if all the difficulties of town and country were solved, travellers might still feel that the more convenient and capacious "'arabanah" yet offered a greater and easier bait to the lawless.

The first suggestion of better road transport came from abroad, and came to nothing. In 1865 a Frenchman, the Conte de Pertheris, journeyed from Damascus to Baghdad and proposed to open up this route for carriages. Of the desert shaikhs *en route* he foresaw no trouble in buying the protection. In Baghdad merchants were found ready to float his company; but Namiq Pasha, already bitter against foreign boats on the Tigris, would not see possible plums of the land route also snatched by strangers. He forbade participation, and warned the Conte against meddling with the tribes.

In Europe meanwhile greater and stranger schemes had been mooted. In 1742 an Irish manufacturer had planned a railway from Calais by Stambul to Calcutta and Pekin—the "Atlas Railway" of William Pane. In 1843 Alexander Campbell proposed an England-to-India railway by the Euphrates valley—a scheme duly propounded to the East India Company, elaborated and mapped. In 1849 John Wright advocated another Euphrates valley alinement. In 1851 Dr. J. B. Thomson died at Stambul, a martyr to zeal in the same cause. Three years later, W. P. Andrew, for years the protagonist of this route to India, gathered a distinguished group of scientists and pioneers—Lynch, Chesney, Macneill, and others, who formed a Company to construct a railway from Mediterranean to Gulf. The track was by Seleucia, Antioch, Aleppo, "Ja'ber Castle", Hit, Baghdad, and thence to Qurnah or Baṣrah. This group was content first to construct only the Seleucia-Euphrates section (of eighty miles), thereafter utilizing the Euphrates by suitable steamers. They emphasized the fear of Russian influence in the East, 'Iraq's great potential riches, the boon to India and to Turkey, the expected trade with the Far East, the engineering simplicity of the scheme, and the readiness of materials in Syria. The enterprise secured official support, including that of Palmerston and Sir Stratford Canning; the Turkish government were favourable; after fifteen years' efforts, however, it was not possible in the end to obtain the necessary finances, and the scheme was abandoned. Local enterprise still showed no life. That of Europeans was stilled in this field, for the time, by the opening of the Suez Canal in 1869.

Postal services were absent from 'Iraq throughout the period, but steam navigation was soon followed by the appearance of the telegraph. This was a recent invention, in itself vulnerable and requiring a considerable volume of traffic to maintain it economically. For both reasons 'Iraq might for the whole nineteenth century have remained without it; but as part of a larger whole, and still more as a land-bridge, the country was to profit by advantages scarcely deserved. Turkey had emerged from the Crimean War prosperous, a member of the European "concert", and a guaranteed sovereign state. Her war experience had shown the need of better communication within her empire, while to England, after the Mutiny, any scheme of quicker contact with the East was welcome. Schemes had already been put forward for a submarine cable from India to Baṣrah, and thence in the bed of the Tigris to Baghdad. In 1856 the Turkish government were approached by the East India Company regarding a land-line from Syria to the Gulf. Stambul refused the funds necessary for a guarantee, without which the Company (behind whom was the European and Indian Junction Telegraph Company) would not proceed; and the granting of a foreign concession was in itself distasteful. In 1857, however, the Turkish and British governments agreed on the erection of lines by British engineers, but as a purely Turkish enterprise; and in the summer of 1861 communication by land-line was in fact established between Stambul and Baghdad.

Discussion followed on the connexion of Baghdad with the

Gulf. The Resident was allowed by Namiq Pasha to survey the Euphrates line in person. A route was selected and work begun late in 1863. Simultaneously a Baghdad-Khaniqin line was commenced. This was working by the next autumn, and that of the Euphrates a few months later. The telegraphs of 'Iraq were now linked with those of Turkey, of Persia (at Khaniqin), and of the Gulf and India (at Fao). Lines were extended successively to Karbala and Najaf, by the Tigris to Kut and 'Amarah, to Badrah and Mandali, and by the Karun to link again with the Persian system at Ahwaz. By the end of the century offices at all the principal towns had been opened. With many shortcomings—decaying instruments, untrained linesmen, constant interruption by the ignorant or malicious, operators to whom official secrecy was unknown—the system worked. What had been strange became indispensable. Better tribal control became possible by quicker concentrations of force, though easy and vulnerable objectives were offered to tribal resentment.

XII

THE LATER NINETEENTH CENTURY

§ 1. *Midhat Pasha.*

On the 30th of April 1869 Midhat Pasha entered Baghdad as Wali. His past career suggested, his present professions verified, that he had come from Europe to this remote province as reformer, modernizer.

Born in Stambul in 1822, his education, interrupted by the transfers of his father from place to place as a subordinate official, was that of the local schools. As a young man he pursued the usual course of junior clerkships, serving in Damascus, Stambul, and Konia. From 1849 to 1851 he took successive upward steps on the official ladder, and gained powerful friends. A successful mission in 1852 to inquire into abuses in the Arab provinces of Damascus and Aleppo was a foretaste of future work in Baghdad. From 1853 to 1858 he held posts in the Balkans, Brusah, and the disturbed Wilayats of Widdin and Silistria; and in the latter year was permitted to spend six months touring the capitals of Europe. Of the following ten years the bulk was spent in the Balkans, the last four in the important and difficult office of Wali of the newly amalgamated Danubian Wilayat. The administration that made this in his time the "model Wilayat" was scrupulously honest, progressive, and tolerant. The application of the Wilayat system and its subdivisions, the agricultural banks, the river-steamers, hospitals, state-industries, were prophetic of the Pasha's similar reforms in 'Iraq. A few months headquarter work in Stambul was followed by his appointment in 1869 to succeed Taqi'l Din Pasha at Baghdad. He was in the prime of his strength and energy, his large black beard still untouched with grey. In the very numerous measures which he instituted in these years of absolute power, civil and military, it is not difficult to find traces of hastiness, of economic considerations mistaken or ignored, of excessive confidence in the catch-words of progress, of a preference for the spectacular to the judicious. In his land-registration system, he permitted the use of official machinery from which an infinity of error, vagueness, and corruption must necessarily result. His river-reclamation schemes were condemned to disastrous failure by lack of preparatory study. His river fleets achieved far less than his hopes; the Shaṭṭ ul 'Arab dredgers never worked; the sea-going steamers did not endure. His projected railways never appeared. His industrial machines, ordered from Europe, failed to arrive. He could not accomplish a darling project of using the treasures of Najf for public works. He failed entirely to suppress corruption. His town improvements but feebly survived him. His destruction of the walls of Baghdad left giant rubbish heaps and a defenceless town. With the bricks he proposed to pay his soldiers, and did not shrink from threatening the fabric of the majestic Arch of Ctesiphon with a similar function. Upon such grounds is the work of Midḥat Pasha assailable.

Yet his vision, his patriotic energy, his absolute integrity performed greater works than his imperfect education could mar. In public buildings, he completed and exceeded the works of Namiq Pasha. A newspaper, military factories, a hospital, an alms-house, an orphanage, numerous schools, a tramway to Kadhimiyyah—these in themselves, and in the associations of beneficent modernity which they connoted, remarkably enlightened and enlivened Baghdad. Reforms military and civil were under Midḥat applied for the first time to Baghdad after long use in other provinces. He enforced conscription, founded municipalities and administrative councils, and applied the new Wilayat system in its entirety. The towns of Naṣiriyyah and Ramadi were (for different reasons) his creations.

Turkish 'Iraq in its latest years was a country so backward and misgoverned that it may seem dubious praise to assign to Midḥat Pasha a paramount influence upon it. Such praise is not unqualified; yet those who would withhold it should reflect on the difference in the relations of government and tribes before and after his Pashaliq—on the comparative security of routes, the spread of primary education, the expansion of the provincial mind. His greatest contribution, a reasoned tribal-agrarian policy intended to reclaim the wide spaces of 'Iraq to settlement and profit while civilizing the tribes, will be described later. To it, and to the changed official outlook which accompanied it, was chiefly due the undoubted stride made in settlement and security in the last quarter of the century. At the same time, many of the numerous defects in government after Midhat Pasha resulted not from applying but from forgetting his methods. The 'Iraq governorship was but an incident in his career;[1] but his name, the most famous intimately connected with 'Iraq in the nineteenth century, is still constantly on the lips of townsmen and tribesmen, and always as that of an enlightened innovator.

Midhat Pasha left his office in Baghdad early in 1872, selling his watch—the story goes—to pay for his travelling expenses to the Capital.

The scale of the present account forbids more than a passing reference to the other personalities of the time. Mosul and Baṣrah, whether as Sanjaqs or Wilayats, did not secure any governor of special mark,[2] nor did their high officials conform by training or birth or outlook to any assignable type. The bulk were Turks; Arabs (chiefly of Syria) were not unknown; Kurds attained to high position, especially in the northern districts. It was rare for 'Iraqis to reach a position more elevated than that of Mutasarrif, though the lower walks of the bureaucracy in 'Iraq were mainly recruited therefrom: Kirkuk (Turkish-speaking) was conspicuous as a nursery of the official class. During the period the recognized leading families of each town were well established, bearing usually a Turkish surname or a place-name of origin; and these, without exception, were glad to enter the official world, often in humble capacities. Of the successors of Midhat Pasha none within our period was of first-class mark.[3] Radif Pasha (1874) was a firm disciplinarian,

[1] He became Grand Wazir in 1872 under Sultan 'Abdu'l 'Aziz and again under 'Abdu'l Ḥamid in 1876. He led, in these years, the Progressive and Liberal party, and was responsible for the abortive Constitution. The clash of his and 'Abdu'l Ḥamid's theories of government ruined him. After semi-banishment to the governorships of Syria and Smyrna, he was exiled and murdered at Ṭa'if near Makkah (1883).

[2] Ḥamdi Pasha (Wali of Baṣrah with interruptions from 1894–1900) passed the average in honesty and capacity. Names and dates of Walis of all three Wilayats are given in the official calendars.

[3] This excludes Nadhim Pasha (1911–12).

'Abdu'l Raḥman (1875–9) a vigorous but bigoted educationalist, 'Akif Pasha the Albanian amiable and extremely corrupt, Qadiri (1878) cosmopolitan and sceptical. Taqi'l Din Pasha, the predecessor of Midḥat, appeared a second time at Baghdad and governed for six years (1880–6). Muṣṭafa 'Aṣim Pasha (1887) bequeathed memories of energetic out-station tours, and of fierce quarrels with the Naqib, Sayyid Salman Effendi. Sirri Pasha was a Cretan littérateur, eager for the material embellishment of his Capital, Ḥaji Ḥasan (1892) a Turk of Stambul of commanding physique and old-fashioned religion, 'Ata'ullah Pasha (1896) a former Qaḍhi punctilious in the law and already of ripe age. The century ended with Namiq Pasha the Less, known for generous piety. Of all these, representing so many types and races, none emerged from the ruck of senior officialdom to a place in history. For other figures equally familiar in the 'Iraq of that time—landowners, 'ulama, merchants, generals—there is here no space: many still live, and the present writer has the acquaintance of not a few.

§ 2. *Expansion in Arabia.*

The later nineteenth century saw a notable attempted expansion of Turkey into the Arabian peninsula. It was not instigated, but was first actively pressed, from 'Iraq by Midḥat Pasha. It intended the absorption of all the independent Arab principalities of Najd and the Gulf coast into the name and machinery of the Ottoman Empire. This independence had lasted without question, in the maritime states, since the sixteenth century, when Turkish fleets by the sudden coast-raid of a day would claim Al Ḥasa,[1] Kuwait or Baḥrain; and in Najd, not Turkish but Egyptian forces[2] had conquered and retired. But if the appeal to history revealed little excuse for this expansion, there were other reasons to justify it. Internal revival, for which Midḥat stood, is commonly accompanied by aggression abroad. The Gulf states were Sunni and fit subjects of the Khalif. The Wahhabi power might well be finally destroyed since a deep division had appeared within it. Overtures reached the Pasha

[1] Al Ḥasa had, however (at least nominally and temporally), been a province of Baṣrah in the days of Ḥusain Pasha: see pp. 38, 111 *supra*.

[2] P. 230 (foot-note) *supra*: the Pasha of Egypt was of course theoretically the instrument of the Sultan.

of 'Iraq from this or that refugee Amir, appeals from any one to anybody being the commonplace of Arab politics. The British position in the Gulf—however nobly earned by long civilizing disinterested work of charting and suppression of piracy—must be disputed. Lastly, and the deepest reason, was the persistent, unceasing land-hunger of the Turks, ever grasping at useless and embarrassing possessions, ever willing to annex fresh hostile subjects and barren sands. As to actual conditions in the seventh decade of the century, Bahrain, torn by civil war, was claimed without visible effect by the Turks as Ottoman, and had been till recently tributary to the Amir of the Wahhabis, while British ships pursued their police duties around its coasts; Al Ḥasa and Qaṭar formed a loose part of the Wahhabi dominions; the Najd oases were still the home and centre of their power. To all these a vague Turkish claim persisted. The long and peaceful reign of Faiṣal bin Turki in Najd ended in 1865, whereafter began the feud of his two sons, 'Abdullah and Sa'ud, for the Wahhabi Amirate. The former, looking for assistance to the Turks, sent an agent to Baghdad in 1866, and in 1870, on the successful rebellion of his brother, appealed to Midhat Pasha, offering vassaldom and tribute in return for reinstation. His message went by way of Kuwait, whose Shaikh 'Abdullah bin Subaḥ had for some years past seen his advantage to lie in close relations with Baṣrah.

Few Turkish statesmen could withhold their hand from an offered province: and in Midhat prudence ever fell behind imagination and vigour. He decided to accept 'Abdullah bin Faiṣal's offer, and if possible to annex the Wahhabi kingdom on the plea of restoring order in the Sultan's remoter territories. He dispatched, by the mouldering transports of the Shaṭṭ ul 'Arab, a force of some thousands of men under Nafidh Pasha. These landed at Ras Tanurah in May 1871, and easily occupied Qaṭif. The professed objective of Nafidh was to confer the delights of Turkish rule upon the settled folk of Al Ḥasa, and to restore 'Abdullah to his place as "Qa'immaqam of Najd". Governors were nominated to the Ḥasa villages, and Qaṭar occupied by a garrison at Daulah. For a few weeks Turkish rule was favourably contrasted with the capricious severities of the Wahhabis; and when 'Abdullah bin Faisal appeared in the

Turkish camp, realized that his return to power was far from their real intentions, and fled, there was little regret in Al Ḥasa.

But, as their first good impression was effaced by experience, so to the Turkish soldiery the occupation was increasingly irksome. Fever, disease, and bad supplies thinned the ranks. Late in 1871 Midḥat Pasha with reinforcements and stores himself left Baghdad on inspection. At Kuwait he was entertained, and invested the Shaikh formally as Qa'immaqam. In Al Ḥasa he evacuated the sickly garrison, replaced it with fit men, proclaimed the territories as the Sultan's without reserve (thus disposing of Wahhabi claims), and appointed Nafidh Pasha "Mutasarrif of Najd". No advance was made into the central oases, and Baḥrain was not touched out of respect to known British objections;[1] but both now and at regular intervals till the close of our period the island was claimed as under Turkish suzerainty, a claim never allowed nor effective.

Midḥat Pasha's arrangement lasted till 1874. It was then found that the direct administration of the Ḥasa Sanjaq was too costly to continue. Naṣir Pasha, the Muntafiq Mutasarrif of Baṣrah, was commissioned to introduce a cheaper régime.[2] He visited Ḥasa, withdrew most of the Turkish garrison, and appointed Shaikh Barrak of the Bani Khalid as Mutasarrif. The move, highly retrograde in character, failed within a few weeks. A Wahhabi counter-rising expelled Barrak, and threatened the few Turkish troops. Naṣir Pasha late in 1874 revisited Ḥasa, sternly restored order, and retired leaving his own son as Mutasarrif. He was succeeded in that office by a line of other officers, and Turkish rule—mean, rapacious, stagnant, hated when not ignored—continued till 1900.[3] The Sanjaq, now nominally part of 'Iraq, at no time developed connexions with it, and has little interest for this history. The attention of the world to its affairs was drawn only by the chronic piracy of its coasts, suppressed by British ships under protest from the nominal suzerain who could and would do nothing.

[1] The *Life of Midhat Pasha* by his son 'Ali Haidar (pp. 59–60) in this respect altogether deserts the facts.

[2] These events were no doubt responsible for the reformation of Baṣrah as a separate wilayat (1875).

[3] And afterwards: Sayyid Ṭalib Pasha, of Baṣrah, was Mutasarrif for two years from 1902.

Kuwait remained definitely Turkophile during the reign of 'Abdullah bin Subaḥ. His successor continued this policy until his assassination in 1896, when Shaikh Mubarak the assassin became Qa'immaqam. Turkish sovereignty over the Kuwait state, however, was very variously assessed by Arab, by Turkish, by European, and by Indian authorities. The British at no time admitted the complete Turkish claims, while themselves refusing more than once the Shaikh's overtures for their protection. In 1898, however, a rumour of Russian railway enterprise changed the position; and in the last months of the century a formal agreement between the Shaikh and the Indian government bound the former to refuse all foreign concessions. As other railways came under discussion, the status of the town became of great importance: but these controversies belong to the twentieth century. With central Najd the governors of 'Iraq had almost no relations during the remaining years of our present period. The intestine wars of the Sa'ud family continued, as well as the struggle between the rival empires of Ḥa'il and Riyaḍh. Appeals to Baghdad by this and that candidate were not uncommon, each promising loyal subjection to the Sultan.[1]

It will be convenient here to mention Persian and other foreign relations, before turning back to domestic affairs. The frontier difficulties, already marked by so many conferences and treaties since 1823, were not lessened by a ceremonial pilgrimage of Naṣiru'l Din Shah to the Holy Cities of 'Iraq in 1871, a visit productive rather of friction than of cordiality. The "carte identique" evolved after twenty years' work by British and Russian draughtsmen did not provide a cure, the Turkish commission claiming a line altogether outside the debated area thus prepared. The dispute, in brief, thus continued in various stages of acrimony till the close of our period. It was acutest in the Panjvin and Zuhab zone of southern Kurdistan, and in the riverain marshes of 'Arabistan. It was marked in the northern area by constant encroachment by each nation into the debated zone, met by the punctual complaints of the other. The mud islands of the Shaṭṭ ul 'Arab were as eagerly claimed. The

[1] Turkish forces under Faiḍhi Pasha occupied Qasim in 1905, divided the country into nominal units on the Turkish pattern, and withdrew.

imposing Turkish fort at Fao (begun in about 1886, but never actually finished), appeared to defy the second Treaty of Erzerum which forbade to fortify the Shaṭṭ. The most vexatious play was made by the Turks with police posts, quarantine stations, and provocative collection of Customs from ships bound for the Karun. The usual points of Perso-Turkish friction were ever present: extortion at the Shia' shrines, robbery of pilgrim caravans, protection of criminal tribes, residence of suspected Persian princes in Baghdad.

Great Britain was represented in 'Iraq by a senior representative[1] at Baghdad, by an Assistant Political Agent (and from 1898 by a Consul) at Baṣrah, and by a Vice-Consul (but not continuously) at Mosul. The influence wielded by these officials did not decrease, nor was less resented by the more suspicious or xenophobe of local officials. The telegraphs, the Residency privileges, the Tigris navigation rights, the Indian post offices[2] were always available to furnish matter for obstruction; but there is every sign that the attitude of British agents was consistently correct and patient. Their special position (acquired after three centuries), however patent to town and tribe alike, was never abused. Frequent advances made by Turkish subjects for their protection were refused, opportunities for acquiring power and for disuniting the Turkish administration were rejected.

A French Consul represented the Republic in Baghdad, and at times in Baṣrah. Russia, the United States, and Germany maintained agents in Baghdad. Their proceedings call for no comment in this history. More vital touch with the 'Iraq people was found by the many archaeological expeditions of the time: more than once the parts of Consul and excavator were united.

§ 3. *The new policy of Settlement.*

In internal affairs this generation brought a new policy and a quickened evolution rather than single striking events. Travellers and residents alike in 1900 could report a notable improvement in settlement and security since 1865; and most agreed that the lines now successfully followed were those of Midḥat.

His predecessors' failure to evolve a policy, to govern with

[1] His designation, "Political Agent" in 1870, was "Resident" later in the period. The new Residency was not built till 1905. [2] p. 317 sub.

sympathy and firmness, had resulted in a wilderness of untilled land and wasted water. To break the power of the great tribes, give safety to roads, and multiply ploughs, it was essential to detach the Shaikhs from an exclusively tribal setting, to win them for government by self-interest; and this in general, from the time of Midḥat Pasha, was the conscious aim of the 'Iraq governors. Already under Geuzliki, the Sardar i Akram, and Namiq, evolution itself was very gradually settling the unsettled, tent by tent. Midḥat accelerated these processes by fresh means which deserve careful attention. His contribution was an approach to the problem of settlement from a new side—that of the land itself.

Lands in 'Iraq were subject to many claims. Estates had been freely bestowed by Daud Pasha, by 'Ali Riḍha; descendants of the old timariots still clung to deeds of feudal title; sale and purchase of state lands had gone on for generations without the knowledge and recognition of government. Mere long possession led both villagers and the shaikhs of wide tribal areas to claim their holdings as *de facto* "mulk". Government's denial of such claims (with consequent crushing demand-rate and scant security of tenure) created uneasy conditions fatal to settlement. All agrarian improvement was checked by the absence of definite rights; and the tribes perceived that to settle merely exposed them to easier exaction and punishment. Briefly, that reasonable alternative life, without which the tribes would never desert nomadism and grazing, had never been provided. The sole such alternative was cultivation. To this, no concessions had been made to attract them. From it, the hard lot of the village cultivator (as well as much in their own character and code) repelled them.

Midḥat Pasha's method was to sell for little and easy payment great or small tracts of state land—upon terms giving full security of tenure (though not actual ownership)—to holders of the doubtfully valid farmans and buyurildis of an earlier age, to villagers who had cleaned a canal or planted a garden, and, most important, to the shaikhs of tribes for their tribal areas. "Tapu" offices were opened, registers filled, titles issued, first instalments paid. Of ever-increasing areas of 'Iraq it could be said that they were "miri tapu", state-owned land whose occupation was secured (with important reservations) to individual holders.

High hopes were formed, not wholly to be unjustified. The shaikh, as rallying-point of anti-government forces, was to lose his terrors, tribalism itself to weaken in the new environment of settled residence, the many interests and relations of the new life to overlay the old outlook of the tribe. As chiefs of an agricultural community the Shaikhs would become accessible, because rooted; vulnerable, by reason of government's power of water-control; taxable, since crops cannot be driven off nor wholly concealed; dependent on government as landlords whose titles—whose very power to collect the "Tapu" crop-share—was from the State. A great increase in man-power and revenue could be expected.

But the method could not wholly succeed in the face of two major difficulties. The first, the ignorance and venality of the Tapu officials, meant that the machinery of Tapu was always inadequate to its functions. The second lay in the faint response of the public to be benefited. Many saw the clear purpose of detribalizing; more suspected any blessing that issued from the Sarai; and more again were still too well content with their own remoteness to accept a change. Vivid fear of conscription kept the tribes from accepting the obligations of settlement, which had other evils enough in accessibility, toil, dependence on canals and markets. There was, in any case, money to be paid. The majority of tribal leaders feared and shunned the new status; some were forestalled as purchasers by a town-dwelling speculator friendly with the Tapu officials; some gladly acquired rights, but in land far from their own people; others paid a first instalment and withheld the rest. Thus, if the aim of Tapu settlement was fixity of tribal-cultivating tenure which should transform shaikh into landlord, it was an aim largely frustrated by the hesitancy of the shaikhs themselves.

Yet it bore notable fruits. The Cha'ab or Muḥaisin shaikh who owned gardens on the Shaṭṭ ul 'Arab had given one valuable hostage. Half-tribal Sayyids in the wild Shamiyyah formed nuclei of settlement. The great Ibn Hadhdhal of the 'Anizah came to possess gardens on the upper Euphrates. Farḥan of the Shammar Jarba was installed on his own lands at Sharqaṭ. On the Kurdish border, many an Agha had lands registered in his name. But the greatest feat of the Tapu system was its death-blow given to the Sa'duns of the Muntafiq. Led by Naṣir Pasha, himself now an Ottoman official, members of the family made haste to buy the rights over vague estates in the tribal dirah. The Muntafiq tribesmen, who had long borne their rulers as tax-farmers and had seen them recently with Ottoman titles of office, were now asked to pay not only the government's, but a landlord's crop-share. No rule is for ever; perhaps the Sa'duns were already doomed; but this acceptance of the role of landlord under Ottoman auspices, joined with a new avarice and new ungenerous quarrels among themselves, was to prove their ruin. The change of status was too sudden for the marshmen. When the wide Muntafiq territories were officially bestowed on this or that Sa'dun, disputes of landlord and tenant began. The great days of the Shaikh ul Masha'ikh were over. Sa'duns were still to live precariously on their estates, to lead sections of the tribe, to fight each other; the Muntafiq region (now a Sanjaq of that name) was still mainly closed to government and paid scanty revenue; but the seeds of settlement were sown, the Sa'duns broken and in part expelled.

The same tribe best illustrates other lines of new policy and their results. Naṣir Pasha, brother of Manṣur, had in 1866 bidden highest for the shaikhship. Under Midḥat he became the Pasha's chosen and willing tool to tame the Muntafiq.[1] He founded Naṣiriyyah, and accepted high government office. But here and elsewhere reaction among the body of the tribe followed hard upon such "betrayal" to the Turks. Manṣur, and later his son Sa'dun, led the old school of hostility to innovation; Naṣir, and then his son Faliḥ, were government nominees to carry out the policy of Ottomanization. The years 1880–1900 form a period of constant struggle between the two factions, wherein personal ambition and hatred joined with a clear issue of policy. The government vacillated between the less resistance of an "old school" appointment (with its retrograde results) and the harder line of maintaining their own man in

[1] In 1872 he was Mutasarrif of his own Liwa; in 1874 he was sent to Al Ḥasa to suppress rebellion; and in 1875 he became Wali of Baṣrah. From that office he was removed to Stambul.

power. Year after year tribal war went on, state forces sometimes participating from their barracks at Khamisiyyah or from outside; civil government appeared almost wholly inoperative; yet settlement and tribe-breaking was all the time half-visibly proceeding. The day of a quiet tithe-paying Muntafiq peasantry was still distant: the fear of a united Muntafiq army was long past.

In the Shammar, a similar position arose by similar reaction against an Ottomanizing shaikh; Farḥan, son of Sufuk, like Naṣir was promoted Pasha, like him was to be the means of settling his nomads. He visited Stambul, gave offence in his tribe by his Turkish airs and town-bred wives, and obediently settled to cultivate on the Tigris. The result was a secession of half the tribe under Faris, protagonist of the claims of desert and freedom. Hostility on familiar lines went on. Farḥan's cultivation was of small account; but the mere break with nomad tradition, the contact with government, the Turkish education of his sons, meant more than victories in tribal battle. In other tribes camel-keeping was becoming more and more a symbol of shaikhly respectability, less an economic necessity. The Dulaim settled from 'Anah to Fallujah, the Zubaid tribes on the Tigris and round Ḥillah, the Shammar Togah from Diyalah nearly to Kut. The tribal map, in fact, assumed its familiar contours of to-day, and the boundary-lines of the settled could be ever more confidently drawn. 'Iraq by 1900 was a country of tribesmen fast losing the old loyalties, less and less able to revert to the old livelihood, attracting local rather than tribal relations, more dependent on order and control—yet still tribal in material equipment, in speech, in ignorance, still easily inflamed to ruin their own interests, still resentful of government and all its works.

The two lines of tribal policy hitherto described—settlement on the land, and Ottomanization—were both damaging to the tribal spirit. There remains another, dating from 1885, very different in tendency. It was the policy not of the 'Iraq pashas, but of the Sultan. Applying only to the Kurds, it was designed less to settle the tribes than to secure their close adhesion to the Khalif by paid employment without deserting tribalism. "Ḥamidiyyah" battalions of Kurdish horse, contributed by every tribal leader who could be formidable, remained in being until the Revolution of 1908 removed their author. Something was gained by this paid attachment of powerful Kurds to government: but the bullying indiscipline of the Ḥamidiyyah, their still doubtful loyalty, their limited fighting uses, and the retrogression implied in their formation, leaves this phase of policy on the whole to be condemned. It affected only the northern fringes of 'Iraq. Ibrahim Pasha Milli—descendant of the Timur Pasha of Buyuk Sulaiman's days—was among those recruited.

Tribal wars loom smaller on the 'Iraq page of these years than on any that we have scanned. Midḥat led a famous expedition to Dagharah. The Shammar were perennially restless, especially after the hanging of 'Abdu'l Karim and the succession of Faris to lead the opposition to Farḥan. The Bani Lam were fighting among themselves in 1879, and their neighbours the Albu Muḥammad in 1880 closed Tigris communications.[1] In the same year occurred anti-Christian outrages in the Hakari country, the work of Shaikh 'Ubaidullah, while in Sulaimaniyyah power fell increasingly into the hands of Shaikh Sa'id, who—now ally and now enemy of government on one side, and of the notorious Hamawand on the other—went far to ruin the place. The Hamawand broke out as the mood took them: routes east of Kirkuk were at their mercy, and even wholesale transplantation[2] did not solve the problem of their enormities which at times brought the government of Sulaimaniyyah to a close. In 1886 fierce combat raged between Shammar and Dulaim, in 1893 between the marsh tribes of the Bani Ḥasan and Fatlah. In the latter year Saihud of the Albu Muḥammad was chastised by Kad͟him Pasha,[3] and Ḥasan ul Khayyun of the Bani Isad driven from his swamps into exile. This list might be extended by scores of small punitive expeditions and intestine tribal quarrels. In some areas it was habitual for government to send a column every few years to collect the accumulated dues; some were still untouched by the settling tendency; yet, with all that, organized

[1] Among other offences, they attacked the Lynch steamer *Khalifah*.
[2] To Sinai in 1882. They fought and robbed their way back.
[3] Brother-in-law of Sultan 'Abdu'l Ḥamid, and kept for political reasons in Baghdad as commander of the cavalry.

tribal opposition to government was by now immensely less than it had been. The Turkish writ ran farther afield, the fez was seen in every village. The recalcitrant could be punished one by one, and failure was rare. The lawlessness of bandits, a brief defiance by single sections, took the place of great confederacies at war with their Pasha. Restlessness and insecurity, superficially still distressing enough, moved from less depths.

The means to meet it were also better. After the return of forces from the Russian war of 1878, new cantonments appeared at Khamisiyyah in the Muntafiq, at Ramadi in the Dulaim, at 'Amarah in the Bani Lam country, and military garrisons improved somewhat in size and discipline. The telegraph (itself sadly vulnerable) gave a new advantage to government forces. The steamboats helped to check the tribes of the lower Tigris. Numerous police-posts along the routes—and particularly by Ramadi to Dair ul Zor, by the Khaliṣ to Kirkuk, and south of Baghdad to Ḥillah and the Holy Cities—made travel tolerably safe for the prudent, though the carrying of arms was universal. The new power of government over its tribes (and its obligations from them) was shown by the effects of the new persistent desertion by the Euphrates of its old bed passing Ḥillah. Each decade of the nineteenth century had seen more and more water follow the Hindiyyah canal.[1] By 1885 the Ḥillah river was almost dry, to the consternation of the tribes not long settled upon it. French engineers[2] were brought to correct the position, and finished their work in 1891. In this all could see a work vital to the tribes, yet impossible without super-tribal agency—an example of their new dependence on government.

[1] The Hindiyyah canal (intended by its Indian author 'Aṣif ul Daulah to supply Najf) was gaining ground by 1800. By 1830 it was necessary to check the stream trying to desert the Ḥillah river in its favour. 'Ali Riḍha and Najib both attempted dams. 'Abdi Pasha diverted the Euphrates and built a strong regulator with brick piers (Loftus, pp. 44 f.). By 1854 it had again broken through. 'Umr Pasha built a great weir of mud and brushwood, also short lived. The repairing of this was the constant care of his successors. The Hindiyyah was by 1880 the main Euphrates.

[2] M. Schoenderfer. His attempt was a solid masonry dam (200 yards wide) with a nitch in the centre. It partially collapsed in 1903, and conditions on the Ḥillah river were bad until the completion of Willcock's Barrage in 1913.

§ 4. *The Government of 'Iraq at the close of the nineteenth century.*

'Iraq shared to a certain extent in the international fortunes of Turkey. It contributed funds to the ruinous extravagance of 'Abdu'l 'Aziz, kissed the farmans of his imbecile successor Murad V, and welcomed the vigorous and promising 'Abdu'l Ḥamid II in 1876. The Russian war of 1877–8 depleted the garrisons of 'Iraq and increased its burden of poverty. The active Sunni propaganda of 'Abdu'l Ḥamid had its effect in the towns and the Kurdish tribes of the 'Iraq provinces who appreciated (as was intended) his skilful playing upon elements the most conservative and reactionary.[1] In the last years of the century faint rumours were perceptible in the Baghdad diwans of a new movement soon to lead to Union and Progress, and of very different and still fainter aspirations for Arab independence. More than this need not be said of 'Iraq's imperial position. Among the most remote and backward of the wilayats, the 'Iraq provinces yet contained all the features of the Ḥamidian régime and, for the rest, cannot have regretted their distance from the Bosphorus.

To review in detail the organization of the various Departments lies outside the scale of the present history. Full information can be found in official handbooks. We are concerned only, and briefly, to notice important changes occurring in this last generation, and to judge in general terms the adequacy of the Turkish machine in this (almost its final) form.

The first act of Midḥat Pasha had been to announce the application to 'Iraq of the Wilayat system, already formulated by him and used on the Danube. By this means were introduced administrative arrangements which survived with little change till 1914. At every town and village, graded according to the importance of its district, were now found the Mutasarrif, the Qa'immaqam, or the Mudir of the Sanjaq, Qadḥa, or Naḥiyyah. At each a fixed cadre of officials performed defined duties, at each an elected council with doubtful powers assisted the administrative head. The vocabulary and machinery of the final period of Turkish 'Iraq now held the field.

[1] The veneration in which 'Abdu'l Ḥamid is still regarded in 'Iraq by the townsmen is very remarkable.

Baṣrah remained a mere Sanjaq of Baghdad until its reconstitution as a Wilayat in 1875. Najd was already considered by the Turks as a Qa'immaqamlik under Baṣrah. Al Ḥasa became a Sanjaq in 1871, and in subsequent years it suited Turkish policy to bestow the names of their official appointments upon various of the Gulf potentates. In 1880 Baṣrah again became a Sanjaq, in 1884 its Wilayat was re-formed. Mosul had been reduced to the office of a Mutasarrif in 1850; in 1879 it again became a Wilayat, with dependent Sanjaqs of Kirkuk and Sulaimaniyyah.[1]

Public order was maintained by regular and reserve forces of the army, by a fleet at Baṣrah, and by gendarmerie. The latter, the Ḍhabṭiyyah, organized by battalions and companies but in fact dispersed in numerous small detached posts, was a shabby, undisciplined force, its officers commonly illiterate[2] and corrupt, the rank and file unpaid and unequipped, and habitually degenerating into mere messengers, tax-collectors, and personal servants of the nearest official. Neither on open roads nor in bazaars were they an adequate police-force. They had little superiority of discipline and arms, little leadership, no specialized training. For tribal robbers they were too weak, for town malefactors too venal; but they contained many hardy and capable men.

[1] Thus in its last phase Turkish 'Iraq was bounded by the Sanjaq of Dair ul Zor (attached to no Wilayat); by the Wilayat of Diyarbakr, with its head-quarter Sanjaq and those of Arghanah and Mardin; and by Persia. It consisted of three Wilayats: *Mosul* contained three Sanjaqs: that of head-quarters (with Qaḍhas of Dohuk, Zakho, 'Amadiyyah, Sinjar, 'Aqrah), Kirkuk (with Qaḍhas of Arbil, Raniyyah, Ruwanduz, Keui Sanjaq, Kifri), and Sulaimaniyyah (with Bazyan, Halabjah, Shahribazar, and Markah). *Baghdad* Wilayat had the head-quarter Sanjaq of Baghdad (with Qaḍhas of 'Anah, Ramadi, Samarra, Kaḍhimain, 'Aziziyyah, Kut, Khaniqin, Ba'qubah, Mandali, Badrah), the Sanjaq of Diwaniyyah (with head-quarters first at Ḥillah and latterly at Diwaniyyah, and Qaḍhas of Ḥillah, Samawah, and Shamiyyah), and the Sanjaq of Karbala (with Hindiyyah, Najf, and the desert Qaḍha of Razazah). *Baṣrah* Wilayat contained the Sanjaq of 'Amarah (with Duwairij, Zubair, and Qal'at Ṣaliḥ), of Baṣrah (with Fao and Qurnah and theoretically Kuwait), of Muntafiq (with Naṣiriyyah the head-quarters, Shaṭrah, Suq ul Shuyukh, and Ḥai). The Sanjaq of Al Ḥasa contained three Qaḍhas, Ḥufuf, Qaṭar, and Qaṭif, while the shadowy Sanjaq of Qasim in central Arabia contained on paper the Qaḍhas of Buraidah and Riyaḍh. The Qasim Sanjaq, however, dates (in that form) properly from 1905.

[2] Literacy became commoner towards the end of the century, and the gendarmerie conditions described above were greatly improved by the reforms of 1906. The urban "Polis" did not appear till after 1900, on the advice of Van der Goltz.

The Shaṭṭ ul 'Arab navy needs no description. It was, and had been for scores of years, a puny, decayed service of no value whatsoever save for firing salutes and precariously convoying troops. The Turkish army cannot be so lightly dismissed; but its full description belongs elsewhere than to the history of 'Iraq. The Nidham Jadid of Maḥmud II was modified after the Russian wars of 1854 and 1879, and was remodelled on the continental territorial system in 1885. Under this organization 'Iraq formed the area of the 6th Army, supporting in peace-time one corps, the 6th, and in war-time, theoretically, three corps, the 6th, 12th, and 18th. The system of recruiting was that of conscription in settled areas, many exemptions being allowed and lots cast among those eligible. The unsettled (tribal) areas paid a house-tax in lieu, and any conscripted person could buy exemption. The organization by Nidham (regular), Radif (first reserve), and Mustaḥfidh (second reserve) was elaborate and on the whole suitable. The staffs, establishments, and strategic instructions were in general those of a modern army. Formation and unit head-quarters were found each in its appointed place. These favourable points, added to the high military qualities of Kurdish and Turkoman recruits, might have led to hopes of a fully efficient army. In practice it was otherwise. Elaborate checks and returns did not prevent all units from being immensely below strength, sometimes to vanishing point. Even regulars were used for unmilitary duties; reservists occasionally resisted mobilization by force, and represented, in the statistics of reserve battalions, the dream or fond hope of the higher command. In equipment there was no uniformity. Arms were of all patterns, uniforms tattered and various, training for all ranks inadequate. Pay was for all habitually in arrears, obtained as a rare favour, and augmented by petty peculation, by pilfering, by bullying and extortion. Over all and in all was the deadness of low standards. No other army would admit the Turkish engineer or doctor or gunner to be such.[1] His sore-backed horses, his non-existent sanitation, his shoddy string-tied harness, his dirty rifles and old-pattern guns, did not indeed prevent occasional successful

[1] These remarks apply to 'Iraq of 1870–1900, not to the last years before the War, and not to *all* Turkish forces in the earlier period. The 6th Army was admittedly the worst.

operations; but they showed vividly certain abiding failings of Turkish rule: the fall in standards ever lower and lower for every mile out of Stambul—the poverty which (due to blind and corrupt administration) intensified the evils from which it sprang—the oriental acquiescence in existing conditions, the ignorance that knew no others. Between men and officers there was no camaraderie, rather the relation of master and servant; among tribesmen and villagers the dread of conscription was such as to impede settlement and terrify waverers from entering the body politic.

Of the judicial system, nothing need be said but that it was a compromise between Islamic simplicity and the Code Napoleon. Clumsy in application (but not excessively), punctilious in process, despairingly slow, it worked by laws ill coded when old, ill drafted when new, and often tacitly unapplied to this or that wilayat. That corruption was universal, that no outrage to justice was beyond the reach of money and influence, is admitted by practically all who were, at the time, parties thereto. From the court, criminal or debtor was conducted to a jail where his relations brought him meals (shared in perfect amity with the jailor); prison clothes, rules, or exercises were unknown, and all curtailments of perfect liberty viewed with regret by a public rarely unfavourable to crime or debt. That every prison official from governor to watchman sold privileges, services, and even liberty, needs not to be said.

Leaving justice and security, we come to municipalities and public services. The former afford the most pleasing feature of public life in Turkish Asia. The elected president and council of the township, meeting regularly to transact their business of watch and ward, street-cleaning and watering and sometimes lighting, bridge repairs, supervision of buildings and the like, had a half-independence under their local governor and a pleasant municipal pride. Too often, indeed, the municipality did little but pay salaries to its staff and entertain visiting and resident officials: its standards were low, its activities excluded most of what Europe demands of city authorities: yet more honesty of purpose, more sense of service were to be found in the Baladiyyah than in the central administration. Many of these bodies were created by Midḥat Pasha, the rest came one by one into existence.

By 1900 every considerable village was so constituted, and Baghdad contained three municipalities. Of public services performed by the State, the department of Nafi'ah (Public Works) was scarcely operative in 'Iraq.[1] Sanitation was in towns a municipal service, elsewhere did not exist. Quarantine stations —maintained at Fao and Baṣrah, at Khaniqin and the Holy Cities, and at certain other points on the pilgrim routes—blended puerile inefficiency with vexatiousness, and were readily made a malicious weapon against foreigners; all could, however, buy complete exemption for a few pence. A public hospital existed at Baghdad, none (during the period) elsewhere. Of all these sanitary and medical services it must be said that, of the familiar oriental blend of scrupulous cleanliness with most offensive filth, the latter was the more in evidence.[2] There was no veterinary service. In education there was little to show, yet far more than nothing. It increased rapidly after the great progressive impulse of Midḥat. From perhaps a half per cent. in 1850, some five to ten per cent. of townspeople were literate by 1900. (In the tribes it was, and is still, confined to rare individuals.) Christian and Jewish schools were found at the largest towns. Among these the establishments of the Alliance Israelite gave the best education; most, in their remoteness from modern subjects and methods, scarcely surpassed the Mullas' schools found in every mosque; but by far the highest proportion of literates was among the non-Muslims. Government maintained, besides military schools, a free primary school at every Qadha headquarters. A boys' secondary school was founded in Baghdad in 1870, a girls' primary in 1898. Of the schoolmasters we may pass over the actual ignorance, the frequent immorality. Of the tuition, the leading feature was the use of Turkish as the medium. This had two results: the lessons were largely uncomprehended, and the young 'Iraqis grew up unable to write tolerable Arabic. Political value in half-transforming Arabs into Turks cannot be denied; it long postponed consciousness of Arab nationality; and it secured the identification of the educated with the official

[1] The very few public works were performed by the army, by the Crown Lands department, and by municipalities. The Hindiyyah Barrage (of M. Shoenderfer, 1891) was an exception.

[2] There were outbreaks of cholera in 1871, 1889, 1894, and 1899; of plague in 1877, 1881, and 1882.

class: educationally, it was disastrous. Two departments remain to mention: that of Tapu (Land Registry) founded with fair hopes by Midḥat Pasha and fundamental in his tribal agrarian policy, and that of Auqaf (Religious Endowments). The former lacked too many essentials to be successful. It had no maps, no surveyors, no sufficiently educated and no honest staff. Therefore exactness, without which a record of land rights had far better not exist, was lost in vagueness and venality; titles were given for lands already held, of doubtful location, unknown boundaries. To this, so easily stated, immense difficulties in subsequent administration must be traced. The Auqaf, influential by reason of strong vested and social-religious interests, succeeded to some degree in its trusteeship of endowments, saving them, at least, from secular misuse; but it did not save the yearly dispatch to Stambul of surplus Waqf revenues while its properties deteriorated, mosques crumbled, and starved officials stole. Worst of official misers and obstructionists, the Auqaf was no better as a landlord, and a firm enemy to the progress that must endanger its own abuses and sinecures.

Of communications, something was said in the previous chapter. Postal arrangements, it was seen, did not exist[1] for a full generation after the Mamluks. In 1868, with the agreement of Taqi'l Din Pasha, British-Indian post offices were opened in Baghdad and Baṣrah. No official objection was raised for ten years, and the post offices extended deliveries to the riverain towns and for a time to the Holy Cities. But in 1878 Turkey participated in the Paris Conference, and subscribed to its Postal Convention. Thereafter, her attitude to the British posts was marked by constant diplomatic battles at Stambul, and a local campaign for suppression in 'Iraq. Turkish post offices were gradually opened: a partial service came into existence, unreliable and not free from abuses, but fairly adequate to 'Iraq's simple needs. The mail-boats, pillar-boxes, and distributors of the Indian post offices were periodically obstructed but never suppressed. The telegraphs were extended to all the larger towns, and 'Iraq

[1] That is, government posts for public use. The Company's camel-mail to Aleppo was of long standing, and did not cease till about 1885; and the Pashas had for centuries maintained touch with Stambul and with each other by Tartar riders.

became, in this regard, one of the open regions of the world. The lack of reliability and secrecy did not diminish.

On the rivers, steam navigation was bound to attract the restless energies of Midḥat. He found the 'Uman-Ottoman administration's fleet inefficient and deteriorating. Its last recruits, *Taufik* and *Rasafa* (ordered by Namiq Pasha), arrived in 1869. He introduced many reforms, appointed a more competent director, and gave instructions to open the old Kin'an canal into the Saqlawiyyah to form a single waterway from river to river. A ship was deputed for Euphrates survey work, a dredger was ordered. His fleet of small steamboats for the upper Euphrates was arriving (in sections) at Baṣrah in his last months; but the exhaustion of funds, the removal of his personality, the unsuitability of the craft themselves, led to the waste of the whole consignment. They remained, their engines never inserted, decaying in the shops at Baṣrah. A single glimpse of achievement was allowed to Midḥat. In his last days in 'Iraq he ascended the Euphrates as far as Maskanah, safely passing through the Saqlawiyyah. This marked the apex of river enterprise in Turkish 'Iraq. No further development was attempted. The Lynch Company were forbidden to enlarge their fleet, and the Turks were fully occupied in keeping their ships afloat. In 1876 the *Dajlah* was sunk and replaced by the *Blosse Lynch*; and in 1883 the Company was suddenly prevented by the Baghdad authorities from sailing at all, on the occasion of the addition of the *Mejidieh* to their fleet. The strongest protests were made by the Company to the Resident; Taqi'l Din was adamant. To a natural xenophobia were added private Baghdad interests and the hope of soaring profits for the Turkish ships. In the end the crisis was resolved by the diplomacy of the respective capitals, and sailings resumed. The condition of the 'Uman steamers, by some twenty years after Midḥat, was desperate. No renewals had been made. One ship was scrapped, one sunk, one burnt. The remaining four reached, and remained in, that state of decay which in Turkey alone does not presage decease.[1]

Land transport was more progressive. The tramway, but not

[1] The 'Uman-Ottoman fleet was bought in 1904 by the Sanniyyah department and renamed the Ḥamidiyyah. The ships ran better and more profitably until the fall of 'Abdu'l Ḥamid, then relapsed to their former state, in which the War found them.

the railways, of Midḥat Pasha materialized. A few carts began to work on the main routes. A Kufah-Najf tramway was made at the close of the century. Otherwise, mule and horse, donkey and camel, still held the field. Railway enterprise (all external in origin) was not dead. In 1878, some years after the failure of Andrew's attempts, another group formed a Tigris Valley project. The route was from Diyarbakr by Mosul to Kuwait; but the British Government's support was not forthcoming, and the scheme dropped. In 1898 British authorities were startled by rumours of a Russian concession, sought in Stambul, for a line from Asia Minor to Kuwait; but the only local result was a tightening of British relations with Shaikh Mubarak of Kuwait, and increasing delicacy in the question of Turkish sovereignty there. Not Russians, however, but Germans were to launch the attack.[1]

There remain to consider the revenue-producing departments of government. The Customs were represented, at all places on sea or land frontiers, by officials of the most notoriously corrupt of all government departments. The usual import duty of eight, and export duty of one per cent. was evaded or lightened in proportion to the generosity shown by the shipper or caravan-master to the Gumrek official. Delay, quarantine, and inflated assessment awaited the ungenerous. This was, however, a main source of revenue. A second was the tax on live stock, convenient and profitable except in the wilder areas; a third, Land Revenue, the officials of which—working with many local variations, many practical difficulties, and too little uprightness—were at every government head-quarters whatever. Methods of assessment were many—estimation of crops, counting of trees and water-lifts, farming of whole estates, bargaining for lump-sum demands; in vast unsurveyed, half-controlled areas, government must rely on

[1] Germany had by 1885 completed Balkan railways giving direct access to Stambul. In 1888 it leased from Turkey the Haidar Pasha-Ismit Line. In 1889 the "Chemin de fer d'Anatolie" was formed with German capital. By 1893 the Angora line was complete, and by 1896 that to Askishahr and Konia, and a concession obtained (but not used) for an Angora-Kaisariyyah-Siwas-Diyarbakr-Baghdad line. By 1900 the German position was paramount in Turkish railways and could not be regarded as merely industrial. In 1899 the Konia-Gulf concession was confirmed, and a German commission visited Kuwait. In 'Iraq from 1903 the coming railway was a burning topic. In 1912 the first tugs and barges arrived, and by 1914 the Baghdad-Samarra section was complete.

wholly unreliable officials, get what it could, and redress the loss by stripping at ruinous rates the more accessible folk. Accountancy was careful and elaborate, unpaid arrears neatly transcribed from year to year until pardon or a military expedition should cancel or collect the accumulated sums. In the whole range of revenue-collecting (the chief function of most of the innumerable officials) was seen government's care for pence, its carelessness of future pounds—the profound distrust between governors and governed—the self-imposed poverty that could afford nothing, improve nothing, develop nothing—the sheer ignorance of the governing arts, whereby everything was taxed, nothing assisted. These fundamental faults were less glaring in administrations under special management. Such were the Sanniyyah Department, Crown-lands of the Sultan's Privy Purse; the Department of Public Debt, collecting the revenues of fisheries, liquor, salt, and stamps for the bond-holders of the International Ottoman Debt; and the Régie,[1] dealing efficiently with tobacco. The Sanniyyah Department, started in 'Iraq in the last years of the century, administered the large and well-selected estates successively acquired from the State by the Sultan by purchase, real or nominal, or by arbitrary transfer. Though the acquisition was never competitive, and the estates unequally favoured by special influences and improved policing (at State expense), the resulting administration was far superior to that of government estates. Their better buildings, cleared canals, chosen and well-treated officials, copious revenues, showed in little on what lines, and how easily, the whole land-administration might have been improved.

§ 5. *Retrospect and judgement.*

Such were features of almost[2] the last phase of Turkish rule in the 'Iraq. It has been traced since its first conquest by the greatest of Ottoman Sultans from the formidable Persia of the

[1] In full, the "Régie Cointéressée des Tabacs de l'Empire Ottoman", a joint-stock company with a monopoly for manufacture and sale of tobacco in Turkey.

[2] The twentieth century lies outside the plan of the present history. It was marked in 'Iraq generally by certain (but disappointing) impulses of progress resultant from the Constitution of 1908. A number of new regulations then introduced did not improve the personnel of the official class:

early Ṣafawis: through nearly a century of Turkish rule, ill recorded but assessable by its results: through scenes of treachery, violence, and brief Persian dominion to an historic day of reconquest: and thereafter through sixty years of uneventful government to more than a century of detachment from the Empire under local rulers, who withstood great foreign assaults and maintained an almost independent Court. The fall of these was followed by seventy more years wherein 'Iraq, a normal province of the Empire, might again expect such benefit as the Sultan held to bestow.

Of Turkish administration, in 'Iraq or elsewhere, there is nothing new to say. Our glance at the 'Iraq of 1900—nearly four centuries from the first conquest by a Turkey at the apex of its power and sway—has shown clearly enough what this wide and rich Muslim country had suffered or benefited: it showed, in fact, almost no progress since the day of Sulaiman Qanuni—progress whether of mind and spirit, or of material wealth and modern method. The country passed from the nineteenth century little less wild and ignorant, as unfitted for self-government, and not less corrupt, than it had entered the sixteenth; nor had its standards of material life outstripped its standards of mind and character. Its resources lay untouched, however clearly indicated by the famous ages of the past and by the very face of the country. Government's essential duty of leading tribe and town together in the way of progress had scarcely been recognized, barely begun, when our period closes; in the yet clearer task of securing liberty and rights to the governed (however backward), it had

and the removal of 'Abdu'l Ḥamid's personality and machinery of propaganda had bad results in relaxing bonds of loyalty to his throne. Direct results of the Constitution were the lapse of all Crown lands back to the State, the further deterioration of steamships of the Ḥamidiyyah Company, the dispersal of Ḥamidiyyah regiments, the introduction of improved gendarmerie and town police. The military reforms of Liman von Sanders took effect. The Samarra-Baghdad section of the railway was begun in 1912, finished in 1914. Yet another Persian Frontier Commission surveyed the border in 1913–14. Najd was invaded and evacuated. Settlement of tribes proceeded steadily, with a set-back when the Ḥillah river dried from 1903 to 1913. Willcocks' Barrage then restored it. The Sa'duns grew ever weaker, the Shammar as divided; their settlement was a failure. Shipping still suffered from the riverain tribes; the Hamawand still laughed at government in Bazyan. The chief personality of these years was Nadhim Pasha, Wali of the three Wilayats in 1911 for some months.

failed more signally perhaps than any government of the time called civilized—failed in spite of long generations of rule in 'Iraq while the Empire passed through prosperity and adversity, in spite of the great advances made simultaneously in Europe and in India, in spite, even, of the material reward which success must have conferred.

A harsh sentence on this seeming crime of neglected opportunities, of perverse backwardness, may be mitigated by several pleas. No Islamic state in modern times has reached the first rank among nations. The conservatism into which the tenets of that great religion are interpreted has proved incompatible with progress as it is ordinarily judged: and in the very air and aspect of the East there seems to lie an acquiescence, a lack of the forward impulse, which critics of an Eastern state should not ignore. Turkey and 'Iraq—not of their own fault or merit—are countries of the East and of Islam; and a generous judge will make fullest allowance for the vast difference of tradition, of outlook, of purpose which these words connote. He will find, at closer quarters, that the blame for a fatal disunity of mind, a deep antipathy, between the Turks and their subject Kurds and Arabs does not attach solely to the rulers; for the ruled did not refuse allegiance and obedience merely to the Turks as such, but to any government whose ways clashed (as must those of any) with their age-long lawlessness and special codes. Any Shia' government would have faced the hostility of Kurdistan, of northern and much of central 'Iraq: any Sunni government must meet the opposition of the Mujtahids of Karbala and Najf, and of the Shia' tribes: and any government whatever—the very justest and noblest—would have found that justice was not everywhere popular, light and leading often resisted—that the coercion of some (necessary for the liberty of all) was a task ever to be renewed and ever resented. In brief, the difficulties of governing 'Iraq would have been profound to whomever the task had fallen, as other than Turks have found and will find again.

The remoteness of these provinces from the heart of Turkey brought special consequences. It exposed 'Iraq to peril from the Shah's empire to which it once fell, once offered a noble resistance. The constant strain of so dangerous a neighbour, so far from imperial help, may somewhat excuse the Turks for their little care of the country internally. To the same remoteness is due in large measure the century-long dominion of the Mamluk Pashas, a period in which the Ottoman government can scarcely be blamed if it did little to assist a seceding province, and nothing to foster it. 'Iraq, again, was neither a land of Turks, nor attractive to them. In the earlier centuries it attracted few Turkish settlers to hold its lands in fief, in the later it must rest content with the second-rate in Turkish officialdom, since none would gladly serve so far from home. With such few exceptions as have been mentioned, inferior officials reached 'Iraq from Stambul, nor did the local recruits surpass them. The services, in every branch, fell short of those nearer to the Capital.

Finally, the faults of Turkish rule in the 'Iraq cannot be judged without reference to the fortunes of the central Empire. Pre-occupation and self-defence at head-quarters must distract from a proper care of distant territories, as the constant need of the central government for men and money must drain them. To an empire in decline, and threatened not distantly with extinction, much may be forgiven. Even so, the last generation of Ottoman dominion in 'Iraq might be thought to show signs of improvement on previous eras, and to hold out whatever hopes were consistent with the Turkish character.

All these pleas of extenuation do not conceal that the Ottoman, after conquering and reconquering the world-famous fertile territories of Chaldaea and Assyria and holding them for nearly four centuries in the Sultan's name, left them still backward and ignorant, still undeveloped and poor, still lawless and resentful of their rulers, still set upon no pathway of progress. Travellers could find in no Turkish province greater potentialities more neglected, misrule more stagnant.

The Turks, endowed with outstanding military and attractive social qualities, are cursed as rulers by the conception of government which their rise and their decline alike have left unchanged, which phrases borrowed from Europe have rather concealed than modified: the principle that the rule of subjects is for the glory and benefit of the ruler. Once the Sultan, then the independent

Pashas, then the narrow class of officials, and later perhaps military adventurers, represented that for which millions must be starved and bullied. Above all temporary and local reasons, this long misrule of 'Iraq that we have studied sprang from the absence of will to govern well. The Turks never admitted by their actions—however plausibly in phrase—that justice mattered more than judgeships, that revenue was a means to benefit the payers, that security of the rights of the weak and the many is the very purpose of Government.

APPENDICES

APPENDIX I

SOURCES OF THE PRESENT WORK

THE present History has been derived from the printed or manuscript works of Turkish and Arab historians, from the accounts of European and other travellers, from various histories and monographs belonging to 'Iraq or to its greater neighbours, from records of the Honourable East India Company, and from the local inquiries of the author. No single item of this list predominates. The travellers are necessarily transient and discontinuous; the bulk of the other sources rather suggest or verify details than constitute a sound basis; even the oriental historians cover restricted periods and must be proportioned and reconciled, being partly from the official historiographers of Turkey (to whom 'Iraq is a theme only when a siege or rebellion has earned a moment's attention of the Empire), and partly 'Iraqi writers, whose whole concern is with their own province. The sources are in several instances unknown in Europe, in others forgotten or not previously used as historical material, and in others inaccessible to all but orientalists.

This Appendix will divide the sources into groups as follows: (i) Previous (oriental) histories devoted to 'Iraq in these centuries; (ii) Travellers; (iii) Records of the East India Company; (iv) General histories of neighbouring countries; (v) Various monographs on 'Iraq and neighbouring countries; (vi) Local inquiries.

(i) *Previous (oriental) histories dealing with 'Iraq in this Period or part of it.*

كلشن خلفا (Gulshan i Khulafa'), written in Turkish in A.H. 1100 (A.D. 1688) by Murtadha Effendi Nadhmizadah, was continued later by the same hand. It covers, thus prolonged, the period from the foundation of Baghdad to A.H. 1130 (A.D. 1717–18).[1] It was printed in Stambul in August 1730;[2] printed copies are, however, rarer than MS., of which there are four in the British Museum Library.[3] Particularly for the period 1638–1717, the source is of high value.

[1] For fuller information, see Huart, Introduction (pp. 1–4). The present writer used both a printed and a manuscript copy.

[2] Von Hammer (xiv, pp. 107 and 494).

[3] Catalogue of Turkish Manuscripts (1888), (p. 41, Add. 7865). These are from Mr. Rich's collection, made in Baghdad in 1808–20.

حديقت الوزرأ (Hadiqatu'l Wuzara') : a MS. history in Arabic of Ḥasan Pasha and Aḥmad Pasha, by Shaikh 'Abdu'l Raḥman bin Shaikh 'Abdullah ul Suwaidi. The author, of a famous Baghdad family, was born in 1722 in Baghdad and died in 1805. No copy has been seen by the present writer, but a careful abridgement (by Sulaiman Effendi ul Dakhil, from a copy seen by him in the library of Ḥikmatullah bin 'Ismatullah Effendi in Stambul) has been used.

دوحت الوزرأ (Duḥatu'l Wuzara') is with Gulshan the most important single source to be mentioned. The author is Rasul Ḥawi Effendi, of Kirkuk. Manuscript copies are rare, printed copies rarer.[1] Composed in ornate Turkish by order of Daud Pasha in (?) 1827–8, it was printed in Baghdad in A. H. 1246 (A. D. 1830) by Mirza Muḥammad Baqir ul Tiflisi. The writer is a sober (but partial) recorder of events of which he was a contemporary witness. His work, which uses Ḥadiqatu'l Wuzara', is professedly a continuation of that of Na͟dhmizadah, and quoted as such by Jaudat Pasha. It covers the period 1718 to 1821.

مطالع السعود (Muṭali'u'l Sa'ud), of Amin bin Ḥasan ul Halwani ul Madini, in Arabic, lithographed in Bombay in A. H. 1303 (A. D. 1885), is itself an abridgement of an unprinted work of Shaikh 'Uthman bin Sanad ul Baṣri. The original work commences at A. H. 1188 (A. D. 1774), the year of Daud Pasha's birth, and stops at A. H. 1242 (A. D. 1826)—a matter of surprise to the editor, Amin bin Ḥasan, since Shaikh 'Uthman lived till A. H. 1250 (A. D. 1834). Amin continues the narrative to 1831. The writers used Duḥatu'l Wuzara', but have enough independent matter to be valuable, Shaikh 'Uthman being strictly contemporary.

زاد المسافر ولهنة المقيم والحاضر (Zadu'l Muṣafari wa luhnatu'l Muqimi wa'l Ḥa͟dhir): a short account in Arabic of the later fortunes of Ḥusain Pasha of Baṣrah (1645–65), by Shaikh Fatḥullah bin 'Alwan ul Ka'abi. It existed in manuscript only (and was thus used by the present writer), but is now printed (Baghdad, 1924). A paraphrase of it forms the *History of Modern Bassorah*, given by Mignon (pp. 269–86).

حروب الايرانيين (Hurubu'l Iraniyyin, of Sulaiman Beg bin Ḥaji Ṭalib Kahya), exists only in manuscript (Turkish). The present writer knows of one copy only, borrowed by him from Ḥamdi Beg Baban in Baghdad.

[1] Huart (op. cit., Introduction, p. 5). It is doubtful whether he has accounted for all copies. The present writer was able to borrow a printed copy from Ḥamdi Beg Baban, and one in manuscript from Shukri Effendi ul Fa͟dhli.

It was composed in about 1880 in Baghdad. It covers the period 1721–46. It is based on the Turkish official historiographers, on Duḥatu'l Wuzara', on the Jihangusha i Nadiri of Mirza Mahdi, and on private information. The latter gives it its value which, however, is not first class.

بغداد کولەمن حکومتنك تشکیلیله انقراضنه دائر رساله (History of the formation and fall of the Mamluk Government in Baghdad) is a booklet, printed in Turkish in Stambul, 1875, ostensibly by "Thabit". It covers 1749–1831. It is in fact the work of Sulaiman Beg bin Ḥaji Ṭalib Kahya, who preferred to use a pseudonym. There are three or four copies in Baghdad, almost certainly one or more in Egypt and probably in Stambul. M. Huart obtained one,[1] and allows it to form an important part of his work. It is an authentic source, though not free from bias natural to the family of the author.[2]

مرأة الزورا (Mira'tu'l Zaura), by the same author, exists only in manuscript and unfinished. Besides covering the same period as the foregoing work, it contains the first seven years of 'Ali Riḍha Pasha, with much information not in "Thabit". The fair copy is said to have been lost on the occasion of the author's banishment. That seen by the present writer is rough and incomplete, on loose leaves; it belongs to Ḥamdi Beg Baban, and is believed to have been copied by various hands. Used carefully, it has great authority.

غايت المرام (Ghayatu'l Muram), in Arabic manuscript, is the work of Yasin ul 'Umari bin Khairullah ul 'Umari ul Khaṭib ul Mauṣili. The author (of the famous 'Umari family of Mosul) was born in 1734. This work contains much geographical, genealogical, and biographical material, and a history of Baghdad, of which the last fifty years (ending in 1805) is original and valuable.

غرائب الاثر (Ghura'ibu'l Athr), by the same author, also in manuscript Arabic, repeats the foregoing in a different form, but adds full details of 1805–11.

This concludes the list of the more important local historical sources: those now following are of far less importance.

زبدة التواريخ (Zubdatu'l Tawarikh), by 'Abdu'l Waḥid bin Shaikh 'Abdullah Basha'yan. The work, in sixteen manuscript volumes of Arabic, is in the possession of Shaikh Aḥmad Basha'yan of Baṣrah. It covers in all the Khalifate as well as the later history of Baṣrah, and makes long excursions into general Turkish and Ḥijaz history. It

[1] Huart (Introduction, p. 4). He speculates on the identity of the author, which is well known in Baghdad learned circles.

[2] Ḥaji Ṭalib was Kahya of Daud Pasha, and himself a Georgian freedman.

consists almost entirely of extracts from other works, notably Muṭali'u'l Sa'ud (*q.v.*); but there are sufficient independent minor points to give it a certain, though very small, value.

The Mosul Wilayat Calendar for A. H. 1325, in Turkish, contains a chapter of Historical Information (pp. 99–191) reprinted also in other years' issue. It is the work of Ḥasan Taufiq Effendi, Maktubchi of the Wilayat. The incidents best recorded are the siege by Nadir Shah (1743) and the reign of Injah Bairaqdar (1835–43). It has a complete list of Mosul Pashas from A. H. 1000.

تأريخ الموصل (History of Mosul) of Sulaiman Sayigh (printed in Cairo, 1924) adds nothing (in our period) to the foregoing. Both are in fact based with great fidelity upon an Arabic manuscript work entitled منهل الاوليا (Minhalu'l 'Auliya) by Muḥammad Amin Effendi ul 'Umari, dealing with Mosul history, which work the present writer has not seen in its original form.

The Baṣrah Wilayat Calendar for A. H. 1306 (A. D. 1887) contains a list of the Walis and Mutasallims of Baṣrah, and a chapter of Historical Information. The latter is apparently all derived from the Basha'yan history.

The Baghdad Wilayat Calendar for A. H. 1322 (A. D. 1904), in Turkish, contains (pp. 50–5) a list of Walis of Baghdad with exact periods of their tenure, from 1639.

خلاصه تأريخ العراق (Summary of 'Iraq History), by Père Anastase (Baṣrah, 1919), gives few pages to our period. It is all derived from various of the sources above mentioned, chiefly from Ghayatu'l Muram.

(ii) *Travellers.*

The bibliography of 'Iraq travellers here offered no doubt falls far short of completeness, so wide and often obscure is the field where further relevant works might be sought. Works have been included whose specific contribution to history is minute: they are nevertheless historical documents, and the reiteration of the conditions which they portray gives the author confidence in the authenticity of his setting. As materials for history they are fragmentary, laborious to collect, often facile and ill informed, but, in the aggregate, highly valuable: they often record, more than the oriental compilers, the data essential to a modern historian. The Turkish and Arab writers, too generally vague and formal, are thus humanized and proportioned.

They will now be mentioned in order of the dates of their travel in 'Iraq, a central year being assigned to those who visited the country more than once or stayed long. Not necessarily the earliest, but the most convenient edition has generally been quoted. In some cases French translations of English travel-books are quoted, merely because they happen to be more easily obtainable. A hint has sometimes been given, by a single adjective, of the historical value of the work. "Interesting" means valuably descriptive of conditions; "historical", that important historical information has been directly presented; "essential", that the work must necessarily be perused by students of the period, in contrast to other works rather of bibliographical or topographical interest. These latter are passed over without remark. This Baedeker method of "starring" the authorities may enable some interested student to get at once to his chief sources. An idea of the itinerary of each traveller is given by the mention, in condensed form, of places or regions visited by him.

Travellers in 'Iraq, as authorities for its History.

1553. Sidi Ali Reis. *Travels and Adventures of the Turkish Admiral Sidi Ali Reis.* (London, Luzac, 1899.)

Translation from Turkish by A. Vambéry. Original "Mira'tu'l Mamalik", published by the Iqdam Library, Stambul, A. H. 1313. Aleppo-Mosul-Baghdad-Euphrates-Baṣrah-Hormuz. Author was Turkish admiral and litterateur. *Interesting.*

1553–4. Anon. Title unknown. (MS., written 1559.)

Portuguese traveller, Syria-'Iraq-Baṣrah. Not seen by author. [See the *Athenaeum*, No. 3830, of March 23, 1901, p. 375, col. 2.]

?–1555. Antonio Tenrreyro. *Itinerario de . . .* (Lisbon, 1829.)

(Reprint of a 1560 edition.) Hormuz-Gulf-Persia. In Portuguese.

1563. Cesare Federici. In Hakluyt's *Voyages.*

Venetian merchant. Aleppo-'Iraq-Baṣrah. Original in Italian.

1575. Dr. Leonard Rauwolff. Travels, collected in *A Collection of Curious Voyages and Travels* (12 vols.), by John Ray. (London, 1693.)

German doctor and trader. Aleppo-Fallujah-Baghdad-Kirkuk-Mosul-Anatolia. From German. *Interesting.*

1579 ff. Gasparo Balbi. *Voyage.* [Purchas, ii: and in Pinkerton, *Voyages and Travels*, ix. 395 ff. (London, 1811).]

Venetian jeweller. Aleppo-Fallujah-Baghdad-Baṣrah. Original in Italian.

1581. John Newberry. [Purchas, ix.]

London merchant. Syria-Baghdad-Hormuz. See Ryley, *Ralph Fitch*, pp. 202 ff.

1583. John Eldred. [Hakluyt, ii, pt. i. Three letters in Purchas.]

1583. Ralph Fitch. [Hakluyt, ii, pt. i. Also edited by Horton Ryley (London, 1897) for Hakluyt Society.]

London merchants. Aleppo-Fallujah-Baghdad-Baṣrah-Hormuz. See Ryley (*passim*) and Murray, *Asia*, iii. 135 ff. *Interesting.*

1589. Sir Anthony Sherley. *The Three Brothers: Travels of Sir Anthony, Sir Robert, and Sir Th. Sherley*: Anon (London, 1825). [From Purchas. See Murray, *Asia*, iii. 23 ff.]

English adventurer, later famous at the Court of Persia. Aleppo-Euphrates-Baghdad-Kasvin.

1604. Pedro Teixeira. *The Travels of* . . . by W. F. Sinclair and D. Ferguson. Hakluyt Society, London, 1902.

Portuguese traveller. Gulf-Baṣrah-Holy Cities-Baghdad-'Anah. *Very interesting.* [Bibliographical information in ed. cit.]

1615. Pietro della Valle. *Suite des fameux Voyages de* . . . (Paris, 1663, 4 vols.)

Roman aristocrat. Vols. i and ii only concern 'Iraq. *Very interesting.*

1625. Ḥaji Khalifah. *Jihan-numa.* (Constantinople, A. H. 1245.)

Turkish traveller and author. In 'Iraq with Khasrau Pasha. *Interesting.*

1629. R. P. Philippe. *Voyage d'Orient.* (Lyon, 1652.)

French Carmelite. Aleppo - Euphrates - Baghdad - Persia (Baṣrah later, ? 1632).

1638. M. D. Thévenot. *Relation d'un Voyage fait au Levant.* (Paris, 1665.)

pp. 569 ff. give a valuable eye-witness account of the capture of Baghdad, in form of a letter from " le Grant fauconnier du Grand Seigneur ".

1638. M. D. Thévenot. *Suite du Voyage de* . . . (Amsterdam, 1727.)

Vol. iv, 557–92: Baṣrah-Haṣa-Qaṭif. *Interesting.*

1638 ff. J. B. Tavernier. *The Six Voyages of . . . through Turkey into Asia.* (" Made English by J. P. ": London, 1678.)

French noble. Bk. II is relevant: journeys in 1638, 1644, and 1663. *Essential.*

1638. Sieur du Loir. *Les Voyages du . . . contenus en pleusieurs lettres* . . . (Paris, 1654.)

See von Hammer (ix. 331). Not seen by the present author.

1649. Sieur de la Boullaye-le-Gouz. *Les Voyages et observations de* . . . (Paris, 1657.)

" Gentil-homme Angevin." Baṣrah-Baghdad-Mosul-Mardin.

1655. Auliya' Chelebi, Travels of. (Stambul, 1314.)

Turkish courtier and traveller. Persia-Kurdistan-Baghdad-Baṣrah. *Interesting.*

1663. Father Manuel Godinho. (Extracts in Murray, *Asia*, i. 395 ff.: Edinburgh, 1820.)

Portuguese Jesuit. Baṣrah-Baghdad-'Anah. Bibliographical details not ascertained.

1671. M. Carré. *Voyages des Indes Orientales.* (Paris, 1699.)

Baṣrah-Baghdad. French traveller.

? 1694. Anon. *Relation de la mort de Shah Soliman Roy de Perse, etc.* (Paris, 1696.)

Persia-Kurdistan. Interesting for Baban origins. Seen by author only in extracts (MS.) relevant to this.

1695. Soares sieur du Val. *Journal de mon voyage des Indes Orientales* (MS. only).

French gentleman. Syria-'Anah-Baghdad-Mandali-Persia. (MS. with Ya'qub Effendi Sarkis, Baghdad.)

1720. Duri effendi. *Relation de Dourry effendi*; دوری افندی سفارتنامهسی [Turkish, lithographed, undated; also translation by M. Petits de la Croix. (Paris, 1820.)]

Turkish ambassador to Persia, 1720. Passed through 'Iraq.

1721 f. Captain A. Hamilton. *A New Account of the East Indies.* (London, 1739.)

Scottish sea-captain. Baṣrah only (I, ch. viii). *Interesting.*

1726. Muṣṭafa bin Kamalu'l Din bin 'Ali ul Sidqi.: كشط الرداً وغسل الران في زيارة العراق (Account of travels in 'Iraq, &c.): [No. 930 of Brown's Handlist (Cambridge Univ. Library)].

Not seen by author.

1733. J. Nicodeme. *Une lettre écrite à S. E. Mons. le Marquis de Villeneuve.*

(In von Hammer, xiv. 514 ff. and xiii. 14.) French physician of Ṭopal 'Uthman. Full description of battle of June 19, 1733. *Historical.*

1736. 'Abdu'l Karim. *Voyage de l'Inde à la Mekke.* (Tr. by Langlés, Paris, 1825.) [English ed., F. Gladwin, London, 1793.]

Persian original not seen by author. Native of Kashmir, favourite of Nadir Shah. Persia-Baghdad-Holy Cities-Kirkuk-Mosul.

1736. M. Otter. *Voyage en Turquie et en Perse.* (Paris, 1748.)

French government agent. With 'Abdu'l Baqi Khan to Mosul-Baghdad-Persia. In 1739, Mandali-Baghdad-Baṣrah; 1741, Baṣrah; 1743, Baṣrah-Baghdad-Mosul-Diyarbakr. *Essential.*

1739. R. Pococke. *A Description of the East.* (London, 1743.)

Doctor and antiquarian. Syria and Jazirah (ii. 162 ff.).

1744. Leandro di S. Cacilia. *Viaggi in Palestina, Persia, Mesopotamia.* (Rome, 1753–7.)

Not seen by author except in summary (Murray, *Asia*, iii. 75 ff.). Italian monk.

1750. M. M. Plaisted et Eliot. *Itinéraire de l'Arabie Déserte.* (Paris, Year V.)

Officials of H. E. I. Company. This is Fr. translation of English original. Baṣrah-Zubair-Najf-Kubaisah-Aleppo. Forms pp. 327–82 of Howell, q. v.

1757. Anon. *Overlandreis von India naar Europa in 1757.* (Utrecht, 1860.)

Forms pp. 124 ff. of Kronijk van Het Historisch Genootschap gevestigd te Utrecht. Dutch. Baṣrah-Aleppo by desert.

1758. Dr. E. Ives. *A Journey from Persia to England.* (London, 1773.)

H. E. I. Coy. Surgeon. Baṣrah-Euphrates-Baghdad-Kirkuk-Mosul-Mardin. *Very interesting.*

1765. C. Niebuhr. *Voyage en Arabie et en d'autres pays circonvoisins.* (Amsterdam, 1776.)

Danish savant. This is French translation. Baṣrah-Euphrates-Baghdad-Kirkuk-Mosul-Mardin. *Historical: Essential.*

1768. Joseph Emin. *Life and Adventures of . . .* (Reprinted and edited by Amy Apcar, Calcutta, 1918. Original published London, 1792.)

Armenian adventurer, born Hamadan 1726. Persian wars. In 1768, Armenia-Baghdad-Ḥillah-Baṣrah; in 1774, Baṣrah-Baghdad-Baṣrah.

1771. (Companion of) Sir Eyre Coote. *Journal of a Journey from Xebeir near Basrah to Aleppo in 1771.* (MS.)

MS. with Ya'qub Effendi Sarkis of Baghdad. Printed, *Journal of Royal Geographical Society*, xxx (1890), p. 199.

1771. Mr. Carmichael. *Journey from Aleppo to Baṣrah over the desert.*

(Forms Appendix to 1772 edition of Grose, *Voyage to the East Indies*, London, 1772: not in the 1766 edition.) H. E. I. Coy. employee. *Amusing.*

1774. A. Parsons. *Travels in Asia and Africa.* (London, 1808.)

Consul, &c., at Alexandretta. Aleppo-Baghdad-Ḥillah-Ḥiskah-Baṣrah (siege, 1775). *Interesting: Historical.*

1778. J. Capper. *Observations on the passage to India, &c.* (London, 1785.)

H. E. I. Coy. Aleppo-desert-Baṣrah. Episodes of Persian occupation of Baṣrah.

1779. Anon. *A journal kept on a Journey from Bassorah to Baghdad, &c. by A Gentleman . . . &c.* (Horsham, 1784.)

Officer of Honourable East India Company. Baṣrah-Baghdad-Aleppo. *Interesting.* (Printed by subscription.)

1781. — Sestini. *Voyage de Constantinople à Bassora en 1781.* (Paris, l'an VI.)

Italian academician. Diyarbakr-Mosul-Baghdad-Baṣrah. In 1782, Baṣrah-Euphrates-Baghdad-Kirkuk-Mosul. *Interesting.*

1781. Eyles Irwin. *A Series of adventures in the course of a Voyage . . . &c.* (London, 1787.)

Traveller. Vol. ii, pp. 312 ff. only are relevant. Euphrates-'Anah-Ḥadithah-Alus-Baghdad-Baṣrah. *Unreliable.*

1781. D. Campbell. *A Narrative of extraordinary adventures and sufferings, &c.* (London, 1797.)

H. E. I. Coy. employee. Mosul-Kirkuk-Baghdad-Mosul.

1782. André Michaux. *Voyage de . . . en Syrie et en Perse.* Ed. par Dr. E. T. Harvey. (Genéve, 1911.)

French traveller. Aleppo-Baghdad-Baṣrah.

1785. Comte de Ferrières-Sauvebœuf. *Mémoires Historiques.* (Paris, 1790.)

Vol. ii only. Itinerary not clear. In Baghdad ? 1785.

1786. J. Griffiths. *Travels in Europe, Asia Minor, and Arabia.* (London, 1805.)

English doctor. Aleppo-desert-Baṣrah.

1787. W. Franklin. *Observations made on a tour from Bengal to Persia in 1786–7.* (London, 1790.)

H. E. I. Coy. At Baṣrah in December 1787. (Thuwaini's occupation.)

1788. T. Howel. *Voyage en retour de l'Inde par terre.* (Paris, l'an V.)

H. E. I. Coy. Original in English. Baṣrah-Euphrates-Baghdad-Kirkuk-Mosul. (Thuwaini at Baṣrah.)

1790. Major Taylor. *Voyage dans l'Inde au travers du Grand Désert.* (Paris, 1807.)

H. E. I. Coy. Original in English. Syria-desert-Baṣrah.

1791. G. A. Olivier. *Voyage dans l'Empire Ottoman, l'Égypte, et la Perse.* (Paris, ix.)

French official agent. (Vol. iv only relevant.) Mardin-Mosul-Kirkuk-Baghdad-Euphrates-Baṣrah. *Essential.*

1797. J. Jackson. *Journey from India towards England in . . . 1797.* (London, 1799.)

H. E. I. Coy. Baṣrah-Euphrates-Baghdad-Mosul. *Interesting.*

1802. Mirza Abu Ṭalib Khan. *The travels of, in Asia, Africa, and Europe, in 1799–1803.* (London, 1810.)

Indian gentleman. Original in Persian. Vol. ii, pp. 273 ff. relevant. Mardin-Mosul-Kirkuk-Baghdad-Holy Cities-Baṣrah. Many absurd mistakes.

c. 1802. H. J. Brydges. See v (b) of this Appendix.

1807. Muḥammad Rafi'. Safaratnamah سفارتنامه. (Record of an embassy to Persia in A. H. 1222.) Stambul, 1330.

Touches on 'Abdu'l Raḥman Pasha Baban.

1807. Adrien Dupré. *Voyage en Perse fait dans les années 1807–9, en traversant la Natolie et le Mesopotamie.* (Paris, 1819.)

French traveller. Vol. i only. Mardin-Nisibin-Jazirah-Mosul-Kirkuk-Baghdad-Persia. *Essential* (but needs care).

1808. J. B. Rousseau. *Voyage de Bagdad à Alep.* (Paris, 1899.)

For author, see v (a) of this Appendix. This work was printed from his MS. after ninety years. Valuable tribal lists.

1808. Anon. *Journal d'un Voyage dans la Turquie d'Asie et la Perse.* (Paris, 1809.)

Persia-Ba'qubah-Baghdad-Mosul. *Interesting.*

1808-16. J. Morier. *A journey through Persia, Armenia, and Asia Minor to Constantinople*, 1808–9. (London, 1812.) *A second journey through Persia.* (London, 1818.)

English diplomat in Persia. Touches on 'Iraq (cf. chs. 44–6 of his "Hajji Baba of Isfahan").

1810 ff. J. M. Kinneir. *Journey through Asia Minor, Armenia, and Kurdistan.* (London, 1818.)

Geological memoir of the Persian empire. (London, 1813.)

Mainly concerned with Persia, but touch northern and eastern 'Iraq.

1816. J. S. Buckingham. *Travels in Mesopotamia.* (London, 1827.)

Vol. i, Diyarbakr-Mardin. Vol. ii, Mosul - Kirkuk - Baghdad - Babylon-Baghdad. *Interesting.*

1816 f. J. S. Buckingham. *Travels in Assyria, Media, and Persia.* (London, 1830.)

Vol. i, Baghdad-Persia; vol. ii, Baṣrah.

1817. W. Heude. *A voyage up the Persian Gulf . . . &c.* (London, 1819.)

H. E. I. Coy. Baṣrah-Euphrates-Gharraf-Baghdad-Mosul. *Interesting: Historical.*

1818. Sir R. K. Porter. *Travels in Georgia, Persia, Armenia, Ancient Babylonia . . . &c.* (London, 1822.)

Archaeologist and dilettante. Vol. ii. 210 ff. Persia-Khaniqin-Baghdad-Kifri-Sulaimaniyyah-Persia. *Interesting.*

1820. C. J. Rich. *Narrative of a Residence in Koordistan.* (London, 1836.)

British Resident in Baghdad, 1808–21. Guest of Maḥmud Pasha Baban at Sulaimaniyyah, 1820. *Interesting: Historical* (for Babans).

1824. Hon. G. Keppel. *Travels in Babylonia, Assyria, Media, and Scythia in . . . 1824.* (London, 1827.)

H. E. I. Coy. Gulf-Baṣrah-Baghdad-Babylon-Baghdad-Ba'qubah-Persia. *Interesting.*

1825. "R.C.M." *Journal of a tour in Persia.* (London, 1828.)

From p. 230. Persia-Ba'qubah-Baghdad-Baṣrah.

1827. R. Mignon. *Travels in Chaldaea.* (London, 1829.)

H. E. I. Coy. Baṣrah-Baghdad-Ḥillah, &c.-Baghdad. pp. 269-86 give paraphrase of "Zad ul Musafir," q. v.

1830–1. J. R. Wellsted. *Travels to the City of the Caliphs.* (London, 1840.)

Indian Navy. Baṣrah-Euphrates-Baghdad-Fallujah-Aleppo. Valuable for the Plague (1831), at times wild. *Interesting.*

1830–1. Rev. A. N. Groves. *Journal of a Residence in Baghdad.* (London, 1832.)

Missionary. Baghdad only, minute and vivid for 1830–1. *Interesting: Historical.*

1831. J. H. Stocqueler. *Fifteen months' pilgrimage through untrodden parts of Khuzistan and Persia.* (London, 1832.)

Journalist. Vol. i, to p. 80, only are relevant, chiefly for Baṣrah.

1831–6. F. R. Chesney. *The expedition for the survey of the rivers Euphrates and Tigris.* (London, 1850.)

Narrative of the Euphrates expedition. (London, 1868.)

Interesting for topography, no historical information.

1834–7. Dr. J. Ross. *Journey from Baghdad to the ruins of Opis and the Median wall in 1834.* (J. R. G. S., XI. ii, pp. 121 ff.)

Notes on a journey from Baghdad to the ruins of Al Ḥadhr. (J. R. G. S., IX. iii, pp. 443 ff.)

Residency doctor. Tribal information and anecdotes.

1834. J. B. Fraser. *Travels in Kurdistan and Mesopotamia.* (London, 1840.)

Professional writer. Ardalan-Shahrizor-Kifri-Baghdad-Euphrates and back to Persia. *Very interesting.*

Memorandum on the present condition of the Pashalic of Baghdad (forms appendix to the *Précis*, q. v.).

Written for submission to government. *Valuable, overdrawn.*

1835. Aucher-Éloy. *Relations de Voyage en Orient, de 1830–1838.* (Ed. Jaubert; Paris, 1843.)

French botanist. Mardin-Mosul-Baghdad-(and Ḥillah)-Persia. pp. 99 ff. describe a campaign of Injah Bairaqdar in 1835.

1835–6. V. Fontanier. *Voyage dans l'Inde et dans la Golfe Persique.* (Paris, 1844.)

French consul, Baṣrah. Baṣrah-Baghdad-Muḥammerah. Vol. i, chaps. 8–18 relevant. Much information, ill arranged and partisan. Strong Anglophobe.

1836 ff. W. F. Ainsworth. *Researches in Assyria, Babylonia, and Chaldaea.* (London, 1838.)

Travels and researches in Asia Minor, Mesopotamia, Chaldaea, and Armenia. (London, 1842.)

Travels in the Track of the Ten Thousand Greeks. (London, 1844.)

Personal Narrative of the Euphrates expedition. (London, 1888.)

Geologist to Chesney. Travelled *passim*, very full for topography and conditions, little historical. *Interesting.*

1836. Mme. Helfer. *Travels of Doctor and Madame Helfer.* (Tr. by G. Sturge: London, 1878.)

Germans. Accompanied Chesney's expedition.

1836. Major Rawlinson. *Notes on a march from Zohab at the foot of Zagros, along the mountains of Khuzistan, &c.* (J. R. G. S., IX. i, pp. 27 ff.)

Interesting for Zohab, Luristan, Bakhtiari, &c.

1837. H. B. Lynch. *Notes on a part of the River Tigris, between Baghdad and Samarra.* (J. R. G. S., IX. iii, pp. 471 ff.)

Survey notes. More are to be found in *Proceedings of Bombay Geographical Society*, Sept. 1841–May 1844, and in vol. xiii (1891).

1838. Rev. H. Southgate. *Narrative of a tour through Armenia, Kurdistan, Persia, and Mesopotamia.* (London, 1840.)

Missionary. Vol. ii only relevant. Persia - Khaniqin - Baghdad - Kifri-Kirkuk-Mosul-Mardin. *Interesting.*

1839. Dr. A. Grant. *The Nestorians.* (London, 1841.)

Medical missionary. Mardin-Mosul-'Aqrah-'Amadiyyah. *Interesting.*

1840–51. A. H. Layard. *Early adventures in Persia, Susiana, and Babylonia.* (London, 1894.)

With Mitford (q.v.) to Baghdad. Bahktiari and 'Arabistan: Baṣrah to Baghdad: down and up Tigris: Luristan: Mosul. *Interesting, little historical use.*

Nineveh and its remains. (London, 1891.)

Nineveh and Babylon. (London, 1853.)

Localities as indicated. Good observation: *interesting.*

1840. E. L. Mitford. *A land march from England to Ceylon forty years ago.* (London, 1884.)

Vol. i only. Jazirah-Mardin-Mosul-Baghdad-Ḥillah-Khaniqin-Persia.

1842–3. Rev. J. P. Fletcher. *Notes from Nineveh.* (London, 1850.)

Missionary. Diyarbakr-Mosul and back.

1848–55. Commander Felix Jones. Various Survey notes, in *Tr. of Bombay Geographical Society*, ix, x, xi (1849 to 1856).

No historical interest.

1849–50. W. K. Loftus. *Travels and Researches in Chaldaea and Susiana.* (London, 1857.)

Member of Frontier Commission, 1849. Mosul-Baghdad-middle Euphrates-Baṣrah-'Arabistan.

1850. Lieut. F. Walpole. *The Ansayrii* (or *Assassins*), *with travels to the further east.* (London, 1851.)

Vol. i, Diyarbakr, Mosul; vol. ii, central Kurdistan and to Persia.

1878. Lady Anne Blunt. *Bedouin tribes of the Euphrates.* (London, 1879.)

A Pilgrimage to Nejd. (London, 1881.)

Syrian desert affairs. Keen observation, little knowledge, no balance. *Interesting.*

1878. G. Geary. *Through Asiatic Turkey.* (London, 1878.)

Journalist. Baṣrah to Mosul and Asia Minor. *Superficial.*

1885. H. Binder. *Au Kurdistan, en Mesopotamie, et en Perse.* (Paris, 1887.)

Kurdistan, Mosul, Baghdad, Persia. *Dull.*

1885. Madame J. Dieulafoy. *La Perse, la Chaldée, et la Susiane.* (Paris, 1887.)

Interesting.

1892. H. S. Cowper. *Through Asiatic Arabia.* (London, 1894.)

Pleasure-traveller. Euphrates to Baghdad-Baṣrah. *Thin.*

1895. J. D. Peters. *Nippur, or Explorations and Adventures on the Euphrates.* (New York, 1897.)

1899–1906. Sir M. Sykes. *Through five Turkish Provinces.* (London, 1900.)

Dar ul Islam. (London, 1904.)

Upper Euphrates, Mosul, central Kurdistan.

The Caliph's last Heritage. (London, 1915.)

Northern Jazirah, Mosul, Kurdistan.
Vivid description, occasional valuable historical hints.

1908–9. E. B. Soane. *To Mesopotamia and Kurdistan in disguise.* (London, 1912.)

Personal and descriptive.

1909. Miss G. L. Bell. *Amurath to Amurath.* (London, 1911.)

Archaeological and descriptive.

1910. D. Fraser. *Persia and Turkey in Revolt.* (Edinburgh, 1910.)
Journalistic.

1913-14. G. E. Hubbard. *From the Gulf to Ararat.* (Edinburgh, 1916.)
Anecdotal, thin.

(iii) *Records of the Honourable East India Company.*

The compilations used for the present work are: *Précis, containing information in regard to the first connexion of the Honourable East India Company with Turkish Arabia*, compiled anonymously, and printed in 1874 at the Foreign Department Press, Calcutta. It consists of an Index (i–xxviii), the Summary itself (pp. 1–137), and five appendices. The relevant information to be extracted from the correspondence of the residents and agents of Baṣrah (and latterly Baghdad) is small in quantity, but often illuminating and highly authoritative.

Secondly, a few dispatches from the *Précis of Turkish Arabia Affairs* by J. A. Saldanha (Simla, 1906) are of value. The compilation, a remarkable storehouse of misprints and errors, is of use only when it quotes dispatches verbatim.

For the Company's records concerned with the Persian Gulf, see Section v (e) of this Appendix.

(iv) *General Histories of adjacent Countries.*

These constitute a source more important than would at first appear. From Persia and Arabia the 'Iraq was divided by an inexact frontier and united by constant dealings, while Turkey—here classified as an "adjacent country"—was not only neighbour but also the body of which 'Iraq was a member.

(a) *Histories of Turkey.*

Of these there is, in general, no great profit to be had from the point of view of the present work, except in the case of the contemporary official Turkish historiographers. Those of this class consulted and quoted are: Na'imah (covering period 1592–1629): Rashid (راشد), 1660–1721, and continuation by Chelebizadah Muṣṭafa 'Aṣim Effendi, 1722–8: Subḥi, 1730–43: 'Izzi, 1744–50: Waṣif (himself an editor of previous historiographers), 1750–74: and Shanizadah, 1805–20. Reference to these is easy in the octavo reprints of their works (Stambul, various dates), events being strictly chronological and well indexed; but very inconvenient in the original folios. Other original

Turkish historians quoted are Sultan Sulaiman himself: Ferdi, Pashawi, and Jalalzadah for the same period: and Nuri, and Qarachelebizadah 'Abdu 'l 'Aziz for the campaigns of Sultan Murad.

These (and possibly similar other works which the present author has failed to locate or secure) are a source of great value for such periods as brought 'Iraq—by rebellion, apostasy, and the like—into the direct light of Imperial scrutiny and record. For periods of normal relations between the provinces and Stambul they are valueless and rarely mention 'Iraq. A later and derived Turkish historian—Jaudat Pasha (Stambul, 6 vols., A. H. 1302)—is an important source for the period 1750–1825, since he has used original authorities not directly accessible, and has a somewhat more modern conception of his task than the historiographers.

Of European historians of Turkey—of whom in all so formidable a list can be compiled—the great majority contain but the meagrest, and often the most inexact, references to 'Iraq affairs. Study of Knolles, Ricaut, Cantamir, and a few others will be rewarded by a rare page or sentence; the latest summarizers of Ottoman affairs—Creasy, Halil Ganem, de la Jonquière, Lamartine, Lane-Poole, Eversley—will enable a general reader to place 'Iraq affairs in the main scheme of Turkish history; and the writers of monographs within the last few years—Gibbons, Miller, Lybyer—present bibliographical information which may stimulate the curious to research; but in general it is not to the Western histories of Turkey that the student of 'Iraq affairs should look for material. To von Hammer alone—and to Jorga in a lesser degree—he must turn constantly (and more especially if not himself a reader of the Turkish originals) for a compendium of the numerous and highly important references to 'Iraq affairs given in the wide and often inaccessible range of sources used by that amazing compiler. The French edition of J. J. Hellert (Paris, 1841, 18 vols.) was used for purposes of the present work.

A large number of works, of which but few can claim close relevance to (or have been used by the historian of) our present subject, is to be found in pp. 319–68 of Gibbons, *Foundation of the Ottoman Empire* (Oxford, 1916), which contain the most ambitious recent bibliography for the earlier period; and in the appropriate parts of the Cambridge Modern History.

(b) *Persia.*

The histories used for the purpose of this work are the *History of Persia* of Sir John Malcolm (1829), of R. G. Watson (1866), and of Sir Percy Sykes (2nd edition, 1921).

References to the monographs of Hanway, Brydges, Krusinski, and Durand will be found in Section v (c) of this Appendix.

(c) *Arabia.*

The only general history used is that of D. G. Hogarth (Oxford, 1922). Important monographs on relevant phases of Arabian history will be found under Section v (b).

v. *Monographs on Matters connected with 'Iraq and neighbouring Countries.*

It will be necessary to mention as sources only those works which have directly contributed to this History, the number and scope of others which could claim some relevancy being extremely large. They will be arranged with regard to the country or viewpoint with which they are associated, and (within such grouping) approximately in their order of composition.

(a) *'Iraq.*

Chronique Syriaque relative au Siège de Mossul par les Persans. A French edition and translation, by M. H. Pognon, of a Syriac manuscript found in a church at Tel Qush, near Mosul. Original written in 1746. Present edition forms pp. 489–503 of *Florilegium Melchior de Vogue.*

Account of the Siege of Mosul by Nadir Shah. A Turkish manuscript forming one (Add. 7867, p. 249 of the Catalogue) of the collection of Turkish manuscripts in the British Museum. The author is apparently a dependant of Ḥaji Ḥusain Jalili, to whom the work is dedicated.

L'Euphrate et le Tigre, by M. d'Anville (Premier Geographe du Roi), Paris, 1779. Purely geographical and not based on personal inspection.

Description du Pashaliq de Baghdad. Anonymous (but understood by the citations of other authors to be J. B. Rousseau). Paris, 1809. Disappointing, but contains several points not elsewhere preserved. Author was French Consul at Baṣrah from about 1780, and at Baghdad 1796–8.

No. CCCLXXXV (p. 147) of the Catalogus Codicum Orientalium M. B. pars secunda (Londoni, 1846): octavo Arabic manuscript بهجه الاخوان فی ذکر الوزیر سلیمان by Maḥmud bin 'Uthman ul Rahbi. In four parts; the fourth consists of an account of "Sulaiman Pasha of Baṣrah".

No. CCCXLII of the same compilation. Quarto Arabic manuscript by Muḥammad Bassam ul Tamini, entitled الدرر الفاخره فی اخبار العرب الاواخر

being an account of the modern tribes of 'Iraq, compiled for Mr. Rich in 1818.

Notes on Mohamrah and the Cha'ab Arabs, etc., by Colonel Sir H. C. Rawlinson. In the Proceedings of the Royal Geographical Society of India, 1855–7.

Memoir of the Euphrates Valley Route to India, London, 1857, by W. P. Andrew.

عنوان المجد فى احوال بغداد وبصرة ونجد by Sayyid Ibrahim Faṣiḥ. An account descriptive, geographical, historical, statistical, and genealogical of Baṣrah, Baghdad, and Najd. Completed in A. H. 1256 (A. D. 1836). Arabic manuscript. Its principal interest, which is not great, lies in pedigrees of leading 'Iraq families.

La Province de Baghdad, by M. Chiha (Cairo, 1900). The work of an Italian long resident in 'Iraq, contains an historical chapter. The middle and late nineteenth century only are of any value.

Histoire de Bagdad dans les Temps Modernes, by M. Clement Huart (Paris, E. Leroux, 1901). He brings to the task the qualifications of a consummate orientalist, and has seen three of the principal oriental sources named above, Gulshan i Khulafa', Muṭali'u'l Sa'ud, and Thabit. With small additions, a paraphrase of these sources forms the work, which is in consequence somewhat disappointing and jejune, and has not the advantage of personal acquaintance with the 'Iraq. The total period covered is that from A. D. 1258 to 1831.

Life of Midhat Pasha, by Ali Haidar Midhat (London, 1903).

(b) *Arabia.*

E. G. Browne's *Hand List of the Muḥammadan Manuscripts* of the University of Cambridge, p. 343, No. 501, shows "Miscellaneous papers" which include "an account of an engagement between the Turks and Wahhabis near Baghdad in September 1809". (Not seen by the author.)

J. B. Rousseau, *Note sur les Wahabis*, is valuable. It is bound with his *Description.* A series of letters appended to the same work contain interesting references.

L. A. Corancez, *Histoire des Wahabis* (Paris, 1810).

J. J. Burckhardt, *Notes on the Bedowins and Wahaubys* (London, 1831).

Sir H. J. Brydges, *A Brief History of the Wáhauby*, forms vol. ii of his *Transactions of His Majesty's Mission to the Court of Persia* (London, 1834), and is particularly valuable in its Notes (Nos. III, VI, VII, VIII, IX, X). The immortal work of C. M. Doughty, *Travels in*

Arabia Deserta, cannot be too often read as the complete account of Arabian conditions. (Cambridge, 1888).

'Uthman bin 'Abdullah's عنوان المجد فى تأريخ نجد was "corrected" by Muḥammad bin 'Abdu'l 'Aziz ul Mani' ul Najdi and Sulaiman ul Dakhil, and printed at the Shahbandar Press, Baghdad, A.H. 1327 (A.D. 1909).

(c) *Persia.*

The تأريخ عالم ارای عباسی of Iskandar Beg Turkoman (folio, lithographed at Teheran, A.H. 1314) is of value for Shah 'Abbas the Great in relation to Baghdad.

Father Krusinski, *History of the Revolution of Persia* (translated by Father de Cerceau, London, 2 volumes, 1728), is a good authority for the Afghan domination and its consequences. Jonas Hanway in the "Revolutions in Persia", which forms the concluding part of his *Historical Account of British Trade over the Caspian* [4 volumes, London, 1753; but the "Revolution" (volumes iii and iv) are commonly bound together as a separate work], is a very important authority for the same period. The Persian work of Mirza Mahdi Khan, chief secretary to Nadir Shah, is not less so, being the fullest contemporary account of the 'Iraq campaigns of the Conqueror. It is entitled *Jihangusha i Nadiri*, and has been paraphrased by William Jones in his *History of the Life of Nadir Shah, King of Persia* (London, 1773). Other relevant but less important works are Sir H. J. Brydges, *The Dynasty of the Kajars* (London, 1834), and H. M. Durand, *Nadir Shah* (London, 1908).

(d) *Kurdistan.*

Of the *Sharafnamah* there are numerous oriental editions, and many manuscript copies. The best-known European edition is that of F. Charmoy (Paris, 6 volumes, 1860–75) as the *Cheref Namah* of "Cheref, Prince de Bidlis".

(e) *Persian Gulf.*

The following sources deal with the Europeans in the Gulf: J. Stevens' translation (London, 3 volumes, 1695) of Manuel de Fariaxy Sousa, bringing Portuguese affairs down to 1640; F. C. Danvers, *Portuguese in India* (London, 2 volumes, 1894); R. C. Whiteway, *Rise of the Portuguese Power in India* (London, 1899); S. B. Miles, *The Portuguese in Eastern Arabia* (in the Persian Gulf Administration Report for 1884–5); M. L. Damas, *The Portuguese and Turks in the Indian Ocean in the Sixteenth Century* (Journal of the Royal Asiatic Society, January, 1921); W. de G. Birch, *Commentaries of Alfonso*

Dalboquerque (Hakluyt Society, London, 1875 ff., 4 volumes); The *Travels* of Teixeira (see this Appendix, § ii) and Hamilton (ditto); Dr. Fryer, *A New Account of East India and Persia, 1672–1681* (London, 1688); E. Monnox (in *Purchas, His Pilgrims*, volume x); Sir T. Herbert, *Some Years' Travels into Asia and Afrique* (London, 1638); Anon., *The Three Brothers* (see § ii); W. Foster's edition of *The Embassy of Sir Thomas Roe* (London, 1899); C. R. Low, *History of the Indian Navy* (London, 2 volumes, 1877); W. Foster (and others), *Letters Received by the East India Company from their Servants in the East* (London, 4 volumes, 1896 ff.); and *English Factories in India* (London, 6 volumes, 1906 ff.); W. N. Sainsbury's official *Calendar of State Papers* for the East Indies and Persia, 1630–4 (1 volume) (London, 1862 ff.); J. Bruce, *Annals of the Honourable East India Company* (London, 3 volumes, 1810); and the official *Selections from the State Papers, Bombay*, by J. A. Saldanha (Simla, 1905).

(vi) *Local Inquiries.*

About this source it is impossible to be precise. The writer feels himself to have profited in knowledge of conditions and topography during more than eight years political and administrative work in 'Iraq, and is indebted to innumerable conversations upon tribal, social, and fiscal history with 'Iraqi friends. For many statements in the text he has the testimony, never reduced to writing, of some descendant of the tribe or family concerned—an authority not free from danger, but unique and irreplaceable.

APPENDIX II. GENEALOGIES

a. The Family of Ḥasan Pasha.
b. The Jalili family.
c. The Baban family.
d. Âl Shabib (of the Muntafiq).

THE FAMILY OF ḤASAN PASHA

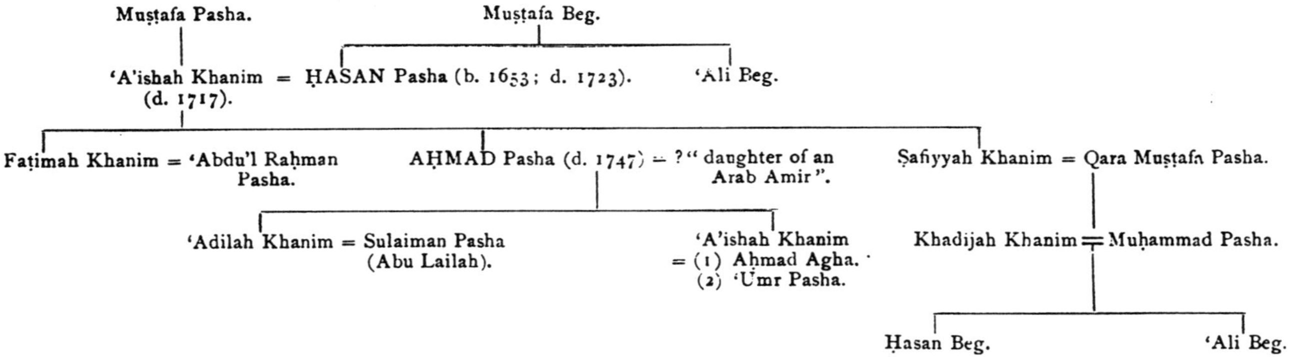

THE JALILI FAMILY

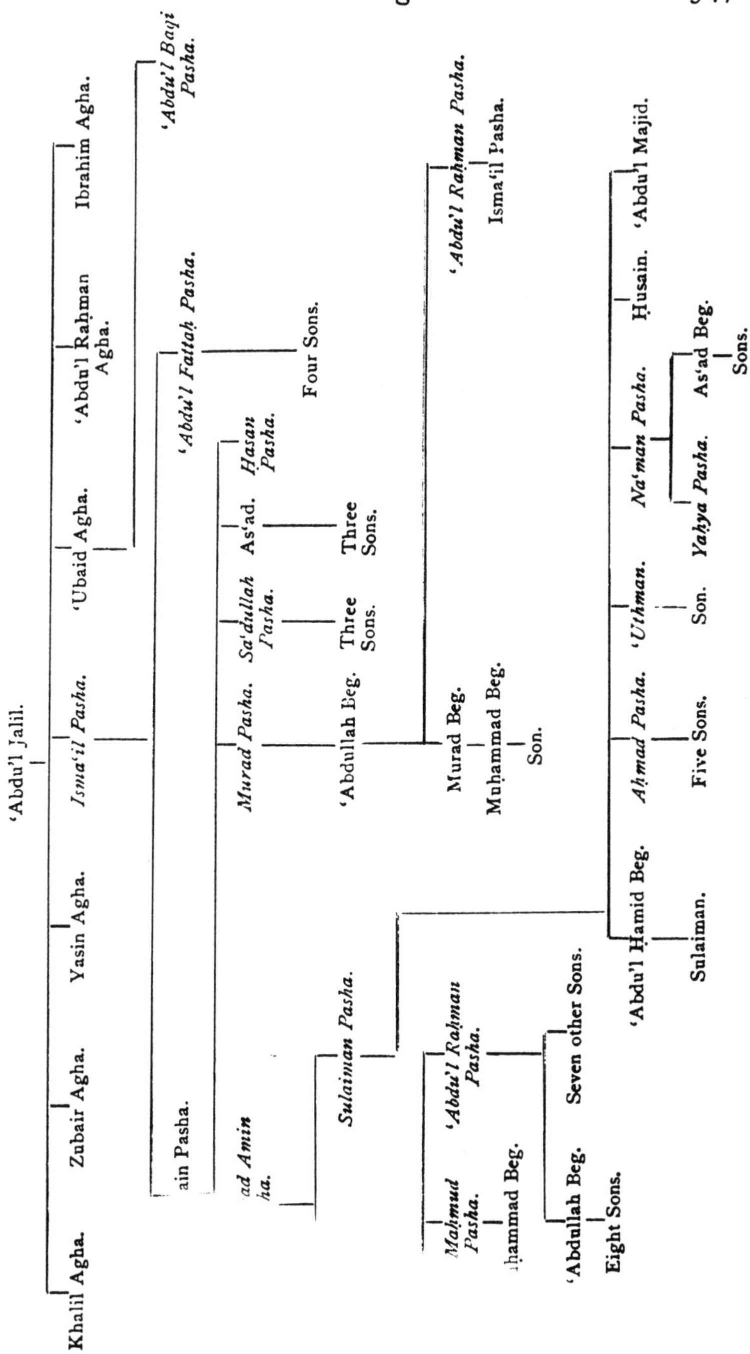

Note 1.—Names italicized are of those who at some time held the Mosul Pashaliq. **2.** Numerous unimportant persons are omitted.

THE BABAN FAMILY

- **Sulaiman Beg** (in second or third generation from Aḥmad ul Faqih).
  - **Khanah Pasha.**
    - **ammad Pasha.**
    - **'Ali Pasha.**
  - **Bakr Beg.**
    - **Salim Pasha.**
    - **Khalid Pasha.**
      - **Aḥmad Pasha.**
        - **Ibrahim Pasha.**
          - **Sulaiman Pasha.**
            - **Qadir Pasha.**
              - **Majid Pasha.**
                - **Jamil Beg.**
        - **'Abdu'l 'Aziz Beg.**
        - **Khalid Pasha.**
          - **Muḥammad Pasha.**
            - **Ḥusain Beg.**
              - **Mustafa Dhihni Pasha.**
              - **Other Sons.**
              - **Ḥamdi Pasha.**
      - **Maḥmud Pasha.**
        - **'Uthman Pasha.**
          - **Muḥammad Pasha.**
        - **Salim Pasha.**
        - **'Abdu'l Raḥman Pasha.**
          - **Sulaiman Pasha.**
            - **Aḥmad Pasha.**
              - **Khalid Beg.**
            - **Muḥammad Pasha.**
              - **Ḥamdi Beg.**
            - **'Abdullah Pasha.**
          - **Maḥmud Pasha.**
            - **Sons.**
          - **'Aziz Beg.**
          - **'Uthman Beg.**
          - **Yusif Beg.**
          - **Ḥasan. Beg.**
        - **'Abdullah Pasha.**
        - **Sulaiman Pasha.**
      - **Muḥammad Pasha.**
      - **Sulaiman Pasha.**
        - **'Ali Khan.**
        - **Ḥasan Beg.**
        - **Maḥmud Pasha.**

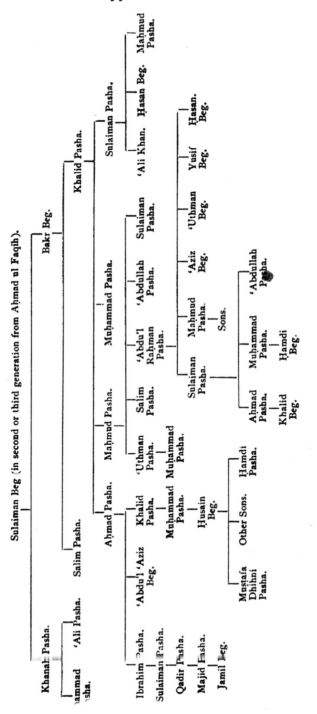

ÂL SHABIB (*Ruling house of the Muntafiq*)

(i) First four generations are conjectural.
(ii) Large numbers of unimportant persons are omitted.
* = founder of the Sa'dun family.
† = Prime Minister of 'Iraq, 1923 and 1925.

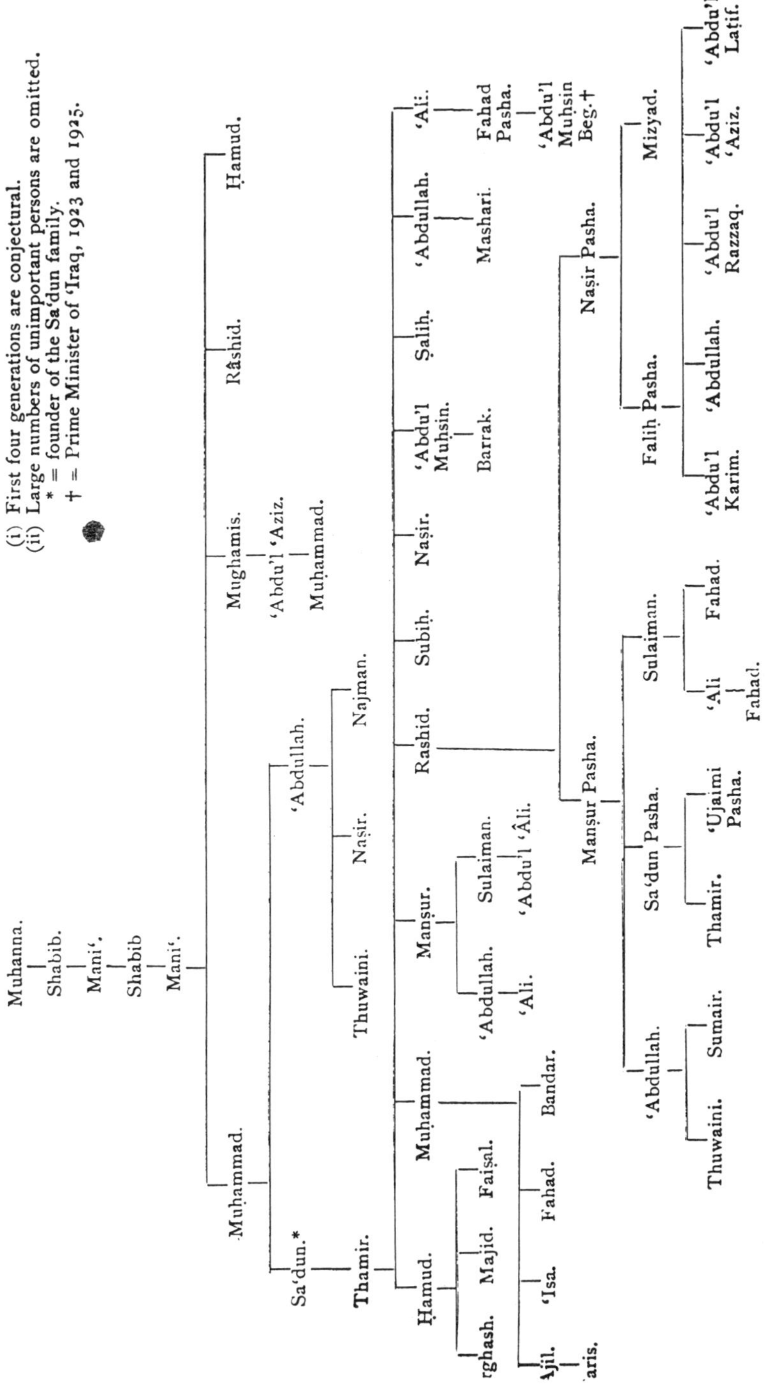

APPENDIX III

CONTEMPORARY MONARCHS OF TURKEY AND PERSIA

Turkey.		Persia.		
Date.	*Name of Sultan.*	*Date.*	*Name of Shah.*	*Remarks.*
1512	Salim I	1500	Isma'il I	
1520	Sulaiman I			
1566	Salim II	1524	Tahmasp I	
1574	Murad III			
		1576	Isma'il II	
		1578	Muḥammad Khuda-bandah	
1595	Muḥammad III			
1603	Aḥmad I	1587	'Abbas the Great	Ṣafawis.
1617	Muṣṭafa I ″			
1618	'Uthman II*			
1622	Muṣṭafa I (2nd time)			
1623	Murad IV	1629	Ṣafi	
1640	Ibrahim ″	1642	'Abbas II	
1648	Muḥammad IV ″	1667	Sulaiman	
1687	Sulaiman II			
1691	Aḥmad II			
1695	Muṣṭafa II @	1694	Ḥusain	
1703	Aḥmad III ″			
		1722	Maḥmud Khan	Afghan.
		1723	Ashraf Khan	Both claiming the throne.
1730	Maḥmud I	1730	Tahmasp II (Ṣafawi)	
		1736	Nadir	Afshars.
		1747	'Adil	
		1749	Shah Rukh and others: anarchy	
1754	'Uthman III			
1757	Muṣṭafa III	1757	Karim Khan	Zand: Regent.
1773	'Abdu'l Ḥamid I	1779	Anarchy	
1789	Salim III ″	1796	Agha Muḥammad	
1807	Muṣṭafa IV ″	1797	Fatḥ 'Ali	
1808	Maḥmud II			
1839	'Abdu'l Majid	1834	Muḥammad	
1861	'Abdu'l 'Aziz ″	1848	Naṣiru'l Din	Qajars.
1876	Murad V ″			
1876	'Abdu'l Ḥamid II ″	1896	Mudhaffaru'l Din	
1908	Muḥammad V	1907	Muḥammad 'Ali	

* Signifies Murdered.
″ Deposed.
@ Abdicated.

APPENDIX IV

ISLAMIC AND CHRISTIAN CHRONOLOGY

Although the chronology of the Christian era has been adopted throughout the present work, the sources from which it is derived almost invariably use the Islamic. It has been thought well to give a ready means of re-converting the dates, and to note shortly, for the general reader, the different chronological systems.

The Islamic Era commences from the new moon of July 15th A.D. 622. The Islamic sacred year, being lunar, is shorter than the Christian (solar) year by ten days, twenty-one hours, fourteen and two-fifths seconds. As the Christian months ignore the moon, and the Islamic exactly follow it, the coincidence of one Christian to one Islamic month is an accident rarely produced. Similarly, new year's day of the Islamic year may occur at any point late or early in the Christian year, and the great Islamic festivals may occur in summer or winter while falling always on the same day of the same Islamic month. The Islamic months in order are Muḥarram, Safar, Rabi'u'l Awwal, Rabi'u'l Akhir, Jamada'l Awwal, Jamada'l Akhir, Rajab, Sha'ban, Ramaḍhan, Shawwal, Dhi'l Qa'dah, Dhi'l Ḥijjah.

The Civil Calendar introduced into Turkey by Sultan Salim III, in A.D. 1789, scarcely concerns us here. It is, in fact, the European "Old Style" Calendar, but with two differences: it accepts the Islamic year (A. H. 1205) as its basis on introduction, and has since then added solar years to the previous total of Islamic lunar years; and it commences on March 1st instead of, as the Christian year, January 1st. This Calendar is known in Turkey as "Rumi", Greek.

A convenient approximate method of converting a Muslim to a Christian year is to divide it by 33, subtract quotient from dividend, and add 622. To convert from Christian to Muslim, subtract 622, divide remainder by 33, and add quotient to dividend. But the results so obtained do not show the extent of correspondence between the two years. The following table will show the Christian date upon which falls the New Year's Day of various Islamic years. It has not been thought necessary to give every year, the constant annual loss of the Islamic to the Christian year (of three hours short of eleven days) making the calculation an easy one over short periods. Every fifth year is given, except that all Christian years are given in which occur the first of Muḥarram of two Islamic years.

A.H.	A.D.	A.H.	A.D.	A.H.	A.D.
906	July 28, 1500.	1045	June 17, 1635.	1189	Mar. 4, 1775.
911	June 4, 1505.	1050	Apr. 23, 1640.	1194	Jan. 8, } 1780.
916	Apr. 10, 1510.	1055	Feb. 27, 1645.	1195	Dec. 28, }
921	Sept. 15, 1515.	1060	Jan. 4, } 1650.	1200	Nov. 4, 1785.
925	Jan. 3, } 1519.	1061	Dec. 25, }	1205	Sept. 10, 1790.
926	Dec. 23, }	1066	Oct. 31, 1655.	1210	July 18, 1795.
927	Dec. 12, 1520.	1071	Sept. 6, 1660.	1215	May 25, 1800.
932	Oct. 18, 1525.	1076	July 14, 1665.	1220	Apr. 1, 1805.
937	Aug. 25, 1530.	1081	May 21, 1670.	1225	Feb. 6, 1810.
942	July 2, 1535.	1086	Mar. 28, 1675.	1228	Jan. 4, } 1813.
947	May 8, 1540.	1091	Feb. 2, 1680.	1229	Dec. 24, }
952	Mar. 15, 1545.	1093	Jan. 10, } 1682.	1231	Dec. 3, 1815.
957	Jan. 20, 1550.	1094	Dec. 31, }	1236	Oct. 9, 1820.
958	Jan. 9, } 1551.	1097	Nov. 28, 1685.	1241	Aug. 16, 1825.
959	Dec. 29, }	1102	Oct. 5, 1690.	1246	June 22, 1830.
963	Nov. 16, 1555.	1107	Aug. 12, 1695.	1251	Apr. 29, 1835.
968	Sept. 22, 1560.	1112	June 18, 1700.	1256	Mar. 5, 1840.
973	July 29, 1565.	1117	Apr. 25, 1705.	1261	Jan. 10, } 1845.
978	June 5, 1570.	1122	Mar. 2, 1710.	1262	Dec. 30, }
983	Apr. 12, 1575.	1127	Jan. 7, } 1715.	1267	Nov. 6, 1850.
988	Feb. 17, 1580.	1128	Dec. 27, }	1272	Sept. 13, 1855.
993	Jan. 3, } 1585.	1133	Nov. 2, 1720.	1277	July 20, 1860.
994	Dec. 23, }	1138	Sept. 9, 1725.	1282	May 27, 1865.
999	Oct. 30, 1590.	1143	July 17, 1730.	1287	Apr. 3, 1870.
1004	Sept. 6, 1595.	1148	May 24, 1735.	1292	Feb. 7, 1875.
1009	July 13, 1600.	1153	Mar. 29, 1740.	1295	Jan. 5, } 1875.
1014	May 19, 1605.	1158	Feb. 3, 1745.	1296	Dec. 26, }
1019	Mar. 26, 1610.	1161	Jan. 2, } 1748.	1298	Dec. 4, 1880.
1024	Jan. 31, 1615.	1162	Dec. 22, }	1303	Oct. 10, 1885.
1026	Jan. 9, } 1617.	1164	Nov. 30, 1750.	1308	Aug. 17, 1890.
1027	Dec. 29, }	1169	Oct. 7, 1755.	1313	June 24, 1895.
1030	Nov. 26, 1620.	1174	Aug. 13, 1760.	1318	May 1, 1900.
1035	Oct. 3, 1625.	1179	Jan. 20, 1765.		
1040	Aug. 10, 1630.	1184	Apr. 27, 1770.		

GLOSSARY

(Abbreviations used : T. = Turkish ; Ar. = Arabic ; P. = Persian.)

Agha (T.): a gentleman or official of middle (sometimes high) rank, military or civil or domestic (in a great household).

'Aim (pl. **'Ulama**) (Ar.): a learned person, especially in Islamic religious lore.

Amiru'l Ḥaj (Ar.): conductor of a formed party of pilgrims to Makkah.

Aq (T.): white.

'Arabanah (Ar.): carriage.

Ashrâf (pl. of *sharif*) (Ar.): leading gentry, notables.

Auqaf (Ar.): properties or funds entailed to pious foundations or purposes. Also name of the department administering these.

Ayalat (Ar.): a province; the largest administrative unit in the Turkish Empire.

'Azab (Ar.): originally a special corps of non-combatant troops connected with the Jebechis. Later, and generally, locally-raised light troops.

Babu'l 'Arab (Ar.): the (Arab) official at the court of a Pasha through whom the Arab tribes of the province dealt with the Governor.

Baladiyyah (Ar.): municipality.

Baleos (from Italian *baglio*): a European consul in Turkey, especially the British Resident at Baghdad.

Baratli (T.): a regiment of regular, but locally-raised, infantry.

Beglerbegi (T.): title of a Pasha of the highest rank and Governor of an ayalat.

Bustanchi (T.): literally "gardener": member of an ancient corps of the Sultan's domestic troops, later incorporated in the Janissaries.

Buyuk (T.): great.

Buyurildi (T.): letters-patent granted by a Pasha, conferring appointment or privilege.

Buzurg (P.): great.

Daftardar (T.): accountant (chief revenue and treasury official) of a province.

Daulah (Ar.): Government, especially the Turkish.

Dere Begi (T.): generic designation for independent (often tribal) rulers of localities nominally within a Turkish province.

Ḍhabiṭ (Ar.): officer (generally military).

Ḍhabṭiyyah (Ar.): gendarmerie (nineteenth century).

Dirah (Ar.): area recognized as the grazing ground of a particular tribe.

Diwan (P.): a formal council or council-place, (1) in a private house, a saloon, (2) the state council of a Pashaliq, (3) that of the Sultan.

Elchi (T.): envoy, ambassador.

Farman (P.): letters-patent granted by the Sultan.

Fatwah (Ar.): a ruling given on a point of religious law by the Mufti.

Gedikli (T.): holder of property or rank by a special (and archaic) type of feudal tenure; in general a vassal, officer, burgess.

Geunul-li (T.): "good-hearted", a special corps of light cavalry.

Ghazu (Ar.): raid by an Arab tribe.

Grand Signor, Seigneur: title (in Europe) of the Sultan.

Gumrek (T.): customs; customs department.

Haitah (T.): irregular gendarmerie or local troops, usually employed and paid by a provincial Governor or adventurer; often of Albanian race.

Ich Aghalari (T.): Aghas of the Interior; members of the retinue of the private portion of a Pasha's palace.

Ich Da'irasi (T.): apartments of the Interior; the private portion of a palace.

Jarid (Ar.): the game of hurling a lance from horseback.

Jebechi (T.): member of the old (imperial) corps of Armourers, in charge of ordnance and magazines.

Kahya (T.): corrupt but usual form of Katkhuda (P.). In general, steward, warder, high officer: in particular, the chief Minister (for all purposes) in a provincial Government under the Pasha.

Kallak (Ar.): square timber raft, floating on inflated skins.

Kulah, Kulaman (T.): slave; freedman (of Circassian race).

Khâṣṣ (Ar.): intimate personal Aghas of the Pasha's household.

Khila' (Ar.): robe of honour.

Khuṭbah (Ar.): the formal sermon pronounced on Fridays in the mosque.

Kuchuk (T.): little.

Lawand (T.): semi-regular, locally-raised troops. In 'Iraq, predominantly of Kurdish and Lurish race.

Liwa (Ar.): (1) sub-province governed by a Mutaṣarrif; (2) a brigade.

Mir Akhor (P.): Master of the Horse (literally, the Stable).

Mirmiran (P.): grade of Pasha below that of Wazir and Beglerbegi.

Mu'adhdhin (Ar.): mosque servant who calls to prayer from the minaret.

Mufti (Ar.): doctor of Islamic religious law, empowered by appointment and by public recognition to give fatwahs (q. v.).

Muḥafidh (Ar.): officer commanding the garrison in the Citadel.

Muhurdar (T.): keeper of the Pasha's seal.

Mujtahid (Ar.): Shia' religious teacher of highest standing, commonly of Persian race.

Muṣaḥib (Ar.): courtier.

Mutasallim (Ar.): deputy-governor of a sanjaq, or of an ayalat when more than one were under the rule of one Pasha.

Mutaṣarrif (Ar.): governor of a liwa or sanjaq.

Naḥiyyah (Ar.): smallest administrative unit, governed by a Mudir.

Naqib (Ar.): semi-official head of the community of Sayyids in a place. Of great consequence in Baghdad.

Nidhamiyyah, Nidham, Nidham Jadid (Ar.): the New System introduced by Sultan Maḥmud II, especially on its military side. Later, the regular (as opposed to reserve) forces.

Padishah (T.): the Sultan.

Pashaliq (T.): (1) the office, (2) the territories of a Pasha.

Qaḍha (Ar.): administrative unit intermediate between sanjaq (or liwa) and naḥiyyah.

Qaḍhi (Ar.): judge, originally both civil and criminal, later only civil and religious; using Shara' code.

Qa'immaqam (Ar.): deputy or deputy-governor, (1) in general, for any post; (2) in particular, administrator of a Qaḍha.

Qal'ah (Ar.): the citadel of a town; any fort or stronghold.

Qalpaq (T.): fur cap, worn very large by the Janissaries, smaller by other troops.

Qalpaqli (T.): regiment of regular local troops wearing the qalpaq.

Qaptan Pasha (from Italian): lord high admiral.

Qapu Quli (T.): "slave of the gate"; imperial, as opposed to local or provincial forces. See p. 48 (footnote).

Qapuchi (T.): "doorman"; chamberlain, imperial messenger.

Qara (T.): black.

Qizlar Aghasi (T.): steward of the private (women's) part of the Sultan's palace; chief eunuch.

Ra'is Effendi (Ar. and T.): abbreviated from "Ra'is ul Kuttab"; Ottoman Minister of Foreign Affairs (under the Grand Wazir) up to the nineteenth century.

Sagban (P.): originally keepers of the Sultan's hounds; then a military corps incorporated with the Janissaries; then loosely for inferior regular troops.

Sanjaq (T.): "banner"; area under a sanjaq begi, serving as unit of feudal rally; thence sub-province of an ayalat, governed by a Mutaṣarrif.

Saqqa (Ar.): water-carrier; corps of that name and duty.

Sarai (T.): palace: Government offices.

Sar'askar (P. and Ar.): Commander-in-Chief.

Sardar (P.): Commander-in-Chief.

Ṣari (T.): yellow.

Sayyid (Ar.): a descendant of the Prophet.

Seiman (T.): vulgar form of Sagban (q. v.), in its loose sense.

Seraglio: European corruption of Sarai.

Shaikh ul Masha'ikh (Ar.): "Shaikh of the shaikhs", high title of tribal rulers, especially of the Sa'dun in the Muntafiq.

Shakhtur (Ar.): flat-bottomed wooden raft.

Shara' (Ar.): Islamic religious law.

Sipahi (P.): horse soldier (1) supplied by fief-holder for temporary service; (2) regular corps of Imperial cavalry.

"Sophy": English version of Ṣafawi.

Ṣu Bashi (T.): "Chief of the Water." By origin (?) irrigational and revenue official; then lieutenant of troops used for police duties in towns.

Tandhimat (Ar.): the body of reforms and new Institutes ordained by Sultan 'Abdu'l Majid.

Tapu (T.? from Greek): a type of land-tenure (nineteenth century); thence this type of registration, and the Department dealing with it.

Timar (P.): hereditary fief, of value less than 20,000 "aqchah" p.a.

Timariot: holder of the above, bound to military service under his sanjaq begi.

Ṭopal (T.): lame.

Ṭopchi (T.): gunner of the Imperial artillery.

Tufenkchi (T.): musketeer, especially of the local regular regiments so called.

'Ugail (Ar.): Arab tribe, originally of Najd but subsequently dispersed, living in organized but detribalized communities, generally on the outskirts of towns, as mercenaries, escorts, guides, &c.

'Ulama (Ar., pl. of **'alim**): persons learned in religious lore.

Valley Begs: *see* Dere Begi.

Waiwodah, waiwode (Slav.): governor; title (common in European provinces but also found at Mardin) corresponding to Mutasallim.

Wali (Ar.): governor-general of a wilayat.

Waqf (Ar.): *see* Auqaf, of which it is the singular.

Wazarat, Wazirate (Ar.): the rank of Wazir.

Wazir (Ar., English "vizier", &c.): the highest Ottoman rank.

Wilayat (Ar.): later form of ayalat, q. v.

Yaramaz (T.): "good-for-nothing". See text, p. 288.

Za'im (Ar.): holder of a zi'amah.

Zi'amah (Ar.): fief, of value of 20,000 "aqchah" p.a. and over.

INDEX OF SOURCES

[Reference to the page where the chief bibliographical information as to each source will be found is given by the use of italics.]

INDEX

[Abbreviations used :—P. = Pasha ; Ag. = Agha ; Eff. = Effendi. Members of the Baban, Jalili, Sa'dun, and Shawi families will be found under the *family* name.]

Printed in England at the Oxford University Press

Folios Archive Library

Fifty-three Years in Syria
Henry H. Jessup
Vol. I • 412pp • 220 x 145 mm • Paper £12.95 • ISBN 1 85964 170 9
Vol. II • 412pp • 220 x 145 mm • Paper £12.95 • ISBN 1 85964 171 7

The Caliphs' Last Heritage: A Short History of the Turkish Empire
Lt. Col. Sir Mark Sykes
644pp • 218 x 135 mm • Paper £12.95 • ISBN 1 85964 168 7

The Dawn of a New Era in Syria
Margaret McGilvary
304pp • 200 x 130 mm • Paper £12.95 • ISBN 1 85964 167 9

Newmarket and Arabia
Roger D. Upton
228pp • 198 x 135 mm • Paper £12.95 • ISBN 1 85964 162 8

The Thistle and the Cedar of Lebanon
Habeeb Risk Allah Effendi
416pp • 202 x 120 mm • Paper £12.95 • ISBN 1 85964 163 6

The Land of Uz
Abdullah Mansûr (G. Wyman Bury)
392pp • 215 x 138 mm • Paper £14.95 • ISBN 1 85964 121 0

Arabia Infelix: Or the Turks in Yamen
G. Wyman Bury
232pp • 215 x 138 mm • Paper £14.95 • ISBN 1 85964 122 9

Narrative of the Residence of Fatalla Sayeghir among the Wandering Arabs of the Great Desert
Collected and translated by M. Alphonse de Lamartine
216pp • 210 x 120 mm • Cased £19.95 • ISBN 1 85964 088 5

The Land of the Date
C. M. Cursetjee
208pp • 235 x 168 mm • Cased £30.00 • ISBN 1 85964 038 9

The History of the Wahabis from their Origin until the End of 1809
Louis Alexandre Olivier de Corancez
224pp • 235 x 168 mm • Cased £25.00 • ISBN 1 85964 036 2

Mount Lebanon: A Ten Years' Residence
Colonel Charles Henry Churchill
Vols. 1–3 • 400pp • 235 x 158 mm • Cased £30.00 • ISBN 1 873938 50 0
ISBN 1 873938 51 9 • ISBN 1 873938 52 7

Mount Lebanon: The Druzes and the Maronites under the Turkish Rule
Colonel Charles Henry Churchill
Vol. 4 • 300pp • 235 x 158 mm • Cased £30.00 • ISBN 1 873938 53 5

Southern Arabia
Theodore and Mabel Bent
504pp • 235 x 168 mm • Cased £45.00 • ISBN 1 85964 035 4

The Countries and Tribes of the Persian Gulf
Colonel Samuel Barrett Miles
644pp • 235 x 168 mm • 4 engravings • Cased £45.00 • ISBN 1 873938 56 X

Travels through Arabia and other Countries in the East
Carsten Niebuhr
212 x 125 mm • Cased £30.00
Vol. I • 464pp • 10pp engravings, 2 maps • ISBN 1 873938 43 8
Vol. II • 456pp • 10pp engravings, 1 map • ISBN 1 873938 54 3

Travels of Ali Bey in Morocco, Tripoli, Cyprus, Egypt, Arabia, Syria and Turkey
235 x 168 mm • Cased £30.00
Vol. I • 383pp • 44 engravings, 2 maps • ISBN 1 873938 39 X
Vol. II • 388pp • 38 engravings, 4 maps • ISBN 1 873938 40 3

Notes on the Bedouins and the Wahabys
John Lewis Burckhardt
Vol. I • 400pp • 235 x 168 mm • Cased £30.00 • ISBN 1 873938 26 8
Vol. II • 400pp • 235 x 168 mm • Cased £30.00 • ISBN 1 873938 32 2

Sinai, the Hedjaz and the Soudan
James Hamilton
440pp • 235 x 168 mm • 1 plate, 1 map • Cased £45.00 • ISBN 1 873938 38 1

A Voyage up the Persian Gulf
Lieutenant William Heude
252pp • 235 x 168 mm • 4 engravings • Cased £45.00 • ISBN 1 873938 44 6

Gazetteer of the Persian Gulf, Oman and Central Arabia
John Gordon Lorimer
10,000pp • 237 x 168 mm • Cased 19-volume set £3,000.00 • ISBN 1 85964 127 X

Contact our Sales Department on +44 (0)118 959 7847 or e-mail on **orders@garnet-ithaca.demon.co.uk** to order copies of these books.